THE AMERICAN PLUTARCH

THE
AMERICAN PLUTARCH

———————— ☼ ————————

18 Lives Selected
from the
Dictionary of American Biography

Edited by
EDWARD T. JAMES

with an Introduction by
HOWARD MUMFORD JONES

———————— ☼ ————————

CHARLES SCRIBNER'S SONS *New York*

PREFATORY NOTE

ADMIRERS of the *Dictionary of American Biography* have long asserted that within its covers were the best existing brief treatments of many of the major figures of American history. Acting on the suggestion of Paul Herman Buck, Carl H. Pforzheimer University Professor and Director of the University Library at Harvard, Charles Scribner's Sons has undertaken in this volume to make a selection of such articles available to a larger audience. Assembled here are biographies of eighteen of the nation's most eminent political and military leaders over the span of its history. In the classic manner of Plutarch's *Lives*, they have been arranged in contrasting pairs.

For the most part the articles are reprinted from the *Dictionary* without change. A few corrections of detail have been made, however, and some of the authors have taken this opportunity to incorporate minor changes of form or interpretation. In addition, the attempt has been made to bring the bibliographies up to date, in most cases by a supplementary paragraph, occasionally by a revision of the original bibliography. Some of the authors of the articles here reprinted are, regretfully, no longer living. Those who are have given willing cooperation in this project, for which the editor and publishers wish to express their appreciation. Thanks are due also to Professor Leonard W. Labaree, Editor of *The Papers of Benjamin Franklin*, for preparing the revised bibliography for the Franklin article; to Professor David Donald of The Johns Hopkins University for preparing the Lincoln bibliography; and to the editors of the papers of Alexander Hamilton and of John C. Calhoun for expert advice.

EDWARD T. JAMES, EDITOR

Dictionary of American Biography

CONTENTS

INTRODUCTION

The American Plutarch

AN INTRODUCTION

by

HOWARD MUMFORD JONES

I

Few readers, one suspects, understand that biography, with such related forms as autobiography, personal memoirs, diaries, and books of reminiscence, is one of the oldest and richest forms of American writing. In North America autobiography commences with the appearance in 1630 of *The True Travels, Adventures, and Observations of Captain John Smith*, the charm of which has outlasted criticism and the truth of which is forever under attack. Biography proper begins with *Abel Being Dead Yet Speaketh: or, the Life and Death of . . . John Cotton* by John Norton, printed in 1630 in order that "such a Light" as Cotton, a mighty figure among the founders of New England, should not be "hid under a Bushel." The first biographical encyclopedia in the future United States was contained in Cotton Mather's *Magnalia Christi Americana*, published in 1702, which includes the lives of seventy ministers and those of various colonial administrators and other worthies. By the opening of the eighteenth century, it is clear, the three great lines of development in biography had been laid down. The eighteenth century added to the charm of autobiography with William Byrd's *History of the Dividing Line* and Benjamin Franklin's *Autobiography*, but the complete text of neither was fully known until well into the nineteenth century or later.

The seventeenth-century impulse towards biography and autobiography arose from the desire to record the wonders of God's providence and the difficulties of creating a culture in the wilderness. The two elements were often fused together, as in the *Narrative of the Captivity and Restoration of Mrs. Mary Rowlandson*, published in 1682, the best known of a long line of narratives, some factual, some with a good deal of imaginative embroidery, concerning capture by the savage Indians. The type is of more than antiquarian interest, for the "Indian captivity narrative," much embellished in the raw-head-and-bloody-bones way, delighted cruder tastes and became standard biographical fare for boys like Tom Sawyer.

After the creation of the republic, piety and commercial shrewdness produced such biographical confections as the *Life of George Washington with Curious Anecdotes equally Honourable to Himself and Exemplary to his Young Countrymen* by Mason L. Weems, which has sold continuously since 1800, the latest edition (1962) being one in which Marcus Cunliffe treats this "classic" with an amused and scholarly gravity. There were, of course, scores of serious biographies. Later on, such collections as the *Library of American Biography* in two series and twenty-five volumes, published from 1834 to 1848, embalmed in reverential prose sixty worthies concerned with the discovery of North America, its settling, or the establishment of the independence of the United States. This was edited by Jared Sparks, who wrote many biographies both for this collection and otherwise, and who secured the help for his *Library* of such notables as William H. Prescott and John G. Palfrey. *The Library of American Biography* belongs to the plaster-cast school of biographical writing. Biography and autobiography were also written in the nineteenth century, however, by virtually every eminent man of letters in the nation, Cooper, Irving, Emerson, Thoreau, Hawthorne, Melville, Parkman, William Gilmore Simms, Mark Twain, Howells, and Henry James being among them.

The nineteenth century produced the first great professional American biographer—that is, a writer making his reputation principally by biographical volumes of enduring value. This was James Parton (1822–1891), who, unlike Sparks, did not sophisticate his source materials, who toiled at research, who was able to organize vast masses of material, and who wrote acceptably. Some of his lives are still consulted by serious students, including his biographies of Aaron Burr, Benjamin Franklin, Thomas Jefferson, Andrew Jackson (and, of all persons, Voltaire!). Parton has to be amplified and corrected, but he cannot be ignored as it is possible to pass over Jared Sparks.

Three leading events or groups of events in the later nineteenth century increased the library of serious biographies—the Civil War, the centennial celebrations of 1876, and the passing of the great nineteenth-century leaders. The war was scarcely over when most of the leaders (and many who were not) broke into print to justify what they had done or to record their experience. Of this vast output the *Personal Memoirs of U. S. Grant*, published in 1885-86, is the outstanding literary classic, a book that approaches Caesar in clarity and terseness and outshines him in modesty. Confederate leaders wrote fully and richly, but did not write quite as well. The enormous work known as *Abraham Lincoln: A History* in ten volumes (1890) by John G. Nicolay and John Hay is probably the longest "biography" of an American ever to be published, but is more than a life of Lincoln. The famous *Battles and Leaders of the Civil War* in four volumes (1890) is a notable collection of statements by leaders of both sides.

The centennial year was followed within a decade by the creation of the American Historical Association in 1884, the first national society of professional historical scholars if one puts by the American Antiquarian Society (1812). The two events, in a sense, played into each other's hands, and both history and biography were scrutinized and revised in the light of new knowledge and higher professional standards. In 1882 under the editorship of John T. Morse, Jr., was launched the "American Statesmen" series, which ran to thirty-one volumes and concerned twenty-eight American public men. In these biographies political considerations were paramount. Meanwhile the "American Men of Letters" series was begun in 1881 under the editorship of Charles Dudley Warner. This ran to twenty-six volumes. Volumes of reminiscence, collections of letters, and of course scores of serious biographies outside these two series were written, published, and read.

In 1856 there appeared the first edition of *Appletons' Cyclopædia of Biography*, the later bibliographical transformations of which have been kaleidoscopic in character. No edition of this work ever quite attained uniform and competent standards of accuracy, though copies of some one of its several transformations still linger on library shelves. It was, therefore, no predecessor of the great *Dictionary of National Biography* that began publication in London in 1882 under the editorship of Leslie (later Sir Leslie) Stephen. Indeed, all American biographical dictionaries, encyclopedias and other compilations seemed to suffer under a mysterious curse of inadequacy, inaccuracy, or illiteracy, so that, when the first volume of the *Dictionary of American Biography* appeared in 1928, its editors could truthfully remark that "the lack of an authoritative dictionary of national biography has been often deplored by American scholars." The *Dictionary of American Biography* accomplished for the United States what the *Dictionary of National Biography* accomplished for Great Britain and the Commonwealth. It was published under the auspices of the American Council of Learned Societies and the editorship of a group of distinguished scholars. The original edition was completed by a twentieth volume in 1937, since which time, at proper intervals, supplementary volumes have appeared, on the model of the supplementary volumes of the *Dictionary of National Biography*. It is hardly necessary to add that the biographical output of American publishers, serious, popular, and fictional, in the twentieth century has been enormous.

II

The biographies in this collection have been chosen from the *Dictionary of American Biography*, reworked wherever necessary in the light of new evidence, and arranged in pairs, the principle of the pairing being contrast and comparison. We have, then, a kind of American Plutarch. This is not a far-fetched nor fantastic notion.

From 1600, when Richard Hakluyt collected all the then available voyage literature concerning the New World into the third volume of the second edition of his great *Principal Navigations, Voyages, Traffiques & Discoveries of the English Nation,* down to the present age when translations of Plutarch in inexpensive editions can be bought in any competent bookstore, Plutarch has meant a great deal to thoughtful Americans. For example, in George Peckham's account of the fateful last voyage and heroic death of Sir Humphrey Gilbert, which can be read in Hakluyt, one finds Peckham citing Plutarch's "Historie of Themystocles," that "right noble and valiant Captain," as an encouragement to the brave. John Smith's account of himself was written with an eye on Plutarch and on the classical historians. Searching for biographical parallels for some of his heroes, Cotton Mather appealed to Plutarch's method as his justification. Washington, the Cincinnatus of the West, was, in innumerable eulogies and some biographies, characterized as the American equivalent of Plutarchian man. When William Preston Johnston delivered a eulogy of Robert E. Lee at Washington College, he said that Lee had all the virtues of Pericles without one blemish, spot, or stain, and we remember that Pericles is one of Plutarch's subjects. In his essay on heroism Emerson says of Plutarch that we "are more deeply indebted to him than to all the [other] ancient writers" and that "each of his 'Lives' is a refutation to the despondency and cowardice of our religious and political theorists." (Incidentally, leaders of the antebellum "Greek democracy" in the South were not unaware of Plutarch.) What is probably the best * English version of Plutarch's *Lives*—Arthur Hugh Clough's reworking of the so-called Dryden translation—was published in Boston in 1859. Nor should it be forgotten that the writer most widely studied in American schools and colleges is William Shakespeare nor that all of Shakespeare's serious plays about antiquity are ultimately based on Plutarch, among them *Coriolanus, Julius Caesar,* and *Antony and Cleopatra.*

The Parallel Lives of Eminent Greeks and Romans by Plutarch, the father of biography (46?–120? A.D.), though it comes down to us battered by time, tampered with by forgers, and rearranged by historians, is a book influential not only in the United States but in the Western world. In founding biography Plutarch gave the form a special tendency and a special preoccupation with public morality or "civil virtue." He looks in his heroes for martial or civic responsibility, and he traces their downfall in many cases to their failure in this quality. His "note" is a concern for the government of men and the management of war and peace by powerful individuals. He can think of no form of greatness worth recording other than that involved in founding a state, giving it laws, expanding its power, or defending its sovereignty. All the persons he writes about, whether they are more or less mythical like Theseus or historical characters like Julius Caesar, are public figures.

Plutarch, whose boyhood was spent under Nero and who died when, in Gibbon's words, "the empire of Rome comprehended the fairest part of the earth and the most civilized portion of mankind," witnessed great political changes. He was born in Chaeronea in Boeotia and he lived in a Greece emptied of all her glory except her culture. He lectured in Greek at Rome, that center of the universe, on philosophy. He probably accepted Roman titles from Trajan and Hadrian. He wrote about morality, religion, geography, and science. He could, it seems clear, no more escape the problem of power and political change than we can escape the problem of atomic science. Of the fifty biographies by him which have come

* Best in point of accuracy. As a literary classic North's translation of Amyot's French translation of Plutarch surpasses the Clough version in style.

down to us (four of them do not belong in his binary scheme of
parallel lives), it has been remarked that the twenty-three sets are
important in the light of two great problems before the ancient
world: (1) why did the city states of Greece, given their unparalleled
wealth in intellect and culture, collapse as political entities? and
(2) what was the relation between the world power of imperial
Rome on the one hand and, on the other, the great constitutional
struggle reaching its climax in the transformation of Octavius into
Augustus Caesar?

For Plutarch great men are, then, political figures—founders of
cities or of kingdoms, law-givers, generals, statesmen, rulers. This
fact should in itself be interesting to a political-minded people like
the Americans, but Plutarch had special meaning to the leaders of
the American Revolution and the founders of the American republic. They all read him, or read in him, and most of them read in
books derived from him. An example of the last is Montesquieu,
whose *Considérations sur les Causes de la Grandeur et de la Déca-
dence des Romans* and the even more famous *L'Esprit des Lois*
owe much to Plutarch and were widely influential in the generation
of the founding fathers. Montesquieu of course cites Plutarch (as
who did not?), and he divides all governments into three categories:
the despotic, in which the governing quality is fear; the monarchical, of which the dominant qualities are honor and ambition; and
the republican, of which the central quality, if the republic is to
live, is virtue. By virtue Montesquieu means *amor patriae*, which
he finds extolled in Plutarch and which is also, he says, a love of
equality. He drew on Plutarch for his statements about law, or
many of them, and on the *Lives* for examples of republican virtue
and its concomitant evil, which is luxury. One has but to read John
Adams or Thomas Jefferson to discover how these examples from
antiquity sank in and how Plutarch was read as a series of practical
lessons in the management of states. For them history, of which
Plutarch's *Lives* was a moving instance, was philosophy taught by
example and precept.

We, too, have had two crucial constitutional struggles. The first
concerned the theory of the British empire; and failure to modernize the structure of that empire resulted in the independence of
the United States. The second was the long constitutional difference
that reached its climax in the Civil War, the outcome of which
reshaped the whole structure of the American state. We have passed
from being a set of random cities (in the wilderness!) to an imperial
power. We have been fascinated and perplexed as Plutarch was by

problems of greatness and demagoguery. Hence the propriety of an American Plutarch, a series of reliable biographies of great public figures so arranged that by comparison and contrast they illumine American development and American problems.

III

The biographies of these leaders are, as in the case of Plutarch, arranged in pairs, Jefferson and Hamilton being an obvious instance. Like Plutarch's *Lives* the accounts concentrate on great problems of historical responsibility and change. The men chosen for inclusion fall, though not symmetrically, into the same general categories as Plutarch's heroes. Some of them—for example, Washington and Jefferson Davis—were founders of nations, the one succeeding, the other failing, partly from temperamental qualities Plutarch would have understood. Some, like Marshall, were law-givers. Some—Lee, Grant, Washington, Jackson—were generals; and on the success or failure of at least three of these men depended the very existence of the state. Others, like Jackson and Clay, believed in extending American dominion. Lincoln sought to maintain it. Theodore Roosevelt and Woodrow Wilson were forced to think imperially; and Wilson, like Caesar Augustus, was compelled, though from different motives, to transform the nature of his office beyond the changes Lincoln had wrought, to consider the problems of the world, and to contend (unsuccessfully in Wilson's case, successfully in that of Caesar Augustus) with a hostile senate. It will be noted also that these biographies are in length comparable to the length of Plutarch's *Lives*.

There are of course three important differences between this collection and the collection of Plutarch. The *Parallel Lives* purport to be the product of a single writer, and with the exception of a few spurious passages are written by this great genius, whereas these eighteen lives are by various and varying writers. Yet a kind of unity appears, imposed by the requirements of the *Dictionary of American Biography* in style and treatment. In the second place Plutarch wrote about Greeks and Romans, opposing a representative of one culture to a representative of the other in a like area of activity. Moreover, for the majority of his pairs as they have come down to us, he institutes a formal comparison of the twain, that of Demosthenes and Cicero or that of Alcibiades and Coriolanus being characteristic. But in this collection all the personages are Americans, and no formal comparisons are drawn. The difference between Plutarch and the present collection in this respect is, however, less crucial than at first sight appears: Plutarch's heroes were, after all, products of a Mediterranean culture that developed toward unity as Greece conquered her conquerors, and the Americans, as will presently appear, are not all of a piece. More important is it to note that Plutarch, although he informed himself as well as he could, liked those small, gossipy, and sometimes apocryphal details that illumine character and personality, whereas the high aim of the contributors to the *Dictionary of American Biography* was the utmost accuracy. Plutarch wrote as a private citizen and a moralist; these scholars contribute, as it were, to an official publication. The governing principle of Plutarch is a kind of happy art; the governing principle in this collection is demonstrable truth. This of course should not be construed to mean that Plutarch is nothing but gossip and that the American scholars have no art.

The central virtue of the Plutarchian system is retained in this collection. Some of the American worthies were reared in the antebellum South—Calhoun and Jefferson Davis, for examples—and others in the North, Franklin and Abraham Lincoln being obvious instances. It has been said of the antebellum South that the ideal of that region, or of a large part of it, was to become a Greek democracy based on slavery and supporting an elegant and responsible minority who were to govern it. The historical parallel is interesting. Both the Greek city states and the antebellum South were defeated as political entities and both passed into larger, more imperial systems by no means unsympathetic with the cultural dreams of the defeated groups (consider the vogue of the romantic South in song and story). It is true the North-South parallelism, though it works neatly in the cases of Jefferson-Hamilton, Lincoln-Davis, and Grant-Lee, will not work consistently, just as the Greek-Roman parallels and oppositions do not work out consistently in Plutarch. Andrew Jackson, for example, was born in South Carolina, matured in Tennessee, and fought his most famous battle in Louisiana, but historians do not agree whether the Southern, the Western, or the national element dominates his career. Though Woodrow Wilson was born in Virginia and Theodore Roosevelt was born in New York, it would be difficult to demonstrate that the likenesses and differences in their political outlooks and programs are basically determined by their places of origin.

The United States is a nation notable for cultural pluralism, so that it is erroneous to think about parallel and opposition in these pairs of lives only or mainly in terms of the Mason and Dixon line. The genuine differences of value and of approach to the problem of creating a nation that separates Franklin from Washington is only partly topographical and springs rather from cultural traditions. Franklin is the enlightened utilitarian, Washington the enlightened aristocrat. Jackson and Marshall are paired. Jackson typifies government by energy, Marshall symbolizes government by law. Yet Marshall, like Oliver Wendell Holmes, sets a strong personal stamp upon his famous decisions, and Jackson, who looks like a Southerner and also expresses the restlessness of the frontier and of "democracy," in a supreme crisis turns to law, as is evident in his toast: "Our Union, it must be preserved," meaning that he proposed to control the illegal nullification movement in South Carolina by asserting the majesty of the constitution. Even the pairing of Roosevelt and Wilson, which looks like a chronological convenience only, is apposite. Roosevelt carried out the Big Stick policy and got the Panama Canal built with what looked like triumphant success but we are nowadays more than a little uneasy about both, whereas Wilson, triumphant in domestic policies we have all accepted, was made unhappy (like the hero of a Greek tragedy) because at the supreme crisis of his career he could control neither the world at Versailles nor the senate at home. Yet world and senate have since moved on lines he laid down.

IV

American biographies written in an older fashion than is here represented, if they were in book form, often postponed to a final chapter the private lives of their subjects and an estimate of the lasting significance of their careers and characters. Such summations, like the peroration of a formal address, either emitted an odd, mortuary air or seemed to be acts of desperation, as if the writer had suddenly remembered his hero was a man who did not live every hour of the twenty-four in the spotlight of immortal destiny. Such final estimates had the purpose of tinting the formality of historical narrative with the strong colors of personality. Today, however, biographers no longer summon the subject into court as if he were a historical suspect, compel him to testify on his own behalf before being dismissed, and indict or clear him after the manner of Macaulay. But how shall the makeup of a personality be made evident?

Plutarch and Boswell assembled the revealing anecdote, the remembered phrase, the traditional (or invented) conversation as they moved slowly and informally over the arc of somebody's life. But writing an account strictly limited in words, to some extent bound to a majority opinion, and for so quasi-official a purpose as that represented by a contribution to the *Dictionary of American Biography* does not permit the formal peroration except in limited degree and cuts down the space one can give to anecdote and quotation. The results in the lives here reprinted are not, however, monotonous but surprisingly varied. There is a famous tag by Goethe,

In der Beschränkung zeigt sich erst der Meister

—"it is in self-limitation that the master first shows himself to be one"—and quite possibly the very limitations imposed upon these writers have led them to the rich variety of means they adopt in their biographies.

It is illuminating to contrast the account of John Marshall by Mr. Corwin with that of Oliver Wendell Holmes by Mr. Justice Frankfurter, or that of Benjamin Franklin with that of Thomas Jefferson, the one by Carl Becker, the other by Dumas Malone. All four have admirable and varied styles. In all four cases a personality comes through the account. It then becomes a fascinating exercise in critical judgment to try to determine the degree to which quotation, anecdote, general history, and general reflections are instrumental in securing their biographical effects. Thus it is possible that if Mr. Corwin had quoted the *ipsissima verba* of John Marshall as often as Mr. Justice Frankfurter quotes the words of Holmes, he would have done Marshall a disservice, not because Marshall's decisions are not clear but because diction has altered and our response to certain categories of phrases has changed. Again, when Theodore Roosevelt died, William Allen White said it was like the ceasing of the playing of a military band. Only those who lived when Roosevelt was active can grasp at once the humor and the criticism in this figure of speech, but would so pungent a metaphor have been appropriate to Mr. Paxson's account of Roosevelt's later embittered years? Problems equally delicate arise when one asks how much military lore should be assembled to "explain" Washington, Lee, and Grant, and whether it is right that Calhoun the man should disappear into Calhoun the constitutional theorist as Mr. Phillips goes about the necessary task of making clear Calhoun's doctrine of concurrent majorities. The Lincoln biography is rather rich in anecdote, especially of Lincoln's boyhood, youth, and young manhood; but this is not true of the life of Clay. But was Clay an anecdotal personage? And how leave out anecdote if one is writing a life of Lincoln? Possibly the characteristic weakness of the biographical article is the lack of a sense of place, since the writer cannot, except in extreme instances, spend his precious words on topography, but, this aside, how widely varied, how economical, yet how sympathetic are the accounts of great American leaders here assembled from the *Dictionary of American Biography!*

HOWARD MUMFORD JONES

Benjamin Franklin

by

CARL L. BECKER

FRANKLIN, BENJAMIN (Jan. 17, 1706–Apr. 17, 1790),
printer, author, philanthropist, inventor, statesman, diplomat, scientist, was born in Milk Street, Boston. His father, Josiah, came to
New England "about 1682" (moving from Banbury to Boston,
1683) from Ecton, Northamptonshire, England, where the parish
records of his Protestant ancestors run back to 1555. His mother,
second wife of Josiah, was Abiah, the daughter of Peter Folger, a
man of liberal views who taught the Indians to read and wrote
some doggerel verse (*A Looking Glass for the Times*). Benjamin
was the tenth son of Josiah, and the youngest son of the youngest
son for five generations. He learned to read at a very early age,
probably taught by his father who destined him for the church as
"the tithe of his sons," and sent him at eight years to the Boston
Grammar School. The expense proving too great, he was transferred
within less than a year to George Brownell's school for writing and
arithmetic. At the age of ten he was taken into his father's business
(tallow chandler and soap boiler). Disliking this, he was apprenticed
at twelve years to his brother James, a printer, who later (1721)
started the *New England Courant,* the fourth newspaper established
in the British colonies. In 1722 James was "taken up, censur'd, and
imprisoned for a month." During this time the paper was issued
under the management of Benjamin, his status as apprentice being
concealed by a "flimsy" (dishonest) device (Smyth, *The Writings of
Benjamin Franklin*, I, 248). Repeated quarrels with his brother led

Benjamin to leave Boston for Philadelphia, where he arrived in October 1723, at the age of seventeen.

At this early age Benjamin was already an expert printer, and had begun that close application to reading, writing, reflection, and self-improvement which, continued through life, was one secret of his intellectual eminence and of his practical success. Besides a few books in his father's house, he had access to the small library of Matthew Adams. Bunyan, Plutarch, Defoe, and Cotton Mather came his way. Tryon's book on "vegetable diet" interested him. Cocker's arithmetic, Seller's work on navigation, and an English grammar (Greenwood?) were studied. Locke's *Essay*, some works of Shaftesbury and Collins, Xenophon's *Memorabilia*, the "Art of Thinking by Messrs. du Port Royal"—all of these were pored over and reflected upon to some purpose. By some happy chance he bought an odd volume of Addison's *Spectator*, which he read "over and over," the style of which he thought "excellent, and wished, if possible, to imitate." Making notes of the ideas in several papers, he laid them by, and after some days "try'd to compleat the papers again. . . . Then I compared my *Spectator* with the original, discovered some of my faults, and corrected them" (*Writings*, I, 241). Thus playing the "sedulous ape," the boy acquired a vocabulary and fashioned his style. One day he composed a labored "essay," signed it Silence Dogood, and secretly slipped it under the door of his brother's shop. To his great delight it was printed. Others followed, fourteen in all—his earliest publications, crude indeed but characteristic.

Franklin arrived in Philadelphia with one Dutch dollar and a copper shilling. Obtaining employment in the print-shop of Samuel Keimer, he soon demonstrated his ability and made a circle of friends. Through his brother-in-law, Robert Homes, he fell under the notice of the eccentric Gov. Keith, who urged him to set up for himself and sent him off to London to buy equipment, promising him letters of credit for the purpose. In London (1724), no letters of credit being forthcoming, Franklin found employment at Palmer's (later at Watts's) printing-house. At the former he set up William Wollaston's *The Religion of Nature Delineated* (1725) which inspired him to write and print a refutation—*A Dissertation on Liberty and Necessity, Pleasure and Pain* (1725), in which he presented, cleverly for a boy, the current theory of necessity. He returned to Philadelphia in October 1726, with Mr. Denham, a Quaker merchant, in whose shop he served as clerk, learning accounts and becoming "expert in selling." Upon the sudden death of

Denham, Franklin was once more employed by Keimer, but in 1728 left him to form a partnership with Hugh Meredith. In 1730 he became sole owner of the business, including *The Pennsylvania Gazette* (founded in 1728 by Keimer) which Franklin and Meredith had purchased in 1729.

Established in business on his own at the age of twenty-four, Franklin settled down. On Sept. 1, 1730, he "took to wife" Deborah Read, the daughter of his first landlady. Since she was already married to a certain Rogers who had deserted her (never afterwards heard of) the marriage was a common-law union. To them two children were born: Francis Folger (1732–1736), and Sarah (1743–1808), later the wife of Richard Bache. Franklin had besides one illegitimate son: William Franklin, later governor of New Jersey and a Loyalist during the Revolution. Franklin's wife was a person of meager education, incapable of sharing, or even of understanding, the importance of his intellectual interests. But she was devoted to him, even taking William Franklin to live in the house for a time, and by her industry and thrift contributed to his material comfort and welfare. "She proved a good and faithful helpmate, assisted me much by attending the shop; we throve together, and have ever mutually endeavor'd to make each other happy" (*Writings*, I, 311). Marrying chiefly in order to relieve the strain of youthful passion, Franklin thus makes the best of a bad business.

From 1730 to 1748 Franklin applied himself to business, won a competence, and laid the foundation of his fame at home and abroad. Industry and thrift contributed to the prosperity of his business. "In order to secure my credit and character as a tradesman, I took care not only to be in *reality* industrious and frugal, but to avoid all appearance to the contrary. I drest plainly; I was seen at no places of idle diversion. I never went out a fishing or shooting; a book, indeed, sometimes debauch'd me from my work, but that was seldom, snug, and gave no scandal; and, to show that I was not above my business, I sometimes brought home the paper I purchas'd at the stores thro' the streets on a wheel-barrow" (*Writings*, I, 307–08). But the chief reason for his success was his capacity for making friends, influential and otherwise, his uncanny instinct for advertising himself and his paper, and above all the sense, novelty, and charm of the things he wrote for it. Nothing better exhibits the man, or better illustrates his ingenuity as an advertiser, than his famous almanac, *Poor Richard* (1733–58). "Richard Saunders," the Philomath of the almanac, was the Sir Roger de Coverley of the masses, pilfering the world's store of aphorisms, and adapting them to the circumstances and the understanding of the poor. "Necessity never made a good bargain." "It is hard for an empty sack to stand upright." "Many dishes make diseases." "The used key is always bright." The almanac was immediately successful, and commonly sold about ten thousand copies. "As poor Richard says" became a current phrase, used to give weight to any counsel of thrift. The work made Franklin's name a household word throughout the colonies, and gave a homespun flavor to American humor. The introduction to Franklin's last almanac (Father Abraham's speech at the auction) spread the fame of Poor Richard in Europe. It was printed in broadsides and posted on walls in England, and, in translation, distributed by the French clergy among their parishioners. It has been translated into fifteen languages, and reprinted at least four hundred times.

Although in origin a business venture, Poor Richard was a genuine expression of Franklin's passion for improving himself and others. He was forever laboring consciously to perfect his mind and his character. He taught himself (beginning in 1733) to read French, Spanish, Italian, and Latin. In 1727 he established the "Junto," a debating club devoted to the discussion of morals, politics, and natural philosophy. He was easily the best informed and the most skilled in discussion. At first he was inclined to be argumentative, given to laying traps for his opponents (a trick learned from Socrates), in order to show up their errors or stupidities. Finding this not useful, since it got him disliked and only confirmed his opponents in their opinions, he deliberately adopted the habit of expressing himself "in terms of modest diffidence; never using . . . the words *certainly, undoubtedly,* . . . but rather say, I conceive or apprehend, . . . or, *it is so, if I am not mistaken.* This habit, I believe, has been of great advantage to me when I have had occasion to inculcate my opinions" (*Writings,* I, 244, 338). Thus early in life Franklin trained himself in the fine art of inducing others to appropriate as their own the ideas or the projects which he wished to have prevail.

In the same pragmatic way Franklin set about devising a religion for the practise of the useful virtues. He regretted his youthful essay on *Liberty and Necessity,* suspecting, from sad experience, that a materialistic doctrine, "tho' it might be true, was not very useful." It seemed to him far more useful to believe in God and to infer that "though certain actions might not be bad *because* they were forbidden [by Revelation] . . . yet probably these actions might be forbidden *because* they were bad" (*Writings,* I, 296). At the age of twenty-two he drafted "Articles of Belief and Acts of Religion" (*Ibid.*, II, 91). The substance of the creed which he held throughout his life was that the one God, who made all things and governs the world through his providence, ought to be worshipped by adoration, prayer, and thanksgiving; that the most acceptable service of God is doing good to men; that the soul is immortal, and that God will certainly reward virtue and punish vice, either here or hereafter. Aiming at "moral perfection," he made a list of the useful virtues, which turned out to be thirteen—Temperance, Silence, Order, Resolution, Frugality, Industry, Sincerity, Justice, Moderation, Cleanliness, Tranquillity, Chastity, and Humility. To each of these in turn he gave "a week's strict attention, marking down in a book the measure of daily success achieved in the practice of each." Thus he went through "a course compleat in thirteen weeks, and four courses a year." He was surprised to find himself "so much fuller of faults" than he had imagined, but persisting for some years he had the satisfaction of "seeing them diminish." To propagate these simple doctrines and practices, Franklin designed (1732) to write a book on "The Art of Virtue," and to unite all men of good will in a society for the practise of it (*Writings*, I, 326; IV, 12, 121; 377; J. G. von Herder, *Sämmtliche Werke*, 1830, XVII, 10, 16).

His passion for improvement made him the leader in many movements for the benefit of his community. He initiated projects for establishing a city police, and for the paving and the better cleaning and lighting of city streets. He was largely instrumental in establishing a circulating library in Philadelphia, the first in America, 1731; in founding in 1743 the American Philosophical Society, incorporated 1780; a city hospital, 1751; and an Academy for the Education of Youth, opened in 1751, incorporated, 1753 (the origin of the University of Pennsylvania). Franklin rarely solicited public office; but he was too public-spirited to avoid such honors. In 1729 he supported the popular demand for paper money. He was clerk of the Pennsylvania Assembly (1736–51); member for Philadelphia (1751–64); deputy postmaster at Philadelphia (1737–53), and, jointly with William Hunter, deputy postmaster-general for the colonies (1753–74). This was one of the few offices he ever solicited. In the latter capacity he made visits of inspection to nearly every colony, and not only increased the frequency and efficiency of the mail deliveries, but made the post-office a financial success as well.

In the intervals of his varied activities as printer, philanthropist, and politician, Franklin found time for the study of science. It was probably in England that his attention was first turned to "Natural

Philosophy." There he met Mandeville, and Dr. Pemberton, the secretary of the Royal Society, and was "extremely desirous" of seeing Newton, then at the height of his fame. Returning to America he was soon discussing, in the Junto, such questions as: "Is sound an entity or a body?" "How may the phenomena of vapors be explained?" As early as 1737 he was writing, in the *Gazette*, on earthquakes. In 1743, prevented from observing an eclipse of the moon by a "northeaster," he was surprised to learn that the storm struck Philadelphia sooner than it struck Boston; which led him to the discovery that northeast storms on the Atlantic coast move against the wind. In the winter of 1739–40 he invented the "Pennsylvania Fireplace," a stove with an open firebox, which heated rooms better with less expense. He contrived a clock which told the hours, minutes, and seconds with only three wheels and two pinions in the movement (improved by James Ferguson, it was known as Ferguson's clock). Every sort of natural phenomenon enlisted his interest and called forth some ingenious idea. In one short letter he speaks of linseed oil, hemp land, swamp draining, variations in climate, northeast storms, the cause of springs on mountains, sea-shell rocks, grass seed, taxation, and smuggling (*Writings*, II, 310). So fascinating was natural philosophy to Franklin that he determined to make it his vocation. Business was a game which he could play with skill, but he cared little for it, or for the money it brought, except as a guarantee of independence. At the age of forty-two he had won a competence. Besides the income from some real estate, his business was worth perhaps £2,000 a year. In 1748 he therefore entered into a partnership with his foreman, David Hall, who was to run the business, relieving Franklin "of all care of the printing office," an arrangement which lasted eighteen years and paid him some £670 annually. "I flatter'd myself that, by the sufficient tho' modest fortune I had acquir'd, I had secured leisure during the rest of my life for philosophical studies and amusements" (*Ibid.*, I, 373–74). The leisure acquired lasted without serious interruptions for no more than six years; but it was during these years that he made those electrical experiments on which his fame as a scientist chiefly rests.

Franklin first witnessed experiments with electricity during a visit to Boston in 1743, and began to make them himself about two years later when Peter Collinson sent to the Philadelphia Library an "electric tube." With this fascinating toy he spent all of his spare time. "I never was before engaged in any study that so totally engrossed my attention" (*Writings*, II, 302). In July 1747 he sent to Collinson an amazingly precise, clear, and intelligible account of his experiments. He noted "the wonderful effect of pointed bodies, both in *drawing off* and *throwing off,* the electrical fire." He noted that a person "standing on wax" was differently affected by the electrical charge than a person standing on the floor; and from this fact, tested in a variety of ways, "there have arisen," he says, "some new terms among us. we say B (and bodies like circumstanced) is electrised *positively;* A, *negatively.* Or, rather, B is electrised *plus;* A, *minus"* (*Ibid.,* II, 302–10). He was soon experimenting with "Muschenbroek's wonderful bottle" (Leyden jar), and was confirmed in his "single fluid" theory (*Ibid.,* I, 95; II, 325). "The eleven experiments, to each of which a single brief paragraph is given, cover the essential phenomena of the condenser. As statements of fact they will stand almost without revision or amendment to the present day" (E. L. Nichols, in *Record of the Celebration of the Two Hundredth Anniversary of the Birth of Benjamin Franklin,* p. iii). Franklin was not the first to suggest the identity of lightning and electricity; but he proposed a method of testing the theory by erecting an iron rod on a high tower or steeple (letter to Collinson, July 29, 1750; *Writings,* II, 426, 437). At first English scientists ignored the proposal, even after Franklin's letters were published in 1751 through Collinson's efforts (*Experiments and Observations on Electricity, Made at Philadelphia in America, by Mr. Benjamin Franklin,* London, 1751). But on May 10, 1752, an assistant of Thomas-François Dalibard, a French scientist who had brought out a translation of the letters, successfully undertook the experiment at Marly-la-Ville. Another Frenchman repeated the "Philadelphia experiment" in Paris about a week later, and in the following summer several Englishmen performed it with equal success. Franklin, not having the means of testing his own method, devised a simpler one. This was the famous kite experiment, performed by Franklin in the summer of 1752, and described by him in the *Pennsylvania Gazette,* Oct. 19. These experiments, together with Franklin's published letters on the subject, established his fame as a scientist. The degree of Master of Arts was conferred on him by Harvard and by Yale (1753), and by William and Mary (1756). His fame pleased as much as it surprised him. More than ever he desired to devote his time to "philosophical studies," which it now seemed might be something more than mere "amusements."

His dream of leisure for philosophical studies was never to be realized. Soon after retiring from private business, public affairs began to claim him in earnest, and during the rest of his life he was chiefly engaged in politics and diplomacy. He was elected to the

Assembly in 1751 and at once became one of its leading members. In 1754 he was sent to represent Pennsylvania at the Albany Congress, called to unite the colonies in the war against the French and Indians. His "Plan of Union" was adopted by the Congress in preference to others; but "its fate was singular: the assemblies did not adopt it, as they all thought there was too much *prerogative* in it, and in England it was judged to have too much of the *democratic*" (*Writings*, I, 388; III, 197). Meantime the war had intensified the old dispute between the Assembly and the proprietors (descendants of William Penn, who lived in England and by the charter were privileged to appoint and instruct the governors of Pennsylvania). The chief grievance was that the proprietors forbade the governor to pass money bills for defense unless the vast proprietary estates were exempt from taxation (report of the Assembly committee, drafted by Franklin, 1757. *Ibid.*, III, 370). The proprietors proving obdurate, the Assembly decided to appeal directly to the British government, and in 1757 Franklin was sent to England to present its case.

The business of his first mission was not settled for nearly three years. In 1760, after two hearings before the Privy Council, a bill of the Assembly taxing the proprietary estates, except unsurveyed waste lands, was allowed by the King. In spite of the long delay, perhaps because of it, Franklin remained in England until 1762. These five years were perhaps the happiest of his life. He resided with Mrs. Margaret Stevenson, at 7 Craven St., where he became at once the beloved and well-cared-for foster father of the family. With Mrs. Stevenson, and especially with her daughter Mary, he formed an enduring friendship. In the Craven Street house he set up an "eletrical machine" and carried on experiments. He indulged his humor by composing "The Craven Street Gazette" in which the doings of Her Majesty's Court were related with becoming solemnity. He made journeys—to Holland, to Scotland, to Cambridge, to the ancestral home at Ecton. He became intimate with Collinson, Fothergill, Priestley, Strahan; and corresponded with Lord Kames and David Hume. He visited the University of Edinburgh, received the degree of LL.D. from St. Andrews (1759), and of D.C.L. from Oxford (1762). He followed the war with interest, opposed the clamor for peace in 1760 by publishing in the *London Chronicle* a satire "On the Meanes of Disposing the Enemie to Peace" (*Writings*, IV, 90); and argued at length the advantages of taking Canada rather than Guadaloupe from France ("The Interest of Great Britain Considered," *Ibid.*, IV, 35). To this pamphlet, which tradition supposes to have had some influence with the government, there was appended a brief paper written in 1751 and first published in 1755 which in some points anticipates the Malthusian theory of population ("Observations concerning the Increase of Mankind, Peopling of Countries, &c.," *Ibid.*, III, 63. See T. R. Malthus, *An Essay on the Principles of Population*, 1803 ed., pp. iv, 2). In these papers he argued: (1) that in America, where land is easily obtained, population doubled every twenty years; (2) that where land is easily obtained manufactures will not develop; (3) that Canada (including the Mississippi Valley) was accordingly more valuable than Guadaloupe since (a) becoming populous it will furnish rich markets for British goods, but (b) remaining indefinitely agricultural it will not compete with British industry.

In 1762 Franklin returned reluctantly to Philadelphia, envying the "petty island" its "sensible, virtuous and elegant Minds" (*Writings*, IV, 194), and flirting with the idea of settling his affairs so that "in two years at farthest . . . I may then remove to England—provided we can persuade the good Woman to cross the seas" (*Ibid.*, IV, 182). Pressure of affairs, or perhaps the "good Woman," persuaded him to conclude that *"old Trees cannot safely be transplanted"* (*Ibid.*, IV, 217); but, new disputes arising with the proprietors, the Assembly once more sent him to England to obtain a recall of the Charter. This object was not attained, was indeed submerged in the greater issue raised by Grenville's proposal to levy a stamp tax in the colonies. In the second interview between Grenville and the colonial agents Franklin was present and protested against the measure, suggesting instead the "usual constitutional method" of raising a revenue. Perceiving that the bill would be enacted, he advised his friends to make the best of it. "We might as well have hindered the sun's setting. . . . But since 'tis down . . . let us make as good a night of it as we can. We may still light candles" (*Ibid.*, IV, 390). When Grenville applied to the colonial agents to recommend Americans for the new office of stamp distributor, Franklin named his friend John Hughes for Philadelphia; and failing to foresee opposition to the act he sent over some stamped papers to be sold by his partner. These acts laid him open to the charge of having urged the law in order to profit by it; his house was menaced, and his wife advised to seek safety; but his prestige was soon restored by his famous "examination" before the House of Commons. In February 1766, during the debates on the repeal of the Stamp Act, he was called before the House (committee of the whole) and questioned on the subject. Of the 174 questions asked, some were put by opponents, some by friends, of the act. The replies, brief, lucid, and to the point, aimed to show that the tax was contrary to custom, and administratively impracticable both on account of the circumstances of the country and the settled opposition of the people. Published immediately and widely read, the performance greatly increased Franklin's influence in America and his reputation abroad. "The questions . . . are answered with such deep and familiar knowledge of the subject, such precision and perspicuity, such temper and yet such spirit, as do the greatest honor to Dr. Franklin, and justify the general opinion of his character and abilities" (*Gentleman's Magazine,* July 1767, p. 368).

In 1766, after the repeal of the Stamp Act, Franklin requested permission to return to Philadelphia, but the Assembly reappointed him its agent. He was also named colonial agent of Georgia (1768), New Jersey (1769), and Massachusetts (1770). Those appointments, together with his outstanding reputation, made Franklin a kind of ambassador extraordinary from the colonies to Great Britain. During those years he worked persistently for reconciliation: urging his American friends to avoid indiscreet conduct; in England defending the colonies in private conversation and by published articles. Until the passing of the coercive acts (1774) he never quite despaired; but as the years passed he became less hopeful. A more serious note creeps into his correspondence; his sympathies become more American, less British. As early as 1768 he complained that all his efforts were without avail except to make him suspect: "In England, of being too much of an American, and in America, of being too much of an Englishman" (*Writings,* V, 182). His close observation of British politics abated both his admiration for the English government and his expectation that conciliatory measures would prevail. In 1768 he wrote, no doubt in an unusually depressed mood: "Some punishment seems preparing for a people, who are ungratefully abusing the best constitution and the best King . . . any nation was ever blessed with, intent on nothing but luxury, licentuousness, power, places, pensions, and plunder" (*Ibid,* V, 133). He welcomed every prospect of returning to America. He had indeed friends enough in England to live there comfortably the rest of his days, "if it were not for my American connections, & the indelible Affection I retain for that dear Country" (*Ibid,* V, 382).

As his admiration for England abated and his love of America deepened, his ideas on American rights became more precise and more advanced. In 1765 he did not doubt the right of Parliament to levy the Stamp Act. In 1766 he defended the distinction between internal and external taxes, contenting himself with an ironical and prophetic comment: "Many arguments have lately been made here to shew them [Americans] . . . that if you have no right to tax them internally you have none to tax them externally, or make any other law to bind them. At present they do not reason so; but in time they may possibly be convinced by these arguments" (*Writings*, IV, 446). By 1768 Franklin was himself convinced. In order to resist the Townshend duties (1767), Dickinson and Samuel Adams had devised ingenious arguments designed to admit the right of Parliament to legislate for the colonies while denying the right to tax them. Franklin caused Dickinson's letters to be published in England, but writing to William Franklin Mar. 13, 1768, he brushed aside these too subtle distinctions. "The more I have thought and read on the subject, the more I find myself confirmed in opinion, that no middle doctrine can be well maintained, I mean not clearly with intelligible arguments. Something might be made of either of the extremes; that Parliament has a power to make *all laws* for us, or that it has a power to make no laws for us; and I think the arguments for the latter more numerous and weighty, than those for the former" (*Ibid.*, V, 115). Two years later he deprecated the use of such phrases as *"supreme authority of Parliament,"* and urged Americans to base their rights on the theory that the colonies and England were united only, "as England and Scotland were before the Union, by having one common Sovereign, the King" (*Ibid.*, V, 260). Thus early did Franklin accept the doctrine later formulated in the Declaration of Independence.

Appointed agent by the Massachusetts House of Representatives, Oct. 24, 1770, Franklin's American sympathies were intensified by the truculent unfriendliness of Hillsborough, who refused to recognize the appointment until approved by Gov. Hutchinson. Too long absent from America to form an independent judgment of the situation in Massachusetts, he was further prejudiced by the colored accounts of it transmitted by Samuel Cooper and Thomas Cushing. Although deprecating violence, and advising the Boston leaders that the government contemplated no new taxes, he agreed with Samuel Adams that good relations could not be established until the British government had repealed the tea duty. He welcomed the establishment of correspondence committees, and suggested, as a means of bringing "the Dispute to a Crisis," that the colonies should "engage . . . with each other . . . never [to] grant Aids to the Crown in any General War, till . . . [their] Rights are recogniz'd by the King and both Houses of Parliament" (1773. *Writings*, VI,

77). He was convinced of Hutchinson's "duplicity," and thought his controversy with the House of Representatives would discredit him in England. While encouraging the anti-British party in Boston, Franklin contrived to exasperate the anti-American party in London. He published two pointed satires, "Edict by the King of Prussia," and "Rules by which a Great Empire may be reduced to a Small one," which did more to aggravate than to compose the quarrel (see Mansfield's opinion, *Ibid.*, VI, 145); and, wittingly or unwittingly, he contributed much to the final breach by his part in the famous affair of the "Hutchinson Letters." In 1772 an unknown member of Parliament showed Franklin certain letters, six of which were written by Gov. Hutchinson in 1768–69, said to have been addressed (the name had been erased) to William Whately, former secretary of Grenville, urging drastic measures on the ground that "there must be an abridgment of what are called English Liberties" (the letters are in J. K. Hosmer, *Life of Hutchinson*, 1896, p. 429). By permission of the possessor, Franklin sent the letters to Thomas Cushing, with the stipulation that they should be returned to him without being either copied or printed. The letters were shortly printed in Boston and circulated in London, the immediate result of which was a duel between Thomas Whately, executor of the estate of William Whately, and John Temple, whom Whately accused of stealing the letters. To exonerate Temple, Franklin declared that he alone had procured and transmitted the letters, and that neither Thomas Whately nor Temple had ever had possession of them (*Writings*, VI, 284). In conservative circles Franklin was at once regarded as an incendiary and a thief; on Jan. 29, 1774, at a hearing before the Privy Council in the Cockpit on a petition of the Massachusetts House to remove Hutchinson, Solicitor General Wedderburn, on the assumption that Franklin had purloined the letters, denounced him in unmeasured terms as a man without honor who would "henceforth esteem it a libel to be called a man of letters: *homo* TRIUM *literarum*"—a man of three letters, *i.e. FUR*, the Latin word for thief (*Ibid.*, X, 269. For full account of the episode, see *Writings*, VI, 258–89; X, 258–72; Van Doren, *post*, pp. 443–51, 458–78; R. H. Lee, *Life of Arthur Lee*, 1829, I, 266; P. O. Hutchinson, *Diary and Letters of Thomas Hutchinson*, 1883, I, 81; J. K. Hosmer, *Hutchinson*, ch. XII). Two days later the government dismissed him from his office as deputy postmaster-general. Supported by his friends, and convinced that the sending of the letters was "one of the best actions of his life" (*Writings*, X, 270), Franklin remained in England, aiding Pitt in his fruitless efforts at conciliation, until Mar. 20, 1775, when he sailed for America.

On May 6, 1775, the day following his return to Philadelphia, Franklin was chosen a member of the second Continental Congress. Conciliation seemed to him now no more than a vain hope. To satisfy the moderates he supported the Petition to the King, giving "Britain . . . one opportunity more of recovering the friendship of the colonies," but "I think she has not sense enough to embrace [it], and so I conclude she has lost them forever" (*Writings*, VI, 408). He sketched a Plan of Union for the colonies; organized the Post-Office, of which he was the first postmaster-general; served on the commissions sent to induce the Canadians to join the colonies, to advise Washington on defense, and to listen to Howe's peace proposals; and on the committee to draft the Declaration of Independence. As a member of the committee appointed Nov. 29, 1775, to correspond "with friends in Great Britain, Ireland, and other parts of the world," he prepared the instructions for Silas Deane, whom the committee sent to France in 1776, and through Barbeu Dubourg, the translator of his works, did much to facilitate Deane's reception by Vergennes. Encouraged by letters from Deane, Congress decided, Sept. 26, 1776, to send a commission of three to negotiate a treaty with France. Franklin, Deane, and Jefferson were first chosen. Upon Jefferson's declination, Arthur Lee was appointed in his place. Franklin was then almost seventy years old: "I am but a fag end, and you may have me for what you please" (*Writings*, X, 301). His last act before leaving Philadelphia (Oct. 26) was to lend Congress some three or four thousand pounds. He arrived in France Dec. 4, 1776.

Unwilling as yet to recognize the rebellious colonies, the French government could not openly receive Franklin; but the French people gave him a welcome rarely if ever accorded to any foreigner. He was already well known in France through two previous visits in 1767 and 1769, and through the translations of his scientific works, parts of Poor Richard, and the examination in Parliament. To the readers of Plutarch and Rousseau nothing could be more appropriate than that this backwoods sage and philosopher should now come to plead the cause of a young nation claiming its "natural right" to freedom from oppression. And Franklin had only to be himself to play the part allotted to him. His fur cap (very rarely worn indeed), covering unpowdered gray locks; his simple dress and unpretentious manners; his countenance, shrewd, placid, benignant; his wit and wisdom, homely indeed but somehow lifted above the provincial; the flexibility of his unwarped and emancipated intelligence, and the natural courtesy with which the sage from Arcady demeaned himself, without arrogance and without servility, in the most sophisticated society in the world—all this made Franklin more than an ambassador: it made him a symbol, the personification of all the ideas dear to the Age of Enlightment. To the French people Franklin was Socrates born again in the imagined state of nature. At Passy, where M. Ray de Chaumont placed at his disposal part of the Hôtel de Valentinois, he lived for nine years, in comparative seclusion, and yet the object of unmeasured adulation. His sayings were treasured and repeated as *bon mots.* His portrait was to be seen everywhere in shop windows and in many private houses. His image was stamped on innumerable medals, medallions, rings, watches, snuff-boxes, and bracelets. John Adams, who later replaced Silas Deane, contrived, in spite of characteristic exaggeration and a certain irascible jealousy, to describe exactly the impression which Franklin made in France. "His reputation was more universal than that of Leibnitz or Newton, Frederick or Voltaire, and his character more beloved and esteemed than any or all of them. . . . His name was familiar to government and people . . . to such a degree that there was scarcely a peasant or a citizen, a *valet de chambre,* coachman or footman, a lady's chambermaid or a scullion in a kitchen who was not familiar with it, and who did not consider him as a friend to human kind. When they spoke of him, they seemed to think he was to restore the Golden Age" (*Works of John Adams,* 1856, I, 660).

Franklin's popularity contributed much to the success of his diplomatic mission. On Dec. 28, 1776, the Commissioners, secretly received by Vergennes, presented their instructions and requested a treaty of commerce; and on Feb. 2 they went so far as to promise that if France became involved in war with Great Britain on account of such a treaty, the United States would not "separately conclude a peace, nor aid Great Britain against France or Spain." Vergennes was more than willing to aid in disrupting the British Empire in order to redress the European balance in favor of France; but he could not take the decisive step until the King consented, and wished not to do so without the cooperation of Spain or until it was clear that the colonies would be content with nothing less than independence. Meantime, Franklin had been in communication with British agents through unofficial messengers; and in April 1778 he negotiated directly with Hartley, a member of Parliament, who came over to Paris. These overtures came to nothing, however, because of the British refusal to grant independence to the American colonies as a condition of peace. Franklin's contribution to the success of Vergennes's policy was indirect, but not unimportant. His mere presence in France, intensifying popular enthusiasm for the Americans and encouraging American privateers to operate from French ports, made it increasingly difficult for the French government to avoid a rupture with Great Britain in any case; while his relations with persons in England gave life to the rumor that the colonies, failing the aid of France, would as a price of independence join Great Britain in the conquest of the French and Spanish West Indies, a rumor which Vergennes, without crediting, made use of to persuade the King. In the actual negotiations for an alliance (Dec. 1777–Feb. 1778), which the King authorized after the Battle of Saratoga, Franklin seems to have desired the French government to guarantee the conquest of the Mississippi Valley (where he was personally interested in certain land grants) as a condition of peace, a point which Vergennes, not wishing to alienate Spain, was unwilling to concede. The final treaties (a treaty of commerce, and a treaty of "defensive alliance . . . to maintain effectively the . . . independence absolute and unlimited of the United States") were signed Feb. 6, 1778. For this occasion Franklin donned the suit of Manchester velvet last worn when Wedderburn denounced him in the Cockpit.

Meantime the relations between the commissioners were anything but cordial. Arthur Lee, an incurably vain, suspicious, and wrong-headed person, charged Beaumarchais and Deane, and by implication Franklin, with incompetence and venality, especially in connection with the supplies furnished the colonies through the dummy company of Beaumarchais, Hortalez et cie. The arrangements between Beaumarchais and Vergennes were made before Franklin arrived in France, and Deane was the American agent in whom Beaumarchais confided. Franklin, leaving the business to Deane, whom he trusted, seems not to have informed himself of the exact nature of the understanding. The most that can rightly be charged against Franklin is that he appointed as his secretary his grandson, Temple Franklin, an incompetent boy; that his accounts were accordingly in confusion; and that he appointed as business agent at Nantes his grand-nephew, Jonathan Williams, who proved incompetent if not venal. Franklin made it a rule never to engage in personal controversies; he had learned early in life that "spots of dirt" thrown on one's character were best left alone since "they would all rub off when they were dry." He suffered Lee's "magisterial snubbings and rebukes" with a serene patience that rarely failed (see, however, *Writings,* VII, 129–38); but he had more important tasks than the hopeless one of setting Arthur Lee right. Being the only American with whom Vergennes cared to deal, the chief burden of the negotiations with the French government fell to him. He also served virtually as consul, judge of admiralty, and director of naval affairs. He negotiated for the exchange of prisoners in England. He was burdened with innumerable applications, from Americans desiring recommendation in France, from Frenchmen desiring recommendation in America. In addition he found time to publish articles designed to strengthen American credit abroad. In April 1778, John Adams, replacing Deane, came to Paris, offended de Chaumont by offering to pay rent for Franklin's house at Passy, helped Franklin to straighten out his account, was made "sick to death" by the Lee-Deane controversy, and recommended that the commission be replaced by a single agent. Lee was of the same opinion, suggesting himself as the proper person. On Sept. 14, 1778, Congress appointed Franklin sole plenipotentiary. With his status made definite his life became pleasanter. He found some time to write on scientific subjects; to carry on gay and frivolous correspondence with Madame Helvetius and Madame Brillon; and to amuse himself and his friends with satires and bagatelles printed on his excellent Passy press. But if his life was pleasanter, his responsibilities were if anything heavier. For three years his chief service was to obtain money; his chief task to persuade Vergennes to overlook irregular methods and to honor debts for which the French government was in no way obligated. Aside from negotiating loans, Franklin was expected to meet the innumerable bills of exchange which were drawn on him, by Congress, by John Adams in Holland, by John Jay in Spain, by ship captains fitting out in any port that was handiest, even by his vilifiers Arthur Lee and Ralph Izard. On Mar. 12, 1781, on the ground that excessive duties were impairing his health, Franklin tendered his resignation to Congress. He was well aware that the friends of Lee, Izard, and Adams were about to move for his recall, and his resignation was probably no more than a shrewd political move designed to defeat the motion. At all events, when Congress voted to continue him, he slyly remarked: "I must . . . buckle again to Business, and thank God my Health & Spirits are of late improved . . . I call this Continuance an Honour . . . greater than my first Appointment, when I consider that all the Interest of my Enemies, united with my own Request, were not sufficient to prevent it" (*Writings,* VIII, 294).

On June 8, 1781, Franklin was named one of the commissioners to negotiate peace with Great Britain. While awaiting the arrival of Jay and Adams he assumed responsibility for the preliminary conversations, of which he wrote a detailed account. Resisting every suggestion that the colonies should make a separate peace, and keeping Vergennes informed of every step, he proposed as a basis of negotiation: (1) independence; (2) the cession of the Mississippi Valley; (3) fishing rights "on the banks of Newfoundland, and elsewhere." He objected to the British claim for the recovery of debts (later he conceded that just debts should be paid). He took the ground that Congress could not compensate the Loyalists, since the confiscation acts were state laws; but he suggested that Britain might contribute much to *real* conciliation by voluntarily ceding Canada, in which case the Loyalists might possibly be compensated by grants of wild lands in that country. Uncertain of the outcome of the naval war, the British government was apparently ready early in June to make peace on Franklin's terms. But at this point two circumstances contributed to give a new direction to the negotiations. Jay, arriving June 23, and suspecting the sincerity of the British, delayed matters by insisting that the British commissioners be authorized to treat with the United States as an independent state. Meantime British naval successes, culminating in the relief of Gibraltar, Oct. 10, strengthened the hands of the British commissioners, who now renewed the demand for compensation to the Loyalists, and objected to the American claim (injected into the negotiations by Adams) of a right to dry fish on British coasts. When the conference reached an impasse on these points, Franklin came forward with a proposal which seems to have turned the scale in favor of the Americans. On Nov. 29, according to Adams, Franklin "produced a paper from his pocket, in which he had drawn up a claim, and he said the first principle of the treaty was equality and reciprocity. Now, they demanded of us payment of debts, and . . . compensation to the refugees. . . . Then he stated the carrying off of goods from Boston, Philadelphia, and the Carolinas, . . . and the burning of towns, etc., and demanded that this might be sent with the rest." After further discussion of Franklin's counter demand for compensation, the British commissioners accepted the American "ultimatum respecting the fishery and the loyalists" (F. Wharton, *Diplomatic Correspondence of the U.S.,* 1889, VI, 87); and on the following day the preliminaries were signed.

In negotiating and signing the preliminaries without keeping the French government informed, the commissioners violated not only the instructions of Congress, but Franklin's earlier agreement with Vergennes. The responsibility for this step rests with Jay and Adams, who were convinced: (1) that Franklin was too subservient to French influence; and especially, (2) that France and Spain were secretly working to restrict the boundaries of the United States to the Alleghanies. The latter was true of Spain; true of France only so far as Vergennes was bound to consider the interest of Spain. Franklin's "subserviency" was only a superior diplomacy; but he yielded to his colleagues in order to maintain harmony. When Adams, shortly after his arrival (Oct. 26), gave Franklin his and Jay's reasons for ignoring Vergennes, "the Doctor," Adams reports, "heard me patiently, but said nothing; but at the next conference with Oswald, he turned to Jay and said: 'I am of your opinion, and will go on with these gentlemen in the business without consulting this court.' He accordingly met with us in most of our conferences, and has gone with us in entire harmony and unanimity throughout" (Wharton, VI, 91). Upon receiving the preliminaries, Vergennes wrote Franklin a sharp formal protest. It is possible that Vergennes, hampered by his obligations to Spain, was really pleased with the outcome, and that his protest was merely formal, and so understood by Franklin. It is difficult to suppose that Vergennes was unaware of the separate negotiations. Earlier he had himself said that each country "will make its own Treaty. All that is necessary . . . is, that the Treaties go hand in hand, and are sign'd all on the same day" (*Writings*, VIII, 512). Although the negotiations had not gone "hand in hand," it was stipulated in the preliminaries that the final treaty "is not to be concluded until terms of peace shall be agreed upon between Great Britain and France" (Wharton, VI, 96). There was therefore some basis for Franklin's reply to Vergennes's protest, in which he admitted that the commissioners had been "guilty of neglecting a point of *bienséance*," but contended that in substance there had been no breach of agreement since "no peace is to take place between us and England till you have concluded yours" (*Ibid.*, 144). He added: *"The English, I just now learn, flatter themselves they have already divided us."* Few diplomats, taking Vergennes's protest at its face value, would have ventured to unite with this bland apology a request for twenty million livres, or have contrived so to word it as to have obtained from the irritated minister a grant of six millions. The final peace was signed Sept. 3, 1783.

On Dec. 26, 1783, Franklin reminded Congress of its promise to recall him after the peace was made. Not until May 2, 1785, did he receive notice of the desired release. He left Passy, July 12, in one of "the King's Litters, carried by mules" (*Writings*, IX, 363), to embark from Havre de Grace. He arrived in Philadelphia Sept. 14, having profitably employed his time on the long voyage in making "Maritime Observations" and writing a detailed account of "The Causes and Cure of Smoky Chimneys." He was shortly chosen president of the executive council of Pennsylvania. While serving in this capacity, he was chosen a member of the Constitutional Convention which met in May 1787. Although suffering from the stone he attended the sessions regularly for over four months. Like Jefferson, this master of discussion was no speechmaker; and his few formal discourses were written out and read. The text of the last speech as printed by Smyth, p. 607, is incomplete and incorrect (see the text in Elliot's *Debates*, 1845, V, 554, which follows more nearly the Franklin autograph original in the Cornell University Library). None of his cardinal ideas was adopted. He favored a single chamber, an executive board, and opposed the payment of salaries to executive officials. Yet Franklin contributed not a little to the final result. His immense prestige, and the persuasive effect of his kindly personality and genial humor, were of great value in calming passions and compromising disputes. When the convention was at a deadlock over the question of representation, Franklin said: "If a property representation takes place, the small states contend that their liberties will be in danger. If an equality of votes is to be put in its place, the large states say their money will be in danger. When a broad table is to be made, and the edges of the planks do not fit, the artist takes a little from both, and makes a good joint" (Elliot's *Debates*, V, 266). Franklin's first proposal for a compromise was not adopted; but he was a member of the committee appointed to adjust the matter, and largely responsible for the compromise actually incorporated in the Constitution. Although the Constitution was not wholly to his liking, he urged in his inimitable manner that it be unanimously adopted. "I confess that there are several parts of this Constitution which I do not at present approve, but I am not sure I shall never approve them. . . . The older I grow, the more apt I am to doubt my own judgment. . . . Though many . . . persons think . . . highly of their own infallibility . . . few express it so naturally as a certain French lady, who . . . said: 'I don't know how it happens, sister, but I meet with nobody but myself who is always in the right'—*il n'y a que moi qui a toujours raison.* . . . On the whole, sir, I cannot help expressing a wish that every member of the Convention . . . would with me, on this occasion, doubt a little of his own infallibility, and, to make manifest our unanimity, put his name to the instrument" (*Ibid.*, 554–55).

During the last five years of his life Franklin lived in a commodious house near Market Street with his daughter (his wife died in 1774) and his grandchildren. He invented a device for lifting books from high shelves, wrote to his numerous friends at home and abroad, entertained his neighbors and the many strangers come to do him homage, enjoying to the last that ceaseless flow of "agreeable and instructive conversation" of which he was the master and the devotee (see Cutler's description, *Writings*, X, 478). His last public act was to sign a memorial to Congress for the abolition of slavery. He died Apr. 17, 1790, at the age of eighty-four years. At his funeral twenty thousand people assembled to do him honor. He was buried in Christ Church Burial Ground under a stone bearing a simple inscription of his own devising: *Benjamin and Deborah Franklin.*

Great men are often hampered by some inner discord or want of harmony with the world in which they live. It was Franklin's good fortune to have been endowed with a rare combination of rare qualities, and to have lived at a time when circumstances favored the development of all his powers to their fullest extent. He was a true child of the Enlightenment, not indeed of the school of Rousseau, but of Defoe and Pope and Swift, of Fontenelle and Montesquieu and Voltaire. He spoke their language, although with a homely accent, a tang of the soil, that bears witness to his lowly and provincial origin. His wit and humor, lacking indeed the cool, quivering brilliance of Voltaire or the corrosive bitterness of Pope and Swift, were all the more effective and humane for their dash of genial and kindly cynicism. He accepted without question and expressed without effort all the characteristic ideas and prepossessions of the century—its aversion to "superstition" and "enthusiasms" and mystery; its contempt for hocus-pocus and its dislike of dim perspectives; its healthy, clarifying scepticism; its passion for freedom and its humane sympathies; its preoccupation with the world that is evident to the senses; its profound faith in common sense, in the efficacy of Reason for the solution of human problems and the advancement of human welfare.

For impressing his age with the validity of these ideas, both by precept and example, Franklin's native qualities were admirably suited. His mind, essentially pragmatic and realistic, by preference occupied itself with what was before it, with the present rather than with the past or the future, with the best of possible rather than with the best of conceivable worlds. He accepted men and things, including himself, as they were, with a grain of salt indeed but with insatiable curiosity, with irrepressible zest and good humor. He took life as it came, with the full-blooded heartiness of a man unacquainted with inhibitions and repressions and spiritual *malaise*, as a game to be played, with honesty and sincerity, but with shrewdness and an eye to the main chance, above all without pontifical solemnity, without self-pity, eschewing vain regrets for lost illusions and vain striving for the light that never was. Both his achievements and his limitations spring from this: that he accepted the world as given with imperturbable serenity; without repining identified himself with it; and brought to the understanding and the mastery of it rare common sense, genuine disinterestedness, a fertile and imaginative curiosity, and a cool, flexible intelligence fortified by exact knowledge and chastened and humanized by practical activities.

Not only was Franklin by temperament disposed to take life as it came and to make the most of it; in addition fate provided him with a rich diversity of experience such as has rarely fallen to the lot of any man. Rising from poverty to affluence, from obscurity to fame, he lived on every social level in turn, was equally at ease with rich and poor, the cultivated and the untutored, and spoke with equal facility the language of vagabonds and kings, politicians and philosophers, men of letters, kitchen girls, and *femmes savantes*. Reared in Boston, a citizen of Philadelphia, residing for sixteen years in London and for nine in Paris, he was equally at home in three countries, knew Europe better than any other American, America better than any European, England better than most Frenchmen, France better than most Englishmen, and was acquainted personally or through correspondence with more men of eminence in letters, science, and politics than any other man of his time. Such a variety of experience would have confused and disoriented any man less happily endowed with a capacity for assimilating it. Franklin took it all easily, relishing it, savoring it, without rest and without haste adding to his knowledge, fortifying and tempering his intelligence, broadening his point of view, humanizing and mellowing his tolerant acceptance of men and things —in short chastening and perfecting the qualities that were natively his; so that in the end he emerges the most universal and cosmopolitan spirit of his age. Far more a "good European," a citi-

zen of the world, than Adams or Jefferson, Washington or Hutchinson, he remained to the end more pungently American than any of
them. Jefferson said that Franklin was the one exception to the
rule that seven years of diplomatic service abroad spoiled an American. Twenty-five years of almost continuous residence abroad did
not spoil Franklin. Acclaimed and decorated as no American had
ever been, he returned to Philadelphia and was immediately at
home again, easily recognizable by his neighbors as the man they
had always known—Ben Franklin, printer.

The secret of Franklin's amazing capacity for assimilating experience without being warped or discolored by it is perhaps to be found
in his disposition to take life with infinite zest and yet with humorous detachment. Always immersed in affairs, he seems never
completely absorbed by them; mastering easily whatever comes his
way, there remain powers in reserve never wholly engaged. It is
significant that his activities, with the exception of his researches
in science, seem to have been the result, not of any compelling
inner impulse or settled purpose, but rather of the pressure of external need or circumstance. He was a business man, and a good
one; but having won a competence he retired. He was an inventor
and a philanthropist, but not by profession; perceiving the need,
he invented a stove or founded a hospital. He was a politician and
a diplomat, and none more skilled; but not from choice; for the
most part he accepted as a duty the offices that were thrust upon
him. He was a writer, a prolific one; yet his writings were nearly
all occasional, prompted by the need of the moment. His one book,
the *Autobiography,* was begun as something that might be useful
to his son; that purpose served, it was never finished. He was a
literary artist of rare merit, the master of a style which for clarity,
precision, and pliable adhesion to the form and pressure of the
idea to be conveyed has rarely been equaled. Yet once having learned
the trade he was little preoccupied with the art of writing, content
to throw off in passing an acute pragmatic definition: Good writing
"ought to have a tendency to benefit the reader. . . . But taking
the question otherwise, an ill man may write an ill thing well. . . .
In this sense, that is well wrote, which is best adapted for obtaining
the end of the writer" (*Writings,* I, 37). It has been said that Franklin was not entrusted with the task of writing the Declaration of
Independence for fear he might conceal a joke in the middle of it.
The myth holds a profound symbolic truth. In all of Franklin's dealings with men and affairs, genuine, sincere, loyal as he surely
was, one feels that he is nevertheless not wholly committed; some

thought remains uncommunicated; some penetrating observation is held in reserve. In spite of his ready attention to the business in hand, there is something casual about his efficient dispatch of it; he manages somehow to remain aloof, a spectator still, with amiable curiosity watching himself functioning effectively in the world. After all men were but children needing to be cajoled; affairs a game not to be played without finesse. Was there not then, on that placid countenance, even at the signing of the great Declaration, the bland smile which seems to say: This is an interesting, alas even a necessary, game; and we are playing it well, according to all the rules; but men being what they are it is perhaps best not to inquire too curiously what its ultimate significance may be.

One exception there was—science: one activity which Franklin pursued without outward prompting, from some compelling inner impulse; one activity from which he never wished to retire, to which he would willingly have devoted his life, to which he always gladly turned in every odd day or hour of leisure, even in the midst of the exacting duties and heavy responsibilities of his public career. Science was after all the one mistress to whom he gave himself without reserve and served neither from a sense of duty nor for any practical purpose. Nature alone met him on equal terms, with a disinterestedness matching his own; needing not to be cajoled or managed with finesse, she enlisted in the solution of her problems the full power of his mind. In dealing with nature he could be, as he could not be in dealing with men and affairs, entirely sincere, pacific, objective, rational, could speak his whole thought without reservation, with no suggestion of a stupendous cosmic joke concealed in the premises. Franklin was indeed "many sided." From the varied facets of his powerful mind he threw a brilliant light on all aspects of human life; it is only in his character of natural philosopher that he emits a light quite unclouded. It is in this character therefore that the essential quality of the man appears to best advantage. Sir Humphry Davy has happily noted it for us. "The experiments adduced by Dr. Franklin . . . were most ingeniously contrived and happily executed. A singular felicity of induction guided all his researches, and by very small means he established very grand truths. The style and manner of his publication [on electricity] are almost as worthy of admiration as the doctrine it contains. He has endeavoured to remove all mystery and obscurity from the subject; he has written equally for the uninitiated and for the philosopher; and he has rendered his details amusing as well as perspicuous, elegant as well as simple. Science appears in his language in a dress wonderfully decorous, the best adapted to display her native loveliness. He has in no case exhibited that false dignity, by which philosophy is kept aloof from common applications, and he has sought rather to make her a useful inmate and servant in the common habitations of man, than to preserve her merely as an object of admiration in temples and palaces" (*Collected Works of Sir Humphry Davy*, 1840, VIII, 264–65).

––––––––––

[REVISED BIBLIOGRAPHY, by Leonard W Labaree. The Franklin Manuscripts are chiefly in five depositories: the Lib. of the Am. Philosophical Soc. at Phila. (16,000 documents in nine languages; for the largest part of these see I. M. Hays, *Calendar of the Papers of Benjamin Franklin in the Lib. of the Am. Philosophical Soc.*, 1908); the Lib. of Cong. (Stevens Collection, 14 vols., nearly 3,000 documents; see W. C. Ford, *List of the Benjamin Franklin Papers in the Lib. of Cong.*, 1905); the Papers of the Continental Congress in the Nat. Archives, about 1,900 documents; the Lib. of the Hist. Soc. of Pa., 1,300 documents; the Lib. of the Univ. of Pa. (800 documents; see "Calendar of the Papers of Benjamin Franklin in the Lib. of the Univ. of Pa.," published as an appendix of the work of I. M. Hays cited above). Other important groups of documents are in the Lib. of the Mass. Hist. Soc., Yale Univ. Lib., the Archives of the French Foreign Office, and Harvard College Lib. The original MS. of the *Autobiography* is in the Huntington Lib. at San Marino, Cal.

Of the many collected editions of Franklin's works the chief are: *Memoirs of the Life and Writings of Benjamin Franklin* . . . (3 vols., 1817–18; 6 vols., 1818–19), by his grandson William Temple Franklin; *The Works of Benjamin Franklin* (10 vols., 1836–40), by Jared Sparks, who "corrected" the text where he thought Franklin guilty of bad taste or vulgarity; *The Complete Works of Benjamin Franklin* (10 vols., 1887–88), by John Bigelow; *The Writings of Benjamin Franklin, Collected and Edited with a Life and Introduction* (10 vols., 1905–07), by Albert Henry Smyth. A comprehensive edition of *The Papers of Benjamin Franklin* (at least forty volumes projected, of which seven have been published, 1959–63), ed. by Leonard W. Labaree and others, includes for the first time systematically the letters addressed to Franklin as well as his own writings. The Smyth edition was used in the preparation of this article. The famous autobiography has been issued in innumerable editions, under various titles, and in a variety of textual versions. The original MS., long lost to sight, was discovered in France in 1867 by John Bigelow; he published it the next year as *Autobiography of Benjamin Franklin. Edited from the Manuscript, with Notes and an Introduction.* The latest and most thoroughly annotated edition, prepared by the editors of the comprehensive edition of the *Papers,* will be published in 1964.

The outstanding biography is Carl Van Doren, *Benjamin Franklin* (1938). Other leading accounts are Jas. Parton, *Life and Times of Benjamin Franklin* (2 vols., 1864), anecdotal, interesting, not too critical, but still useful in spite of its age; and Verner W. Crane, *Benjamin Franklin and a Rising People* (1954), brief and readable, emphasizing Franklin's political activities. Useful general treatments are Paul Leicester Ford, *The Many Sided Franklin* (1899), and Bernard Faÿ, *Franklin, the Apostle of Modern Times* (1929). Gerald Stourzh, *Benjamin Franklin and Am. Foreign Policy* (1954), is a much broader analysis of his political thought than the title suggests. I. Bernard Cohen, *Benjamin Franklin's Experiments* (1941), and the same author's *Franklin and Newton* (1956) are the most important treatments of his scientific contributions. Edward E. Hale and Edward E. Hale, Jr., *Franklin in France* (2 vols., 1887–88); Antonio Pace, *Benjamin Franklin and Italy* (1958); Alfred Owen Aldridge, *Franklin and His French Contemporaries* (1957); Lewis J. Carey, *Frankin's Economic Views* (1928); and Luther S. Livingston, *Franklin and His Press at Passy* (1914), are also useful on other special topics. *Meet Dr. Franklin* (1943) is a collection of lectures by Carl Van Doren and other authorities on a variety of subjects. For Franklin bibliography before 1889, see P. L. Ford, *Franklin Bibliography: A List of Books Written by or Relating to Benjamin Franklin* (1889).]

George Washington

by

JOHN C. FITZPATRICK

WASHINGTON, GEORGE (Feb. 11/22, 1732–Dec. 14, 1799), first president of the United States, was born in Westmoreland County, Va., on the estate of his father lying between Bridges Creek and Popes Creek and later known as "Wakefield." The eldest son of Augustine Washington and his second wife, Mary Ball (1708–1789), of "Epping Forest," Va., he was descended from Lawrence of Sulgrave, Northampton, England, who was of the fourth generation from John of Whitfield. Four generations later John, son of Lawrence the rector of Purleigh, emigrated to Virginia in 1657–58 and settled in Westmoreland County (Ford, *Writings*, XIV, 331–409; chart opp. p. 319). Augustine Washington was the grandson of John and the son of Lawrence of Bridges Creek, Westmoreland County. He lived in Westmoreland until 1735, when he removed to Little Hunting Creek, on the Potomac. After his homestead there was burned he moved to "Ferry Farm" in King George County, on the Rappahannock nearly opposite Fredericksburg. Augustine died in 1743 and the next half-dozen years of George Washington's life were spent with relatives in Westmoreland and the Chotank region, at "Ferry Farm," and at "Mount Vernon," the home of his elder half-brother Lawrence, who had married Ann Fairfax.

During this period George Washington received the major part of his school training, which totaled seven or eight years. His father and his elder half-brother Lawrence seem to have been his principal, if not his only teachers. The extent of his mother's influence

27

upon Washington cannot be accurately appraised, but from the great respect he accorded her, and the scrupulous manner in which he fulfilled his filial duty, it is justifiable to credit her with a decided influence in the way of discipline and morals. His training in mathematics extended to trigonometry and surveying, which helped develop a natural talent for draftsmanship that found expression in map-making, in designing tabular memoranda, and in giving the pages of his letters an unusual but characteristic pictorial quality. He had a certain appreciation of beauty and a decided appreciation of music and the drama. Early memoranda give an indication of his reading habits and his accounts show purchases of books dealing with military affairs, agriculture, history, and biography, and a fair number of the great novels of the day, such as *Tom Jones, Humphry Clinker,* and *Peregrine Pickle.* He purchased a number of ethical works and ordered and used a bookplate. The quotations that are sprinkled sparingly through his correspondence cover a wide range, and show his familiarity with such authors as Pope and Addison, while his Biblical allusions are varied enough to prove a satisfactory acquaintance with the Book of books. A letter to Lafayette in 1788 (Ford, *Writings,* XI, 265–66) suggests the general outline of his historical and literary knowledge, while his statement to James McHenry in 1797 that he had "not looked into a book" since he came home *(Ibid.,* XIII, 392) adds to the cumulative evidence that he appreciated fully the value of the printed word in his own cultural development. The social intimacy between "Belvoir" and "Mount Vernon," where one of the Fairfax fledglings had nested, brought Washington, at an impressionable age, into contact with the courtly manners and customs of the best English culture. His youthful idealism responded to this stimulus, as it did to the stateliness of the drama, and the two combined to produce the dignity and poise which were characteristic of his maturity.

Through the Fairfax association developed the first important adventure of his career. When, in 1748, Lord Fairfax sent James Genn, county surveyor of Prince William County, to survey his Shenandoah lands for tenantry, George William Fairfax and George Washington were permitted to go along. The two young men were gone a month, worked hard, and encountered many inconveniences, but gained valuable experience *(Diaries,* I, 3–12). A year later Washington was appointed county surveyor for Culpeper. His duty carried him into wild country where he encountered many hardships, yet his surveys required exactitude and gave him insight into the importance of land ownership. This work was interrupted by the call of duty to accompany Lawrence Washington on his health-seeking voyage to Barbadoes. George was stricken with smallpox on that island and so rendered immune to the disease which raged among the troops he commanded during the Revolutionary War. He returned alone to Virginia to be followed by Lawrence, who died in July 1752, bequeathing the "Mount Vernon" estate in such wise that it shortly became the property of George.

That year he was appointed by Governor Dinwiddie district adjutant for the southern district of Virginia, but was soon transferred to that of the Northern Neck and Eastern Shore. Washington's military ambition, first stimulated by his half-brother's service with Admiral Vernon, was reawakened and increased by his experience in military musters and drills of the Virginia militia. When the French encroached, as was claimed, on the English lands in the Ohio country, he accepted without hesitancy Dinwiddie's appointment (1753) to carry an ultimatum to the trespassers. Though the mission was one of hardship and downright danger, it appealed to Washington as one of honor and possible glory. It certainly was unusual that a colonial governor should appoint a young man of twenty-one to so important a mission, and the exact reasons for the selection are conjectural. Washington was also instructed to strengthen the friendship of the Six Nations with the English. With a party of six frontiersmen, he left Will's Creek in the middle of November 1753 and a week later reached the forks of the Ohio, where he had expected to find the French. But the French had withdrawn for the winter and Washington was faced with a decision between giving up the delivery of the ultimatum, and traveling sixty miles farther into the wintry wilderness to reach the next French post. Before starting on this new journey he endeavored to fulfil the second part of his instructions by holding, at Logstown on the Ohio, a council with such of the chiefs of the Six Nations as he could gather together; but he accomplished little, as the Indians were wary of the English assurances, unbacked by any display of force, when the French were already on the ground with troops and cannon. He found the French at Venango, but the officer there refused to receive his message and directed Washington to the commandant at Fort Le Beouf. Unwilling to return without accomplishing his main mission, he was forced to proceed one hundred miles farther, through winter-clogged swamp-land, nearly to the shores of Lake Erie. After five days of difficult travel he reached the fort and received in writing a polite refusal to pay any attention to Dinwiddie's ultimatum. On the return journey Washington's horses gave out, and with his guide, Christopher Gist, he undertook to walk back to Will's Creek. He was shot at by a prowling French Indian, nearly drowned in crossing the ice-choked Allegheny on an improvised raft, and nearly frozen from exposure (*Diaries*, I, 40–67). His report to Dinwiddie was printed by the Governor as *The Journal of Major George Washington* . . . (1754) and created a stir in England as well as America.

Washington had described a position at the forks of the Ohio (the present location of Pittsburgh) as the best place for an outpost and Dinwiddie dispatched a small force to forestall the French in building a fort there. He commissioned Washington a lieutenant-colonel and ordered him to reinforce the forks with the militia then assembling at Alexandria. These amounted to 150 men and with them on Apr. 2, 1754, Washington marched. He was met on the way by the news that the French had captured the fort. They named it Fort Duquesne. His force was too small for him to attempt to recapture it but Washington, nevertheless, advanced to Red Stone, the Ohio Company's trading post about forty miles from Fort Duquesne, and began a road for the expedition which Dinwiddie was virtually obligated to undertake. At Great Meadows, Pa., on rumors of a French advance, he built an entrenched camp which he called Fort Necessity, and when informed by friendly Indians of the approach of a French scouting party he marched forward to intercept it. Aided by the Indians, he succeeded in surprising and defeating the French (May 27); their leader, Jumonville, was killed. In reprisal the French advanced in force from Fort Duquesne and Washington fell back to Great Meadows; the retreat would have been continued to Will's Creek, but he feared being overtaken at some less defensible place than Fort Necessity (*Diaries,* I, 101 n.; *Writings,* Bicentennial ed., I, 87). The attack of the French was sustained for ten hours, then they proposed a parley. The terms offered Washington were generous but contained a bit of clever roguery, unnoticed by his translator, which made the signing of them an admission by Washington that Jumonville had been "assassinated." It was part and parcel of the age-old practice of placing the blame for starting a war; it created a stir at the time, but the truth of the matter has long been understood. The tangled condition into which Virginia's military affairs had been brought by Dinwiddie's management made Washington liable to be commanded by junior and inferior officers and, no relief being granted, he resigned near the end of the year 1754.

In 1755 Great Britain sent an expedition of regulars under General Braddock against Fort Duquesne. For reasons not entirely clear, though Washington's knowledge of the country and the influence of Dinwiddie are the probable explanations, Braddock offered Washington the position of aide on his staff. His military ambitions were still alive and this opportunity to serve under a professional soldier appealed to him. The tradition that his advice was scornfully rejected by Braddock is largely a misapplication of the suggestions Washington made later on the Forbes expedition. On the march toward Duquesne he was taken violently ill and left behind, rejoining Braddock only the day before the action at the Monongahela. In that action, weak and debilitated though he was, he strove to carry out Braddock's orders; he had two horses shot under him and four bullets through his coat before every one, along with the fatally wounded general, was swept from the field by the rush of panic-stricken soldiery. With Braddock's death his appointment as aide ended and he returned to "Mount Vernon." Not having resigned his adjutancy of the Northern Neck he issued a call for the militia of his district to be ready for muster and inspection (*Writings,* Bicentennial ed., I, 158). This was the limit of his authority, but to that extent he prepared Virginia for the expected French and Indian invasion of the frontier.

In the fall of 1755 Dinwiddie appointed him colonel and commander in chief of all Virginia forces, thrusting upon him at the age of twenty-three the responsibility of defending 300 miles of mountainous frontier with about 300 men. It was in this savage, frontier warfare (averaging two engagements a month with raiding Indians), that Washington acquired the habit of thinking and acting for the welfare of a people, and the experience of conducting military operations, however poorly, over an extensive expanse of territory. His letters show the depths to which he was stirred by the plight and suffering of the inhabitants, and his strenuous efforts to protect them from the ravages of the Indians. They also show the causes of his partial failure. With too few troops and inadequate supplies, lacking sufficient authority with which to maintain complete discipline, and hampered by an antagonistic governor, he faced difficulties which closely paralleled those that he met in the Revolution. He encountered in 1756, as he had once before, the supercilious arrogance of the British army officer who called in question his right to command because of a pretended difference between a commission signed by the king and one signed by a colonial governor. Washington rode from Winchester to Boston to obtain a settlement of the difficulty, which otherwise might have disrupted Virginia's frontier defense. The journey had an unexpected but important effect in broadening Washington's viewpoint in respect to the people of the other colonies. It was the longest horseback journey he had made up to that time; but there were few Americans, then and for some years later, who were so continuously in the saddle and few who traveled over so large an expanse of the country as did Washington. With the matter of rank settled to his satisfaction, he returned to Virginia and the disheartening duty of defending the frontier. Lacking pay for his men, lacking clothes, shoes, powder, and even food at times, Washington managed nevertheless to protect the frontier so well that fewer inhabitants fell victims to savage fury in Virginia than in the other colonies (*Writings*, Bicentennial ed., II, 11). He continually urged the capture of Fort Duquesne, but with the governor and legislature at loggerheads, Virginia could not raise a force sufficient to undertake it and Washington's efforts to secure cooperation from Maryland and Pennsylvania in the enterprise were unsuccessful. In 1758, however, Great Britain again sent a force of regulars under Gen. John Forbes against the post and Washington, with the title of brigadier (there being then two Virginia regiments) was ordered to cooperate. On this expedition Washington suggested an order of march for the British that was remarkably near the modern open-order method of fighting. It was ignored. The fort was abandoned by the French on the near approach of the British (November 1758) and, the main objective of Virginia's frontier defense being thus accomplished, Washington resigned shortly thereafter.

He married, on Jan. 6, 1759, Martha (Dandridge) Custis, widow of Daniel Parke Custis, and settled down to the life of a gentleman-farmer at "Mount Vernon." Through Mrs. Custis's offspring by her first husband, Washington's strong, natural love of children, nowhere attested better than in his expense accounts, found ample vent. In the death of young "Patsy" Custis (1773), he experienced one of the great emotional shocks of his life. His troubles with "Jacky" Custis brought home to him the difficult problem of the education of youth, and broadened his viewpoint in educational matters. At various times he contributed generously to educational organizations: to Washington College in Maryland, to Liberty Hall (later Washington and Lee) in Virginia, to the Alexandria Academy, to an academy in Kentucky, and to an academy in the Southwestern Territory. He urged the establishment of a national university in the Federal City and provided an endowment for it in his will. The basis of this idea was largely the "indescribable regret" with which he had "seen the youth of the United States migrating to foreign countries, in order to acquire the higher branches of erudition, and to obtain a knowledge of the sciences." His fear that they would imbibe "maxims not congenial with republicanism" was not based on his doubt of republicanism, but on his perception of the danger of sending youth abroad among other political systems before they had "well learned the value of their own" (Ford, *Writings*, XIII, 52).

He had been elected a burgess from Frederick in 1758, after having been defeated in 1755 and 1757, and took his seat in the session of 1759, when he was thanked by the House for his military services. The succeeding fifteen years of Washington's career were uneventful in a public way but undoubtedly were the most enjoyable of his life. They were spent in developing the farming possibilities of the "Mount Vernon" estate, with the variation of trips to Williamsburg to attend the sessions of the legislature, of neighborly visits to Alexandria, Dumfries, and Fredericksburg, of attendance on the Annapolis races and theatre, of fox-hunts and fishing trips. To his taste for theatricals was added an interest in strange animals which was akin to his interest in unusual plants. In his expense accounts one notes payments for seeing a lioness, a tiger, an elk, a camel, and other animals, and once a reference to a sleight of hand performance. Card-games, billiards, boat-racing, in addition to horse-racing, the theatre, dancing, fishing, gunning, and fox-hunting with horse and hounds—all the usual sports and amusements were enjoyed by Washington. His accounts unintentionally show how often he bore the major part of the necessary expenses and how often he made loans to his friends. From these accounts are to be gleaned much information about Washington's personal tastes and fancies. His snuff-taking and pipe-smoking habits were pre-Revolutionary and temporary; but his liking for oysters, watermelons, Madeira wine, and other delicacies was permanent.

But the pleasant, busy life at "Mount Vernon" was not without its annoyances. Many of these were of such nature as to create and gradually strengthen a conviction of the general unfairness of all things British. It was necessary to purchase practically all the supplies needed for "Mount Vernon": farm implements, tools of all sorts, paint, hardware, even textiles for clothing, needles, and thread. Washington's yearly invoices of goods purchased from Liverpool and London list great quantities of supplies, for he was buying for the annual consumption of a community of village proportions; when the estates of the Custis children were added to those of "Mount Vernon" the combined needs were enormous. The British commercial restrictions imposed needless hardships upon most business transactions and to these were added the sharp practices of the English factors, who were used by every Virginia planter in transacting his yearly business with the English markets. Complaints were easily passed over as the intervening distance and the time necessary for correspondence gave the Virginian little power to enforce redress. By a process of gradual accretion Washington's disappointing experiences in the Braddock and Forbes campaigns were built upon by these commercial annoyances, and a subconscious antagonism was created which even his strong sense of duty and loyalty could not hold in check.

He was successively reelected as a burgess from Fairfax, faithfully attended the sessions, and shouldered his share of the legislative duties. From 1760 to 1774 he was also a justice of Fairfax, holding court in Alexandria. His experiences in court and as a burgess did much to clarify his view of the handicapping influences of the British colonial system on America. The Stamp Act brought to a focus the developing colonial antagonism and Washington expressed with the logic of common sense the American attitude towards the claims of Parliament. It "hath no more right to put their hands into my pocket, without my consent, than I have to put my hands into yours for money" (*Writings*, Bicentennial ed., III, 233). He pointed out the practical difficulties which lay in the path of the enforcement of the act. "Our Courts of Judicature must inevitably be shut up . . . for . . . we have no Money to pay the Stamps . . . and if a stop be put to our judicial proceedings I fancy the Merchants of G. Britain trading to the Colonies will not be among the last to wish for a Repeal of it" (*Ibid.*, II, 426). The British prohibition of colonial paper money was one of the major grievances; with the balance of trade always against them, paper money was a primal necessity to the colonists. A personal matter was the effort to obtain for the officers and men of the old Virginia regiment the bounty land allotted to them for their services in the French and Indian War. Elected their attorney and agent under a prorata agreement as to expenses, Washington pushed the matter to a conclusion, advanced his own funds, some of which he did not get back, and made a hazardous canoe trip with a small party in 1770, down the Ohio and up the Great Kanawha, to locate the land (*Diaries*, I, 401–52). This journey revived his interest in the western territory and increased the knowledge which he had early acquired of its value to the development of the Atlantic seaboard; to an extent, it laid the foundation of his western land policy when president. On this trip Washington killed several buffalo. These animals, it seemed to him, might in the future supply meat for America, so he undertook an experiment with them. At his death, nearly thirty years later, a buffalo cow still remained among the stock animals at "Mount Vernon."

After 1770 the question of British taxes assumed increasing importance in the colonies, and in four short years became the major problem. The device of non-importation was tried, in resistance to British political and economic aggression. Washington strongly supported it, yet prophesied, before 1775, "that more blood will be spilt on this occasion, if the ministry are determined to push matters to extremity, than history has ever yet furnished instances of in the annals of North America" (*Writings,* Bicentennial ed., III, 246). He did not approve of the Boston Tea Party (*Ibid.,* III, 224), while thoroughly in sympathy with the refusal of Massachusetts to submit to the British restrictions. He was one of the burgesses who met in the Raleigh Tavern on May 27, 1774, after the Assembly had been dissolved by the governor, and signed the proceedings of that unauthorized but important meeting, and on July 18 he acted as chairman of a meeting in Alexandria, at which the important Fairfax Resolutions, the work of George Mason, were adopted. He was next chosen one of Virginia's delegates to the First Continental Congress, 1774, which did little beyond petitioning Great Britain for a redress of grievances. In the interval between that and the Second Congress, Washington was chosen to command the independent militia companies of Frederick, Fairfax, Prince William, Richmond, and Spotsylvania counties and authorized by them to procure equipment, which he did in Philadelphia. The buff and blue uniform chosen by the Fairfax company was the uniform worn by Washington throughout the Revolution, and so has become fixed in the public mind as the Continental Army uniform. At the March session of the Virginia legislature he was elected a delegate to the Second Continental Congress, which convened in Philadelphia May 1775. In that body his most important work was on the committee for drafting the army regulations and planning the defense of New York City. The latter assignment was to exercise a hampering influence upon him later.

His election to command the armies, June 15, 1775, was the result of a compromise between the northern and southern factions which existed, thus early, in Congress. The Massachusetts delegates knew that their only hope was to have the war, which up to then had been centered in the siege of Boston, taken over by the Continental Congress. In bringing about Washington's nomination and unanimous election John and Samuel Adams were the prime movers, and it was natural that Congress should confer the supreme command upon one of its own members when that member was the most prominent southern military character known to it. In his speech of acceptance Washington refused all pay for the arduous employment which he accepted as a duty "at the expense of my domestick ease and happiness" (*Writings,* Bicentennial ed., III, 292). He asked only that he be reimbursed his necessary expenses, of which he kept the account himself with such exactness that after eight years of nerve-wracking warfare his balance was less than a dollar wrong in a total of some £24,700.

When Washington took command of the army at Cambridge on July 3, 1775, he found it little better than a loosely organized mob of raw New England militia whose terms of service were to expire at the end of that year, or sooner. Earlier than most, Washington gave up as hopeless the idea of an accommodation with Great Britain, and the king's speech in October 1775 confirmed him in his belief that no compromise was to be expected (*Writings,* Bicentennial ed., IV, 321). The belief which persisted in others of the possibility of an accommodation was a hampering influence that prevented the colonies from exerting their full power in opposition to the British; it was, in large measure, the cause not only of lukewarm support of Washington but also of the growth of downright opposition to him, centering in a clique in Congress. The problems of supply and pay for the troops, which Congress had taken over, became a vexation that grew with the months. Efforts to establish discipline encountered bitter hostility; democratic ideas stood in the way and caused to be construed as a snobbish display of fancied superiority the authority necessary to create an efficient military machine. Opposing disciplinary measures, the New Englanders at the same time criticized Washington for the army's lack of it. Fear of a standing army was another difficulty. Obsessed with this fear, in which the phantom of an accommodation with Great Britain played its part, Congress hesitated to decree long-term enlistments for the troops. Washington stood almost alone in his plea for men who could be held in service long enough to make them seasoned soldiers. At the siege of Boston, he was forced to replace one army by another while holding in check twenty seasoned British regiments, and in the New York campaign the main cause of the so-called retreat through the Jerseys was the inability to collect troops to replace the losses caused by expired enlistments and desertions.

At Cambridge scarcity of powder held Washington back from any major operation until 1776; but when a sufficient quantity was accumulated he seized and fortified Dorchester Heights, a position which threatened Boston with bombardment and placed the British fleet in jeopardy. The city was evacuated Mar. 17, 1776, and with his army of newly enlisted troops Washington marched for New York City, which was the next logical base of operations for the enemy. He had already sent Maj.-Gen. Charles Lee to supervise the work of fortification at that place, so that Washington on his arrival found himself partially committed to a plan of defense mapped out by others. He improved the three months before the British arrived by training his army as well as he could, handicapped by an appalling lack of experienced officers, and in preparing against the inevitable consequences of the decree of Congress that New York must be defended. He had sixteen miles of water-front lines to defend with 10,000 men, and when the British had assembled their whole force in New York Bay they numbered 30,000 trained troops, exclusive of a naval force of over 100 vessels. Any defense worthy of the name, under such conditions, was impossible, yet Washington attempted the impossible from his concept of duty to obey the orders of Congress, and from a disinclination to insist upon his own judgment where he believed his military knowledge and experience inadequate. This hesitancy was more evident throughout the New York campaign than at any other period of the Revolution.

The British tactics in that campaign were far from masterly, though ample to insure success. Howe's choice of Long Island as the point of attack was a safe and sure step. Washington was obliged to divide his force as a result. He sent ten regiments to reinforce Brooklyn, a pitiful few to oppose a veteran force of 30,000; but the main body of Americans had to be held on Manhattan to oppose the attack of the British fleet, which only a strong headwind frustrated. Washington himself crossed over to Brooklyn as soon as it was seen that the British ships could not make way against the wind; but the enemy had already outflanked Sullivan and the tragedy was beyond repair. Howe delayed his assault on the Brooklyn fortifications and, on the night of Aug. 29, Washington moved all the troops over to New York. His arrangements were perfect; the British were kept in ignorance and the retreat was rightly considered a military masterpiece. On Sept. 15, the British landed at Kip's Bay and, despite Washington's presence and desperate attempts to rally his men, they fled in panic and a retreat to Harlem Heights became a necessity. British flanking moves pushed Washington, though not without some sharp skirmishing, back to a strong natural position at White Plains. Howe desisted and returned to New York, on the way gathering in Fort Washington, which had been held against Washington's better judgment but not against his orders.

His report to Congress laid down the general principle on which he was waging the war. "We should on all Occasions avoid a general Action, or put anything to the Risque, unless compelled by a necessity, into which we ought never to be drawn" (*Writings,* Bicentennial ed., VI, 28). Inexperienced troops, always inferior in numbers to the British, made this the only possible course of action until Congress was willing to create a permanent army. The odds against him were heavy. His great need was time: time to make a reluctant Congress realize the necessity of his recommendations; time to raise a permanent army after it was finally authorized; and time to train it to fight after it was raised. Dogged perseverance, a straining to the limit of the scant means in his hands, together with British lethargy, gained him some of the time he needed. He could complain bitterly to his brother that he was "wearied almost to death with the retrograde Motions of things" (*Ibid.,* VI, 246), and could warn Congress in October 1776 that its army was again "upon the eve of its political dissolution" (*Ibid.,* VI, 152). His belief in the moral righteousness of the American struggle for liberty was based on his sense of the injustice and unfairness of the British course. To him rebellion against the king and change of allegiance were matters demanding scrupulous moral honesty. Not until his concept of honor approved the change did he make it; but the step once taken, turning back was for him unthinkable and impossible. As he wrote to his brother: "Under a full persuasion of the justice of our Cause, I cannot . . . entertain an Idea that it will finally sink tho' it may remain for sometime under a Cloud" (*Ibid.,* VI, 399). The fortitude with which he met overwhelming difficulties was based upon his faith; defeats to him were merely temporary setbacks and victories merely longer or shorter steps toward final success.

The loss of Fort Lee, on the Jersey shore, resulted from the same misplaced confidence in his generals which had lost Fort Washington, yet both disasters were unrecognized blessings. They freed the Continental Army from responsibility for fixed fortifications, in which it had small chance against the trained British forces, and made it a mobile, maneuvering force which could be handled in accordance with Washington's ideas. The Pennsylvania and Jersey militia failed to answer his appeals and, with a steadily dwindling force, he fell back as the British pushed forward. The so-called retreat through New Jersey was a perfect example of Washington's military principle, for it was a retirement before a superior force of the enemy, conducted so slowly and so cleverly that the British expected to encounter strong opposition at almost every point. His grasp of military science, for all his modest disclaimers, was far above that of any of his generals. His plea at this time to Congress for artillery showed a far-sighted comprehension that few could boast (*Writings,* Bicentennial ed., VI, 280–81).

His calls, while retiring through New Jersey, to Maj.-Gen. Charles Lee for reinforcements revealed the first serious military opposition within his own army. Lee delayed marching, apparently with the idea of contesting the supreme command with Washington as soon as the latter's army dissolved or was defeated. The British solved this difficulty by the surprise and capture of Lee, whose troops were promptly marched to Washington's support by the officer next in command. With an army of barely 5,000, Washington reached the Delaware River, swept up all the boats, called in the Princeton rearguard, and crossed into Pennsylvania, where from the west bank he watched the enemy make futile marches up and down the east side, seeking means to cross. The British settled into winter quarters in a series of posts along the Delaware at and near Trenton and in a line across New Jersey to Amboy, confident that the end of the year 1776 would mark the end of the rebel army and of the rebellion. "Short enlistments and a dependence upon militia," Washington felt, would "prove the downfall of our cause" (*Writings,* Bicentennial ed., VI, 347). Yet, under heavy discouragements, he could write to Congress that he conceived "it to be my duty, and it corrisponds [*sic*] with my Inclination, to make head against them [the British] as soon as there shall be the least probability of doing it" (*Ibid.,* VI, 330).

Congress fled to Baltimore, and the protection of Philadelphia forthwith becoming relatively unimportant in Washington's judgment, he fixed his eyes on Morristown, N. J., as the place most threatening to the British arrangements. That place was designated as the rendezvous of the militia and recruits for the army of 1777 and, with the remnant of the army of 1776, on Christmas night Washington crossed the Delaware amid driving ice, crushed the Hessians at Trenton, and dislocated the entire line of British posts along the river. The failure of his two supporting detachments to get across the river postponed the movement to Morristown, of which the Trenton victory was intended to be the first phase. Washington returned to Pennsylvania with nearly a thousand prisoners. A few days sufficed to rest his troops and he again crossed into Jersey, to move northward. Checked by the British reinforcements advancing from New York, he fought the stubborn engagement of the Assunpink, by a forced night march outwitted the enemy, and struck and pierced their line at Princeton. Once he was at Morristown, his position was such a strategic threat to the British that they abandoned their entire New Jersey line and retreated to Brunswick.

Six days before the victory at Trenton he had applied to the Congress, which had fled to Baltimore, for power to handle "every matter that in its nature is self evident," since a necessity of waiting until such things were referred a hundred and thirty or forty miles would in itself defeat the end in view. He had "no lust after power but wish with as much fervency as any Man upon this wide extended Continent, for an oppertunity [sic] of turning the Sword into a plow share" (*Writings*, Bicentennial ed., VI, 402). Congress responded with a grant of powers greater than he had asked and for a term of six months; but when Washington used this authority to compel all citizens who had taken out British protection papers to deliver them up and take the oath of allegiance to the United States, or remove at once within the British lines, he was violently criticized in Congress. It took Washington a year and a half to shake himself free from the entanglements which had been created by the interference and mismanagement of Congress; but from 1777 troops could be enlisted for three years or the war, and in January of that year Washington began to build a permanent military machine that could "bid Defiance to Great Britain, and her foreign Auxiliaries" (*Ibid.*, VII, 199). But the exorbitant bounties offered by the states for home-guard and militia service operated to check enlistments for the Continental Army. Washington was still forced to rely upon the militia for swelling his force to a respectable total at times when the British threatened or actually moved against him. He expressed his opinion of the militia to Congress more than once. If 40,000 men had been kept in constant pay since the commencement of hostilities, and the militia never called out, the expense of the war would not have been nearly so great as it was; when the losses sustained for want of good troops were taken into account the certainty of this was placed beyond a doubt. To this he added his pungent and deft characterization of militia which has seldom been bettered. They "come in you cannot tell how, go, you cannot tell when; and act, you cannot tell where; consume your Provisions, exhaust your Stores, and leave you at last in a critical moment" (*Ibid.*, VI, 403). At Morristown the army grew slowly and slowly acquired discipline. Washington's hope was to "be able to rub along till the new army is raised," but how he was to do it he did not know. "Providence has heretofore saved us in a remarkable manner, and on this we must principally rely" (*Ibid.*, VII, 53). His own efforts to "keep the Life and Soul of this Army together" (*Ibid.*, VII, 225) were barely successful and this accomplishment, as much as anything, measures the power of his personality. Congress, he wrote not without satire, thought that when difficulties were distant from them, it had but to say "Presto begone, and everything is done."

Washington's handling of this small, green, poorly equipped army in the spring of 1777 was remarkable. He managed to keep the enemy from plundering New Jersey at will, checking their forays by vigorous skirmishing which proved costly to the enemy and had a valuable seasoning effect on the Continental troops. It also convinced Howe that the risk of marching across New Jersey again to take Philadelphia was too great and, the capture of that town being a major object with him, Howe set about taking it by sea. He succeeded in puzzling Washington completely, for the logical move was up the Hudson River to cooperate with Burgoyne's advance from Canada, and until Howe finally appeared in Chesapeake Bay Washington was kept in a state of wearing suspense. But, with the suspense dissolved, Washington marched south and on Sept. 11, 1777, met Howe at Brandywine Creek. Here his right wing, under Sullivan, was out-flanked by the British and Washington was forced to retreat. Nevertheless, Washington's proximity, for though defeated he refused to withdraw, and the skirmish at Yellow Springs which was interrupted by a cloud-burst, delayed Howe's entry into Philadelphia two weeks.

The Congress adjourned to Lancaster and then to York, Pa., and again entrusted Washington with dictatorial powers for a six-day period, but he used this authority sparingly. Washington's recognition of the necessity of according first place to the civil power made him always willing to exhaust every means before using the military. He admitted to Congress that "a reluctance to give distress may have restrained me too far," and realizing the "prevalent jealousy of military power" among the people, he avoided every act that would increase it (*Writings*, Bicentennial ed., X, 159). Some months later he wisely used justices of the peace to impress provisions, which through them were obtained without causing a murmur. His method of waging the war admitted of attacking the British only when the possible gain was worth the sacrifice involved. He was cautious always, and with reason, for he was unbelievably handicapped by a paucity of information even where he should have been kept informed. "I am as totally unacquainted with the political state of things, and what is going forward in the great national council, as if I was an alien," he wrote somewhat bitterly to Edmund Randolph, "when a competent knowledge of the temper and designs of our allies . . . might . . . have a considerable influence on the operations of our army" (Sparks, *Writings*, VI, 314).

There have been few generals who have had to husband their men and supplies so carefully as did Washington and fewer who have been more ready to expend them on a proper occasion. At Germantown (Oct. 3–4, 1777) Washington thought the probable gain outbalanced the probable loss and his surprise attack on the British was less a move to regain Philadelphia than to destroy Howe's army. It failed through no fault of plan, but to some extent it contributed to Howe's later resignation, and both Brandywine and Germantown are to be credited with large influence in the decision of France to aid the United States. Valley Forge and the Conway Cabal were to follow these defeats, and at the time the states should have whole-heartedly supported Washington for their own preservation the intrigue to supplant him in command of the army reached its crisis. The victory of Horatio Gates at Saratoga on Oct. 17, 1777, furnished Washington's enemies in Congress the opportunity to draw invidious comparisons. The intrigue was at bottom the culmination of the continuous effort of Massachusetts since 1775 to regain control of the war, which would be an accomplished fact with Gates at the head of the army. Opposition to Washington, engineered by this influence, had been steadily growing, for every criticism was cleverly directed to this end. But James Wilkinson, a bibulous aide of Gates, babbled of a letter from Maj.-Gen. Thomas Conway to Gates; Washington wrote a brief note to Conway with no other purpose than to let that gentleman know that he was not unaware of Conway's intriguing disposition, and this note became the bomb that shattered the secrecy of the cabal. Once in the open, the innate character of the cabal and its purposes roused resentments and antagonisms in Congress which compelled its adherents to abandon the move (in some instances even to deny their connection with the plot) and, lacking congressional support, the military part of the scheme collapsed.

But Washington held no resentments; his eyes were fixed upon the purpose of the war, and, since the cause of the nation had not been harmed by the cabal, he did not allow the episode to interfere with more important things. The criticism of contemporaries occasionally wounded his feelings but signally failed to disturb his steady course; it only marked the critics as men of less vision or, as was sometimes the case, of less honesty. For Washington did not doubt "that the candid part of Mankind, if they are convinc'd of my Integrity, will make proper allowance for my inexperience, and Frailities" (*Writings,* Bicentennial ed., VIII, 295). "We have some among Us, and I dare say Generals," he wrote, "who wish to make themselves popular at the expense of others; or, who think the cause is not to be advanc'd otherwise than by fighting; the peculiar circumstances under which it is to be done, and the consequences which may follow, are objects too trivial for their attention, but as I have one great end in view, I shall, maugre all strokes of this kind, steadily pursue the means which in my judgment, leads to the accomplishment of it" (*Ibid.*). His calm self-restraint allowed him to write to Lafayette, who found himself ensnarled in the Conway coil: "I have no doubt but that every thing happens so for the best . . . and that we . . . shall, in the end, be ultimately happy; when, My Dear Marquis, if you will give me your Company in Virginia, we will laugh at our past difficulties and the folly of others" (*Ibid.,* X, 237). Without such self-control it may be doubted if his success would have been so complete.

The Continental Army emerged from the suffering of Valley Forge better trained, as the result of months of steady drill under Baron von Steuben, and both the army and the country had been heartened by the news of the alliance with France, in March 1778. Here again Washington's value to the Revolution is manifest for, despite every effort of Congress and its commissioners in Paris and regardless of the French secret aid which had been given for nearly two years, France was not ready openly to assist the Americans until convinced that they would not compromise with Great Britain. The battles of Trenton, Brandywine, and Germantown went far toward convincing France, but the main assurance was the character and purpose of George Washington. Gerard, the French minister, who held long interviews with him, became convinced that Washington's attitude was uncompromising and that the army would, to a man, follow him. This confidence Gerard succeeded in instilling in Vergennes, the French minister of foreign affairs, and so, in turn, influencing the French king. The Saratoga victory, far from being the deciding element, merely contributed to the convincing effect of Washington's indomitable purpose and honesty of character.

Sir Henry Clinton, succeeding Howe in supreme command in America, abandoned Philadelphia as a consequence of the French Alliance and undertook to march across New Jersey to New York. Washington pursued, and the line of march of the two armies converging, he overtook the British at Monmouth. The resulting conflict (June 28, 1778) not only proved that the Continental Army had developed into a fighting machine of considerable efficiency, but also demonstrated anew Washington's ability as a general. He checked the disorderly and unnecessary retreat of General Lee and turned the confusion into an obstinate and successful holding of a battlefield, from which the British slipped away during the night and made good their retreat to New York City. France's first open aid was D'Estaing's fleet, but his ships, unfortunately, drew too much water to enter New York Bay. The French admiral sailed to attack the British force in Rhode Island, but a storm and the conduct of Maj.-Gen. John Sullivan brought this attempt to naught, and created anti-French feeling that required all of Washington's influence and tact to smooth over successfully. D'Estaing sailed for the West Indies and Washington quartered his army for the winter in New Jersey.

Lafayette, who had been with Washington since the summer of 1777, now conceived a plan of returning to France and obtaining a force to conquer Canada. Congress, more attracted by distant glittering schemes than by nearby everyday realities, approved Lafayette's idea, but had the saving sense to send the plan to Washington for an opinion. The calm common sense of his report (*Writings*, Bicentennial ed., XIII, 223–32; see also 254–57) dissolved the dream and showed Congress again that the commander of its armies, despite his keeping his hand scrupulously clear of civil matters, could reason upon them more intelligently than Congress itself. After pointing out the impossibility of collecting the necessary men and supplies, he dwelt upon the consequences of having France and the Indian tribes as neighbors on the north, while Spain would be on the west and south. His analysis was clear even to an obtuse Congress and the plan was laid aside. Lafayette, on his part, met with a refusal from Vergennes to consider the scheme.

The French Alliance, instead of stimulating the Americans to greater effort, operated as a sedative and to Washington's dismay things went from bad to worse. In spite of his urgent pleas to Congress and to the states for supplies and men a disheartening lethargy was displayed everywhere. Unable to move in a major operation, because of lack of troops and supplies (even a lack of powder in August 1779), Washington yet succeeded in sending an expedition into the Indian country under Sullivan, which broke the power of the Six Nations and freed the frontiers from the horrors of Indian warfare. The bright spots in the prevailing gloom were Wayne's victory at Stony Point and "Light-Horse Harry" Lee's capture of Powles Hook. In July 1780 a French army under the Comte de Rochambeau arrived in Rhode Island, the British force there having been withdrawn to New York, but lack of supplies and men prevented real cooperation by Washington. A conference with Rochambeau at Hartford on Sept. 22, 1780, compelled Washington to lay bare the real situation. The conference could only decide upon a future attack upon New York when the expected second division of the French arrived, or, if this was then impracticable, to transfer the campaign to the South. The situation was described bluntly by Washington: "We have no magazines, nor money to form them; and in a little time we shall have no men. . . . We have lived upon expedients till we can live no longer . . . the history of the war is a history of false hopes and temporary devices, instead of system and œconomy" (Ford, *Writings*, VIII, 468). Another conference with Rochambeau was held in Wethersfield May 21–22, 1781, and the tentative plan of attacking New York without waiting for the expected second French expedition was decided upon. The French marched to the Hudson and joined the American troops; and the combined forces closed in on the British northern defenses of New York City. Then De Grasse arrived with his fleet in the Chesapeake. The siege of the city was abandoned for a move against Cornwallis in Virginia. Leaving a force to threaten New York, Washington, with a detachment of Americans and the whole of the French army, marched southward for a cooperation with De Grasse. The transportation and quartermaster arrangements on this march were all made by Washington. The armies arrived on schedule and the siege of Yorktown progressed steadily to its triumphant conclusion (Oct. 19, 1781) in three short weeks. De Grasse sailed to the West Indies, Rochambeau's army went into winter quarters in Virginia, and Washington led his troops back to the Hudson, making headquarters at Newburgh.

The states now became more supine than before, and Washington's urgent pleas for exertion and his arguments for the necessity of continued effort had small effect. He urged that "unless we strenuously exert ourselves to profit by these successes, we shall not only lose all the solid advantages that might be derived from them, but we shall become contemptible in our own eyes, in the eyes of our enemy, in the opinion of posterity, and even in the estimation of the whole world, which will consider us as a nation unworthy of prosperity, because we know not how to make a right use of it" (Ford, *Writings*, IX, 437). But he was compelled to possess his soul in patience while his countrymen indulged in an orgy of profiteering, even to the extent of carrying on clandestine trade with the British, as they had done at the beginning of the struggle. It was impossible for Washington to stop these things; they were civil matters to be handled by Congress and the states, but very little was done by either. He was certain the war was not yet over. The king's speech at the opening of Parliament (1782) showed little signs of yielding and the war continued for two dreary years; but no military events of importance took place after Yorktown.

Though the enemy was reduced to inactivity through Washington's efforts, domestic conditions were slowly going from bad to worse. The army, more dissatisfied than ever from neglect and chronic lack of pay, showed an unrest which increased Washington's anxiety daily. The first open display of what was seething underneath came in the shape of a personal letter from Col. Lewis Nicola, of the Invalid regiment, who submitted to him a plan for using the army to make Washington a king. The army, at least, would benefit by it and Nicola stated that the idea was prevalent in camp. The proposal shook Washington's soul, for it swept away all that he had so painfully built up during the war, and hinted that the very men on whom he most relied were ready to support him in an apostasy, in a forswearing of honor and principle, for personal power. It was this, more than the idea of a crown, that stunned Washington. He saw his lifework threatened with dissolution through the political and short-sighted muddling of those responsible for the welfare of the army. To find that the men who had followed and trusted him through years of hunger, nakedness, suffering, and bloodshed were now, with victory in sight, ready to fail him, was bitter; and his answer (May 22, 1782) to the proposal was a withering blast which shrivelled the idea of kingship into the ashes of impossibility (Ford, *Writings*, X, 21–24). For a time the dissatisfaction subsided but a few more months saw it rise again in serious form. Anonymous addresses were posted in camp calling on the officers to meet for a discussion of their condition, to address Congress, and to be prepared to take by force, if necessary, what was unjustly denied them. Washington met the situation with a tact, wisdom, and sincerity which neutralized the danger and substituted for overt action further forbearance; and his letter to Congress urging a compliance with the officers' petition put the matter upon personal grounds with unusual emphasis. " 'If, retiring from the field, they [the officers] are to grow old in poverty, wretchedness and contempt; if they are to wade thro' the vile mire of dependency, and owe the miserable remnant of that life to charity, which has hitherto been spent in honor'; then shall I have learned what ingratitude is, then shall I have realized a tale, which will embitter every moment of my future life" (Ibid., X, 181).

Not content with this, he later addressed to the states a circular letter which was largely a plea for justice to the officers and men of the fast-disbanding Continental Army, with which he had ever considered his own military reputation inseparably connected. More than that, it contained some wise advice on civil matters which ranks it with the Farewell Address, thirteen years later. Now as then he was retiring, as he believed forever, from public service and so felt privileged to speak his mind plainly. In this circular he unconsciously reveals how close to his heart was the national principle for which he had fought, and how earnest his desire that the country prove worthy of the liberty it had gained. Again and again in his letters he showed how important he considered it that the country should take high rank among the nations of the world, and that high rank, he knew, was only to be gained and held by a strong union and by honorable conduct. Four things, he stated, were essential to respectable national existence: (1) "An indissoluble union of the States under one federal head"; (2) "a sacred regard to public justice"; (3) the adoption of a proper national defense; and (4) a spirit of cooperation, and the suppression of local prejudices (Ford, Writings, X, 257). He pleaded with the states for the army as he had pleaded with Congress, for the states were really the ultimate powers, and what Congress had promised in the form of half-pay was, he said, the price of the officers' "blood and your independency; it is therefore more than a common debt, it is a debt of honor" (Ibid., X, 262).

There was little of the dramatic in the closing scenes of the war, but Washington intentionally fixed the date for the cessation of hostilities as Apr. 19, 1783, the anniversary of the battle of Lexington. He entered New York, at the head of the troops which still remained in service, as the British evacuated it; he bade farewell to his officers at Fraunces Tavern and set off for Annapolis to resign his commission to Congress. There is some evidence that a slight uneasiness existed in Congress that he might at the last moment decide to become dictator. No such idea could have been entertained by Washington, who resigned "with satisfaction the appointment I accepted with diffidence" (Ford, *Writings,* X, 339). On Christmas eve (1783) he reached "Mount Vernon" and soon afterward could write to a friend: "I feel now, however, as I conceive a wearied traveller must do, who, after treading many a painful step with a heavy burthen on his shoulders, is eased of the latter . . . and from his housetop is looking back, and tracing with an eager eye the meanders by which he escaped the quicksands and mires which lay in his way; and into which none but the all-powerful Guide and Dispenser of human events could have prevented his falling" (*Ibid.,* X, 358). The evidences of Washington's faith in the intervention of Providence in the affairs of man that are scattered through his letters admit of no doubt of his sincerity. Equally apparent are an unusual lack of egoism and a complete absorption in the successful working out of the problem that confronted him.

His financial condition at the close of the war was far from satisfactory. "Mount Vernon," lacking his careful guidance, had deteriorated and now was not even self-supporting. But despite his own financial stringencies, the quiet, unostentatious charity which is so clearly shown in his accounts was undiminished; the almost weekly entries of donations to needy applicants continued, and his running accounts were balanced by loss entries in cases of widows and helpless children, and of men who had died in his debt. He had suffered from the depreciation of the Continental currency; amounts owing him from before the war had been liquidated in Continental bills, which he had grimly received because he would not stand accused of repudiating the national money, even though these payments were, on their face, plain subterfuge in debt cancellation. A financial statement of his investments in Continental loan-office certificates, drawn up after the war, shows also that he had loaned every spare dollar to the government in the years of greatest depression and at the times when the outcome of the Revolution was the most doubtful (Washington MSS., 1784, Photostats, Lib. of Cong.).

He had time now (1784) to devote to the idea of opening a route to the western country from tidewater Virginia, by connecting the Potomac and Ohio rivers. This was one of the favorite projects of his life. Before the Revolution, in the Virginia legislature, he was one of the committee appointed to prepare a bill granting authority to form a company for this purpose (J. P. Kennedy, *Journals of the House of Burgesses of Virginia, 1770–1772*, 1906, pp. 292, 297, 304–05). In furtherance of that idea he undertook a horseback journey of observation into the West in the autumn of 1784 (*Diaries*, II, 279–328). He traveled over 650 miles, and returned with knowledge which stood him in good stead later. But his real interest lay in the development of the farms at "Mount Vernon." His efforts to bring the estate back to a self-supporting condition were discouraging. Slave labor, the only kind available, had proved its inefficiency. No matter how carefully Washington planned, the results went awry because of the clumsy and unintelligent way the work was carried on. Unable either to free his slaves or to develop them into a self-supporting group, he was convinced that the gradual abolition of slavery would prevent much future mischief (P. L. Ford, *The True George Washington*, 1896, p. 154). To gradual abolition, by legislative authority, he pledged his vote. "But," he said, "when slaves, who are happy and contented with their present masters, are tampered with and seduced to leave them; when masters are taken unawares by these practices; when a conduct of this sort begets discontent on one side and resentment on the other; when it happens to fall on a man whose purse will not measure with that of the society [which works to free the slave], and he loses his property for want of means to defend it; it is oppression in such a case, and not humanity in any, because it introduces more evils than it can cure" (Ford, *Writings*, XI, 25–26). Washington had more Negroes than he could profitably employ on his farms. "To sell the overplus I cannot, because I am principled against this kind of traffic." Yet he was steadily being pushed toward bankruptcy and may have been saved from it only by his death (*Ibid.*, XIV, 196).

The agreement between Virginia and Maryland in regard to the navigation of the Potomac had led, through meetings at Alexandria and "Mount Vernon," to a call for what is known as the Annapolis Convention, and through this Washington was again to be brought into public life. But at first, in his absorption in the management of "Mount Vernon" and in the affairs of the Potomac Company, this was not clear to him. Life at "Mount Vernon" was pleasantly calm, and his wife's grandchildren filled the measure of his interest. As he wrote to Lafayette: "I have not only retired from all public employments, but I am retiring within myself. . . . Envious of none, I am determined to be pleased with all; and this, my dear friend, being the order for my march, I will move gently down the stream of life, until I sleep with my fathers" (Ford, *Writings*, X, 347). In 1786 this philosophic calm was interrupted by the disturbing news of the rebellion of Daniel Shays in Massachusetts, which forced his thoughts again to public affairs. The outbreak added weight to his conviction, which had been steadily growing, that the Articles of Confederation needed revision in the interests of a strong central government. The memories of Valley Forge, of Morristown, of Trenton, of all the instances of needless suffering and difficulty caused by lack of a central power, were vivid, and he wrote vigorously to his friends of the need of strengthening the government and more closely cementing the states. He attended the Federal Convention reluctantly, but as was characteristic when once he decided to do a thing, he gave to the work his full energy and thought. As president of the Convention, possessing the full confidence of every member, he supplied a ground anchor to the proceedings. Much of the confidence afterwards displayed in the Constitution was due to that fact. When its adoption was opposed he admitted that it had imperfections, but maintained that it was the best plan obtainable at that time (*Ibid.*, XI, 205–06; see also a collection of his letters in Max Farrand, ed., *The Records of the Federal Convention*, 1911, vol. III). Since workable machinery was provided for amending the imperfections, his logic was to adopt, and then make the alterations. He saw no choice between this procedure and chaos. In the contest that raged over adoption he expressed two, among many, typically Washingtonian ideas of government. One was that the purpose of the new Constitution was to "establish good order and government and to render the nation happy at home and respected abroad"; and the other, apropos of the theoretical fear of a self-perpetuating president, that "when a people shall have become incapable of governing themselves, and fit for a master, it is of little consequence from what quarter he comes" (Ford, *Writings*, XI, 257). That Washington had completely discarded the idea of monarchy as a just system of government is not open to doubt nor can it be doubted that he was sincere in his belief that the people should govern themselves. He was "sure the mass of citizens in these United States *mean well,* and I firmly believe they will always *act well* whenever they can obtain a right understanding of matters" (*Ibid.*, XIII, 188). Yet it must be admitted that the plan of government which he signed as president of the Federal Convention provided necessary protection for the conservative, property-owning class of citizens and by an elaborate system of counterbalance and check seriously handicapped the common people in exerting much influence upon the course of the government. The explanation of this apparent contradiction lies in the conditions of the time; certainly Washington's justice and honesty are amply proven, and he, less than almost any one else in the Convention, was swayed by considerations of personal property.

Even before the Constitution was adopted, public opinion had fixed on Washington as the first president. He repelled the suggestion when it was made to him and opposed it wherever he decently could. Fame he had never coveted and the purely military ambition of his youth had long since been burned out, as he had gained close acquaintance with the scourge of war. At the age of fifty-six he had no "wish beyond that of living and dying an honest man on my own farm" (Ford, *Writings*, XI, 258). The sense of humor with which he was liberally endowed was usually flavored late in life with a sardonic saltiness, the result of the long, bitter years of the war. "My movements to the chair of government," he wrote, after he had decided to accept and the unanimous election had settled the matter, "will be accompanied by feelings not unlike those of a culprit, who is going to the place of his execution"; for he realized that he was "embarking the voice of the people, and a good name of my own, on this voyage; but what returns will be made for them, Heaven alone can foretell" (*Ibid.*, XI, 379–80). He was sure of his own integrity and firmness, but he could not think with calmness of the possibility of appearing in the light of a bungler and an incompetent. The fortunate outcome of the Revolution, in which he had risked not only his reputation but also his life and fortune, was due, he believed, to the interposition of Providence, and his self-abnegation prevented him from taking credit for the victory. He regarded the Revolution as a great movement of a people and was content with the thought that he had played his part therein with honor. He was as doubtful of his ability to administer the government successfully as he had been of his ability to command the army successfully, and, having already seen the lengths to which partisanship, prejudice, and jealousy could go, he was well aware that this new task would be difficult.

Being unwilling to leave Virginia to become president of the United States with several debts against him, he was compelled to borrow money to clear up local obligations and pay his traveling expenses to the seat of government. He took the oath of office Apr. 30, 1789, on the balcony of the United States Building in New York (the site of the Washington statue, at the old Sub-Treasury building) and delivered his inaugural address in the Senate chamber before both houses of Congress. In it he declined a salary, as he had done when elected commander in chief, but Congress later voted $25,000 annually for the president. Washington accepted this amount for defraying the expenses incident to the office, which in his case exceeded it. The realization that the motive of his every action could be subject to a double interpretation and that by his conduct in any instance he might create a precedent, did not tend to lessen the strain upon his fifty-seven years. In the Revolutionary War he had passed through a long siege of emotional repression, which was part of the price he paid for victory, and he was not quite ready to subject his temper to the same sort of strain, if it could be avoided. He was tired; the tinsel and power of high office did not appeal; and his honesty of thought did not permit him to discount the heavy responsibilities of the presidency. Nothing but that same rigorous sense of duty which had carried him through the Revolution could have drawn him again into public life.

Organizing and coordinating the various parts of the governmental machine and appointing the necessary officials occupied the better part of the year 1789; and in this Washington moved with steady caution. As was natural, he thought first of the men whose measure he had taken during the Revolution. Few offers of high place were made without reasonable confidence, or assurance, that they would be accepted and in these offers Washington's personality counted more heavily with the individuals approached than the power or honor that were involved. Even in the minor appointments, Washington moved cautiously. "A single disgust," he wrote, "excited in a particular State, on this account, might perhaps raise a flame of opposition that could not easily, if ever, be extinguished. . . . Perfectly convinced I am, that if injudicious or unpopular measures should be taken by the executive under the new government, with regard to appointments, the government itself would be in the utmost danger of being utterly subverted by those measures" (Ford, *Writings,* XI, 368). When Congress adjourned in September, Washington toured the New England states in an effort to learn for himself the feeling of the people of that region toward the new government. This tour was productive of little other than a warm welcome from the inhabitants and an unnecessary test of official strength between the President of the United States and Gov. John Hancock of Massachusetts, in which the latter came off second best, to the great glee of the citizens of Boston.

The pressing domestic problem was that of attaining financial stability for the nation; this necessarily involved the encouragement of manufacturing and commerce. Besides the existence of commercial restrictions, the retention of the western posts by Great Britain constituted the main foreign problem. Nearly every difficulty which developed bitterness during Washington's two administrations seems to have taken its start from a ramification of one or the other of these problems. Divergent theories of government were the basis of the struggle between Hamilton and Jefferson out of which the well-defined Federalist and Republican groups emerged, but personal factors were evident to Washington. In the Revolution he had wasted no time on anything personal and he could not conceive of anything being more important than the question of national independence; so now as president he could not conceive of a personal quarrel being more important than the task of establishing the government on a firm foundation. To him that task was so formidable as to require the aid of every man, and the only parties he recognized, in his singleness of purpose, were those which supported the government, and the group which, for considerations of private advantage, opposed it. Yet for all his uncompromising attitude toward those things which interfered with the development of nationality, his forbearance toward both Jefferson and Hamilton seems that of a wise parent toward wayward sons. He pleaded with both men to compromise, convinced that the country needed their services, and a fair indication of his estimate of both may be gathered from the character of the plea which he made to each (Ford, *Writings*, XII, 174–79).

Methods and means of strengthening the government were in Washington's view debatable, but not the strengthening itself. All during the Revolution he had labored to dissolve local prejudice of every kind, and to substitute for the provincialism he found in the army a national pride and fellowship in being an American. Despite the acknowledgment that he had failed in this, his efforts had borne some fruit as the soldier returned to civil life at the expiration of his term, carrying with him the somewhat broadened view which he had acquired almost unconsciously and which leavened, to an extent, the ideas of the people among whom he lived. The first displays of military force by the new government proved disastrous. Both Harmar's and St. Clair's expeditions against the Indians failed; but Washington proudly repelled covert suggestions that Great Britain was willing to cooperate against the savages. His purpose was to "keep the United States free from political connexions with *every* other country, to see them independent of *all* and under the influence of none. In a word, I want an *American* character that the powers of Europe may be convinced we act for *ourselves,* and not for *others"* (Ford, *Writings,* XIII, 119–20).

The display of political partisanship on the part of the Hamilton-Jefferson factions was an influence in Washington's decision to serve a second term, when his overwhelming desire was to spend the remainder of his life in peace and quiet at "Mount Vernon"; but the foreign situation was undoubtedly the main factor in his decision. France's declaration of war on Great Britain stirred up an emotional enthusiasm that was easily developed into criticism of the President's neutrality, and from criticism to opposition to other acts of his administration. Though sympathizing with the French revolutionists at first, Washington was keenly aware of probable developments. As early as 1789 he saw that the disturbance in France was a "revolution   of too great magnitude to be effected in so short a space with the loss of so little blood" (Ford, *Writings,* XI, 435), and when the expected excesses began he speedily sickened of the spectacle. He was unopposed in his reëlection, but during his second term he was subjected to the heaviest strains and to vilification and abuse which went beyond the bounds of common decency. Washington believed that twenty years of tranquillity would make the United States strong enough to "bid defiance in a just cause to any power whatever" (*Ibid.,* XIII, 151). He could not comprehend an attitude that could place any other problem ahead of this. In this light must be viewed all his decisions, which were strongly Federalist; they were moves designed to strengthen the national government.

The somewhat hysterical criticism of Washington's official formality and dignified, presidential ceremonial was similar to the democratic opposition he had encountered in establishing discipline in the Continental Army. In 1775 discipline was necessary to make the army efficient, in 1789–90 official ceremony was necessary to insure respect for the new government and clothe it with authoritative dignity. Without precedent to guide him, Washington was feeling his way carefully toward a goal which was as clear to him as was the goal of victory in the Revolutionary War. He defined it in his fifth annual message to Congress. "There is a rank due to the United States among nations, which will be withheld if not absolutely lost, by the reputation of weakness" (Ford, *Writings,* XII, 352). His whole course as president was governed by the purpose of obtaining that rank for the United States. The national bank, the excise tax, and the development of the army and navy into permanent, trained organizations, all common-sense projects of value to the nation, yet gave rise to feelings of uneasiness in many honest but provincial-minded men, who in some instances followed the lead of the unscrupulous. The proclamation of neutrality (1793) and the arrival of Genet furnished an exceptional opportunity to embarrass the administration and to demonstrate sympathy for the French. Genet's recall was finally demanded and all the political frenzy that centered around him subsided with unexpected rapidity. The French danger past, there yet remained the British commercial restrictions, while their retention of the western posts and encouragement of the Indians were also matters demanding prompt and careful attention. Wayne's crushing defeat of the savages at Fallen Timbers eliminated the immediate Indian problem in 1794. To attempt a settlement of the other questions Washington appointed John Jay envoy extraordinary to Great Britain.

Domestic trouble of a serious kind arose in Pennsylvania over resistance to the excise tax. This, the so-called Whiskey Rebellion, was a popular defiance of the tax collectors, accompanied by rioting and violence. It demonstrated that the same state indifference to the national welfare which had increased Washington's difficulties in the Revolution fourfold was still to be reckoned with, for, the tax being a federal one and the collection of it a federal matter, Pennsylvania's governor virtually ignored the situation. In the face of growing opposition, which seemed to Washington not a mere natural objection to a tax but a movement sponsored by the democratic societies to overthrow the government (Ford, *Writings*, XII, 451–52, 454–55), he was not at all confident of commanding sufficient support to suppress the outbreak of violence, and when the militia responded to his call with heartening alacrity and spirit his relief was great. The rebellion collapsed and the ringleaders were seized. Again Washington displayed that broad understanding which he had manifested in his attitude toward the Loyalists in the Revolution and toward the malcontents of Shays's Rebellion; he felt that the country could not afford to lose such a number of inhabitants by harsh measures of reprisal. In a short time he granted full pardon to all the insurgents who had signed the oath of submission and allegiance to the United States.

In the year 1795, by the Pinckney Treaty, the southern boundary of the United States was established and the coveted navigation of the Mississippi was secured, with port facilities at New Orleans. Offsetting this came the outburst of criticism over the Jay Treaty. Less than a year after the ratification of the treaty it became plain that none of the dire predictions of its opponents had come true;

trade was actually improving and before a year was out the hysterical opposition had subsided. The treaty was no more satisfactory to Washington than to its critics (Ford, *Writings*, XIII, 63–66). Even on some of the points which he considered of prime importance it was not as definite as he desired; but he thought it was the best treaty that could be obtained at the time and it did settle the particular matters in controversy with Great Britain which would have made war probable had they remained in controversy much longer. He withstood this storm of opposition as he had withstood others, confident of his integrity of purpose and sure that the honor and welfare of the nation were served; but he likened the bitter attack to a cry against a mad dog, couched in "such exaggerated and indecent terms as could scarcely be applied to a Nero, a notorious defaulter, or even to a common pickpocket" (*Ibid.,* XIII, 76, 291). To the demand of the House of Representatives for the papers relating to Jay's negotiations he firmly refused to yield, being convinced that what the House really wanted was to establish the precedent that its concurrence was necessary in treaty making. His firmness settled the matter and the question has not been raised since.

In his first administration he had mentioned to Jefferson that he "really felt himself growing old, his bodily health less firm, his memory, always bad, becoming worse, and perhaps the other faculties of his mind showing a decay to others of which he was insensible himself" (P. L. Ford, *The Writings of Thomas Jefferson*, I, 1892, p. 175). In 1796 he set about the preparation of an address that would announce to the people his determination to retire from public life. The increasing weight of years admonished him that retirement was as necessary as it would be welcome. Solicitude for the welfare of the nation to which he had given so much of his thought and strength led him to take advantage of the opportunity to give the disinterested advice "of a parting friend, who can possibly have no personal motive to bias his counsels" (Ford, *Writings,* XIII, 285). He knew, however, that in announcing his retirement he risked being charged with a "conviction of fallen popularity, and despair of being re-elected" (*Ibid.,* XIII, 192).

He had assumed the presidency when the United States was little but a name, without power, prestige, or credit; when he retired from office the country was well on the road to international importance. He had given it dignity, as when he rebuked the French minister for presumption in a diplomatic negotiation (1791) and demanded the recall of Genet; he had demonstrated its power by crushing the Indians and suppressing the Whiskey Rebellion; and he had firmly fixed its credit, through Alexander Hamilton. Treaties with Spain and Great Britain had amicably settled the questions of the navigation of the Mississippi and the Florida and eastern boundaries. For the prosperity of the country he had worked unremittingly, and, though he abhorred war, none knew better than he that unpreparedness added to its horrors. In his first annual message to Congress he enunciated the principle: "To be prepared for war is one of the most effectual means of preserving peace" (Ford, *Writings*, XI, 456). The Farewell Address is partly an explanation of his course as president, with main emphasis upon the necessity of a firm union and a strong central government, for which he had labored incessantly the major part of his public life, and which were not in 1796 so taken for granted as they have finally come to be. Respect for the authority of that government and a solemn warning against the spirit of party he made equally important. The activities of political parties which came under Washington's observation were directed, he thought, solely to the subversion of good government, to a usurpation of power for personal ends, and would logically result in the loss of liberty. Morality and education were urged as necessities for a people's happiness, prosperity, and safety; good faith and justice toward all nations, but favors to none, were enjoined, and a warning was given against the insidious wiles of foreign influence. He hoped that these counsels would "be productive of some partial benefit; some occasional good; that they may now and then recur to moderate the fury of party spirit, to warn against the mischiefs of foreign intrigue, to guard against the impostures of pretended patriotism" (*Ibid.*, XIII, 320).

Washington's steadfast fortitude under the most trying difficulties is to be attributed largely to an unusual knowledge of self. No one would have yielded more quickly, he said, to a standard of infallibility in public matters, had there been such a thing; but lacking that, "upright intentions and close investigation" were his guides (Ford, *Writings*, XIII, 105). Dominated by the single idea and purpose of finding out, if possible, what was of greatest benefit to the nation, and bending all his energies toward accomplishing it, Washington could not comprehend acts of opposition to his carefully considered measures as anything other than so many attempts to destroy the government. Brissot de Warville stated that he never saw Washington "divest himself of that coolness by which he is characterized, and become warm, but when speaking of the present state of America" (*Nouveau Voyage dans les États Unis . . . en 1788*, 1791, Vol. II, 269).

Duty, with Washington, became a moral obligation which was not to be evaded even by honorable means; and the barest outline of his spiritual development reveals the heavy sacrifice of personal inclination to that obligation. Resigning his first military commission in 1754, with no expectation of again entering upon a military career, he was unexpectedly appointed an aide by Braddock, and after Braddock's death he was appointed by Dinwiddie to protect the Virginia frontier; resigning again in 1758 to marry Mrs. Custis, he was appointed to command the American armies at the outbreak of the Revolution; resigning at the end of that war, he confidently expected to live the remainder of his life untroubled by public cares; drafted against his will to be president of the United States, he wished to retire in 1793, but was forced by circumstances to remain; retiring in 1797, as he hoped for good, he was again forced to accept command of the army that was being raised in expectation of war with France in 1798. Half his life was spent fulfilling what he conceived to be his duty at the expense of his domestic ease and happiness. He calmly analyzed the opposition to Adams's administration in 1798–99, as hanging upon and clogging the wheels of government, "Torturing every act, by unnatural construction, into a design to violate the Constitution—Introduce Monarchy—& to establish an aristocracy." Yet he was still able to "Hope well, because I have always believed, and trusted, that that Providence which has carried us through a long and painful War with one of the most powerful nations in Europe, will not suffer the discontented among ourselves to produce more than a temporary interruption to the permanent Peace and happiness of this rising Empire" (Ford, *Writings*, XIV, 142–43). President Adams, following popular will, appointed Washington lieutenant-general and commander in chief of the army it seemed necessary to raise. He accepted, with the understanding that he would not take the field until the troops actually were raised and equipped. He insisted on Hamilton's being second in command, and a heated contest of wills between him and Adams ensued. In the end Adams gave in, but the Provisional Army was not needed and was never personally commanded by Washington. Under pressure of danger to his beloved country the military fire of the Revolution had flamed again, though Washington's steadfast conviction was that war was an unmitigated evil. Changing conditions in France steadily reduced the chance of conflict and Washington once more allotted a greater and greater part of his time to the management of "Mount Vernon." He was not granted opportunity to bring his farms to the point of efficiency he planned, though he had worked out a scheme of rotation of crops in his fields that carried over into the nineteenth century.

His death occurred with startling suddenness. A neglected cold developed into a malignant type of cynache trachealis with which the limited medical knowledge and skill of the time were unable to cope. With his physical strength sapped by mistaken blood-lettings, he fought a losing battle for nearly twenty-four hours. The philosophical calm of his remark that it was "the debt which we all must pay" was only exceeded by the high courage of his declaration, toward the end, "I am not afraid to go" (Ford, *Writings,* XIV, 249). He died at 11:30, Saturday, Dec. 14, 1799. The physical hardships of the Virginia colonial warfare and the later strains of the Revolution had much to do with his final collapse. Though he was a physical giant, over six feet in height and weighing 190 to 200 pounds, with no surplus flesh, he drove himself unsparingly and often beyond his strength; a check-up of the number of letters written daily from headquarters and consideration of the other daily, necessary business justifies the conclusion that, during the Revolutionary War, Washington seldom obtained more than three or four hours of consecutive sleep in any twenty-four.

All contemporaneous descriptions of Washington's appearance agree as to his dignity and impressiveness, many of them enthusiastically so, but Capt. George Mercer, his aide in the Virginia colonial service before Washington obtained world-wide fame, penned a description in 1760 which still remains the best. His frame, Mercer said, gave the impression of great muscular strength. "His bones and joints are large as are his hands and feet . . . rather long arms and legs . . . all the muscles of his face under perfect control, though flexible and expressive of deep feeling when moved by emotion. In conversation he looks you full in the face, is deliberate, deferential and engaging. His voice is agreeable . . . he is a splendid horseman" (P. L. Ford, *George Washington,* 20 ed., pp. 38–39). An anonymous writer stated that his smile was extraordinarily attractive. His personal charm is attested in many letters of his friends, in the expressed regret of the Virginia colonial officers, on his resignation, at the loss of "such a sincere Friend, and so affable a Companion" (*Writings,* Bicentennial ed., II, 316 n.), in the farewell to his officers, and in the Virginia woman's remark to her friend, that when General Washington becomes "the chatty agreeable Companion, he can be down right impudent sometimes; such impudence, Fanny, as you and I like" (Ford, *George Washington*, 20 ed., p. 110). Add to this the French abbé's note that "The Americans, that cool and sedate people . . . are roused, animated, and in-flamed at the very mention of his name" (Abbé C. C. Robin, *New Travels Through North America*, 1783, p. 35), and we have an ap-proximation of the feeling of the people toward him. Leaders of the time, and Washington would have been the last to deny the value of their assistance, followed and supported him with confi-dence and enthusiasm: Greene, Sullivan, Wayne in the army; Ham-ilton, Wolcott, Jay, and Pickering in civil authority. Curiously, the men who opposed him were generally those whose personal ambi-tions were dependent upon the success of that opposition.

The evolution of Washington's fame until his name was placed high upon the scroll of the world's great, began in 1776–77, when the victories of Trenton and Princeton focused European attention on the hopeless-looking struggle of American backwoodsmen with the most powerful nation in the world. The addition of France to that struggle insured Europe's careful watchfulness of every phase of the conflict and, as Lord John Russell put it, "The success of America was owing, next to the errors of her adversaries, to the conduct and character of General Washington" (*Memorials and Correspondence of Charles James Fox*, Vol. I, 1853, p. 153). Liberty, the basis of the American struggle, was becoming more than an academic definition in European thought and Washington per-fectly personified the awakening. As Chateaubriand aptly said (*Travels in America and Italy*, Eng. ed., 1828, vol. I, 106): "He aimed at that which it was his duty to aim at . . . blended his existence with that of his country. . . . The name of Washington will spread with liberty from age to age."

[The miscellaneous Washington MSS. in the Lib. of Cong. are bound in 302 vols., the original letter-books in 35 additional vols., original diaries and account books in over 50 vols., and the contemporaneous Varick Transcript of Washington's letters during the Revolutionary War in 44 vols. Of Wash-ington letters elsewhere, the Lib. of Cong. possesses 21 boxes and a number of bound volumes of photostats. There are also numerous volumes of copies of miscellaneous Washington records, the originals of some of which cannot now be traced. Numerous letters from and to Washington are in the Con-tinental Congress MSS. in the Lib. of Cong., so that the Washington papers in that library are a more nearly complete collection than that of any other distinguished American. The mass of them is, however, so vast that no comprehensive or complete publication was attempted prior to the Bicentennial ed. of his *Writings*, begun in 1931 (*post*). J. C. Fitzpatrick, *Calendar of the Correspondence of George Washington . . . with the Continental Congress* (1906), and *Calendar of the Correspondence of George Washington . . . with the Officers* (4 vols., 1915), have been published.

W. C. Ford, *The Writings of George Washington* (14 vols., 1889–93), is the most useful edition, but must be supplemented by that of Jared Sparks (12 vols., 1834–37), which contains some hundreds of letters omitted in the Ford ed., and by J. C. Fitzpatrick, ed., *The Diaries of George Washington* (4 vols., 1925). The Sparks ed. suffers from unjustifiable textual alterations and unnoted omissions. Both the Ford and Sparks eds. are being supplanted by *The Writings of George Washington. . . . Prepared under the Direction of the U. S. George Washington Bicentennial Commission* (1931), ed. by J. C. Fitzpatrick, which will probably extend to 30 vols.; it will be the first complete ed. of Washington's letters. Other valuable sources in print are: S. M. Hamilton, *Letters to Washington, 1752–1775* (4 vols., 1898–1902); Jared Sparks, *Correspondence of the Am. Revolution; Being Letters of Eminent Men to George Washington* (4 vols., 1853); *George Washington's Accounts of Expenses while Commander-in-Chief* (Facsim., 1917), with annotations by J. C. Fitzpatrick; *Letters from His Excellency George Washington, to Arthur Young . . . and Sir John Sinclair* (1803 and other eds.); M. D. Conway, *George Washington and Mount Vernon* (1889), mainly agricultural letters to William Pearce and James Anderson (in vol. IV of the *Memoirs of the Long Island Hist. Soc.*); *Letters from George Washington to Tobias Lear . . . from the Collection of Mr. William K. Bixby* (1905). J. D. Richardson, *A Compilation of the Messages and Papers of the Presidents*, vol. I (1896), gives the texts of the important communications to Congress. Washington's travels through the United States are described in J. C. Fitzpatrick, *George Washington, Colonial Traveller, 1732–75* (1927); W. S. Baker, *Itinerary of General George Washington . . . 1775 to 1783* (1892), and *Washington after the Revolution, MDCCLXXXIV–MDCCXCIX* (1898).

Nearly every biographer of Washington has fallen under the spell to which Sparks succumbed and has followed, more or less, the example set by the latter in idealizing the man, though some recent biographies have gone to the other extreme. Mention should be made of M. L. Weems, *A History, of the Life and Death, Virtues, and Exploits, of General George Washington* (1800), though no reliance should be placed on this famous work. Washington Irving, *Life of George Washington* (5 vols., 1855–59), is satisfactory from most viewpoints, though its reliance on Sparks lessens the confidence it would otherwise command; John Marshall, *The Life of George Washington* (5 vols., 1804–07), ranks with Irving, but its Federalist bias during the presidential period should be discounted; Vol. I (1837) of Sparks's ed. of the *Writings* is given over to a life of Washington, the interpretations of which must be used with caution. W. R. Thayer, *George Washington* (1922), is an orthodox life; Woodrow Wilson, *George Washington* (1903), is clear and readable but is also an orthodox interpretation; H. C. Lodge, *George Washington* (2 vols., 1898), is more expansive than Thayer and Wilson, but like them is based upon the partial publications of the *Writings;* Norman Hapgood, *George Washington* (1901), is a modern treatment of merit; Rupert Hughes, *George Washington* (3 vols., 1926–30), should be used with great caution, but contains bibliographical aids of unusual value; P. L. Ford, *The True George Washington* (1896), republished as *George Washington* (1924), a refreshing study of Washington from various angles, contains a wealth of interesting material which is unnoted as to source and difficult to trace; J. C. Fitzpatrick, *George Washington Himself* (1933), written from his manuscripts, presents many hitherto undeveloped sides of Washington's character. Other recent biographies are S. M. Little, *George Washington* (1929); L. M. Sears, *George Washington* (1932).

G. W. P. Custis, *Recollections and Private Memoirs of Washington* (1861), is the source of most of the unprovable traditions about Washington; B. J. Lossing, *Mount Vernon and Its Associations* (1886), is somewhat more dependable than Custis. The following studies of special phases of Washington's life can be used with confidence: P. L. Haworth, *George Washington, Farmer* (1915), republished as *George Washington, Country Gentleman* (1925); T. G. Frothingham, *Washington, Commander in Chief* (1930); H. L. Ritter, *Washington as a Business Man* (1931); W. C. Ford, *Washington as an Employer and Importer of Labor* (1889); J. H. Penniman, *George Washington as Man of Letters* (1918); P. L. Ford, *Washington and the Theatre* (1899); J. M. Toner, *General Washington as an Inventor* (1892); C. H. Ambler, *George Washington and the West* (1936). J. C. Fitzpatrick, *The George Washington Scandals* (1929), among other things, fixes the authorship of the "Spurious Letters." Stephen Decatur, Jr., *Private Affairs of George Washington from the Records and Accounts of Tobias Lear, 1789–92* (1933), is the cash account of the President's expenses and the only financial record (except the *Accounts of Expenses while Commander-in-Chief, ante*) so far published. H. B. Carrington, *Battles of the American Revolution* (1876), supplies collateral background for the military side; J. C. Fitzpatrick, *The Spirit of the Revolution* (1924), furnishes details of Continental Army headquarters and of Washington's aides; Paul Wilstach, *Mount Vernon* (1930), is useful to any study of Washington's home life. E. E. Prussing, *The Estate of George Washington* (1927), is an able analysis of Washington's fortune. The best genealogy is in Vol. XIV of Ford's ed. of the *Writings,* which should be supplemented by the material in *Hist. of the U. S. George Washington Bicentennial Celebration, Literature Series* (1932), vol. III. This series also contains many full texts and extracts, carefully compared in most instances with the manuscripts of Washington's letters and state papers.

The number of portraits of Washington is amazing, yet the really reliable portraits are few. Not all the artists who painted or sketched him from life were competent, and their results are heterogeneous and largely mediocre, while the work of those who never saw him can only be classified as efforts of enthusiastic imagination. The Houdon bust, modeled from life at "Mount Vernon," and Gilbert Stuart's Boston Athenaeum portrait are beyond just criticism. Other portraits by Stuart, notably the Channing-Gibbs, and some of Trumbull's work, the St. Memin print, and Sharples's best profile also deserve consideration. See Gustav Eisen, *Portraits of Washington* (3 vols., 1932).]

[SUPPLEMENTARY BIBLIOGRAPHY. The Fitzpatrick edition of *The Writings of George Washington*, in 39 vols., was completed in 1944. The fullest recent biography of Washington is Douglas S. Freeman's monumental *George Washington* (7 vols., 1948–57, the last volume by John A. Carroll and Mary W. Ashworth). The most recent short treatment is Marcus Cunliffe, *George Washington: Man and Monument* (1958). Other biographies include Nathaniel W. Stephenson, *George Washington* (2 vols., completed and revised by W. H. Dunn, 1940); Francis R. Bellamy, *The Private Life of George Washington* (1951); and Howard Swiggett, *Great Man: George Washington as a Human Being* (1953). See also Samuel Eliot Morison's essay "The Young Man Washington," reprinted in his *By Land and By Sea* (1953). Three recent treatments of Washington's role in the American Revolution are Bernhard Knollenberg, *Washington and the Revolution, A Reappraisal* (1940); Curtis P. Nettels, *George Washington and Am. Independence* (1951); and Esmond Wright, *Washington and the Am. Revolution* (1957). Washington's political ideas are treated in Harold W. Bradley, "The Political Thinking of George Washington," *Jour. of Southern Hist.*, Nov. 1945; Saul K. Padover, "George Washington—Portrait of a True Conservative," *Social Research*, Summer 1955; and Louis M. Sears, *George Washington and the French Revolution* (1960). Two works which indirectly treat specific aspects of Washington's public career are James Hart, *The Am. Presidency in Action, 1789* (1948); and Willard M. Wallace, *Appeal to Arms: A Military Hist. of the Am. Revolution* (1951). Recent books on the Federalist era which include much useful material on Washington are Leonard D. White, *The Federalists* (1948); Nathan Schachner, *The Founding Fathers* (1954); and Alexander DeConde, *Entangling Alliance: Politics and Diplomacy under George Washington* (1958). The treatment of Washington in American letters is the subject of William A. Bryan's *George Washington in Am. Literature, 1775–1865* (1952).]

Thomas Jefferson

by

DUMAS MALONE

JEFFERSON, THOMAS (Apr. 2/13, 1743–July 4, 1826), statesman, diplomat, author, scientist, architect, apostle of freedom and enlightenment, was born at "Shadwell" in Goochland (now Albemarle) County, Va., then on the fringe of western settlement. Whether or not the first Jefferson in the colony came from Wales, as the family tradition held, a Thomas Jefferson was living in Henrico County in 1679 and married Mary Branch. Their son Thomas, who married Mary Field, lived at "Osbornes" in what is now Chesterfield County, where on the last day in February, 1707/08, Peter Jefferson was born. His father was a "gentleman justice," but Peter enjoyed few educational opportunities and had largely to shift for himself. Becoming a surveyor, he removed to Goochland County, where by 1734 he was a magistrate. The next year he patented 1000 acres on the south side of the Rivanna River and shortly thereafter purchased from William Randolph of "Tuckahoe," for a bowl of punch, 400 acres more, containing the site north of the river upon which he erected a plain frame house about 1741. Thither he brought his wife and there Thomas, his third child, was born.

Jane Randolph, who became Peter Jefferson's wife at nineteen, first-cousin of William of "Tuckahoe" and the eldest surviving child of Isham Randolph of "Dungeness" and his wife, Jane Rogers, connected her husband with perhaps the most distinguished family in the province and assured the social standing of his children. Peter Jefferson's career closely followed that of Joshua Fry, under whom he served as deputy surveyor in Albemarle, with whom he continued the boundary line between Virginia and North Carolina and made the first accurate map of Virginia, and whom he succeeded as burgess and county lieutenant. Thomas Jefferson had great respect for his father's map and from him doubtless acquired much of his zest for exploring and drawing and his liking for untrodden paths. From him he inherited a vigorous, if less powerful, body, and perhaps his fondness for mathematical subjects. Of the ten children of Peter Jefferson, eight survived his death, Aug. 17, 1757. He left Thomas, the elder of his two sons, about 5000 acres of land and an established position in the community.

Seven of the first nine years of Jefferson's life were spent at "Tuckahoe," on the James a few miles above the present Richmond, whither his father removed in pursuance of a promise to William Randolph to act as guardian of the latter's son. Here he began his education at the "English school." The red hills of Albemarle became his permanent home, however, at the age of nine and held ever thereafter an unrivaled place in his affections. At this time he began the study of Latin and Greek under the Rev. William Douglas, who also introduced him to French. Of Douglas's abilities Jefferson later expressed a low opinion. After the death of his father, he studied with the Rev. James Maury, whom he later described as "a correct classical scholar." Whoever may deserve the credit for it, Jefferson gained an early mastery of the classical tongues and ever found the literature of Greece and Rome a "rich source of delight." In March 1760 he entered the College of William and Mary, from which he was graduated two years later. Here, at the seat of the provincial government, he was enabled to view history in the making and politics in practice. His chief intellectual stimulus while a student came from his association with Dr. William Small, who held first the chair of mathematics and then *ad interim* that of philosophy. Small aroused in him the interest in scientific questions which was destined to remain active all his life, and introduced him to the "familiar table" of Gov. Francis Fauquier and to George Wythe, most noted teacher of law of his generation in Virginia, under whose guidance Jefferson prepared himself for practice.

During these years he appears to have been a recognized member of the close-knit social group that the children of the great families of Virginia constituted. He visited homes, made wagers with girls, gossiped about love affairs, served at weddings. Tall, loose-jointed, sandy-haired, and freckled, he was not prepossessing in appearance, but he was a skilled horseman, played on the violin, and seems to have been a gay companion. The strain of seriousness in his nature, however, was soon apparent; it may have been accentuated by the unhappy outcome of his love affair with Rebecca Burwell. Before he became a prominent actor on the stage of public life, he had formulated for himself a stern code of personal conduct and had disciplined himself to habits of study as few of his contemporaries ever found strength to do. Some time after 1764, perhaps, he began to apply historical tests to the Bible, lost faith in conventional religion, though without questioning conventional morality, and for inspiration turned to the great classical writers. That he prepared himself with unusual care for his profession, by the study of legal history as well as of procedure, is apparent from the notebook in which he abridged his legal reading (Chinard, *The Commonplace Book of Thomas Jefferson*, 1927). He was admitted to the bar in 1767, and, despite his dislike of court practice, was distinctly successful in the law until on the eve of the Revolution he abandoned it as a profession. His legal training, however, left a permanent impress upon him. In his most famous state papers he is the advocate pleading a cause and buttressing it with precedents.

On Jan. 1, 1772, Jefferson was married to Martha (Wayles) Skelton, then in her twenty-fourth year, the daughter of John Wayles of Charles City County and his wife, Martha Eppes. She was the widow of Bathurst Skelton and had borne him a son, who died in infancy. In the ten years of their married life she bore Jefferson six children, only three of whom survived her and only two of whom, Martha and Mary (or Maria), attained maturity. She is reputed to have been beautiful, and certainly her second husband lavished upon her notable devotion. The young couple began their married life in the only part of "Monticello" then finished, the southeastern "pavilion." Jefferson had moved to his adored mountain-top after the nearby house at "Shadwell" burned, together with his cherished library, in 1770, and had begun the building operations which were to extend over a generation. From the estate of his father-in-law he acquired in behalf of his wife, soon after his marriage, holdings practically equivalent to his own. With them, however, went a huge debt from the effects of which he never entirely escaped. Throughout most of his mature life he was the owner of approximately ten thousand acres of land and from one to two hundred slaves. Nothing if not methodical, he made periodical records of everything connected with his plantations—his slaves, his horses and cattle, the trees planted, the temperature at "Monticello," the dates at which birds and flowers first appeared.

In 1770 Jefferson was appointed county lieutenant of Albemarle. In May 1769 he had become a member of the House of Burgesses, as he continued to be until the House ceased to function in 1775, though he did not attend in 1772. He says he had been intimate for almost a decade with Patrick Henry, whose eloquence had enthralled him in his student days. Never an effective public speaker, Jefferson himself did greatest service in legislative bodies on committees, where his marked talents as a literary draftsman were employed. Identified from the outset with the aggressive anti-British group, he was one of those who drew up the resolves creating the Virginia Committee of Correspondence and was appointed a member of the committee of eleven, though not of the select committee of three. In 1774 he was one of the champions of the resolution for a fast day, on the day the Boston Port Act was to go into effect, which resolution led to the dissolution of the House. In 1775 he was on the committee appointed to draw up an address to Dunmore rejecting Lord North's conciliatory offer, and says that he drafted the address adopted. Prevented by illness from attending the Virginia convention of 1774, after he had drawn up the resolutions of his county and been appointed a delegate, he sent a paper, later published as *A Summary View of the Rights of British America,* which proved to be his greatest literary contribution to the American Revolution next to the Declaration of Independence and which reveals, as perhaps no other document does, his point of view in that struggle. Though approved by many, it was not adopted because regarded as too advanced. Emphasizing the "natural" right of emigration and the right of conquest, exercised by the first English settlers in America as by the Saxons in England, he denied all parliamentary authority over the colonies and claimed that the only political tie with Great Britain was supplied by the King, to whom the colonists had voluntarily submitted. The aids rendered by the mother country, he felt, had been solely for commercial benefit and were repayable only in trade privileges. He advocated, not separation, but freedom of trade in articles that the British could not use, and the relinquishment of all British claims in regard to taxation. This powerful pamphlet, distinctly legalistic in tone, reveals no adequate conception of the value of early English protection or of the contemporary British imperial problem. Throughout his career as a Revolutionary patriot he emphasized "rights as derived from the laws of nature," not a king; and here, as elsewhere, he strove for the "revindication of Saxon liberties" (Chinard, *Commonplace Book,* p. 57).

Elected by the Virginia convention to serve in Congress in case Peyton Randolph should be required at home, Jefferson sat in that body during the summer and autumn of 1775. Though he drew drafts of several papers, these were too strongly anti-British in tone to be acceptable while there was hope of conciliation. He was not present in Congress from Dec. 28, 1775, to May 14, 1776. Probably called home by the illness of his mother, who died Mar. 31, and by the needs of his family, he also had duties to perform as county lieutenant and commander of the militia of Albemarle, to which office he had been appointed by the Virginia Committee of Safety on Sept. 26. Following the famous resolutions introduced into Congress on June 7, 1776, by Richard Henry Lee, Jefferson was elected four days later, with John Adams, Franklin, Roger Sherman, and Robert R. Livingston, to draw up a declaration of independence. The reasons for the prominence in this connection of one so young as Jefferson, and especially for his selection over Lee, have been much disputed. Now only thirty-three years old, he had been a "silent member" on the floor of Congress, though outspoken and decisive in committees. The "reputation of a masterly pen," however, stood him in good stead and opened the door of dangerous but glorious opportunity.

More changes in his draft of the Declaration were made at the instance of Adams, and particularly of Franklin, than he later remembered, and some were made by Congress itself; but this most famous American political document as a composition belongs indisputably to Jefferson. The philosophical portion strikingly resembles the first three sections of George Mason's Declaration of Rights, itself a notable summary of current revolutionary philosophy. Jefferson probably availed himself of this, but he improved upon it. The doctrines are essentially those of John Locke, in which the more radical of the patriots were steeped. Jefferson himself did not believe in absolute human equality, and, though he had no fears of revolution, he preferred that the "social compact" be renewed by periodical, peaceful revisions. That government should be based on popular consent and secure the "inalienable" rights of man, among which he included the pursuit of happiness rather than property, that it should be a means to human well-being and not an end in itself, he steadfastly believed. He gave here a matchless expression of his faith. The charges against the King, who is singled out because all claims of parliamentary authority are implicitly denied, are in general an improved version of those that had already been drawn up by Jefferson and adopted as the preamble of the Virginia constitution of 1776. Relentless in their reiteration, they constitute a statement of the specific grievances of the revolting party, powerfully and persuasively presented at the bar of public opinion. The Declaration is notable for both its clarity and subtlety of expression, and it abounds in the felicities that are characteristic of Jefferson's unlabored prose. More nearly impassioned than any other of his important writings, it is eloquent in its sustained elevation of style and remains his noblest literary monument.

Desiring to be nearer his family and feeling that he could be more useful in furthering the "reformation" of Virginia than in Congress, Jefferson left the latter body in September 1776, and, entering the House of Delegates on Oct. 7, served there until his election to the governorship in June 1779. While a member of Congress, he had submitted to the Virginia convention of 1776 a constitution and preamble, only the latter of which was adopted. With the new constitution and government, which were marked by little change in law and social organization, he was soon profoundly dissatisfied. To him the Revolution meant more than a redress of grievances. Against the continuance of an established church, divorced from England, which the conservatives favored, he desired the entire separation of church and state. He was determined to rid his "country," as he long called Virginia, of the artificial aristocracy of wealth and birth, and to facilitate through education the development of a natural aristocracy of talent and virtue and an enlightened electorate. He felt that the legal code should be adapted to republican government "with a single eye to reason, & the good of those for whose government it was formed." Because of his skill as a legislator, the definiteness of his carefully formulated program, and the almost religious zeal with which he pressed it, he immediately assumed the leadership of the progressive group. He deserves the chief credit not only for an unparalleled program but also for legislative achievements that have rarely been equaled in American history.

He struck the first blow at the aristocratic system by procuring the abolition of land-holding in fee-tail. On Oct. 12, 1776, he moved the revision of the laws. Elected to the board of revisors with four others, of whom only Wythe and Edmund Pendleton served to the end, he labored two years with scholarly thoroughness on his share of the revision, including the law of descent and the criminal law. The report of the board (June 18, 1779), comprised 126 bills, most of which were ultimately enacted in substance. Primogeniture was abolished in 1785. His bill for Establishing Religious Freedom (Ford, *post*, II, 237-39), presented in 1779 by John Harvie of Albemarle and passed, with slight but significant modifications in the preamble (Hening, *post*, XII, 84-86), in 1786 when Jefferson was in France, was regarded by him as one of his greatest contributions to humanity. In its assertion that the mind is not subject to coercion, that civil rights have no dependence on religious opinions, and that the opinions of men are not the concern of civil government, it is indeed one of the great American charters of freedom.

Jefferson's educational bills, which represented the constructive part of his program, were unsuccessful. Of his extraordinary Bill for the More General Diffusion of Knowledge (Ford, II, 220-29), which summarizes his educational philosophy, only the part dealing with elementary schools was acted on, in 1796, and a provision was inserted which in effect defeated its purpose. His attempts to amend the constitution of his old college and to establish a public library entirely failed. During his governorship, however, as a visitor of William and Mary, he effected the abolishment of the professorships of Hebrew, theology, and ancient languages and the establishment of professorships of anatomy and medicine, law, and modern languages, the two latter being the first of their kind in America. Though he did not originate the idea of removing the capital to Richmond, he framed a bill for that purpose and the measure which was passed in 1779 included his preamble and provisions for handsome public buildings such as he had favored. His plans for his state were never fully carried out, but he may properly be termed the architect of Virginia government.

His election to the governorship (June 1, 1779) in succession to Patrick Henry was the natural consequence of his preëminence as a legislator and his unchallenged leadership of the progressive group. The philosophical qualities that made him so conspicuous as a planner and prophet were of little avail to him, however, as an executive. Resourceful in counsel, he was hesitant in the exercise of authority, the very necessity of which he deplored. His position as a war-governor was rendered the more difficult by the constitutional limitations upon his authority and the diminution of the state's resources. In handling the countless details of his office he was extraordinarily industrious and conscientious (H. R. McIlwaine, *Official Letters of the Governors of the State of Virginia*, II, 1928). The chief weaknesses charged against him were his unwillingness, even in time of acute crisis, to use means of doubtful legality and his characteristic reliance upon the militia (Eckenrode, *post*, ch. VIII). He managed sufficiently well during the first year of his governorship and was duly reëlected, but in the spring of 1781, when the British seriously invaded Virginia, the state was at their mercy. Richmond being in British hands, the legislature was called to meet at Charlottesville May 24. Jefferson proceeded to "Monticello" and last exercised the functions of his office June 3, interpreting his term to continue only one year and not until his successor qualified. As he put it, he "resigned" the governorship, recommending that the military and civil agencies be combined by the election of Gen. Thomas Nelson, but his act was a virtual abdication. On June 4, Tarleton made a raid on "Monticello." The supposed governor and the legislators who were his guests all escaped, Jefferson the last among them. He returned the next day, but soon removed his family to "Poplar Forest," where late in June he was thrown from his horse and disabled. Thus did his administration come to an unheroic end.

What was left of the Assembly, meeting beyond the mountains at Staunton, elected Nelson and ordered (June 12, 1781) that an investigation of Jefferson's conduct as governor be made at the next session. Judging from the heads of charges proposed by his neighbor and subsequent supporter, George Nicholas (Randall, *post*, I, 354-55; Jefferson Papers, Library of Congress), there was no allegation of personal cowardice, such as was made later by political enemies. The conduct of the assemblymen, indeed, had been marked by even greater prudence. All the charges had to do with the lack of military precaution and expedition. After the crisis actually arose, Jefferson seems to have done everything possible and with as great speed as could have been expected. Whether or not he had made such previous preparation for an impending crisis as he might have is questionable. By autumn, however, the storm had stilled. On Dec. 12 a committee appointed by the House of Delegates to inquire into his conduct as governor reported that no information had been offered them except rumors, which they regarded as groundless, and on Dec. 19 resolutions of thanks were finally adopted. Formally vindicated, Jefferson soon recovered his prestige in Virginia. For a time the state government passed into conservative hands, but during his long absence in France (1784-89) the progressives, under the able leadership of Madison, again gained ascendancy, and Jefferson came to be regarded as the prophet of the new order, as indeed he was.

Now persuaded, however, that public service and private misery were inseparable, Jefferson retired to his neglected farms, his cherished books, and his beloved family, convinced that nothing could again separate him from them. He took advantage of the leisure forced upon him by his fall from his horse to organize the careful memoranda about Virginia which he had made over a long period of years. Arranging these in the order of the queries submitted in 1781 by Barbé-Marbois, secretary of the French legation, he somewhat corrected and enlarged them during the winter of 1782–83, and at length had them printed in France in 1785. The *Notes on the State of Virginia* went through many editions and laid the foundations of Jefferson's high contemporary reputation as a universal scholar and of his present fame as a pioneer American scientist. Unpretentious in form and statistical in character, this extraordinarily informing and generally interesting book may still be consulted with profit about the geography and productions, the social and political life, of eighteenth-century Virginia. With ardent patriotism as well as zeal for truth Jefferson combatted the theories of Buffon and Raynal in regard to the degeneracy of animal and intellectual life in America, and he manifested great optimism in regard to the future of the country, but he included "strictures" on slavery and the government of Virginia. In 1783 he drafted another proposed constitution for his state, which was published in 1786 and ultimately bound with the *Notes* as an appendix.

But for the death of his wife, Sept. 6, 1782, he might have remained in philosophic retirement. He lavished upon his motherless daughters extraordinary tenderness and solicitude, but he was now glad to abandon "Monticello" and seek relief from personal woe in public activity. Appointed peace commissioner to Europe, Nov. 12, 1782, he was prepared to sail when, his mission having become unnecessary, his appointment was withdrawn. In June 1783 he was elected a delegate to Congress and during six months' service in that body the following winter he was a member of almost every important committee and drafted an extraordinary number of state papers (Ford, I, xxviii–xxx). Some of these were of the first importance, especially his notes on the coinage, in which he advocated the adoption of the dollar, to be divided into tenths and hundredths, and his successive reports on the government of the western territory. The report of Mar. 22, 1784, which has been ranked second in importance only to the Declaration of Independence among Jefferson's state papers, contained most of the features of the epoch-making Ordinance of 1787. If it had been adopted as Jefferson presented it, slavery would have been forbidden in all the western territory after 1800, and the secession of any part of that region would have been rendered indisputably illegal. Jefferson had earlier drafted a deed of cession of the northwestern territory claimed by Virginia, and he drew up a land ordinance which failed of adoption. Certainly he was a major architect of American expansion.

As a member of Congress he drafted a report on the definitive treaty of peace which was eventually adopted. He drew up, on Dec. 20, 1783, a report which was agreed to as the basis of procedure in the negotiation of treaties of commerce, and was himself appointed, May 7, 1784, to assist Franklin and Adams in this work. Arriving in Paris on Aug. 6 with his daughter Martha, he was appointed in 1785 Franklin's successor as minister to France and remained in that country until October 1789. Rightly regarded in France as a savant, he carried on the tradition of Franklin, but until the end of his own stay he was overshadowed by Franklin's immense reputation. Jefferson's attitude toward his predecessor, whom he regarded as the greatest American, was one of becoming modesty without a tinge of jealousy. During his ministry he was likewise overshadowed by Lafayette, who was regarded as the French symbol of American ideas and ideals and the protector of American interests. Jefferson took full advantage of Lafayette's invaluable cooperation and associated with him on terms of intimacy and affection, content to be relatively inconspicuous if he might be useful.

Though he later characterized his official activities in France as unimportant, Jefferson proved a diligent and skilful diplomat. He and his colleagues succeeded in negotiating, in 1785, a treaty of commerce with Prussia. Early in 1786 he joined Adams in London, but their efforts to negotiate a treaty were futile. He made careful note of English domestic gardening and mechanical appliances, but of their architecture and manners had few kind words to say. He supported Thomas Barclay in the negotiation of a treaty with Morocco in 1787, but was convinced that the Barbary pirates could be restrained only by force and worked out a scheme for concerted action on the part of a league of nations. This was accepted by Congress, but aroused no enthusiasm in Europe. He negotiated with France a consular convention, signed Nov. 14, 1788, which was the first of the sort agreed to by the United States. Though he could not hope to make much of a breach in the wall of commercial exclusiveness, he gained some relaxation of French duties on American products, and by his arguments against the tobacco monopoly of the Farmers General, which he attacked as a system, made a definite impression on Vergennes and his successor, Montmorin. Jefferson left Europe with the feeling that the French had granted all the commercial concessions possible, that they had few interests in America, and that they had great sentimental attachment to the young Republic. He was convinced that the United States should be friendly to France, both because of gratitude and because of her value as a counterpoise against the British, whom he regarded as hostile in sentiment and entirely selfish in policy. He gained the impression, however, that Great Britain and Spain would pay much for American neutrality if they should become involved in European controversy. The hope that the United States would ultimately gain great advantages from the troubles of Europe profoundly affected his subsequent foreign policy, predisposing him to ways of peace.

At a time when there was a flood of sentimental French writings about America, Jefferson endeavored to present the American cause adequately and accurately. These motives in part caused him to distribute his own *Notes on the State of Virginia,* and the Virginia statute of religious freedom. Appealed to for information by many writers, he furnished extensive materials in particular to his former neighbor, Philip Mazzei, whose *Recherches Historiques et Politiques sur les États-Unis* (4 vols., 1788) was the most accurate work of the period on America, and to Démeunier, whose article, "États-Unis," in the *Encyclopédie Methodique: Économie Politique et Diplomatique* (1786), greatly embarrassed the American minister by its inaccuracies and its fulsome praise of him. To interested friends at home, he wrote about inventions in dozens of letters; and for Madison, Monroe, and others he continually purchased books. In 1787 he went into northern Italy to see the machines used there for cleaning rice, smuggled out samples of rice seed to South Carolina and Georgia, forwarded information about the olive tree, and at Nîmes gazed for hours at the Maison Carrée, "like a lover at his mistress." To his native Virginia he sent a plan for the new state capitol, modeled on this temple, and thus served to initiate the classical revival in American architecture. On another tour in 1788, he made numerous observations in Germany. This keen-eyed, serious-minded, reflective traveler purposed that his mission should prove educative to his fellow citizens as well as himself and never lost sight of his obligation to be useful.

Though greatly impressed with French manners, he was strongly opposed to any aping of them by Americans. He was attracted by the cuisine and wines and found the French a temperate people, but thought their life lacking in domestic happiness and on the whole rather futile. Life for him was empty when not purposeful. He thought little of French science, but was enthusiastic about their arts—architecture, painting, and, most of all, music, which he valued the more perhaps because a fractured wrist had ended his days as a violinist. It is doubtful whether he ever mastered French as a spoken language, but he read it well enough. Distressed by the inequality of conditions, he came to think less than ever of royalty, nobility, and priests. His experiences and observations did not give him a new philosophy, for, like the French reformers, he had already drunk at the fountain of liberal English political thought. Many of the writings of Condorcet might have come from Jefferson's own pen; he shared with Du Pont de Nemours the passionate desire to remove economic and intellectual barriers; like the early revolutionists, he had profound faith in the indefinite improvability of mankind and made a veritable religion of enlightenment. From his stay in France he gained, not new doctrines, but an emotional stimulus, returning to America strengthened in his civic faith.

The course of the Revolution until his departure Jefferson followed closely and reported in detail. Though he strove to maintain strict official neutrality, this skilled political architect suggested to Lafayette's aunt, Mme. de Tessé, a desirable course of procedure for the Assembly of Notables, and to Lafayette himself he submitted a proposed charter for France (June 3, 1789, Ford, V, 199–202). A meeting of the leaders of the Patriot party, arranged by Lafayette, met at Jefferson's house in the effort to arrive at a compromise on the questions of the royal veto and the constitution of the Assembly. Intimate and sympathetic with the moderate reformers, he deplored the violence of later days but retained the conviction that the Revolution had done more good than ill; and, in his ripe old age, he declared that every traveled man would prefer France as a place of residence to any country but his own.

Having been granted a leave of absence to settle his private affairs and to take home his two daughters, the younger of whom, Mary, had joined him in Paris in 1787, Jefferson sailed in October 1789 and arrived at "Monticello" two days before Christmas, to be welcomed tumultuously by his rejoicing slaves. Soon after he landed, he received from Washington the offer of the appointment to the Department of State, then being temporarily administered by John Jay. Jefferson's dislike for publicity and shrinking from censure made him reluctant to enter the storm of politics, from which in France he had been relatively aloof, but on patriotic grounds he at length accepted the eminently appropriate appointment. After giving his daughter Martha in marriage to her cousin, Thomas Mann Randolph, Jr., he proceeded to New York, where, on Mar. 22,

1790, he became the first secretary of state under the Constitution.

Though he had kept in close touch with American developments through extensive correspondence, Jefferson was not fully aware of the conservative reaction which had taken place in his own country while he was in the midst of political ferment in France. He had seen nothing threatening in the commotions that had marked the last years of the Confederation, but thought dangerous liberty distinctly preferable to quiet slavery and had regarded the government, despite its imperfections, as "without comparison the best existing or that ever did exist." None the less, he had viewed with distinct favor the movement for strengthening the federal government and had given the new Constitution his general approval, objecting chiefly to the absence of a bill of rights, which was later supplied, and the perpetual re-eligibility of the president. He had denied that he was of the party of federalists, but had stated that he was much farther from the anti-federalists. He cannot be justly charged with factiousness because he came to be regarded, before his retirement from office, as the leader of the group opposed to the policies of Alexander Hamilton. To distinguish themselves from their opponents, whom they termed monarchists, Jefferson and his sympathizers soon called themselves republicans. They may have subsequently exaggerated their charges for political effect, but he believed until the end of his life that his early fears of an American monarchy were warranted and it would seem that they were at the time not unnatural and not without foundation. Undoubtedly he was distressed by the social atmosphere in which he found himself. He had enjoyed a considerable social experience in monarchical France, where theoretical democracy and even republicanism were fashionable, but in the aristocratic Federalist court, at first in New York and soon in Philadelphia, he was ever ill at ease.

With Hamilton, nearly a dozen years his junior, who had already assumed the first place in the counsels of the government, he strove at the outset to cooperate. His subsequent statement that he was duped by his colleague in connection with the Assumption Bill is unconvincing as well as uncomplimentary to his own intelligence. His contemporary letters show clearly that he was at the time convinced that some compromise was essential for peace and the preservation of the Union. When at length better provision for Virginia was made in the bill, and the location of the Federal City on the banks of the Potomac was agreed to, he gave his approval to the measure. He did not yet fully perceive that Hamilton's whole financial policy was least advantageous to the agrarian groups in which—for broad social rather than narrow economic reasons—he himself was most interested.

The first serious difference of opinion between the two men was over a question of foreign policy. Fully convinced that the British would not yield the Northwest posts or grant commercial privileges unless forced to do so, Jefferson favored the employment of commercial discrimination as a weapon against them. This policy, advocated in Congress by Madison, was opposed by Hamilton, who feared the loss of revenue from British imports. The movement in Congress for discrimination was strengthened by successive able reports of Jefferson on matters of commercial policy, but thanks to Hamilton it was blocked in February 1791 and ultimately abandoned. Meanwhile, the Secretary of the Treasury had maintained a surprising intimacy with George Beckwith, the unofficial British representative (1789–91), with whom the Secretary of State properly refused to have anything to do.

In February 1791, at the request of his chief, Jefferson drew up an opinion on the constitutionality of the Bank of the United States to which Hamilton replied, though neither paper was published until long afterward. Jefferson, who opposed monopolistic tendencies anyway, argued that the powers assumed by Hamilton's bill were not among those enumerated in the Constitution as belonging to the federal government, nor within either of its general phrases, which he interpreted narrowly and literally. He subsequently declared that he did not view constitutions with "sanctimonious reverence," and he favored their periodical revision, but this critic of the Scriptures here set up the Constitution as a sort of sacred law. His fears that liberal construction might result in the unbridled power of the federal government were undoubtedly heightened by his growing distrust of Hamilton, and this perhaps led him to go to extremes in the statement of his own theoretical position. Strict construction had its uses as a check on the tyranny of the national majority, but thorough-going application of Jefferson's arguments would have rendered the federal government feeble and inflexible, as he himself in practice later found. None the less, he had suffered a second defeat at the hands of Hamilton.

In the spring of 1791 Thomas Paine's *Rights of Man* appeared in America, with an extract from a private note of the Secretary of State as a preface. Jefferson's statement that he was glad that something was to be said publicly against "the political heresies" that had sprung up was interpreted both as an approval of Paine, who was anathema to the Anglomen in America, and as a reflection upon

John Adams, whose expatiations on the faults of democratic systems, indeed, Jefferson had actually in mind. His statement of regret that he and his old friend had been "thrown on the public stage as public antagonists" may be accepted as sincere by others, as it was by Adams. The incident, however, identified Jefferson with criticism of the aristocratic tendencies of the government and in the end was politically advantageous to him. Fortuitous circumstances thus served to make a popular figure of one who abhorred controversy, who preferred to work behind the scenes, and who lacked the personal aggressiveness commonly associated with political leadership.

In May–June 1791 he and Madison made a botanical trip to New England, during which they doubtless gave some thought to politics; and, on Oct. 31, Philip Freneau published in Philadelphia the first number of the *National Gazette,* in opposition to the *Gazette of the United States,* published by John Fenno. Jefferson, knowing Freneau to be an ardent republican, had given him the small post of translator in the Department of State, as Hamilton had already given Fenno the more lucrative printing at his disposal and was later to give him personal financial assistance. With the increasingly bitter criticism of Hamilton in Congress during the winter of 1791–92 Jefferson afterward claimed that he had nothing to do, except that he expressed hostility in conversation with and letters to his friends. His leadership at this time was less active than has been commonly supposed, but he had undoubtedly become the symbol of anti-Hamiltonianism, and, though more scrupulous of proprieties than his colleague, he served to inspire forces which he did not now or ever essay to command.

Hamilton had established with George Hammond, who presented in November 1791 his credentials as British minister, an intimacy similar to that which Beckwith had enjoyed. Hammond, forced by Jefferson to admit that he had no power to negotiate a new treaty, unwisely undertook to debate with the American Secretary the infractions of the treaty of peace. Jefferson's magnificent reply of May 29, 1792 (*American State Papers, Foreign Relations,* I, 1832, pp. 201–37), which completely demolished the mediocre case of the Britisher, was submitted in draft to Hamilton in advance, and, with the latter's relatively minor criticisms, to Washington, who heartily approved it. To Hammond, however, the Secretary of the Treasury lamented the "intemperate violence" of Jefferson, and stated that the reply had not been read by Washington and did not represent the position of the government. Thus fortified by assurances which nullified Jefferson's arguments, the British minister submitted the matter to his superiors at home, who felt safe in ignoring it (Bemis, *Jay's Treaty,* ch. V). The full extent of Hamilton's intrigue has only recently been disclosed, but Jefferson was undoubtedly aware that he owed his undeserved defeat to his colleague.

By the summer of 1792 the hostility of the two men had become implacable. In the spring Jefferson had expressed in no uncertain terms to Washington his opinion that the causes of public discontent lay in Hamilton's policy, particularly in the "corruption" that had accompanied the financial measures of the latter and that had extended to the legislature itself. A formal list of the objections Jefferson had cited was submitted by the President to Hamilton on July 29 and was replied to by the latter three weeks later. In the meantime, Hamilton, smarting under the barbs of Freneau, had made an anonymous attack on the democratic editor and through him upon Jefferson. Washington's letters to his two secretaries, deploring the dissensions within the government, elicited lengthy replies in which each man presented his case, not only to his chief but also to posterity (see J. Sparks, *The Writings of George Washington,* X, 1836, pp. 249–55, 515–26; *The Works of Alexander Hamilton,* 1904, II, 426–72, VII, 303–06; Ford, *Writings of Thomas Jefferson,* VI, 101–09, 123–24). Washington did not succeed in stilling the troubled waters. Hamilton, indeed, during the autumn of 1792 published in the newspapers a series of ferocious anonymous attacks on his colleague, with the definite object of driving him from office. Jefferson, with greater dignity or greater discretion, refrained from newspaper controversy, leaving his defense to his friends. He probably played a part, however, in drafting the resolutions of William Branch Giles, presented early in 1793, which were severely critical of Hamilton's conduct of the Treasury.

His hostility to Hamilton, apart from his justifiable resentment at the interference of the latter in the conduct of his department, was like that of a religious devotee to an enemy of his faith. He was convinced that Hamilton's system "flowed from principles adverse to liberty, and was calculated to undermine and demolish the republic, by creating an influence of his department over the members of the legislature." Hamilton's hostility to Jefferson, apart from resentment that his power had been challenged, was like that of a practical man of affairs who found specific projects impeded by one whom he regarded as a quibbling theorist. Washington, reluctant to admit the existence of parties, valued both men and wanted both to remain in office, utilized both, and followed the policies of neither exclusively. The invaluable service rendered by each in his own field of activity vindicates the judgment of the patient President.

Yielding to the request of his Chief, Jefferson remained in office until the last day of 1793, during a critical period of foreign affairs. Though the course of the Revolution in France had been followed with growing concern by the conservative groups in America, popular opinion was still rather favorable to the French when the war in Europe was extended to Great Britain (Feb. 1, 1793) and a new minister, Edmond Charles Genet, came to the United States (Apr. 8, 1793). Jefferson was determined that his country should take no action that would imply opposition to the principles of the French Revolution, but he fully shared the feeling of Washington and Hamilton that American neutrality was imperative. He successfully urged the avoidance of the word "neutrality" in Washington's proclamation, however, in order to offend the French as little as possible and in the hope of gaining from the British some concessions in the definition of contraband. He also prevailed upon Washington to receive Genet without qualification and to postpone consideration of the treaty until the French should demand execution of the guarantee, which he thought they would not do. He agreed with Hamilton that payments on the debt to France should not be anticipated, but urged a softening of the refusal. Though he received Genet kindly, rejoiced in the popular enthusiasm for democracy that the fiery emissary kindled, and, through a letter of introduction, came dangerously near conniving with the Frenchman in his projected expedition against Louisiana, he strove with diligence to maintain neutrality and bore with patience the immense labors that the American position imposed upon him. When Genet persisted in intolerable practices and criticisms Jefferson lost patience with him and joined his colleagues in asking his recall.

Though he protested vigorously against British infringements of American neutral rights during the war, Jefferson was unable as secretary of state to solve the problem of British relations, and he regarded Jay's Treaty, which was later negotiated under the influence of Hamilton, as an ignominious surrender of American claims. The negotiations instituted by him with Spain were equally unsuccessful during his term of office, though the American objectives which he had formulated were attained in the treaty of 1795. His tangible achievements as secretary of state were not commensurate with his devoted labors, but he had fully justified Washington's confidence in him. If in the heat of the controversy with Hamilton he was at times guilty of extravagant assertion, he performed an inestimable service to the Republic by calling attention to the dangers of his colleague's policy, by formulating the chief grounds of opposition to it, and by inspiring the forces that were to effect its modification after it had achieved its most significant results.

Now in his fifty-first year, Jefferson felt that his second retirement from public life was final. Soon he gathered all the members of his immediate family under the paternal roof, and he at length resumed building operations at "Monticello," following revised plans that had grown out of his architectural observations abroad. By a system of crop rotation he tried to restore his lands, he experimented with mechanical devices, built a grist-mill, set up a nail-factory, and directed his large but relatively unprofitable establishment with characteristic diligence and attention to minute details. His renewed and increased enthusiasm for agriculture quite got the better of his love of study. At no other period of his mature life, perhaps, did he read so little and write so rarely. His days on horseback soon restored his health to the vigor that he feared it had permanently lost, and he brought some order into his tangled finances. During his years as an office-holder he had largely lived upon his small salary, yet the profits from his plantations and even sales of slaves and lands had been insufficient to rid him of the old Wayles debt, which in 1795 was increased by a judgment against the executors as security for the late Richard Randolph. Like so many of his fellow Virginians, Jefferson was unable to realize upon his assets and was eaten up by interest to British creditors. His personal generosity, however, which had been manifested in Philadelphia by loans to friends more distressed than he, continued unabated.

To Madison, whom he regarded as the logical Republican candidate for the presidency, he wrote, Apr. 27, 1795, that the "little spice of ambition" he had had in his younger days had long since evaporated and that the question of his own candidacy was forever closed. He remained, however, the symbol and the prophet of a political faith and when the leaders of his party determined to support him in 1796 did not gainsay them. He would have been willing to go into the presidency for a while, he said, in order "to put our vessel on her republican tack before she should be thrown too much to leeward of her true principles," but he was surprisingly content to run second to Adams, who was his senior and whom he perhaps regarded as the only barrier against Hamilton. After it appeared that Adams had won, and that he was second by three votes, he even suggested that some understanding be reached with the President-Elect. He proved himself a more realistic observer and a better political strategist, however, when he wrote Madison: "Let us cultivate Pennsylvania & we need not fear the universe."

The vice-presidency provided a salary which Jefferson undoubtedly needed, enabled him to spend much time at "Monticello," and afforded him relative leisure. The chief significance of his service as presiding officer of the Senate lies in the fact that out of it emerged his *Manual of Parliamentary Practice* (1801), subsequently published in many editions and translated into several languages, and even now the basis of parliamentary usage in the Senate. Despite the conciliatory spirit that marked his early relations with Adams, Jefferson played no part in the conduct of the administration, in which the hand of Hamilton was soon apparent. Since the Vice-President belonged to the opposing group, his complete abstention from politics was not to be expected. He was characteristically discreet in public utterance, but his general attitude toward the questions of the day was undoubtedly well known; and he was inevitably the target of the Federalist press, which continued to regard him as the personification of his party. The publication in the United States in May 1797 of a private letter of his to Philip Mazzei (Apr. 24, 1796), which originally appeared in a Florentine paper and was somewhat altered in form by successive translations, gave wide currency to his earlier criticisms of the Federalists. Certain vehement phrases were interpreted as reflecting upon Washington and served to alienate the latter from his former secretary. Jefferson made no effort to disavow a letter which was in substance his, suffering in silence while the Federalist press termed him "libeler," "liar," and "assassin" while he was practically ostracized by polite society.

He had approved of Monroe's conduct in France, which aroused so much hostile Federalist comment, and felt that the bellicose spirit which swept the country after the publication of the "X. Y. Z. despatches" was aggravated by the Hamiltonians, with a view to advancing their own interests and embroiling the United States on the side of the British. He himself was sympathetic with Elbridge Gerry, the commissioner who proved more amenable than his colleagues to French influence, and suggested that Gerry publish an account of his experiences. At all times, however, Jefferson was a patriotic American, and he had now no enthusiasm for the existing order in France. He was glad to drop the disastrous French issue when, at the height of the war fever, the Federalists provided a better one by passing the Alien and Sedition Acts. Jefferson rightly regarded hysterical hostility to aliens, such as his friends Volney and

Joseph Priestley, and attacks upon freedom of speech as a menace to the ideals he most cherished. Since the Sedition Law was applied chiefly to Republican editors, partisan as well as philosophical motives were conjoined in his opposition.

His most notable contribution to the campaign of discussion consisted of the Kentucky Resolutions of 1798, which, it appeared years later, he drafted. The Virginia Resolutions, drawn by Madison, were similar in tenor though more moderate. The constitutional doctrines advanced by Jefferson—that the government of the United States originated in a compact, that acts of the federal government unauthorized by the delegated powers are void, and that a state has the right to judge of infractions of its powers and to determine the mode of redress—were much emphasized in later years. His dominant purpose, however, was to attack the offensive laws as an unconstitutional and unwarranted infringement upon individual freedom, a denial of rights that could not be alienated. The language of what was in effect a party platform was in the nature of the case extravagant, but Jefferson and Madison had no intention of carrying matters to extremes, and such indorsement as their party ultimately received was of their protest, not of their method (F. M. Anderson, in *American Historical Review,* October 1899, pp. 45–63, January 1900, pp. 225–52). More important from the practical point of view than any promulgation of constitutional theory was the vindication of the right of public discussion and political opposition.

Nominated by a congressional caucus for the presidency and by no means indifferent to the outcome as he had been four years earlier, Jefferson owed his success in the election of 1800 as much to Federalist dissensions as to any formal issues that had been raised. To the Republican victory, his running mate, Aaron Burr, also made no small contribution. By fault of the electoral machinery, soon to be remedied, the two Republicans received an identical vote and the choice of a president was left to the House of Representatives. Despite the personal hostility of many of the Federalists to Jefferson, the feeling, to which Hamilton contributed, that he was the safer man of the two and would not revolutionize the government, caused Congress ultimately to yield to the undoubted desire of the Republicans and to elect him. His own reference to the "revolution" of 1800 was one of his political exaggerations, but the elevation to the highest executive office of one who, almost twenty years before, had unheroically relinquished the reins of gubernatorial power undoubtedly marked a revolution in his own political fortunes. The popular success of Jefferson, whose diffidence and lack of spectacular qualities would have constituted in a later day an insuperable handicap, and whose relative freedom from personal ambition makes it impossible to characterize him as a demagogue, was due in considerable part to his identification of himself with causes for which time was fighting, and to his remarkable sensitiveness to fluctuations in public opinion, combined with an ability to utilize and to develop agencies of popular appeal. As a practical politician he worked through other men, whom he energized and who gave him to an extraordinary degree their devoted cooperation. His unchallenged leadership was due, not to self-assertiveness and imperiousness of will, but to the fact that circumstances had made him a symbolic figure, and that to an acute intelligence and unceasing industry he joined a dauntless and contagious faith. The long struggle between his partisans and the Federalists has been variously interpreted as one between democracy and aristocracy, state rights and centralization, agrarianism and capitalism. His election, however, had more immediate significance in marking the vindication of political opposition, the repudiation of a reactionary régime, and the accession of more representative leaders to power.

Jefferson, the first president inaugurated in Washington, had himself drawn a plan for the city, part of which survives in the Mall. As secretary of state, to whom the commissioners of the District were responsible, he had suggested the competition for the new federal buildings and he was considerably responsible for the selection of classical designs. As president he appointed Benjamin H. Latrobe surveyor of public buildings and fully cooperated in planning for the future development of a monumental city. In his day, pomp and ceremony, to which on principle and for political reasons he was opposed, would have been preposterous in the wilderness village. Remaining until the last at Conrad's boardinghouse, where his democratic simplicity was marked, he walked to the nearby Senate chamber of the incompleted capitol, to receive the oath of office from his cousin and inveterate political foe, Chief Justice John Marshall. Though aware of the last efforts of the Federalists to renew the Sedition Act and entrench themselves in the judiciary, he felt that after the long "contest of opinion" the danger of monarchy was now removed, and in his benevolent inaugural he sought to woo the more moderate of his opponents by making acquiescence in the will of the majority as easy as possible. Though he challenged the assertion that a republican government could not be strong, he defined its functions as essentially negative. It should restrain men from injuring one another, he said, but otherwise leave them to regulate their own concerns. He declared against special privileges and urged encouragement, not of industry, but of agriculture and of commerce "as its handmaid." He reiterated his conviction that the federal government should chiefly concern itself with foreign affairs, leaving to the states the administration of local matters. War, he felt, could be avoided by peaceable coercion through the weapon of commerce.

Inaugurated in his fifty-eighth year, he made his official residence in the boxlike and incompletely plastered President's House, though he continued to spend as much time as possible at "Monticello," where he was still directing building operations. His beautiful second daughter, now the wife of her cousin John Wayles Eppes, though far less prolific than her sister, had also by this time made him a grandfather. (She was to sadden her father's life by her untimely death in 1804.) Generally deprived of adequate feminine supervision while in Washington, Jefferson lived there in sartorial indifference and dispensed generous but informal hospitality, as he was accustomed to do at home, to the consternation of diplomats jealous of precedence. His manners, after he had overcome his constitutional diffidence, were easy though not polished. To hostile observers his democratic simplicity was a pose, to his friends the naturalness of one who had achieved and thought enough to dare to be himself. His loose gait and habit of lounging, together with his discursive though highly informing conversation, doubtless contributed to the common but erroneous impression among his foes that this most scholarly of politicians was a careless thinker. "His external appearance," according to an admirer, "had no pretensions to elegance, but it was neither coarse nor awkward, and it must be owned that his greatest personal attraction was a countenance beaming with benevolence and intelligence" (Margaret Bayard Smith, *First Forty Years of Washington Society*, 1906, pp. 385–86).

Chief in his harmonious official family were Madison, the secretary of state, and Gallatin, who as secretary of the treasury was to carry out with considerable success his program of economy. Jefferson found nearly all the minor offices filled by Federalists and, though anxious to conciliate his former foes, sympathized with his own followers in their insistence that the balance be restored. This could only be done by removals, for, as he said, vacancies "by death are few; by resignation none." He proceeded to treat as null and void Federalist appointments which seemed to him of questionable legality, such as those of the "midnight judges" and others made by Adams after the latter's defeat was apparent. Finding his policy a political success, he extended it, until by the summer of 1803 the balance was restored and removals ceased. No non-partisan standard was adopted, however, and the Republicans came to dominate the civil service as the Federalists had done. Since Jefferson's appointments involved some recognition of party service, they constituted a technical introduction of the spoils system. The standards of the federal service, however, were not perceptibly lowered, and, except in New England, the people were generally satisfied.

Though Jefferson, whose voice could hardly be heard upon a public occasion anyway, abandoned the custom of delivering messages in person, he maintained over Congress indirect and tactful but efficacious control. The repeal of the Federalist Judiciary Act of 1801 was distinctly a measure of the administration. The severe rebuke administered to him and Madison by Marshall in *Marbury vs. Madison* (1803) did not predispose him to concede the right of the Supreme Court to invalidate an act of Congress. Indeed, in pardoning victims of the Sedition Law, he himself pronounced that statute unconstitutional, as he felt he was called upon to do. He thoroughly approved of the use of the weapon of impeachment against offensively partisan judges and deeply regretted its practical failure, notably in the case of Justice Samuel Chase. Though the federal judges learned better to observe the proprieties, Jefferson never receded from his position that the Federalists, from the battery of the judiciary, were endeavoring to beat down the works of Republicanism and defeat the will of the people, as in a sense they were.

Rumors of the retrocession of Louisiana by Spain to France led Jefferson to write the American minister to France, Robert R. Livingston, on Apr. 18, 1802, that the possessor of New Orleans was the natural enemy of the United States and that by placing herself there France assumed an attitude of defiance. Following the independent announcement by the Spanish intendant, Oct. 16, 1802, of the closure of the Mississippi and Federalist talk in Congress of warlike measures, he despatched Monroe to France as special minister. The purchase which Livingston and Monroe made, and for which Jefferson gave them full credit, was a diplomatic triumph of the first magnitude but it required him to disregard many scruples and to compromise cherished constitutional principles. In his proper anxiety to preserve the freedom of navigation of the Mississippi, he felt compelled at one time to consider a rapprochement with Great

Britain, his traditional foe, and ultimately to increase the debt which he was striving so hard to reduce. Doubting the power of the federal government, under the Constitution, to acquire territory and, even more, the power to incorporate it, he believed that broad construction would make blank paper of that supreme safeguard against tyranny. After the treaty was negotiated he favored the submission of a constitutional amendment, but yielded to the insistence of his political friends that no amendment was necessary and that delay was perilous, doubtless consoling himself with the thought that in Republican hands the Constitution was safe. The ratification of the treaty, effected in response to overwhelming public opinion, has been interpreted as a death-blow to strict construction. The Louisiana Purchase can be best regarded, however, as a striking example of Jefferson's pragmatic statesmanship. He had assured the physical greatness of his country and the future success of his party, which was symbolized by his own triumphant reëlection. Western discontent was stilled and the Federalists were reduced to sectional impotence. For all of this his momentary theoretical inconsistency seemed to his partisans a small price to pay, but his subsequent silence about the greatest constructive accomplishment of his presidency suggests that he viewed it with some misgivings. The purchase served, however, to facilitate the expedition for which he had already commissioned Meriwether Lewis and prepared elaborate instructions. He himself wrote for the *History of the Expedition under the Command of Captains Lewis and Clark* (1814), the best biography of his former secretary, and no one more than he rejoiced in the discoveries the explorers made.

Livingston and Monroe had bought a vaguely defined region which they soon persuaded themselves included West Florida as well as Louisiana. Jefferson subsequently embodied similar views in a pamphlet which determined the attitude of the administration and its supporters (in *Documents Relating to the Purchase & Exploration of Louisiana,* 1904; Cox, *post,* pp. 80–87). The Mobile Act of Feb. 24, 1804, assumed the acquisition of West Florida, but Jefferson, finding that the Spanish were not acquiescent as he had expected, practically annulled its offensive features by proclamation and sent Monroe on what proved to be a futile mission to Spain. In his public message to Congress, on Dec. 4, 1805 (Ford, VIII, 384–96), he adopted a tone of belligerency, apparently with the idea of frightening the Spanish, then, by revealing to Congress his purpose to acquire Florida by what John Randolph of Roanoke regarded as a bribe to France, confounded his supporters and alienated that vitriolic leader, already incensed by the settlement of the Yazoo claims. A proposal went to Napoleon too late to be of any use and the perplexing question of Florida remained unsettled during Jefferson's administration. His tortuous policy had served only to diminish his influence in Congress and weaken his hand against the British.

His policy of peaceable negotiation did not extend to the Barbary pirates, to whom he applied more force than had any previous American president. Following the repudiation of his treaty by the Bey of Tripoli in 1801, Jefferson dispatched against him a naval force which blockaded his ports. Subsequently Jefferson also employed naval force against the Sultan of Morocco. The treaty at length negotiated with Tripoli, though it included provisions for the ransom of American prisoners, granted the United States the most favorable terms yet given any nation by that piratical power.

Long before the trial of Aaron Burr in 1807 on charges of treason, Jefferson had lost faith in his former associate, but he gave little heed to the mystifying western expedition of the adventurer until it was well on its way. On Nov. 27, 1806, Jefferson issued a proclamation of warning against an illegal expedition against Spain, and, after Burr's arrest, publicly expressing himself as convinced of the latter's guilt, exerted powerful influence to bring about his conviction. Burr's trial in Richmond before John Marshall developed into a political duel between the Chief Justice and the President. Burr's counsel, including Luther Martin, raised against Jefferson a cry of persecution which echoed through the land, and, attacking the credibility of the chief witness for the prosecution, the vulnerable James Wilkinson, through him assailed the man who had appointed him to command the army and had sent him to protect Louisiana against the Spanish. Marshall was distinctly hostile to Jefferson throughout the proceedings and, by his definition of treason, made the conviction of Burr impossible. Jefferson wished to press the charge of misdemeanor, possibly to find grounds for the impeachment of the Chief Justice, but had to abandon his plans because the whole case rested on Wilkinson. Though Marshall's conduct was by no means unexceptionable, this famous trial proved more discomforting to Jefferson than to the Chief Justice and strengthened the hands of his political enemies, who charged him with an original indifference which gave way to credulity, and with a measure of vindictiveness wholly inconsistent with his expressed convictions in regard to the sacred rights of the individual.

The difficulties which Jefferson faced during his second administration as the head of a neutral nation in a time of ruthless general European war, were inescapable and could probably have been successfully met by no American statesman. During his first term, though he had done little to prepare for a possible conflict of arms, he had managed sufficiently well by employing ordinary diplomatic methods. Until 1805 the British had in practice granted sufficient concessions to permit large prosperity to the American carrying trade, but, following the *Essex* decision of that year, they tightened their control and seized many American vessels. Also, the impressment of seamen remained a grievance, which the British would do nothing to remove. Then, in the battle of Orders in Council and Napoleonic decrees, the neutral American Republic, unable to meet both sets of requirements and threatened with the confiscation of commercial vessels in case either were violated, was placed in an intolerable position.

Of the possible courses of action open to him, war did not commend itself to Jefferson, who did not want to take sides with either of the European rivals, though, after the *Leopard* fired on the *Chesapeake* in June 1807, a declaration against the British might have been supported by the American people. In this instance, Jefferson's belligerency vented itself in a proclamation, regarded by his foes as pusillanimous, denying to British armed vessels the hospitality of American waters. He had previously sent William Pinkney to London to serve with Monroe on a mission extraordinary, and had tried to strengthen the hands of the negotiators by the Non-Importation Act of 1806, which was to become effective some months later. His reliance was on diplomacy, supplemented by the threat of economic pressure, and when diplomacy failed he fell back on economic pressure. The only other apparent alternatives were intolerable submission or some sort of cooperation with the British against Napoleon. The Embargo constituted perhaps Jefferson's most original and daring measure of statesmanship; it proved to be his greatest practical failure. Adopted in December 1807, after an inadequate debate and by an overwhelming vote because of his political dominance and still enormous popularity, the measure combined with the Non-Intercourse Act to bring about a theoretical suspension of foreign commerce for an indefinite period.

The attempts to enforce the Embargo involved an exercise of arbitrary power by the federal government and an inevitable and increasing infringement on individual rights which were contrary to Jefferson's most cherished ideals. He opposed war in large part because of the corruption and repression which were its accompaniments, little realizing that his peaceful substitute would be attended with the same evils and that negative heroism would in the end prove galling. He counted too heavily on British liberal opinion, which had opposed the Orders in Council as affecting the United States, and he did not anticipate the developments in Spain and the Spanish colonies which did so much to relieve the pressure on Great Britain. He claimed, with considerable justification, that the Embargo was not in effect long enough to attain its objective, and it may well be that under other circumstances some measure of the sort might prove an efficacious weapon. But in 1808–09, employed by a weak power, it served chiefly to impoverish the sections that supported Jefferson most loyally, to give a new lease on life to partisan opposition in New England, and to bring his second executive venture to an inglorious consummation. Forced to yield to a rebellious Congress, on Mar. 1, 1809, he signed the Non-Intercourse Act, which partially raised the Embargo, and shortly afterward retired to Albemarle, discredited and disillusioned, though unconvinced that he had erred in policy. He correctly described himself as a wave-worn mariner approaching the shore, as a prisoner emerging from the shackles, and declared that Nature had intended him for the tranquil pursuits of science, in which he found infinite delight.

During the past eight years this earnest advocate of the freedom of the press had been subjected to a flood of personal calumny. Long regarded in ecclesiastical circles, especially in New England, as the embodiment of foreign infidelity, he not unnaturally aroused a storm of indignation, soon after his first inauguration, by offering to Thomas Paine passage to America on a sloop-of-war and by expressing the hope that his "useful labours" would be continued. The following year an indefensible assault was launched by a disgruntled pamphleteer to whom Jefferson had previously made monetary gifts which he himself designated as charity but which could be readily interpreted as a form of subsidy. To the charges of cowardice, dishonesty, and personal immorality made in 1802 by James Thomson Callender in the Richmond *Recorder* almost every subsequent story reflecting on Jefferson's private life can ultimately be traced. Given nation-wide currency by the Federalist press, these were discussed in 1805 in the House of Representatives of Massachusetts, where a motion to dismiss the printers of the House for publishing in the *New-England Palladium* (Jan. 18, 1805) libels on the President failed of adoption. One only of these charges was admitted by Jefferson (W. C. Ford, *Thomas Jefferson Correspondence*, 1916, p. 115). This referred to an instance of highly improper conduct on his part, while yet a young man and single, for which he made restitution. Of the other allegations of immorality, it is quite sufficient to say with Henry Adams that Jefferson, a model husband and father, was "more refined than many women in the delicacy of his private relations."

For the wide acceptance, by persons of the better sort, of the extravagant charges of an unscrupulous drunkard, the sensitive President was disposed to blame his old theological foes, especially in New England. There his followers were assaulting the ancient alliance between church and state, for the final overthrow of which they deserve considerable credit. It may well be, as Henry Adams says, that Jefferson did not understand the New Englanders, but it is certain that they did not understand him. Though sanguine in temperament, he was as serious-minded and almost as devoid of humor as any Puritan; and had he lived a generation later he would have been more at home in liberal religious circles in New England than anywhere else in America. He loathed Calvinism, but he objected to Unitarianism only because it also was another sect. At many times he paid grateful tribute to Epicurus and Epictetus, but as early as 1803 he began to select from the Gospels the passages which he believed came from Jesus. Toward the end of his life this amateur higher critic placed parallel texts, in four languages, in a "wee-little book," which he entitled the "Morals of Jesus" (published in 1904 as *House Doc. No. 755, 58* Cong., 2 Sess.). This proved, he felt, that he was "a *real Christian*, that is to say a disciple of the doctrines of Jesus."

During the remaining seventeen years of his life, Jefferson ventured only a few miles from his haven at "Monticello." The Embargo and its aftermath were ruinous to him, as to so many Virginia planters, and because of the demands of incessant hospitality he could not live as simply as he desired. After the War of 1812, however, the sale of his library of some 10,000 volumes to the government, for the Library of Congress, served for several years to relieve his financial burdens; and his grandson, Thomas Jefferson Randolph, took over the management of his lands. Laborious correspondence occupied a disproportionate amount of his time, but he enjoyed exchanging ideas with John Adams (with whom his old friendship was beautifully restored), his friends in France, Thomas Cooper, and others, and has left in the letters of these years a mine of treasure. He gave his counsel to his disciples Madison and Monroe when they asked it; and some of his expressions on public policy, as, for example, on the Missouri Compromise and on the attitude of the United States toward Europe and the Latin-American republics, are notable.

The chief public problem to which he addressed himself, however, was that of education in Virginia, which he again called his "country." He never ceased to advocate a comprehensive state-wide plan of education, such as he had proposed in 1779. "Enlighten the people generally," he wrote Du Pont de Nemours in 1816, "and tyranny and oppressions of both mind and body will vanish like evil spirits at the dawn of day." Popular education, however, he regarded as more than a defensive weapon and a guarantor of freedom. His proposals of 1779 had been marked by a unique provision whereby youths of great promise were to be advanced from one grade of instruction to another without cost, and he hoped that these "geniuses . . . raked from the rubbish" would serve the state as governors or enlarge the domains of human knowledge. He formulated, as perhaps no other American of his generation, an educational philosophy for a democratic state; and in his last years he declared himself in favor of a literacy test for citizenship.

Having failed in his earlier efforts to transform the College of William and Mary, by 1800 at least Jefferson had hopes of establishing in the more salubrious upper country a university on a broad, liberal, and modern plan. Whatever interest he may have had, during his presidency, in the creation of a national university contingent upon the amendment of the Constitution, Virginia was central in all his thoughts after 1809. Indeed, his regret that so many of his "countrymen" went to be educated among "foreigners" (as at Princeton) or were taught at home by "beggars" (Northern tutors) was partly due to the fear that their political principles were being contaminated. His representations may have stimulated Gov. John Tyler to send to the Assembly in 1809 his strong message on education which resulted in the establishment, the following year, of the Literary Fund. Jefferson regarded this as an inadequate provision for general education but it later made possible the creation of an institution of higher learning.

By happy chance, Jefferson in 1814 became associated as a trustee with the unorganized Albemarle Academy. Transformed into Central College, this became the germ from which the University of Virginia developed, under his adroit management at every stage. His letter of Sept. 7, 1814, to Peter Carr, outlining in masterly fashion his views of a state system, probably inspired the resolution, adopted by the General Assembly on Feb. 24, 1816, which required a report on a scheme of public instruction. Shortly thereafter, Jefferson himself drafted a bill (Honeywell, *post,* appendix H), which contained most of the features of his more famous proposal of 1779 and included a provision for a university. This was rejected and for a time it appeared that, after an appropriation for elementary schools (which Jefferson always felt should be supported locally), no funds would be available for a higher institution. At length, in 1818, by a compromise, appropriations were authorized for elementary, but not for intermediate, schools and for a university.

Jefferson was appointed a member, and became chairman, of the Rockfish Gap Commission, empowered to recommend a site. By skilful use of geographical arguments, he gained the victory for Central College in August 1818. The report, which he had drafted beforehand, incorporated his ideas of what a university should be and remains one of his greatest educational papers (Cabell, *post,* pp. 432 ff.). After a legislative battle in which he acted only behind the scenes, the report was adopted, and in 1819 the University of Virginia was chartered. Though the services of Joseph C. Cabell and John H. Cocke in launching the institution were invaluable, Jefferson, who was inevitably appointed a member of the first board of visitors and elected rector, remained until his death the dominant factor in its affairs. He received architectural suggestions from Benjamin H. Latrobe and to a lesser extent from William Thornton, but the plan of an academical village was his own. Many of the specifications were drawn up by him and the "pavilions," "hotels," dormitories, colonnades, and arcades were constructed under his immediate supervision. At his death, only the Rotunda, modeled by him on the Pantheon at Rome, was incomplete.

The courses of study followed closely those of Jefferson's suggestions that seemed immediately practicable. Upon the organization of the institution, he left his most characteristic impress perhaps in the establishment of independent, diploma-conferring "schools," capable of indefinite expansion, in the provision for entire freedom in the election of courses, in the complete disregard of the conventional grouping of students into classes, in the arrangement for a rotating chairmanship of the faculty, without a president, and in the prohibition of honorary degrees. Despite his insistence that Republican, rather than Federalist, principles be taught in the school of law, to a remarkable extent he freed the institution from hampering restrictions and made it in spirit a university. He can hardly be blamed that it subsequently suffered because of the lack of contributing colleges, the need of which he clearly envisaged, and that circumstances combined to make it a more aristocratic institution than he had anticipated or desired. Though he was disappointed in his full hopes of drawing from Europe to the faculty "the first characters in science," the mission of Francis Walker Gilmer was measurably successful, the new institution had from the outset a flavor of cosmopolitanism, and several of the first professors achieved distinction. The "Old Sachem" lived to see the university opened and for more than a year in operation.

During his own lifetime, Jefferson received not only American but also international recognition as a man, and as a patron, of learning. Elected president of the American Philosophical Society on Jan. 6, 1797, he remained the head of this notable organization until 1815 and actively cooperated with it in the advancement and dissemination of knowledge. By introducing to his colleagues, on Mar. 10, 1797, his megalonyx he fired the "signal gun of American paleontology." To them he read on May 4, 1798, a description of a mould-board of least resistance for a plow, for which invention he received in 1805 a gold medal from a French society (*Mémoires de la Société d'Agriculture du Département de la Seine et Oise*, VII, 1805, pp. xlix–lviii). In due course he became associated with an extraordinary number of important societies in various countries of Europe, as he had long been with the chief learned, and almost all the agricultural, societies of America. Much but by no means all of his recognition was due to his political prominence. His election, Dec. 26, 1801, as *associé étranger* of the Institute of France, if due to his position at all, was due to his presidency of the American Philosophical Society. This signal honor, which during his lifetime was shared by no other man of American birth and residence, may best be attributed to his reputation in France as the most conspicuous American intellectual. He himself interpreted it as "an evidence of the brotherly spirit of Science, which unites into one family all its votaries of whatever grade, and however widely dispersed throughout the different quarters of the globe." He corresponded throughout his life with an extraordinary number of scientists and philosophers in other lands, as well as in America, and sought to make available in his own country the best of foreign thought and discovery.

Modern scholars have recognized Jefferson as an American pioneer in numerous branches of science, notably paleontology, ethnology, geography, and botany. Living before the age of specialization, he was for his day a careful investigator, no more credulous than his learned contemporaries, and notable among them for his effort in all fields to attain scientific exactitude. In state papers he is commonly the lawyer, pleading a cause; in the heat of political controversy he doubtless compromised his intellectual ideals and certainly indulged in exaggeration; but his procedure in arriving at his fundamental opinions, the habits of his life, and his temperament were essentially those of a scholar. As secretary of state, he was in effect the first commissioner of patents and the first patent examiner. He himself invented or adapted to personal uses numerous ingenious devices, the best known of which is his polygraph.

At home in French, Italian, and Spanish, as well as Greek and Latin, he wrote *An Essay towards Facilitating Instruction in the Anglo-Saxon and Modern Dialects of the English Language* (1851); and during a generation he amassed an extraordinary collection of Indian vocabularies, only to have them cast upon the waters by thieves in 1809. He owned one of the best private collections of paintings and statuary in the country, and has been termed "the first American connoisseur and patron of the arts" (Kimball, *Thomas Jefferson, Architect,* p. 86). Besides the Virginia state capitol, "Monticello," and the original buildings of the University of Virginia, he designed wholly or in part numerous Virginia houses, among them his own "Poplar Forest," "Farmington," and "Barboursville." Before the advent of professional architects in America, he began to collect books on architecture and discovered Palladio, from whom his careful and extensive observations abroad never weaned him. Always himself a Romanist, he did more than any other man to stimulate the classical revival in America. His own work, while always ingenious, is academic, precise, and orderly, but, because of the fortunate necessity of using brick and wood, the new creation was a blend, with a pleasing domesticity. He created a definite school of builders in Virginia, sought to establish formal instruction in architecture, stimulated and encouraged, among others, Bulfinch and Thornton, and, except for the fact that he accepted no pay for his services, was as truly a professional as they. It is probably no exaggeration to say with Fiske Kimball that he was "the father of our national architecture." (p. 89).

Few other American statesmen have been such careful and unremitting students of political thought and history as was Jefferson, or have been more concerned with ultimate ends. Yet he has left no treatise on political philosophy, and all general statements about his theoretical position are subject to qualification. It is impossible to grant eternal validity to the principles adduced by him to support his position in particular circumstances; he was always more interested in applications than in speculation, and he was forced to modify his own philosophy in practice. But, despite unquestionable inconsistencies, the general trend of his policies and his major aims are unmistakable. A homely aristocrat in manner of life and personal tastes, he distrusted all rulers and feared the rise of an industrial proletariat, but, more than any of his eminent contemporaries, he trusted the common man, if measurably enlightened and kept in rural virtue; though pained and angered when the free press made him the victim of its license, he was a passionate advocate of human liberty and laid supreme stress on the individual; though he clearly realized the value of union, he emphasized the importance of the states and of local agencies of government; an intellectual internationalist, he gave whole-hearted support to the policy of political isolation, and anticipated the development on the North American continent of a dominant nation, unique in civilization. He is notable, not for his harmony with the life of his age, but rather for his being a step or several steps ahead of it; no other American more deserves to be termed a major prophet, a supreme pioneer. A philosophical statesman rather than a political philosopher, he contributed to democracy and liberalism a faith rather than a body of doctrine. By his works alone he must be adjudged one of the greatest of all Americans, while the influence of his energizing faith is immeasurable.

Regarded by Hamilton as ambitious and temporizing, by Marshall as untrustworthy, loved by John Adams despite rivalry and misunderstanding, honored as a kindly master by a group of disciples the like of which has assembled around no other American statesman, Jefferson, by the very contradictions of his subtle and complex personality, of his bold mind and highly sensitive nature, has both vexed and fascinated all who have attempted to interpret him. As Henry Adams said: "Almost every other American statesman might be described in a parenthesis. A few broad strokes of the brush would paint the portraits of all the early Presidents with this exception, . . . but Jefferson could be painted only touch by touch, with a fine pencil, and the perfection of the likeness depended upon the shifting and uncertain flicker of its semi-transparent shadows" (*History*, I, 277).

The last years of this most enigmatical and probably the most versatile of great Americans were marked by philosophical serenity in the face of impending financial disaster. Ruined by the failure in 1819 of his friend Wilson Cary Nicholas, whose note for $20,000 he had indorsed, he tried vainly to find a purchaser for his lands, and secured legislative permission, in the last year of his life, to dispose of most of them by the common method of a lottery. The public strongly protested against this indignity to him and some voluntary contributions were made, so the project was abandoned. Jefferson died believing that his debts would be paid, fortunately not realizing that "Monticello" was soon to pass from the hands of his heirs forever. A beloved and revered patriarch in the extensive family circle, he retained extraordinary intellectual vigor and rode his horse daily until almost the end of his ordered and temperate life. His death occurred, with dramatic appropriateness, on the fiftieth anniversary of the Declaration of Independence, shortly after noon and a few hours before that of John Adams. His daughter, Martha Randolph, with ten of her children and their progeny, and his grandson, Francis Eppes, survived him. On the simple stone over his grave in the family burying-ground at "Monticello" he is described as he wished to be remembered, not as the holder of great offices, but as the author of the Declaration of Independence and the Virginia statute for religious freedom, and the father of the University of Virginia.

[The Jefferson manuscripts in the Lib. of Cong. comprise, in addition to other important items, 236 vols. of correspondence (*c.* 40,000 pieces), partially calendared in the *Calendar of the Correspondence of Thos. Jefferson* (Parts I–III, 1894–1903). The collection in the Mass. Hist. Soc. consists of 67 vols. (*c.* 10,000 pieces), and some of his most interesting personal records, including account books, his Garden Book, his Farm Book, and the catalogue of his library. Other papers are in the Mo. Hist. Soc., St. Louis, the library of the Univ. of Va., and various other depositories, and some are still in private hands.

P. L. Ford, *The Writings of Thos. Jefferson* (10 vols., 1892–99), is the most useful edition, but this should be supplemented by the more extensive Memorial Ed. (20 vols., 1903–04), and by the edition of H. A. Washington (9 vols., 1853–54). Both the "Autobiography" and the preface to "The Anas" were written in old age and carry less authority than contemporary documents. The following are valuable sources: "The Jefferson Papers," *Collections of the Mass. Hist. Soc.,* 7 ser., vol. I (1900); *Thos. Jefferson Correspondence, Printed from Originals in the Collections of Wm. K. Bixby,* with notes by W. C. Ford

(1916); G. Chinard, *The Commonplace Book of Thos. Jefferson* (1927), *The Literary Bible of Thos. Jefferson* (1928), *The Letters of Lafayette and Jefferson* (1929), the *Correspondence of Jefferson and Du Pont de Nemours with an Introduction on Jefferson and the Physiocrats* (1931); D. Malone, *Correspondence between Thos. Jefferson and P. S. du Pont de Nemours, 1798–1817* (1930); P. Wilstach, *Correspondence between John Adams and Thos. Jefferson* (1925). Numerous letters to and from Jefferson are contained in G. Chinard, *Volney et L'Amérique* (1923), *Jefferson et Les Idéologues* (1925), and *Trois Amitiés Françaises de Jefferson* (1927). John P. Foley, *The Jefferson Cyclopedia* (1900), is a useful compilation.

Of the older biographies, H. S. Randall, *The Life of Thos. Jefferson* (3 vols., 1858), though eulogistic, is still extremely valuable, as is S. N. Randolph, *The Domestic Life of Thos. Jefferson* (1871), which contains many family letters. The most important of the recent biographies are G. Chinard, *Thos. Jefferson: The Apostle of Americanism* (1929), and A. J. Nock, *Jefferson* (1926), both of which emphasize the intellectual aspect of his career. More general treatments are P. L. Ford, *Thos. Jefferson* (1904); D. S. Muzzey, *Thos. Jefferson* (1918). A hostile Federalist work is Theo. Dwight, *The Character of Thos. Jefferson, as Exhibited in His Own Writings* (1839). C. G. Bowers, *Jefferson and Hamilton* (1925), is dramatic and favorable; F. W. Hirst, *Life and Letters of Thos. Jefferson* (1926), is eulogistic.

For genealogical materials, the family background, and his early life, see *Tyler's Quart. Hist. and Genealog. Mag.*, Jan., Apr., July, Oct. 1925; Jan., July 1926; Wm. C. Bruce, *John Randolph of Roanoke* (1922), I, 9 ff.; E. Woods, *Albemarle County in Va.* (1901); *Wm. and Mary Quart. Hist. Mag.*, Jan. 1921, p. 34, and F. Harrison, *Ibid.*, Jan. 1924, p. 15. For his public career and political position, see *Jour. of the House of Burgesses of Va.*, 1766–76 (3 vols., 1905–06); W. W. Hening, *The Statutes at Large . . . of Va.* (13 vols., 1809–23); Carl Becker, *The Declaration of Independence* (1922); J. C. Fitzpatrick, *The Spirit of the Revolution* (1924), chs. I, II; H. J. Eckenrode, *The Revolution in Va.* (1916); C. R. Lingley, "The Transition in Va. from Colony to Commonwealth," *Columbia Univ. Studies in Hist., Economics and Pub. Law,* vol. XXXVI, no. 2 (1910); B. Faÿ, *L'Esprit Révolutionnaire en France et aux États-Unis à la Fin du XVIIIᵉ Siècle* (1925); L. B. Dunbar, *A Study of "Monarchical" Tendencies in the U. S.* (1922); S. F. Bemis, *Jay's Treaty* (1923), *Pinckney's Treaty* (1926), *The Am. Secretaries of State and Their Diplomacy*, II (1927), 3–93; W. K. Woolery, "The Relation of Thos. Jefferson to Am. Foreign Policy, 1783–1793," *Johns Hopkins Univ. Studies in Hist. and Pol. Science,* vol. XLV, no. 2 (1927); Chas. A. Beard, *Economic Origins of Jeffersonian Democracy* (1915); C. R. Fish, *The Civil Service and the Patronage* (1905); A. J. Beveridge, *The Life of John Marshall* (4 vols., 1916); I. J. Cox, *The W. Fla. Controversy, 1798–1813* (1918); L. M. Sears, *Jefferson and the Embargo* (1927); Henry Adams, *Hist. of the U. S. of Am.*, vols. I–IV (1889–90); C. E. Merriam, *A Hist. of Am. Pol. Theories* (1910), ch. IV; V. L. Parrington, *Main Currents in Am. Thought,* I (1927), 342–56; E. S. Brown, *Wm. Plumer's Memorandum of Procs. in the U. S. Senate* (1923); *The Defense of Young and Mims, Printers to the State . . .* (Boston, 1805).

For the Univ. of Va., see N. F. Cabell, *Early Hist. of the Univ. of Va. as Contained in the Letters of Thos. Jefferson and Jos. C. Cabell* (1856); P. A. Bruce, *Hist. of the Univ. of Va.*, vols. I, II (1922); R. J. Honeywell, *The Educational Work of Thos. Jefferson* (1931). For architecture, see Fiske Kimball, "Thos. Jefferson as Architect: Monticello and Shadwell," *Architectural Quart. of Harvard Univ.*, June 1914, *Thos. Jefferson and the First Monument of the Classical Revival in Am.* (1915), *Thos. Jefferson, Architect* (1916); W. B. Bryan, *A Hist. of the Nat. Capital*, vol. I (1914). For his scientific work, see Wm. E. Curtis, *The True Thos. Jefferson* (1901), ch. XII; Alex. F. Chamberlain, "Thos. Jefferson's Ethnological Opinions and Activities," *Am. Anthropologist*, July–Sept. 1907; Geo. T. Surface, "Thos. Jefferson: a Pioneer Student of Am. Geography," *Bulletin of the Am. Geog. Soc.*, Dec. 1909; F. A. Lucas, "Thos. Jefferson—Paleontologist," *Nat. Hist.*, May–June, 1926; H. F. Osborn, "Thos. Jefferson, The Pioneer of Am. Paleontology," *Science*, Apr. 19, 1929; Wm. I. Wyman, "Thos. Jefferson and the Patent System," *Jour. of the Patent Office Soc.*, Sept. 1918. For a personal picture, see D. Malone, "Polly Jefferson and Her Father," *Va. Quart. Rev.*, Jan. 1931. A life mask is reproduced in C. H. Hart, *Browere's Life Masks of Great Americans* (1899).]

[SUPPLEMENTARY BIBLIOGRAPHY. Most of the Jefferson manuscripts, including those in the Lib. of Cong., the Mass. Hist. Soc., and the Huntington Lib., are now available on microfilm in one library or another, and photoduplicates of all that are known to exist are on file in the office of the Papers of Thomas Jefferson in the Princeton Univ. Lib., though these are not open to the public. Nearly everything is available in some form in the Alderman Lib., Univ. of Va. The greatly enlarged collection there includes, besides Jefferson papers proper, the Edgehill Randolph Papers, the Carr and Cary Papers, and others relating to his personal life, family, and the Univ. of Va.

All previous printed collections are being superseded by *The Papers of Thomas Jefferson* (1950–   ), ed. by J. P. Boyd. Projected in more than 50 vols., this exhaustive work, containing letters to Jefferson and many enclosures as well as his own letters, has reached vol. 16 at this writing (1962) and carries the record to July 4, 1790. E. M. Sowerby, *Catalogue of the Library of Thomas Jefferson* (5 vols., 1952–59), with his own comments on his books, is a work of magnitude and great interest. E. M. Betts, *Thomas Jefferson's Garden Book, 1766–1824* (1944), and *Thomas Jefferson's Farm Book* (1953), both of which contain relevant extracts from other writings, are invaluable for life at Monticello. The value and interest of the following, which are listed under the names of the editors, is suggested by the titles themselves: L. J. Cappon, *The Adams-Jefferson Letters: The Complete Correspondence between Thomas Jefferson and John and Abigail Adams* (2 vols., 1959); T. P. Abernethy, *A Summary View of the Rights of British America* (1943); J. P. Boyd, *The Declaration of Independence. The Evolution of the Text as Shown in Facsimiles of Various Drafts by its Author, Thomas Jefferson* (revised ed., 1945); William Peden, *Notes on the State of Vir-*

ginia (1955); Coolie Verner, *A Further Checklist of the Separate Editions of Jefferson's Notes on the State of Virginia* (1950); S. K. Padover, *Thomas Jefferson and the National Capital, 1783–1819* (1946), containing notes and correspondence; Bernard Mayo, *Thomas Jefferson and his Unknown Brother Randolph* (1942); J. M. Dorsey, *The Jefferson-Dunglinson Letters* (1960), bearing on Jefferson's final illness; Marie Kimball, *Thomas Jefferson's Cook Book* (1936).

In making minor changes in the text of this article, the author has drawn to some extent on the published volumes of the comprehensive biography which embodies his later studies, *Jefferson and His Time:* namely, *Jefferson the Virginian* (1948); *Jefferson and the Rights of Man* (1951); *Jefferson and the Ordeal of Liberty* (1962). They carry the story through Jefferson's election as president and each contains a select bibliography. Nathan Schachner, in *Thomas Jefferson, A Biography* (2 vols., 1951), covers the whole life. Marie Kimball gets to 1789 in *Jefferson: The Road to Glory* (1943), *Jefferson: War and Peace* (1947), and *Jefferson: The Scene of Europe* (1950), works which are particularly valuable for his domestic and artistic life. C. G. Bowers completes his trilogy, in reverse order, with *Jefferson in Power* (1936) and *The Young Jefferson, 1743–1789* (1945); neither of these comes up to his *Jefferson and Hamilton* (1925), and his excessively political emphasis is outmoded. H. D. Bulluck, *My Head and My Heart. A Little History of Thomas Jefferson and Maria Cosway* (1945), is strictly personal. F. C. Rosenberger, *Jefferson Reader. A Treasury of Writings about Thomas Jefferson* (1953), is a good collection.

Valuable works of a more specialized nature are: Edward Dumbauld, *Thomas Jefferson: Am. Tourist* (1946); N. E. Cunningham, Jr., *The Jeffersonian Republicans . . . 1789–1801* (1957); L. D. White, *The Jeffersonians: A Study in Administrative History* (1951); Adrienne Koch, *Jefferson and Madison* (1950), and *The Philosophy of Thomas Jefferson* (1943); Sidney Hook, *The Paradoxes of Freedom* (1962), bearing on Jefferson's philosophy; J. B. Conant, *Thomas Jefferson and the Development of Am. Public Education* (1962); R. M. Healey, *Jefferson on Religion in Public Education* (1962); E. T. Martin, *Thomas Jefferson: Scientist* (1952); E. D. Berman, *Thomas Jefferson among the Arts* (1947); Karl Lehmann, *Thomas Jefferson: Am. Humanist* (1947); F. D. Nichols, *Thomas Jefferson's Architectural Drawings* (revised ed., copyright 1961), with commentary and check list—an excellent supplement to Fiske Kimball's *Thomas Jefferson, Architect;* Fiske Kimball, "The Life Portraits of Thomas Jefferson and their Replicas," *Proc. Am. Philosophical Soc.*, Dec. 1944; A. L. Bush, *The Life Portraits of Thomas Jefferson* (1962); C. M. Wiltse, *The Jeffersonian Tradition in Am. Democracy* (1935); D. J. Boorstin, *The Lost World of Thomas Jefferson* (1948); M. D. Peterson, *The Jefferson Image in the Am. Mind* (1960); Dumas Malone, "The Relevance of Mr. Jefferson," *Va. Quart. Rev.*, Summer 1961.]

Alexander Hamilton

by

ALLAN NEVINS

HAMILTON, ALEXANDER (Jan. 11, 1757?–July 12, 1804),
statesman, was born in the British West Indies colony of Nevis, one
of the Leeward Islands. Though 1757 was long universally accepted
as his birth year, and he himself made repeated statements assuming or asserting that date, a record in the probate court archives
of Christiansted on the island of St. Croix, written just after his
mother's death, indicates that the year was 1755. His family was
good, his father being a Scottish merchant of St. Kitts, the fourth
son of Alexander Hamilton of Grange in Ayrshire, and his mother
Rachel Fawcett (Faucett), the daughter of a French Huguenot
physician and planter of Nevis. She had been carefully educated, had
made an unhappy marriage with a Danish landholder of St. Croix
named John Michael Levine (Lavien), had separated from him, and
after meeting James Hamilton had made unavailing efforts to obtain complete freedom from her husband. Her union with Hamilton, though legally irregular, was on an irreproachable moral
foundation, and she was socially recognized as his wife. But the
home was not prosperous. James Hamilton's affairs, as his son later
wrote, soon "went to wreck," and Rachel was living apart from him
and dependent upon relatives in St. Croix when she died in 1768.

Alexander Hamilton was thus practically an orphan as early as
eleven, though his father survived until 1799. After receiving some
desultory education from his mother and a Presbyterian clergyman
at St. Croix, and learning to speak French fluently, at twelve he had

to go to work in the general store of Nicholas Cruger in Christiansted. From this position he was rescued by his intense ambition for a college education, his brilliancy (particularly demonstrated by a newspaper letter descriptive of a hurricane which swept St. Croix in 1772), and the generosity of friends, who probably included admiring business associates and clients of Cruger. He sailed for Boston in 1772 or possibly 1773, but after a few months removed to New York. After some preliminary training at Francis Barber's grammar school at Elizabethtown, N. J., he entered King's College (now Columbia University) in the autumn of 1773. Already he had formed habits of persistent study which he retained throughout life, while his letters of the time display astonishing maturity.

The preliminaries of the Revolution interrupted Hamilton's college work and gave him opportunities for distinction which he seized with characteristic dash and address. Little weight need be attached to his statement that he temporarily inclined toward the royal side; from the time that he was a guest of William Livingston's at Elizabethtown he accepted the patriot views, and Robert Troup's story that it required a trip to Boston in 1774 to confirm his Whig opinions appears improbable. According to an unconfirmed account by his son J. C. Hamilton, which now seems dubious, he spoke against British measures at a mass-meeting in "the Fields" (now City Hall Park) on July 6, 1774; but it is certain that he at once began writing for Holt's *New York Journal, or General Advertiser* with a vigor which attracted attention. In December 1774 he contributed to the pamphlet war of the day *A Full Vindication of the Measures of Congress from the Calumnies of Their Enemies*, in some 14,000 words, and when the Rev. Dr. Samuel Seabury replied, he continued the debate in *The Farmer Refuted; or, a More Comprehensive and Impartial View of the Disputes Between Great Britain and the Colonies*, this reaching 35,000 words. These anonymous pamphlets showed such grasp of the issues, so much knowledge of British and American government, and such argumentative power, that they were attributed to John Jay, and Dr. Myles Cooper of King's College was incredulous that a lad of seventeen could have written them. Hamilton's position was that of a moderate who loyally defended the King's sovereignty and the British connection but rejected the pretensions of Parliament. His conduct was as restrained as his pen, and there is evidence that he several times acted to allay mob excitement, once (Nov. 26, 1775) protesting to John Jay when a party under Isaac Sears destroyed Rivington's press.

As the Revolutionary movement gained headway, however, he

was gladly borne into its full current. Robert Troup's statement that in 1775 Hamilton and he formed a volunteer company called "Hearts of Oak" is probably true; while early in 1776 he applied for the command of an artillery company authorized by the provincial Convention, was examined, and on Mar. 14 received his commission. His skill in drilling his company attracted attention, and Gen. Nathanael Greene is said to have been so impressed that he introduced Hamilton to Washington (G. W. P. Custis, *Recollections and Private Memoirs of Washington*, 1859); it is certain that Lord Stirling made a fruitless effort to obtain him for his staff. During the summer and fall campaign he fought with Washington on Long Island, helped fortify Harlem Heights, commanded two guns at White Plains, and was in the New Jersey retreat, while that winter he shared in the descents upon Trenton and Princeton. Though he thirsted for military glory, promotion would have been slow. It was fortunate for him that Washington, doubtless impressed by the reputation of his pamphlets, made him a secretary, and (Mar. 1, 1777) aide-de-camp, with the rank of lieutenant-colonel. His true weapon was the pen.

As secretary and aide, Hamilton held a position of great responsibility, and his duties were by no means confined to giving literary assistance to Washington. He became a trusted adviser. Since Washington was not only commanding general but virtually secretary of war, an enormous amount of business passed through his headquarters, which Hamilton did much to organize and systematize; while he inevitably came to take minor decisions into his own hands. He complained of the labor, writing that it was hard "to have the mind always upon the stretch, scarce ever unbent, and no hours for recreation." But though he was allowed to take part in a few skirmishing expeditions, and on one of these was the officer who warned Congress to remove from Philadelphia to Lancaster, Washington wisely kept him at his desk. Intercourse with the General, correspondence with Congress and the states, and occasional military missions, gave him an unrivaled opportunity for learning the situation of the army and nation. It was a characteristic of Hamilton's genius that he should not only grasp a state of affairs with lightning speed, but be seized with a passionate desire to offer constructive remedies. Before he had been at headquarters a year he had drafted the first of a series of important reports on the defects of the military system and the best mode of improving it. Among these papers are the report of Jan. 28, 1778, on the reorganization of the army; the report of May 5, 1778, on the work of the inspector-general's office; and the plan for this office as adopted by Congress on Feb. 18, 1779. Hamilton also prepared a comprehensive set of military regulations which he laid before Washington. Meanwhile, he was giving attention not only to the management of the army but to the problem of invigorating the whole government, and in facing this his flair for bold political theorizing again awakened.

The growth of Hamilton's political ideas, and the extraordinary ripeness and incisiveness of his thought, are exhibited in his correspondence with a committee of the New York state convention (Gouverneur Morris, Robert Livingston, William Allison), and also with Robert Morris, James Sullivan, James Duane, and other leaders, the whole covering the years 1777–81. He was a stanch believer in representative government, then widely distrusted. In a letter of May 19, 1777, to Gouverneur Morris he ascribed the supposed instability of democracies to the fact that most of them had really been "compound governments," with a partitioned authority, and declared that "a representative democracy, where the right of election is well secured and regulated, and the exercise of the legislative, executive, and judiciary authorities is vested in select persons, chosen really and not nominally by the people, will, in my opinion, be most likely to be happy, regular, and durable" (*Works*, 1904, IX, 72). But he insisted from the first that his democracy should have a highly centralized authority, armed with powers for every exigency. He sent Robert Morris a 14,000-word letter (Apr. 30, 1781) embodying a systematic treatise on finance as part of this strongly centralized system, and containing a proposal for a national bank; its financial ideas were defective, but as William Graham Sumner said, its statesmanship was superb. Writing to Duane (Sept. 3, 1780), he vigorously exposed the defects of government under the Confederation, condemned the timidity, indecision, and dependence of Congress, and set forth a detailed plan for a revised form of government—a plan, it has been observed, almost exactly paralleled in the very successful Swiss government of later days (H. J. Ford, *Alexander Hamilton*, 1920, p. 92). In this letter he made the first proposal for a constitutional convention, suggesting that Congress should call a representation of all the states, and that this body should grant to Congress "complete sovereignty in all that relates to war, peace, trade, finance"—much more power than it enjoys today, though Hamilton would have reserved all internal taxation to the states. This willingness to entrust to Congress vastly increased authority at a time of general disgust with its inefficiency, vacillation, and corruption, is another proof of Hamilton's political discernment. One secret of his success was his belief in the possibility of a rapid renovation of political instruments.

Meanwhile, Hamilton had allied himself with one of the richest and most influential families of New York by his marriage late in 1780 to Elizabeth, second daughter of Gen. Philip Schuyler. "It is impossible to be happier than I am in a wife," he wrote in 1797, and he was always tenderly devoted to her (*Works*, 1904, X, 260; A. M. Hamilton, *post*, pp. 95 ff.). They had eight children, one of whom, James Alexander Hamilton, became a prominent Democrat in the Jackson era; the first child, Philip, was born Jan. 22, 1782. Hamilton had meanwhile detached himself from Washington's staff in a last attempt to gain military distinction. The excuse for this he found in a quarrel in February 1781, when Washington administered a reprimand to his aide because the latter kept him waiting for a few minutes. The manner in which Hamilton resented this entirely proper rebuke, his rejection of Washington's subsequent advances, and his private slurs upon Washington's abilities, do him grave discredit. Unfortunately it was far from the last example of his hastiness and irascibility. Through Washington's magnanimity he was appointed to head an infantry regiment in Lafayette's corps, and at the siege of Yorktown commanded a brilliant attack upon one of the two principal British redoubts. Returning to Albany as hostilities ended, he rented a house, took Robert Troup to live with him, and after less than five months' study was admitted to the bar. His intention, he wrote Lafayette, was "to throw away a few months more in public life, and then retire a simple citizen and good paterfamilias."

The public service of which he spoke was a term in the Continental Congress, which he entered in November 1782, finding it the weak flywheel of a deplorably ramshackle government. Chafing at the feebleness he saw all about him, he did what little he could to arouse a greater vigor. His efforts included the composition of the spirited but impotent reply of Congress to the refusal of Rhode Island to consent to the five per cent impost plan (Dec. 16, 1782; *Works*, 1904, II, 179–223); the introduction that same winter of a resolution asserting the absolute necessity of "the establishment of permanent and adequate funds to operate generally throughout the United States, to be collected by Congress"; and letters to Washington somewhat officiously but shrewdly urging him to preserve the confidence of the army for use in a possible crisis. He would have introduced resolutions calling for a constitutional convention if he had not foreseen their total failure.

Though Hamilton retired from Congress in 1783 to devote himself to the law, opening an office in New York at 57 Wall St., he continued to throw his energies into the movement for a stronger federal government. Part of his legal work involved a defense of federal authority against the excesses of state law. In the noted case of *Rutgers* vs. *Waddington* he maintained that the peace treaty between the United States and Great Britain overrode the laws of New York, and particularly the Trespass Act, under which the widow Rutgers had claimed arrears of rent from a Loyalist who had occupied her property during the Revolution; his masterly argument, of which only the long brief remains, carried the case in the mayor's court, though the legislature formally reaffirmed its authority. He was an alert spectator of the growing confusion of 1784–86, and eager for an opportunity to act. The commercial negotiations of Virginia and Maryland, and the call for a general commercial convention to meet at Annapolis in September 1786, furnished the opening he desired. He secured appointment as one of the two New York delegates to the Annapolis meeting; when it failed to reach an agreement, he saw the possibility of driving home the lesson that commercial harmony was impossible without political unity; and he secured the unanimous adoption of an address recommending that the states appoint commissioners to meet in Philadelphia the following May "to take into consideration the situation of the United States, to devise such further provisions as shall seem to them necessary to render the Constitution of the Federal Government adequate to the exigencies of the Union, and to report an act for that purpose to the United States in Congress assembled." It was one of the most adroit and timely of all his strokes. The timidity of the other delegates made the terms of the call vague, but Hamilton unquestionably looked forward to the adoption of an entirely new Constitution.

In the legislature of 1787, in which the support of the New York business community gave him a seat, he led a spirited but mainly unsuccessful fight against the state laws which contravened the treaty with Great Britain. Late in the session, the bill for New York's complete adherence to the impost measure asked by Congress was brought up, and in its behalf Hamilton made one of his greatest speeches. "I well remember," Chancellor Kent later wrote of the address, "how much it was admired, for the comprehensive views which it took of the state of the nation, the warm appeals which it made to the public patriotism, the imminent perils which it pointed out, and the absolute necessity which it showed of some such financial measure" (William Kent, *Memoirs and Letters of James Kent*, 1898, p. 297). He met defeat in the Assembly, 36 to 21, but he had aroused public sentiment. Seizing the day after the impost vote, he introduced a motion instructing the New York delegates in the Continental Congress to support a constitutional convention, and despite the efforts of Gov. George Clinton's followers to weaken it, carried it in both houses. When the legislature named three delegates to the proposed convention, Hamilton as a federalist was offset by two anti-federalists, Robert Yates and John Lansing. Clinton and his powerful state-rights group took the most hostile attitude toward his labors, declaring that the Articles of Confederation required only slight amendment. But, as Hamilton gained the support of a solid body of merchants and other capitalists, he was able in increasing degree to place the anti-federalists upon the defensive.

Hamilton's rôle in the Constitutional Convention was not of the first importance; his rôle at home in New York was. Because of legal work his attendance in Philadelphia was irregular, his longest stay being from May 27 to June 29; his influence was lessened by the fact that Yates and Lansing could carry the state's vote against him; and his theories of centralization made him an object of distrust to many delegates. On June 18 he introduced his "propositions" for a Constitution, proposing that the senators and the chief executive serve during good behavior, that the governors of each state be appointed by the federal government, and that all state laws be strictly subordinate to national laws (*Works*, 1904, I, 347–69). Naturally they had little influence. During the debates he argued strongly in favor of the popular election of members of the House of Representatives, and in the contest between the small and large states supported the latter, though ready to compromise. At the close of the sessions he made a moving plea for unanimity in signing the Constitution, declaring that no true patriot could hesitate between it and the grave probability of anarchy and convulsion. Since Lansing and Yates had quit the convention, he signed alone for New York.

Already (July 24) he had fired the first shot in a fierce war of newspaper essays over the Constitution, attacking Clinton for his hostility. The rejoinders were instant. But rising with characteristic ardor to the occasion, he carried the war into the enemy's camp by planning the "Federalist" series, the memorable first number of which he wrote in the cabin of a sloop while returning from legal work in Albany. Of this truly magnificent sequence of eighty-five expository and argumentative articles, publication of which began Oct. 27, 1787, in the *Independent Journal* and continued for seven months, he wrote at least fifty alone, and several others in conjunction with Madison. That is, he bore much the largest hand in the whole work. The authorship of fifteen of the eighty-five essays remains in dispute. By the printing of these papers he accomplished his first preëminent service in the adoption of the Constitution; the second lay in securing the adherence of New York. The state convention which met at Poughkeepsie in June 1788 was found to contain at first forty-six anti-federalists or doubtful men to only nineteen assured federalists. "Two thirds of the convention and four sevenths of the people are against us," wrote Hamilton. But with Jay and Robert Livingston as lieutenants, he led a spectacularly effective fight on the floor of the convention. His opponents argued first for postponement, then for rejection, and then for conditional ratification, but Hamilton overthrew every one of their contentions. Fortunately for history, his irresistible speeches were reported with considerable fullness (*Works*, 1904, II, 3–99). The turning point came with his conversion of Melancthon Smith, and on July 26 the final vote showed a majority of three for the Constitution. This convention offers one of the few outstanding instances in American history of the decision of a deliberate body being changed by sheer power of sustained argument. In political management and general political contests Hamilton was one among several able leaders of his day, and was likely to err through passion or prejudice; but in parliamentary battle he was to have no real equal until the senatorial giants of the generation of Webster and Clay appeared.

The next task was to secure able and loyal officers for the new government, and Hamilton doubtless realized from the outset that he would be one of these. He sat again in the Continental Congress in February 1788, and introduced the ordinance fixing the dates and place for giving effect to the new government. By hard work in the state elections he also carried both branches of the legislature, and thus made it possible to send two federalists, Philip Schuyler and Rufus King, to the United States Senate. Nervous lest Washington refuse to become the first president, he wrote him an insistent letter. He was thus much in the foreground till the new government was organized in April 1789, and when Robert Morris proved unavailable for the Treasury Department, his selection for that post was universally expected. Commissioned on Sept. 11, 1789, he spent the following year at work in New York, removing to Philadelphia in the fall of 1790.

Though he had no practical experience with the management of finances, his labors were marked by his usual rapidity. The organization of a collecting and disbursing force throughout the country had to be carried on simultaneously with the preparation of a plan for placing the public credit upon an adequate basis. No interest had been paid for years on the foreign loans, the domestic debt was heavily and generally regarded as of dubious validity, and paper emissions and partial repudiation had demoralized public opinion. Hamilton's report was ready when Congress met on Jan. 4, 1790, but its delivery was delayed. He had hoped that he would be permitted to present his comprehensive and energetic scheme on the floor of the House, and labor there for its enactment, and he was deeply disappointed when, at the instance of Madison and others who feared his forensic talents, the representatives insisted that he report only in writing. He had to convert his brief for the speech into a written argument, which he laid before the House on Jan. 14 (*Works,* 1904, II, 227–89). Unquestionably this famous document is one of the greatest of his state papers, but its originality has often been exaggerated; he drew heavily upon features of the British financial system as it had been developed up to the time of Pitt (C. F. Dunbar, "Some Precedents Followed by Alexander Hamilton," *Quarterly Journal of Economics,* October 1888). Yet in its boldness, grasp, and courage the plan was admirable.

Hamilton based his proposals upon the assumption that the government would completely and punctually meet its engagements. It is the opinion of an expert student that nine congressmen in ten had come to the capital with the expectation of scaling down the debt (Edward Channing, *A History of the United States,* IV, 1917, p. 69). But Hamilton argued at length against the general view that a discrimination should be made between the original holders of public securities and actual holders by purchase, many of the latter being speculators who had paid a small fraction of the face value; and he proved the impolicy as well as impracticability of such action. He also argued that the federal government should assume the debts contracted by the states during the war, these having been shouldered for the common cause of independence. His tabulation placed the foreign debt at slightly over $11,700,000, the domestic debt at slightly more than $42,000,000, and the state debts at approximately $25,000,000. Since the interest on these sums would be excessive, he proposed several alternative schemes for funding the debt on a basis that would postpone full interest charges, offering the creditors various options, including part payment in lands and in annuities. To provide the annual revenue of $2,240,000 that he estimated was required by the government, he proposed to levy both import duties and an excise.

Hamilton's plans met fierce opposition, Maclay of Pennsylvania characterizing them as "a monument of political absurdity"; it was argued that they played into the hands of a "corrupt squadron" of "gladiators" and "speculators." Madison argued stubbornly in favor of discrimination between the first holders and the later purchasers of public securities, but was defeated by a vote of 36 to 13. After a sharp debate the bill for the assumption of the state debts was temporarily beaten, but Hamilton finally carried it to success through his famous bargain with Jefferson and Madison for the location of the national capital. The funding and assumption measures, combined in one bill of a more rigid type than Hamilton's original proposals, became law on Aug. 4, 1791.

He immediately made use of these achievements to undertake further steps. On Dec. 13, 1790, he presented to the House his plan for an excise on spirits; the next day he offered his elaborate plan for a national bank; and on Jan. 28, 1791, he reported on the establishment of a mint (*Works*, 1904, II, 337–51; III, 388–443; IV, 3–58). All three proposals were accepted. The palpable need for revenue carried the excise bill past bitter opposition; and the bank was established by a law of 1791, though not until Hamilton had clashed with Madison, Edmund Randolph, and Jefferson on the constitutionality of the measure, and had given the first exposition of the doctrine of implied powers to justify his position. As a capstone for his financial and economic structure, he presented to Congress at the winter session of 1791–92 his report on manufactures, a cardinal feature of which was the proposal that protection be given to infant industries by either import duties or bounties. As the successive reports of the Secretary were studied, the scale of his ideas gradually became evident. He was not merely planning a fiscal system, but doing it in such a way as to strengthen the central government and develop the resources of the country, to stimulate trade and capitalistic enterprises, and to bring about a more symmetrical balance between agriculture and industry.

Unquestionably the secretaryship of the treasury represented the climax of Hamilton's career. Dealing with a field so complex and novel, he could not hope to avoid errors, and his opponents have since made the most of some of them. Speculation in federal and state certificates of debt became a veritable mania, with general over-expansion, and ended in a panic and business depression. Hamilton miscalculated future interest rates, expecting them to fall though national growth caused them to rise. Not seeing how rapidly wealth would accumulate, he gave the debt too long a tenure. He has also been criticized for instituting a financial system that was too drastic and firm for the day and that placed an unwise strain upon the new government; even though disaster was avoided, he dangerously stimulated political passions, aroused an armed rebellion against the excise, and founded a protective system that has grown to exaggerated proportions. But the best vindication of his measures lies in their results. He created as from a void a firm public credit; he strengthened the government by not merely placing it on a sure financial foundation, but also uniting great propertied interests behind it; and he gave the country a stable circulating medium, more adequate banking facilities, and important new industries. He saw the importance of what he called "energy in the administration" (*Works*, 1904, II, 57), and if only because he went further than any other member of the government in exercising the powers of the Constitution, he must rank as one of the boldest and most farsighted of the founders of the nation.

Hamilton's natural aggressiveness, his belief that he was the virtual premier of Washington's administration, which led to improper interferences with other departments, and his unnecessary offenses to the susceptibilities of Jefferson, Madison, and others, accentuated the party divisions which sprang naturally from differences in principles. Both he and Jefferson honestly believed that the policy of the other would tend to the destruction of the government and Constitution. They formed also a personal dislike; Hamilton wrote of Jefferson in 1792 that he was a man of "profound ambition and violent passions" (*Works*, 1904, IX, 535), while Jefferson assailed Hamilton in private and protested to Washington against the "corrupt squadron" of the Treasury Department (P. L. Ford, *The Writings of Thomas Jefferson*, VI, 1895, pp. 101–09).

The struggle between the federalists and anti-federalists, between Hamiltonians and Jeffersonians, was carried on by letters circulated among public men, by efforts on both sides to influence Washington, greatly distressing the latter, by congressional oratory, and by newspaper broadsides. It shortly reached a point of great bitterness, and perhaps proved the unwisdom of Washington's attempt to set up an amalgamation cabinet, representing opposite points of view.

The President wrote both secretaries in an effort to moderate their feelings, but without success. Hamilton had encouraged John Fenno to establish the *Gazette of the United States* in New York in 1789, and to transfer it a year later to Philadelphia, while in October 1791 the *National Gazette* of Philip Freneau appeared under the patronage of Jefferson. Both were soon full of severe articles, with not a few personalities. The assaults on Hamilton culminated in a demand, planned by Jefferson and Madison but presented in the House by William Branch Giles, that he furnish full information concerning the loans which had been effected, their terms, and the application of the proceeds. The scarcely veiled charge of the Republicans was that Hamilton had taken funds raised in Europe, which should have been used to pay debts there, and deposited them in the Bank of the United States in order to extend its "special items" and increase its profits. Giles was indiscreet enough to make still more serious charges. In a series of replies early in 1793, Hamilton completely vindicated himself and routed his accusers, and Giles's nine resolutions of censure were overwhelmingly defeated.

When the French revolutionary wars and the arrival of Genet (Apr. 8, 1793) added fuel to the party flames, Hamilton succeeded in winning Washington to his stand that the administration should show a stricter neutrality between France and Great Britain than most of his party opponents desired. Genet, as Jefferson wished, was received without reservations, and Jefferson's view that the treaty of alliance with France was merely suspended instead of dead was also adopted; but Washington issued what amounted to a proclamation of neutrality and Hamilton followed it with strict instructions to the collectors of customs for enforcement. When the British minister demanded restitution of the British vessels captured by privateers which Genet had illegally fitted out in America, Hamilton's opinion that restitution should be made was adopted by Washington over Jefferson's protests. In this troubled period Hamilton maintained close relations with the British envoy. He succeeded also in having John Jay sent to London to negotiate a treaty covering the commercial and other disputes between Great Britain and the United States, and he carefully controlled Jay's work in the interests of his financial policy at home (S. F. Bemis, *Jay's Treaty*, 1923; for Hamilton's instructions to Jay, see *Works*, 1904, V, 121–31). The breach between Jefferson and Hamilton grew steadily more open and embarrassing until Jefferson's resignation as secretary of state in December 1793, and Jefferson continued to try to discredit the Hamiltonian party by connecting it with speculation at home and

British interests abroad. While it is commonly said that Hamilton enjoyed the decisive favor of Washington, there were points in foreign affairs upon which Washington rightly preferred Jefferson's counsel, and some upon which the three men had no real disagreement. Neutrality was a clearly defined American policy before Hamilton ever asserted it, and Jefferson had been fully committed to it.

But in home affairs Hamilton's place was secure, and when the Whiskey Rebellion occurred in 1794 he played the chief rôle in its suppression, attending Gen. Henry Lee's punitive force as a superintending official. He regarded the insurrection as an opportunity for the federal government to vindicate its strength. Soon afterward financial pressure, for his office paid only $3,500 a year, caused him to resign (Jan. 31, 1795). Even after he left the cabinet, however, he did much to advise Washington, as in the recall of Monroe from France and the sending of C. C. Pinckney in his stead; and he assisted Washington to give final form to his Farewell Address (Horace Binney, *An Inquiry into the Formation of Washington's Farewell Address*, 1859).

Until his death, Hamilton remained out of civil office. His best work had all been done; his cruellest errors remained to be committed. When Jay returned home with his treaty to meet a storm of criticism, Hamilton brought his pen into play in its behalf, writing two powerful series of newspaper articles signed "Camillus" and "Philo-Camillus." Their ability extorted from Jefferson a remarkable tribute. "Hamilton," he wrote to Madison, on Sept. 21, 1795, "is really a colossus to the anti-republican party. Without numbers, he is an host within himself" (P. L. Ford, *The Writings of Thomas Jefferson*, VII, 1896, p. 32). Though he was the leader of his party in 1796, he showed no aspiration for the presidency, to which because of the hostility of the South his election would have been impossible. He returned with zest to his work at the New York bar, of which he was regarded as the foremost member and where his earnings shortly reached $12,000 a year. A great favorite with the merchants of the city, he was "employed in every important and especially in every commercial case" (*Memoirs and Letters of James Kent*, 1898, p. 317); of insurance business he had "an overwhelming share." He took delight in his leisure for domestic life, building for his large family in 1802–03 a new home, "The Grange," at what is now Amsterdam Avenue and 141st–145th streets. Had he been discreet his pathway might have been fairly smooth, but discretion repeatedly failed him. In 1797 a baseless accusation against his honesty as secretary of the treasury, brought by Monroe and others, forced him to make public confession of his intrigue some years previous with a Mrs. Reynolds; an avowal which had the merit of a proud bravery, for it showed him willing to endure any personal humiliation rather than a slur on his public integrity.

From the beginning of John Adams's administration he was on ill terms with the President, partly because of an old mutual dislike, and partly because in 1796 Hamilton had encouraged the Federalist electors to cast a unanimous vote for Adam's running-mate Thomas Pinckney, frankly declaring that he would rejoice if this gave Pinckney the presidency in place of Adams. Hamilton also attempted to maintain a steady influence over the acts of Timothy Pickering, Oliver Wolcott, and James McHenry as secretaries of state, the treasury, and war, and succeeded until the President discovered the connection and angrily reorganized his cabinet. To the end of his life Adams cherished resentment over this "intrigue," condemning Hamilton and Pickering (though not Wolcott) in the strongest terms. The natural ill-feeling between two men so unlike in temperament and principles resulted in a series of clashes. Hamilton and Adams disagreed upon the personnel of the diplomatic commission to be sent to France, the former resenting the appointment of Elbridge Gerry; they disagreed upon the Alien and Sedition Acts, which Hamilton with his usual shrewdness condemned as "violence without energy"; and upon the course which was to be pursued when the French Directory, in the X.Y.Z. Affair, outraged American feeling.

When war threatened with France in 1798, Hamilton again entertained dreams of military achievement. Following the passage of a law for raising a provisional army, Washington, who was to command it, suggested Hamilton's appointment as inspector-general with the rank of major-general, his plan being to make his old aide second in command. Gen. Henry Knox forthwith raised the question of precedence, refusing to serve if the generals were ranked according to the order of Washington's published list. Adams acceded to this view, ordering the commissions to be dated to give Knox the first rank. Washington thereupon threatened to resign, and Adams reluctantly yielded. Commissioned as inspector-general on July 25, 1798, Hamilton was busy for several months with plans for organizing a force of 50,000 and for offensive operations against Louisiana and the Floridas. He hoped to effect conquests upon an impressive scale. When suddenly Adams dissipated both the war cloud and these dreams of glory by his wise stroke in dispatching a new minister to France, Hamilton and his supporters were filled with angry consternation. With outward good grace, Hamilton advised his friends in the Senate that "the measure must go into effect with the additional idea of a commission of three," but his inward resentment was extreme. He realized that the French mission, rending the Federalist party in two, had struck it what would probably be its death-blow. A short time later he heard that Adams had accused him of being under British influence. After writing twice to the President and receiving no answer, he rashly gave way to his feelings. In what he called "a very belligerent humor," he wrote a letter harshly arraigning Adams as unfit for the presidency and letting out much confidential cabinet information. Against his friends' protests he circulated it widely; a copy was obtained by Aaron Burr, and the Republicans saw that it went through at least five printings during the year 1800 (*Letter from Alexander Hamilton Concerning the Public Conduct and Character of John Adams, Esq., President of the United States*, 1800). It was a blunder of the first magnitude, and represented so palpable a surrender to personal irritation that it was without excuse.

Yet, after this surrender to petty motives, Hamilton magnificently rose above them during the Jefferson-Burr contest for the presidency in the election of 1800–01, while three years later he was to perform a still more signal service for the Republic. When the Jefferson-Burr tie went to the House, he might have joined other Federalists in attempting to revenge themselves upon Jefferson by throwing the election to his rival, but believing that Burr was an ill-equipped and dangerous man, Hamilton cast his influence into the opposite scale. After Jefferson's election he necessarily played a minor part in national politics, though he watched public affairs alertly and in 1801 joined with some friends in founding the New York *Evening Post* to increase his influence. He trenchantly criticized Jefferson's first message, he supported the acquisition of Louisiana, and he occasionally wrote on other questions. The rising tide of disaffection with the Republican administration in certain New England circles, and the half-covert talk of secession there and in New York, found in him an immovable opponent. When in 1804 Burr again sought the governorship of New York, and it was suspected that if victorious he meant to join the New England malcontents in the formation of a Northern confederacy, Hamilton immediately took the offensive with his old dash. He succeeded in stemming the tide which had set in behind Burr's Independent and Federalist ticket, and the Republican candidate, Morgan Lewis, was easily elected. It was a brilliant achievement, scotching the best hopes of the secessionists.

Burr's defeat left him thirsting for revenge, and he found his opportunity in a statement published by Dr. Charles D. Cooper, declaring that Hamilton had called Burr "dangerous" and had expressed privately "a still more despicable opinion of him." A challenge for a duel passed, and Hamilton lacked courage to defy public opinion by rejecting it, though he accepted with the utmost reluctance. The encounter took place on the early morning of July 11, 1804, under the Weehawken heights on the banks of the Hudson, and Hamilton fell mortally wounded at the first shot. He was carried back to the home of William Bayard at 80 Jane St., and after excruciating suffering died the next afternoon. It was the end of both a brilliant career and a dastardly plot against the Union. "The death of Hamilton and the Vice President's flight, with their accessories of summer-morning sunlight on rocky and wooded heights, tranquil river, and distant city, and behind all, their dark background of moral gloom, double treason, and political despair, still stand as the most dramatic moment in the early politics of the Union" (Henry Adams, *History of the United States of America*, 1890, II, p. 191).

Hamilton was below the middle height, being five feet seven inches tall, slender, remarkably erect, and quick and energetic in his movements. His complexion was clear and ruddy, his hair reddish brown, his eyes deep blue, and his whole countenance recognizably Scottish. It was often observed that his face had a double aspect, the eyes being intent and severe, the mouth kindly and winning. Few could resist his captivating traits, and even his enemies acknowledged the charm of his graceful person, frank manners, and lively conversation. He possessed a quick and powerful pride, which Gouverneur Morris somewhat unfairly called vanity. When at work, and he worked almost incessantly, he had a marvelous faculty of concentration; many observers spoke of his ability to reach conclusions as by a lightning flash—to divine them. *"Hamilton avait deviné l'Europe,"* said Talleyrand (*Life, Letters and Journals of George Ticknor*, 1876, I, 261). In his political activities he displayed a taste for intrigue, which he sometimes carried too far. His machinations against Adams in 1796, his confidential correspondence with the British minister while he sat in Washington's cabinet, his proposal to trick the Republicans in 1800 out of New York's presidential electors—a proposal which Governor Jay quietly set aside as one "which it would not become me to adopt"—can all be counted heavily against him. Apart from this, his character was of the highest stamp, while his patriotism was unquestioned. His power as an orator was the greatest of his time, but it was characteristic of him that he chose to exert it upon select bodies of influential men, not upon the multitude. His abilities as a political leader were surpassed by few, but again he chose to work upon and through small groups rather than upon the masses. His intellect was hard, incisive, and logical, but wanting in imagination and in subtlety.

Hamilton's political principles were clearly formed by the time he was twenty-five, were pursued unremittingly throughout his life, and have probably laid a clearer impress upon the Republic than those of any other single man. He did not believe in the people, but instead profoundly distrusted the political capacity of the common man, believing him too ignorant, selfish, and ill-controlled to be capable of wise self-government. "Take mankind in general, they are vicious, their passions may be operated upon," he said in the Federal Convention (*Works,* 1904, I, 408); and again he referred to the people as a "great beast." He recognized that the ideas and enthusiasms of the time made large concessions to popular and republican government necessary, but he strove to hold them within close bounds. The main instruments of power, he believed, should be kept in the hands of selected groups, comprising those with intelligence and education enough to govern, and those with property interests for government to protect. This implied a concentration of strength in the central government.

His belief in a powerful federal authority, springing thus from his political philosophy, was confirmed and made aggressive by his observations of the evils of the Confederation, with its feebleness and its disintegrating emphasis on state rights. At the time of the Federal Convention he believed the complete extinction of all the states desirable but impossible (*Works,* 1904, I, 397 ff.), and the plan which he actually brought forward would have reduced the states to shadows and have placed a tremendous authority in the hands of the federal executive. As a member of the cabinet, he wished to go beyond the words of the Constitution in invigorating the government, and hence proclaimed his doctrine of implied powers; a doctrine which, as developed under Marshall and since, has tremendously strengthened the national as compared with the state sovereignties.

Accepting representative institutions, he perceived the necessity of creating an economic element devoted to a strong government and eager to uphold it for selfish as well as patriotic reasons, hence his funding measures and his views in the reports on the national credit and on manufactures. In the *Federalist,* which is a keen study in the economic interpretation of politics, he had remarked: "Every institution will grow and flourish in proportion to the quantity and extent of the means concentrated towards its formation and support"; as administrator he simply gave this principle application. He thought much of governmental strength, but little of liberty. He emphasized national wealth, power, and order, and neglected local attachments and autonomy. He believed in governmental measures for helping whole classes to grow prosperous, but he paid no attention to the aspirations of the individual for greater happiness, opportunity, and wisdom. He was a hard, efficient realist, whose work was invaluable to the nation at the time it was done, but whose narrow aristocratic political ideas needed correction from the doctrines of Jefferson and Lincoln.

[Hamilton's papers were purchased by the government in 1849 and are now in the Lib. of Cong. *Hist. of the Republic of the U. S. of America, as Traced in the Writings of Alexander Hamilton* (6 vols., 1857–60), by his son John Church Hamilton, is a documentary life on an excessively grand scale. J. C. Hamilton also published a seven-volume edition of the *Works* (1850–51), which is supplemented rather than supplanted by the editions of Henry Cabot Lodge (9 vols., 1885–88; 12 vols., 1904). Two lives strongly biased in Hamilton's favor are Lodge, *Alexander Hamilton* (1882), and J. T. Morse, *Life of Alexander Hamilton* (1876). Still more partisan, and full of dubious if interesting theorizing, is F. S. Oliver, *Alexander Hamilton: An Essay on Am. Union* (1906). More impartiality is shown in W. G. Sumner, *Alexander Hamilton* (1890); James Schouler, *Alexander Hamilton* (1901); and H. J. Ford's thoughtful but often inaccurate *Alexander Hamilton* (1920). In Claude G. Bowers, *Jefferson and Hamilton* (1925), and Francis W. Hirst, *Life and Letters of Thomas Jefferson* (1926), the point of view is frankly hostile to Hamilton. There is material of value in *The Intimate Life of Alexander Hamilton* (1910), by his grandson Allan McLane Hamilton, and there are interesting sidelights in E. S. Maclay, *Jour. of Wm. Maclay* (1890). Hamilton's connections with journalism are treated in Allan Nevins, *The Evening Post: A Century of Journalism* (1922). For a study of the background, two books by Charles A. Beard, *An Economic Interpretation of the Constitution of the U.S.* (1913) and *Economic Origins of Jeffersonian Democracy* (1915), are invaluable. Gertrude Atherton, who published *A Few of Hamilton's*

Letters (1903), put much original research into her historical novel upon him, *The Conqueror* (1902). Paul Leicester Ford compiled a *Bibliotheca Hamiltoniana* (1886) which should be brought down to date. Among articles on special phases of his work may be cited the following: A. D. Morse, "Alexander Hamilton," *Pol. Sci. Quart.*, Mar. 1890; E. G. Bourne, "Alexander Hamilton and Adam Smith," *Quart. Jour. of Economics*, Apr. 1894; E. C. Lunt, "Hamilton as a Pol. Economist," *Jour. of Pol. Economy*, June 1895; W. C. Ford, "Alexander Hamilton's Notes on the Federal Convention of 1787," *Am. Hist. Rev.*, Oct. 1904. See also the published writings of Washington, Adams, Jefferson, Madison, and Monroe.]

[SUPPLEMENTARY BIBLIOGRAPHY. *The Papers of Alexander Hamilton* are being collected and edited at Columbia Univ. under the direction of Harold C. Syrett, ed., and Jacob E. Cooke, associate ed.; seven volumes have been published to date (1963). Recent selections from Hamilton's writings include Richard B. Morris, ed., *Alexander Hamilton and the Founding of the Nation* (1957), and Saul K. Padover, ed., *The Mind of Alexander Hamilton* (1958). The most recent biographies are Nathan Schachner's *Alexander Hamilton* (1946), Broadus Mitchell's *Alexander Hamilton* (2 vols., 1957–62), and John C. Miller's *Alexander Hamilton, Portrait in Paradox* (1959). See also Harold Larson, "Alexander Hamilton: The Fact and Fiction of His Early Years," *William and Mary Quart.*, Apr. 1952. Recent treatments of Hamilton's ideas are found in Lynton K. Caldwell, *Administrative Theories of Hamilton and Jefferson: Their Contribution to Thought on Public Administration* (1944); Joseph Dorfman, *The Economic Mind in Am. Civilization*, vol. I (1946); and Louis M. Hacker, *Alexander Hamilton in the Am. Tradition* (1957). Other writings bearing on specific aspects of Hamilton's career are William B. Munro, "Hamilton and the Economic Supremacy of the Federal Government," in *The Makers of the Unwritten Constitution* (1930); James O. Wettereau, "New Light on the First Bank," *Pa. Mag. of Hist. and Biog.*, July 1937; Rexford G. Tugwell and Joseph Dorfman, "Alexander Hamilton, Nation Maker," *Columbia Univ. Quart.*, Dec. 1937 and Mar. 1938; and Aly Bower, *The Rhetoric of Alexander Hamilton* (1941). Also of interest is the Hamilton bicentennial number of the *William and Mary Quart.*, Apr. 1955; this includes an article by Joseph Charles on Washington and Hamilton also to be found in his *The Origins of the Am. Party System, Three Essays* (1956). Other works on the Federalist era in general containing useful material on Hamilton are E. Wilder Spaulding, *N. Y. in the Critical Period, 1783–1789* (1932); Leonard D. White, *The Federalists* (1948); Nathan Schachner, *The Founding Fathers* (1954); and Alexander DeConde, *Entangling Alliance: Politics and Diplomacy under George Washington* (1958).]

John Jay

by

SAMUEL FLAGG BEMIS

JAY, JOHN (Dec. 12, 1745–May 17, 1829), statesman, diplomatist, was the sixth son, in a family of eight children, of Peter and Mary (Van Cortlandt) Jay, and was born in New York City. The families of both his father and mother were among the most influential in the colony. His paternal grandfather, Augustus Jay, was a French Huguenot exile who settled in New York about 1686. His father, Peter Jay, was a rich and reputable colonial merchant. John Jay, never of a democratic nature of persuasion, grew up under the most careful family protection. His education went on, with private tutors, under the watchful guidance of his father. Bookish and pious in temperament, the boy is described in contemporary family letters as "serious," "grave," "sedate." Self-confidence and self-satisfaction, rather than ambition, were characteristic of his career. In after life he never once solicited an appointment to public service—except for a successful application for a commission in the New York militia—though he attained, aside from the presidency of the United States, the most important offices which his country could bestow. After graduating from King's College in 1764 he prepared for the bar in the office of Benjamin Kissam of New York. Lindley Murray, a fellow student in the same office, wrote, in his autobiography, of Jay: "He was remarkable for strong reasoning powers, comprehensive views, indefatigable application, and uncommon firmness of mind" (Pellew, *post*, pp. 15–16). These qualities, with a certain lucidity of literary expression—the styles of Jay and Hamilton were similar—marked him from the beginning as a man of unusual intellectual power. His fellow citizens early sought out his service. As years went on Jay's self-confidence begat a not disagreeable vanity, and literary facility sometimes gave way to pretentious oracular utterance.

Following his admission to the bar in 1768, Jay lived the pleasant life of a serious, well-established and well-liked lawyer (he was associated for a time with Robert R. Livingston), prosperously busy, surrounded by friends and clubmates. His was a town-man's life. It drew its principal interest from proper social contacts. There is no indication that he had a liking for sports or strenuous physical exercise, though he was fond of animals, and, of necessity, a horse-back rider. Possessed of a fairly wiry and robust constitution, he was nevertheless frequently ailing in health throughout his long life. As a young man he was tall, slender, and graceful, with highly arched eyebrows, a prominent Gallic nose, a pleasing mouth, and a long chin; he had an honest and a refined face, neither grave nor light, with a certain spiritual beauty. He married, on Apr. 28, 1774, Sarah Van Brugh Livingston, the youngest daughter of William Livingston, later the revolutionary governor of New Jersey.

Jay's first public employment was as secretary, in 1773, of a royal commission for settling the boundary between New Jersey and New York. The dispute was eventually settled by means of a mixed arbitration, a device which must have appealed to Jay's philosophic disposition; it may have been the example for the mixed commissions which were later such prominent features of Jay's Treaty of 1794 with Great Britain, and were repeated in principle in other American treaties thereafter. The advent of the American Revolution put an end forever to Jay's law practice and started his career of public life. He became a conservative member of the New York committee (of fifty-one) of correspondence and soon was sent as a delegate of his colony to the first, and later to the second, Continental Congress. As an indefatigable worker in the Congress he reflected the interests of the conservative colonial merchants who were opposed to independence because they feared it might be followed by an upheaval of mob rule and democracy. But once the Declaration was adopted, in Jay's absence attending the New York provincial congress, he threw his life and fortune unreservedly into the scales, and no man became more jealous against any imputation of the permanency or completeness of American independence. Jay's part in the peace negotiations of 1782 testified abundantly to his conviction. In the spring of 1776 his energies were absorbed in affairs of the new state of New York rather than in the second Continental Congress. As a member of the provincial congress, he not only helped to ratify the Declaration of Independence, but also provided the guiding hand which drafted the constitution of the state. He served until 1779 as chief justice of New York, interpreting the constitution which he had drafted. He was also a colonel in the state militia, but never saw active service.

Jay resumed his seat in the Continental Congress in December 1778, and on the tenth of that month was elected president of the Congress, a position which he continued to hold until elected minister plenipotentiary to Spain, Sept. 27, 1779. Jay's career as a diplomatist begins—if we omit his experience as a member of the secret committee of the Second Continental Congress, for corresponding with foreign powers—with his departure for Spain. He was the most able and distinguished man whom the Congress could spare for this important mission to plead for recognition and assistance at the Court of Madrid, taking with him, as he did, the prestige of "the first office on the continent." After a perilous voyage by way of the West Indies, Jay reached Cadiz, with his wife, on Jan. 22, 1780. From the beginning the mission was a hopeless one. Spain had no intention of recognizing the independence of the United States, much less of making an alliance with the insurrectionists, or even of joining with her ally, France, in a Franco-American combination. Floridablanca had tied Vergennes to a secret treaty, by the terms of which France had agreed not to make a peace with Great Britain except jointly with Spain, and with Gibraltar secured for Spain. On the other hand, France had agreed with the United States not to make peace with Great Britain except jointly with the United States and on the basis of the absolute and unlimited independence of that republic. Thus was the cause of American independence chained to the European rock of Gibraltar. With Jay the Spanish ministry would go no farther than to continue its policy of secret assistance in munitions and money in order to keep the American insurrection going; and Floridablanca made a "loan" (without taking titles for payment) of approximately $170,000. This relieved Jay of the cruel embarrassment caused by the writing of drafts on him by Congress under the unwarranted expectation that he would have meanwhile gotten some money out of Spain. "His two chief points," Floridablanca wrote, concerning Jay, to the Spanish ambassador at Paris, "were: Spain, recognize our independence; Spain, give us more money" (Bemis, *Pinckney's Treaty*, p. 38).

In the spring of 1782 Jay was summoned to Paris by Franklin to assume his post as joint commissioner for negotiating a peace with Great Britain. Despite "bad roads, fleas, and bugs" he reached the city, after a pleasant journey overland, on June 23. The most controversial question in the study of Jay's diplomatic career is whether he upset the American diplomatic apple-cart which had been so cleverly trundled along by Franklin in his preliminary conversations with the British peace representatives, before the arrival of Jay. The latter insisted that the British representative, Richard Oswald, be expressly empowered to treat with representatives of the United States of America, not of the "Colonies," which designation had at first seemed sufficient to Franklin, and to Vergennes, whose good faith Jay suspected. Jay privately communicated to Shelburne, the British prime minister, advice to close quickly with the Americans, recognizing them as plenipotentiaries of the United States. His insistence won out in the end, but delayed the negotiations—in the early course of which Franklin had craftily been proposing the cession of Canada, without provoking active opposition—until after the relief of Gibraltar had greatly strengthened the British negotiating position.

It is not possible to say that Lord Shelburne would have agreed to Franklin's ideas as to the desirability of ceding Canada, and Shelburne's instructions make it certain that if articles of independence should not have been agreed to, the situation was to remain the same as if the negotiation had never been opened, namely one of warfare against a rebellion of colonies. Whether in that instance the world would have construed unsuccessful negotiations with plenipotentiaries of the United States, as a definitive recognition of American independence is extremely doubtful.

Jay and Adams convinced Franklin that they should sign the preliminary articles of peace, as agreed on with Great Britain, without the privity of the French Minister. In this they certainly violated their own instructions to negotiate only with the full confidence of the French ministry. They did not violate the Franco-American treaty of alliance, for the peace was not to go into effect until preliminaries of peace should also have been ratified between Great Britain and France. France could not make peace till Spain was ready. Undoubtedly the American preliminaries, together with the relief of Gibraltar, opened the way for Vergennes to bring Spain into line. Articles between Spain and Great Britain, and between France and Great Britain, were signed on Jan. 20, 1783, without the cession of Gibraltar. The preliminaries of peace thus became complete. Hostilities ceased. Jay further had participated in the peace negotiations by suggesting to the British the reconquest of West Florida before the armistice; and a secret article was inserted in the preliminaries providing that, in case of such reconquest, the southern boundary of the United States should commence at the latitude of the Yazoo River, instead of thirty-one degrees north latitude. Jay's object in making this suggestion was to keep Spain away from the east bank of the Mississippi by keeping Great Britain in West Florida. In the definitive peace treaty of 1783 this was not included, as Florida had been yielded to Great Britain by Spain.

Jay declined the post of minister to Great Britain after the war, as well as that to France, in order to return home and resume his law practice and the delights of private life. When he arrived in New York, July 24, 1784, he found that Congress had already drafted him into service as secretary of foreign affairs. For the position, which amounted to that of minister of foreign affairs of the United States, Jay was the best qualified man available. He put aside personal desires and accepted the unremunerative responsibility which had been thrust upon him. Jay remained in this office until after the adoption of the Constitution and the organization of the new government. In fact, as secretary *ad interim* he administered the business of the new Department of State until Mar. 22, 1790, pending the arrival of Thomas Jefferson to be sworn in as secretary. In addition to the negotiation of treaties of commerce with Prussia and Morocco, and discussions of the same with Austria, Denmark, Portugal, and Tuscany, the handling of the hopeless Barbary corsairs question, and negotiation of a consular convention with France, Jay's principal diplomatic problems as secretary of foreign affairs were connected with Great Britain and with Spain. The dispute with the former involved the retention of the Northwest Posts, in which British garrisons had remained in defiance of the terms of the treaty of peace. The British justified their position on the ground that Congress had not complied with its own treaty obligations in respect to facilitating the payment of pre-war debts to English creditors, and to the proper protection of the Loyalists. We know now that, on the day before the proclamation of the treaty of peace by George III, secret orders were sent out from Whitehall not to evacuate the posts. Without going into the controversy which arose, or the mutual recriminations, during a time that Great Britain refused to send a diplomatic representative to the United States, it may be said that Jay—who naturally remained ignorant of secret orders which have only recently been disclosed—was so impressed by the laxity of Congress in enforcing its own obligations that he could not make progress with Great Britain on this issue; it continued into the national period and was not actually settled until Jay's Treaty of 1794.

With Spain the controversy was somewhat similar. Spanish garrisons continued to occupy alleged American soil up to the latitude of the mouth of the Yazoo River, although the boundary of the United States as laid down by the Anglo-American treaty of peace stipulated the line of thirty-one degrees between the Mississippi and the Apalachicola. Spain also closed the navigation of the Mississippi where it flowed between exclusively Spanish banks. In justice to the Spanish contention it should be recognized that Spain's title to the lower east bank of the Mississippi was at least as good as that of the United States, and that her right to close the navigation of the river was not and could not be estopped by anything in the treaty of peace between the United States and Great Britain. A protracted negotiation between Gardoqui, first Spanish diplomatic representative accredited to the United States, and Jay, between 1784 and 1789, reached no settlement of the question. When in Spain, Jay had not believed in acknowledging exclusive Spanish navigation of the Mississippi, even though, upon instructions received from Congress, he had made such an offer as a condition of Spanish recognition of American independence and the making of a treaty. But during the period of the Confederation Jay became convinced, as did Washington, that the only way to come to terms with Spain was to forbear to use the navigation of the river for a period of twenty-five years or so, while the West could fill up with a population of fighting men. He reached an agreement in principle with Gardoqui on that basis, coupled with some articles of alliance by which each guaranteed the territory of the other power. Congress refused to ratify the Mississippi articles, and Jay never revealed the mutual guaranty clauses to Congress once he saw that the main Mississippi article would not succeed.

Jay's position as secretary of foreign affairs was weakened in power and effect by the impotence of the Union under the Articles of Confederation. He became one of the strongest advocates of a new government under a stronger constitution. After the adoption of the Constitution in 1787 he joined with Hamilton and Madison in the writing of the "Federalist" papers. Illness prevented him from contributing more than five essays—on the Constitution and foreign affairs. When Jefferson arrived to take the post of secretary of state, Jay had already been nominated chief justice of the United States.

The first five years were the formative period of the Supreme Court so far as procedure was concerned. The most important case decided by Jay was *Chisholm* vs. *Georgia,* which involved the suability of a state by a citizen of another state. Jay in his decision pointed out that the Constitution specifically gave a citizen of one state the right to sue another state, and that suability and state sovereignty were incompatible. It was a vigorous exposition of nationalism, too vigorous for the day. Georgia lost the case by default, but before any judgment could be executed, her sister states, alarmed, quickly passed the Eleventh Amendment to the Constitution. While chief justice, Jay was frequently consulted by the President on state decisions, and it was he who wrote (albeit subject to Hamilton's suggestions) a first draft of the famous neutrality proclamation of 1793. After the proclamation, actually indited by Edmund Randolph, and before the appropriate legislation by Congress for the enforcement of neutrality, Jay, in making a charge to the grand jury at Richmond, May 22, 1793, laid down the principle that the proclamation of the President must implicitly be held declaratory of existing law, that is, of the law of nations (Johnston, *post,* III, 478).

It was while still holding the office of chief justice that Jay was sent on the celebrated diplomatic mission to arrange a peaceful settlement of existing controversies with Great Britain. The war crisis, which arose in the spring of 1794, was caused principally by the British occupation of the Northwest Posts, and the still pending question of private debts to British creditors, together with the spoliations made by British cruisers on American neutral shipping during the Anglo-French war. By this time Alexander Hamilton had come to be the principal influence in Washington's administration. Hamilton's new credit system depended on tariff revenues, and nine-tenths of these came from imposts on imported British goods. War with Great Britain, or even suspension of commercial intercourse for any extended period, such as the Republicans advocated, would have meant, in Hamilton's words, cutting up credit by the roots; the collapse of credit would have brought the downfall of the new government, and with it the possible end of American nationality. Jay spent the summer of 1794 in England coming to an arrangement with Lord Grenville on terms mainly suggested by Hamilton. The resulting treaty might more appropriately have gone down in history as Hamilton's than as Jay's Treaty. Without securing any acknowledgment of the illegality of British maritime procedure under which the spoliations had been made, the United States agreed that all spoliation claims which should not receive ultimate justice after running the gamut of British courts of law should go to a mixed claims commission for settlement; similarly all British claims for the collection of private debts should go to a mixed commission, and the United States should be answerable for payment of the awards in sterling money; British troops were to evacuate the Northwest Territory; commissions were to settle boundary controversies on the northeast and the northwest frontier; and the free navigation of the Mississippi, with particular trade privileges for British ships, was guaranteed the citizens and subjects of each nation. By refusing to enforce in the face of Great Britain the rules of international law accepted in the Franco-American treaty of 1778, the United States gave great umbrage to France; this led to a serious but not vital controversy with that country, in which there is something to be said for the French point of view. Jay's Treaty was the price paid by the Federalists for the maintenance of peace and financial stability at a time when both were vitally necessary for the establishment of American nationality under the new Constitution. He was vilified for his part in the negotiation and Hamilton was stoned while speaking in defense of the treaty; but the Senate ratified it, Washington proclaimed it, and history has justified it as a sort of necessary evil.

While chief justice, Jay had already been a candidate of the Federalist party against George Clinton for the governorship of New York, in 1792, and had been defeated by the action of a partisan board of electoral canvassers which threw out many Federalist ballots on technicalities. When he returned home from England in 1795 he found himself already nominated and elected governor. There was little choice but to accept. Jay's two terms, of six years altogether, furnished the state with an upright and conservative administration. Despite the ordinary petty political disputes in which Jay, as a Federalist governor, must needs have his share, no overwhelming political issue arose. In 1800 the victory of the Republicans in the next gubernatorial election was imminent, and Jay had decided to retire from public life. He declined to become a candidate for reëlection, and refused to be considered for renomination as chief justice of the United States. In view of John Marshall's subsequent career in that office, Jay's reasons for declining it are interesting if not amusing: he felt that the Supreme Court lacked "the energy, weight, and dignity which are essential to its affording due support to the national Government" (Johnston, IV, 285).

The presidential election of 1800 afforded an opportunity to test the purity of Jay's political virtue. Believing that the presidency depended on the vote of New York, where the newly elected Republican legislature would be sure to choose Jeffersonian electors, Alexander Hamilton urged Governor Jay to call a special session of the expiring (Federalist) legislature that would choose Federalist electors. Jay refused to countenance this trickery. On Hamilton's letter proposing the plan, he wrote the indorsement: "Proposing a measure for party purposes which I think it would not become me to adopt." The remaining twenty-eight years of Jay's life were spent in complete retirement, saddened by the early death of his wife. He settled down at his 800-acre farm at Bedford, Westchester County, N. Y. Here he died May 17, 1829. He had two sons, Peter Augustus Jay and William Jay. Only one of his five daughters married and she had no children that survived.

Jay was a very able man but not a genius. His principal and invaluable contribution to American public life flowed from his character as he steadfastly performed the day's work. He brought consistent intellectual vigor and moral tone into every office which he held. He belonged to a school of rigid self-disciplinarians and high-minded men who invested the foundations of American nationality with a peculiar mantle of righteousness and dignity. He was second to none of the "Fathers" in the fineness of his principles, uncompromising moral rectitude, uprightness of private life, and firmness, even fervor, of religious conviction. A communicant of the Episcopal Church, he did not scruple to unite with his fellow Christians of other denominations. He owned slaves, to emancipate them; and as governor of New York he signed the act for the abolition of slavery in that state. In retirement Jay took an active interest in church affairs; he became president in 1818 of the Westchester Bible Society, and, in 1821, of the American Bible Society. As a political sage in retirement at Bedford he left these lines: "The post, once a week, brings me our newspapers, which furnish a history of the times. By this history, as well as by that of former times, we are taught the vanity of expecting, that from the perfectability of human nature and the lights of philosophy the multitude will become virtuous or wise, or their demagogues candid and honest" (William Jay, *post*, I, 431).

[The best biography is by a descendant, George Pellew, *John Jay* (1890), and is based on the Jay family papers which in their entirety have not been exploited by any non-family writer. A selected part of these was published by H. P. Johnston, *Correspondence and Public Papers of John Jay* (4 vols., 1890–93). There is a group of Jay papers relating to the Treaty of 1794 in the N. Y. Hist. Soc. The son, William Jay, wrote a filial biography, *The Life of John Jay* (2 vols., 1833), which published for the first time the papers more fully printed by Johnston. Wm. Whitelock, *The Life and Times of John Jay* (1887), is not adequate. Jay as chief justice is portrayed in Henry Flanders, *The Lives and Times of the Chief Justices of the Supreme Court of the U. S.*, vol. I (1855). There are two interesting short sketches: W. W. Spooner, *Historic Families of America* (1907); and Elbert Hubbard, *Little Journeys to the Homes of Famous People* (1922). S. F. Bemis has dealt with Jay's diplomacy in *The Am. Secretaries of State and Their Diplomacy*, vol. I (1927), in *Jay's Treaty; a Study in Commerce and Diplomacy* (1923), and *Pinckney's Treaty; a Study of America's Advantage from Europe's Distress* (1926). An account of Jay's participation in the peace negotiations of 1782, written by a descendant, John Jay, is in Justin Winsor, *Narrative and Critical Hist. of America*, vol. VII (1888). For the Supreme Court in Jay's time see Charles Warren, *The Supreme Court in U. S. Hist.*, vol. I (1922). See also *Memorials of Peter A. Jay, Compiled for his Descendants by his Great-grandson, John Jay* (1905, reprinted 1929).]

[SUPPLEMENTARY BIBLIOGRAPHY. The papers of John Jay are being collected and edited by Richard B. Morris at Columbia Univ. The only recent biography is Frank Monaghan's *John Jay* (1935). Jay's contribution as chief justice is most thoroughly discussed in Charles G. Haines, *The Role of the Supreme Court in Am. Government and Politics, 1789–1835* (1944). Other works which deal extensively with Jay are Samuel F. Bemis, *The Diplomacy of the Am. Revolution* (1935); Nathan Schachner, *The Founding Fathers* (1954); and Alexander De-Conde, *Entangling Alliance: Politics and Diplomacy under George Washington* (1958).]

James Madison

by

JULIUS W. PRATT

MADISON, JAMES (Mar. 5/16, 1750/51–June 28, 1836), fourth president of the United States, was the eldest of ten children. He was born at Port Conway, Va., the home of his maternal grandparents, but soon thereafter mother and son returned to the Madison home in Orange County. According to a statement which, if not written by James Madison, was at least indorsed by him, "his ancestors, on both sides, were not among the most wealthy of the country, but in independent and comfortable circumstances" (Gay, *post*, p. 5). We can safely trace the family no farther back than to John Madison, a ship-carpenter of Gloucester County, who received considerable grants of Virginia land in 1653 and succeeding years and who died prior to Apr. 16, 1683 (*William and Mary College Quarterly*, July 1900, pp. 37–40); and this is one generation farther back than James Madison himself traced it. The Madison blood descended through a second John, Ambrose, and James, Sr., whose mother was Frances Taylor. The mother of the younger James Madison was Eleanor Rose (or, as he himself seems always to have spoken of her, Nelly) Conway, who also contributed the Catlett strain derived from her mother.

James Madison began his formal schooling at twelve years of age under Donald Robertson in King and Queen County, where he studied the classics, French, and Spanish. The inadequacy of the "Scotch French" acquired from Robertson was a favorite theme of jest with him in later years. After further tutoring under the Rev.

Thomas Martin in his home parish, he entered the College of New Jersey (Princeton) in 1769. There he was a diligent student, especially of history and government, and was one of the founders of the American Whig Society, a debating club. The college was already imbued with the spirit of resistance to British demands (Hunt, *Writings of James Madison*, I, 7). After receiving the B.A. degree (Oct. 7, 1771), Madison continued another year at Princeton, studying Hebrew and ethics under President Witherspoon— a fact which some have thought an indication that he contemplated entering the ministry.

He continued his semi-theological course of study after his return to Virginia, meanwhile undertaking to instruct his "brothers and sisters in some of the first rudiments of literature" (*Ibid.*, I, 12). He passed through a period of melancholy at this time, forming the conviction that he could not "expect a long or healthy life" and therefore taking little interest in things which would be "useless in possessing after one has exchanged time for eternity" (*Ibid.*, I, 10–11). From this depressed state of mind he was aroused to interest and activity by the political struggle with the mother country and the local controversy over religious toleration. On the latter question, despite his rearing in a good Anglican family, he felt with especial keenness. In letters to a friend in Philadelphia he contrasted the religious freedom of Pennsylvania with its reverse in Virginia, where "that diabolical, hell-conceived principle of persecution rages among some," and where, he said, "I have squabbled and scolded, abused and ridiculed, so long about it to little purpose, that I am without common patience" (*Ibid.*, I, 21). That the melancholy youth had by this time shaken off his absorption in the preparation for eternity is indicated not only by this vigorous language but also by his election the same year to the Committee of Safety for Orange County, and in 1776 to the Virginia convention, where he was a member of the committee which framed the constitution and declaration of rights. His chief contribution to this was a resolution, offered from the floor, which made the free exercise of religion a matter of right rather than of toleration and which, had it been accepted in the form in which he offered it, would have resulted at once in the disestablishment of the Anglican Church in Virginia. A member of the first Assembly under the new constitution, Madison was defeated for reëlection because (according to tradition) he refused to canvass or treat for votes. The Assembly, however, elected him to the governor's Council in 1778 and in 1780 made him a delegate to the Continental Congress.

Madison took his seat in Congress Mar. 20, 1780, and served until December 1783. He was, during this time, in almost constant attendance, and from Nov. 4, 1782, to June 21, 1783, he kept notes on the debates which are a useful supplement to the official *Journal*. He was a consistent advocate of a federal revenue to be raised by duties on imports for twenty-five years. He wrote the instructions of Oct. 17, 1780, to John Jay, minister to the court of Spain, supplying him with arguments for the free navigation of the Mississippi by the United States (*Ibid.,* I, 82–91). Upon receipt of the draft of the preliminary treaty of peace with Great Britain in March 1783, Madison joined Hamilton in mild criticism of the American commissioners for breaking their instructions and working behind the backs of the French; like Hamilton he believed that the secret clause regarding the Florida boundary should be made known to France (*Ibid.,* I, 415, 417–19). He stood up stoutly for Virginia's claims to western territory against the assaults of the smaller states and was instrumental in working out the compromise of September 1783 by which Congress accepted Virginia's cession of the Northwest with most of the conditions that the state had sought to impose (Rives, *Madison,* I, 445–64; *Journals of the Continental Congress,* Sept. 13, 1783, pp. 559–64). In the debate on a proposal to change the basis of state contributions from land values to population, he broke a deadlock by suggesting that five slaves be counted as three free persons, thereby becoming the parent of the "federal ratio" later to be incorporated in the Constitution (Hunt, *Writings,* I, 400, 434–35). Altogether, he served his state and country well. His state requited his services by a chronic failure to pay his salary. He was continually in money difficulties and was often saved from serious embarrassment by a philanthropic money lender, Haym Salomon, who made loans to necessitous members of Congress without interest (Gay, p. 25). The last few months of his term in Congress were spent at Princeton, whither Congress had fled out of fear of the mutinous Pennsylvania troops and where, as he wrote, he and a colleague were "lodged in a room not 10 feet square without a single accommodation for writing." In December 1783, he returned to Virginia because of "the solicitude of a tender and infirm parent," abandoning a half-formed plan for a winter of "close reading" in Philadelphia (Hunt, *Writings,* II, 18–22).

At home at "Montpellier" (now spelled "Montpelier"), he threw himself into a variety of intellectual pursuits. He took up the study of law although, as he wrote Edmund Randolph, he was "far from being determined ever to make a professional use of it" (*Ibid.,* II,

154). He wrote Jefferson, who was in Philadelphia and later in Paris, to make for him occasional purchases of "rare and valuable books," especially "whatever may throw light on the general constitution & droit public of the several confederacies which have existed" (*Ibid.*, II, 43). He secured through Jefferson a set of Buffon and set about studying the natural history of his county, sending Jefferson detailed measurements and descriptions of moles and weasels, and, confessing to the same friend "a little itch to gain a smattering of chymistry," he requested a treatise on the subject and a set of apparatus, not to cost "more than a couple of Louis" (*Ibid.*, II, 249–53).

His time for such pursuits, however, had to be found in the intervals permitted by public business. Within a few months after his return to Virginia he was elected to the House of Delegates as member from Orange County, and he filled this office to the end of 1786. He became almost at once a leader in the Assembly. His hand is to be seen in nearly every legislative project of the three years—in the efforts to develop the state's resources, improve her commerce, defend her credit against the paper-money craze, and modernize her laws. He defeated a project of Patrick Henry and other conservative leaders to impose a general assessment for the support of religion and followed up his victory by a measure completing the disestablishment of the Anglican Church begun in 1779 by Jefferson. He showed a sympathetic interest in Virginia's western district, Kentucky; favored its admission to statehood under proper safeguards for Virginia's rights; inaugurated a series of surveys for the improvement of transmontane communications; and stoutly defended the "natural right" of the West to the use of the Mississippi outlet. Measures which he advocated in vain would have established a general system of common schools and have made proper provision for the payment of pre-Revolutionary debts to British creditors and of the state's obligations to the federal government. He favored the limiting of Virginia's foreign trade to two ports in the hope of thus securing better regulation and building up "a Philad*a* or a Baltimore among ourselves" (*Ibid.*, II, 148), but he saw steadily and clearly that the effectual regulation of commerce and commercial concessions from foreign nations could be secured only by the adoption by the states of a united commercial policy. In the pursuance of this object he urged in the Assembly a grant to Congress of the power to regulate commerce, and took a prominent part in bringing about the series of interstate conferences which led through the Annapolis Convention of 1786 to the Federal Con-

vention at Philadelphia in 1787. Madison went as a delegate of
Virginia to the Annapolis Convention, knowing that many wished
to make that meeting "subservient to a plenipotentiary Convention
for amending the Confederation." He himself dared not hope for
so much; in fact, he almost despaired of the meeting's producing
even a commercial reform (*Ibid.*, II, 262), and he was in gloomy
apprehension lest the growing friction among the states would
result in a breakup of the Confederation. When the few delegates
who attended the Annapolis meeting issued a call for a convention
of all the states to revise the Articles, and when the Assembly of
Virginia resolved unanimously to accept the call, Madison wrote
Washington that at last he had "some ground for leaning to the
side of Hope" (*Ibid.*, II, 283).

From February to May 1787, Madison was again in Congress.
According to his own statement, made many years later, his main
object in returning to Congress had been "to bring about, if possible, the canceling of Mr. Jay's project for shutting the Mississippi"
(Gay, p. 84). The seven northern states had, in 1786, voted to authorize John Jay, in his negotiations with Gardoqui, the Spanish
minister, to agree that the United States would for twenty-five
years forego the right to use the Mississippi River, in order to obtain
commercial concessions favorable to the maritime states. In a report
of Apr. 11, 1787, Jay informed Congress that he and Gardoqui had
"adjusted" an article embodying the proposal. Thereupon Madison
made two motions, one to transfer the negotiations with Spain to
Madrid and send Jefferson from Paris to take charge of them, and
one declaring the vote of seven states insufficient to effect the above-
mentioned change in Jay's instructions. Neither proposal was
adopted, but the ensuing discussion and votes made it plain that
two northern states now sided with the South and thus put an end
to the proposal to abandon the Mississippi.

Madison had been named one of the Virginia delegation to the
Philadelphia convention. While not sanguine as to the probable
results of that assemblage, he believed that its failure would be
followed by either a recourse to monarchy or, more likely, a breakup
of the Confederation into "three more practicable and energetic
Governments" (Hunt, *Writings*, II, 319). Determined to use every
endeavor to prevent such an outcome, Madison busied himself with
preparations for the approaching convention. The results of his
years of study of the history of confederacies ancient and modern
he embodied in a paper exhibiting the form and failings of each
(*Ibid.*, II, 369–90). In another paper, entitled "Vices of the Political

system of the U. States," he set down what he had learned through his own experience of the weaknesses of the existing federal system and of the constitutions of the states (*Ibid.*, II, 361–69). His constructive suggestions were set forth in letters to Jefferson, Edmund Randolph, and Washington in March and April 1787. His principal proposals were: (1) a change in the principle of representation which would give the large states a more just influence; (2) the arming of the national government "with positive and compleat [*sic*] authority in all cases which require uniformity"; (3) "a negative *in all cases whatsoever* on the legislative acts of the States," perhaps to be lodged in the less numerous house of the legislature; (4) the extension of the "national supremacy" also to the "Judiciary departments"; (5) a legislature of two houses with differing terms of office; (6) a national executive; (7) an article "expressly guarantying the tranquillity of the States against internal as well as external dangers"; (8) an express declaration of the right of coercion; (9) ratification "obtained from the people, and not merely from the ordinary authority of the Legislatures" (*Ibid.*, II, 345–49).

Madison's suggestions were, in substance, embodied in the resolutions drawn up by the Virginia delegates and submitted to the Convention on May 29, known thereafter as the Virginia or Randolph Plan. The actual authorship of these resolutions is not claimed for Madison, but his influence is evident. In the Convention, Madison took a prominent part from the first and became the acknowledged leader of the group favoring a strong central government. "Every Person," wrote one delegate of Madison, "seems to acknowledge his greatness. He blends together the profound politician, with the Scholar. In the management of every great question he evidently took the lead in the Convention, and tho' he cannot be called an Orator, he is a most agreeable, eloquent, and convincing Speaker. . . . The affairs of the United States, he perhaps, has the most correct knowledge of, of any Man in the Union" (*Ibid.*, III, 42 note). He held out strongly for representation of the states in Congress according to population, contending truly that the real conflicts of interest were between sections, not between the large and the small states, and voting against the compromise which gave the small states equality of representation in the Senate. He advocated popular election of members of the federal legislature and of the executive, ratification of the Constitution by state conventions popularly elected for that purpose, and grants to the federal government of wide powers, including the authority to create a national bank and to charter corporations of other kinds (Max Farrand, *The*

Framing of the Constitution of the United States, 1913). He opposed the clause forbidding for twenty years the prohibition of the slave trade. While many of his ideas failed of adoption, his influence upon the Convention's work was so great that he has been aptly described as "the master-builder of the constitution" (*Ibid.,* p. 196). His most conspicuous quality was perhaps his practical sense which sought solutions in the realm of past experience rather than in untried theory. Madison was not only the dominating spirit of the Convention; he was the chief recorder of its proceedings. From its first sitting on May 25 to its adjournment on Sept. 17, he was daily at his post, not missing "more than a casual fraction of an hour in any day" (Hunt, *Writings,* II, 411). Although not the official secretary of the body, he had resolved to make the most complete notes of its deliberations that time permitted, and he carried out his purpose with an industry that, as he said, almost killed him. The result, his "Journal of the Federal Convention," first published in 1840, is by far the most complete record of the proceedings (*Ibid.,* vols. III, IV).

Though he wrote Jefferson that the new Constitution would neither sufficiently strengthen the national government nor "prevent the local mischiefs" (Max Farrand, *Records of the Federal Convention,* 1911, III, 77), he threw himself energetically into the fight for its adoption. In Congress he was instrumental in overcoming the opposition of Richard Henry Lee and others and in securing the reference of the Constitution unamended to the states. While in New York in attendance upon Congress he cooperated with Hamilton and Jay in the series of essays published in several New York newspapers over the signature of "Publius," later collected and published (1788) under the title of *The Federalist.* While these essays have, from the time of their publication, been accepted as an authoritative exposition of the new Constitution and "regarded as the most important contribution of our country to political science" (E. G. Bourne, *Ibid.,* April 1897, p. 443), the full significance of Madison's contribution has been pointed out only in recent years (see especially C. A. Beard, *An Economic Interpretation of the Constitution of the United States,* 1913). In *The Federalist* (No. 10) Madison depicts the problem of government as primarily that of reconciling the rivalries among the various economic groups which compose society and argues that the form of government provided in the proposed Constitution is more likely than any other to hold the balance even among these groups and to prevent any one economic interest from unduly exploiting its rivals. Thus, to a large degree, he anticipates the views of economic historians of the modern school. Almost equally noteworthy is the wide departure in these essays from the radical democratic philosophy which had marked the literature of the Revolution; for while the political science of *The Federalist* is based upon the idea of popular sovereignty, it places emphasis upon the protection of property interests against the attacks of popular majorities, not the protection of "the people" against the exactions of executives. Perhaps Madison is most remarkable in this combination of faith in popular government with an open-eyed realization that a popular majority can be quite as tyrannical as a monarch. (See C. E. Merriam, *A History of American Political Theories*, 1903, pp. 100–22). Emphasis upon the dual nature of the new government, federal in the extent of its powers, national in their operation (*Federalist*, No. 39); and the idea that to form effective checks upon one another the legislative, executive, and judicial branches must not be entirely distinct but must be interrelated (*Federalist*, No. 48) are other noteworthy points in Madison's exposition of the Constitution. In these as elsewhere there is apparent a determination to see realities, an unwillingness to be bound by the clichés of current political thinking.

Madison had not intended to take part in the contest over ratification in Virginia, but when it became evident that the foes of ratification were developing great strength in the state, he yielded to the arguments of his friends and stood successfully for election to the ratifying convention as a delegate from Orange County. In the convention, which met in June 1788 and was almost equally divided between the advocates and the opponents of ratification, Madison found himself ranged against Patrick Henry and George Mason as leaders of the opposition. In the ensuing debates, Madison's quiet but cogent reasoning was in striking contrast with Henry's rambling and flamboyant oratory. His knowledge of recent events in Congress he used with telling effect when he answered Henry's prediction of the loss of the Mississippi by revealing that two northern states now stood with the South on that issue, thus assuring a majority against surrendering the right of navigation (Hunt, *Madison*, ch. xvi; *Writings*, V, 123–234; Jonathan Elliott, *The Debates . . . on the Adoption of the Federal Constitution*, vol. II, 1828). This assurance allayed the chief fear of the delegates from the Kentucky district, with the result that most of them voted for ratification. The final vote on June 25 showed a narrow majority of 89 to 79 in favor of ratification. Four days earlier, New

Hampshire had become the ninth state to ratify, thus completing the number necessary to launch the new venture. The adherence of Virginia, followed a month later by that of New York, made certain the support of all the greater states.

Madison was again chosen by the Virginia Assembly to represent the state in the expiring Congress. His election to the new United States Senate was blocked by Henry, but Henry's attempt to prevent his election to the House of Representatives by what would have been later described as a gerrymander of his district was unsuccessful, and thus Madison from the beginning participated in the new government which he had had so large a share in building (Hunt, *Madison*, ch. xvii). In the first session of the first Congress he took a leading part in the passage of revenue legislation, in the creation of the executive departments, and in the framing of the first ten amendments to the Constitution, sometimes known as the Bill of Rights (*Ibid.*, ch. xviii). In the second session of the same Congress, and thereafter, Madison was increasingly critical of Hamilton's financial measures, and from an ardent Federalist became a recognized leader of the opposition, the Jeffersonian or Democratic-Republican party. He wished to provide compensation for original holders of federal securities who had sold them at a loss. He opposed assumption of the state debts by the federal treasury, though it appears that his opposition was in part silenced by the agreement to locate the capital on the Potomac (*Ibid.*, pp. 184–85, 197–99). He opposed the creation of the United States Bank on constitutional grounds, though his letters show that he was more shocked by the "stock-jobbing" connected with Hamilton's measures and by the profits and power which they gave to northern capitalists than by their questionable constitutionality (Hunt, *Writings*, VI, 55 note, 81 note; Beard, *Economic Origins of Jeffersonian Democracy*, 1915, pp. 51–52). He was also wholly out of sympathy with the pro-British trend of Hamilton's policy. He wished the United States to remain at peace and he roundly condemned the behavior of "Citizen" Genet; but his sympathies in the European conflict were with France, and he believed that Washington, through Hamilton's influence, was unnecessarily subservient to Great Britain. In a series of letters in the *Gazette of the United States* (Aug. 24–Sept. 18, 1793) over the signature "Helvidius" he criticized the form of the President's neutrality proclamation, which Hamilton as "Pacificus" had defended in the same paper (Hunt, *Writings*, VI, 138–88). He advocated harsh measures of retaliation to meet British violations of American rights and voted against the measures for putting the Jay treaty into effect (Hunt, *Madison,* ch. xxiii; Bemis, *post,* III, 5). Down to 1792, at least, his relations with Washington remained cordial. In fact, when Jefferson retired as secretary of state in July 1793, Washington spoke of Madison as a possible successor. Thereafter the relations of the two men became cooler, though there was never an open break.

Madison's marriage to Dolly Payne Todd, a young widow of Philadelphia, which occurred Sept. 15, 1794, was the beginning of an extraordinarily happy married life. After two years more in Congress he voluntarily retired from public service (Mar. 4, 1797), expecting to devote his time to scientific farming and the pleasures of Virginia rural life. The Federalists were now in full control of the federal government. They signalized their victory by the passage of some rather hysterical legislation against aliens and even against native-born critics of their administration—the famous Alien and Sedition Acts. The chief answer to these ill-advised laws was the resolutions drawn by Madison and Jefferson in 1798 and adopted by the Virginia and Kentucky legislatures, respectively. Both these documents, whose authorship was not revealed until many years later, asserted the right of the states, in the last resort, to judge of the constitutionality of acts of Congress; both argued that the Alien and Sedition Acts were unconstitutional. The Virginia Resolutions, penned by Madison, declared that "in case of a deliberate, palpable, and dangerous exercise of other powers not granted by the said compact, the States, who are parties thereto, have the right and are in duty bound to interpose for arresting the progress of the evil, and for maintaining within their respective limits the authorities, rights, and liberties appertaining to them," and invited the other states to join Virginia in declaring the obnoxious acts unconstitutional and "maintaining unimpaired the authorities, rights, and liberties reserved to the States respectively, or to the people" (Hunt, *Writings,* VI, 326, 331). The precise meaning of these Resolutions became a matter of controversy and is even today difficult, if not impossible, to determine. In a report drawn by Madison in 1799 (after his election to the Virginia House of Delegates) in which he defended the Resolutions against hostile criticisms passed by the legislatures of seven northern states, he stated that declarations such as those of Virginia and Kentucky were "expressions of opinion, unaccompanied with any other effect than what they may produce on opinion by exciting reflection" (*Ibid.,* VI, 402). In later years, when the South Carolina nullifiers appealed to the authority of the Virginia and Kentucky Resolutions as supporting their doctrine, Madison took great pains to explain that there was no threat of actual nullification in the Resolutions drawn by him and by his friend Jefferson; that what they proposed was merely cooperation among the states for securing the repeal of the laws or the amendment of the Constitution. He found it very difficult, however, to place a satisfactory construction upon the assertion that it was the right and duty of the states to maintain "within their respective limits the authorities, rights, and liberties appertaining to them." "The pretext," he wrote (Dec. 23, 1832), "for the liberty taken with those [resolutions] of Virginia is the word *respective*, prefixed to the 'rights' &c to be secured within the States. Could the abuse of the expression have been foreseen or suspected, the form of it would doubtless have been varied" (*Ibid.,* IX, 491). It seems clear that in the interplay between the two friends, Jefferson's radicalism had been toned down, while on the other hand, Jefferson's influence had led the more cautious Madison to use language which in a calmer moment he would have avoided (Koch, *post,* ch. vii; Brant, *post,* III, 452–71).

The overthrow of the Federalists in the election of 1800 and the inauguration of Jefferson brought Madison again into a prominent position in public life. His long friendship with Jefferson and the almost complete accord between the two men on public policies made it only natural that Madison should become the new President's secretary of state and chief adviser. It is evident that Jefferson had offered this post to Madison before the close of the year 1800 and before the outcome of the election was known. Though appointed to the office Mar. 5, 1801, and at once confirmed by the Senate, he did not actually take up its duties until May 2, being detained at home by his father's illness and death (Feb. 27) and the resulting cares. While inexperienced in diplomacy, Madison brought to the office a well-informed mind, a knowledge of men, a quiet dignity, and a good-humored affability which did much to promote his popularity with foreign diplomats in Washington. Since the President and Vice-President were both widowers, Mrs. Madison became the capital's leading lady, and her establishment was conducted on a liberal scale. Her personal charm gave her great popularity in Washington society, which easily survived some embarrassing experiences resulting from the application of Jefferson's democratic rules of etiquette. From the outset, however, a faction within the Republican party distrusted Madison, partly because of his earlier association with Federalists, partly because he, like Gallatin, refused to make sufficient places for political followers by ousting

Federalist officeholders (Henry Adams, *post*, I, 236, 261). This hostile faction, headed at first by Duane of Pennsylvania and Senator W. B. Giles of Virginia, came later to embrace the brilliant but erratic John Randolph of Roanoke, and still later, the influential Robert and Samuel Smith of Maryland. The opposition of these men was to be responsible for some bitter defeats during Madison's presidency.

The principal problems of foreign policy confronting the new Secretary of State arose from the relation of the United States to the war between Great Britain and Napoleonic France. Both belligerents had paid scant regard to rights of neutrals on the high seas. For the moment, no crisis with either threatened. The Jay treaty of 1794 had smoothed over the chief sources of friction with Great Britain, and a few weeks before Jefferson's inauguration the Senate had advised ratification (with amendment) of a treaty with France which removed the immediate causes of difficulty with that country. Madison believed the prospects for peace with both to be good, resting that faith in part upon the supposed vital need of both for the services of the United States. "France," he wrote to Jefferson, Jan. 10, 1801, "has sufficiently manifested her friendly disposition, and what is more, seems to be duly impressed with the interest she has in being at peace with us. G[reat] B[ritain], however intoxicated with her maritime ascendency is more dependent every day on our commerce for her resources, must for a considerable length of time look in a great degree to this Country, for bread for herself, and absolutely for all the necessaries for her islands. . . . Besides these cogent motives to peace and moderation, her subjects will not fail to remind her of the great pecuniary pledge they have in this Country, and which under any interruption of peace or commerce with it, must fall under great embarrassments, if nothing worse" (Hunt, *Writings*, VI, 414–15). In this letter, written two months before Jefferson's inauguration, may be seen the germ of the policy of "peaceful coercion" adopted in the Embargo Act of 1807.

The Peace of Amiens (preliminaries signed Oct. 1, 1801) interposed a breathing spell in the European war. The relief afforded the United States by that event gave way to alarm as rumors of a sale of Louisiana by Spain to France were followed by definite confirmation of the transaction and that in turn by the abrogation of the right of deposit at New Orleans, which had been guaranteed to the people of the United States by the Spanish treaty of 1795. In the ensuing negotiations with France, culminating in the purchase of

Louisiana in 1803, it would appear that Madison played merely a formal part, penning the instructions which carried out Jefferson's policy. Thus, although one biographer has termed the Louisiana purchase "the only completed act of Madison's term as Secretary of State" (Hunt, *Madison*, p. 298), such credit as is due to American statesmen for accepting what fate and Napoleon placed in their hands should probably be assigned principally to Jefferson and to Robert R. Livingston, minister in Paris. In the subsequent attempts to make the boundaries of Louisiana include portions of Florida and, by dickering with Napoleon, to force Spain to sell Florida to the United States, Madison seems also to have been merely carrying out the ideas of his chief.

With the renewal of the European war in 1803, American commerce and American seamen were again subjected to losses and indignities by the belligerents. Seamen on American ships—of whom some were deserters from British ships, some naturalized American citizens who under British law remained British subjects, and some native-born Americans—were seized on the high seas and even in American and neutral ports and pressed into service in the Royal Navy. Great Britain invoked the "Rule of 1756," which forbade neutrals to engage in the trade between France or Spain and the French or Spanish colonies; and in applying it British courts invented the "doctrine of continuous voyage," under which the rule could not be evaded by stopping at an American port en route. Finally, Great Britain and France launched at each other a series of Orders in Council on the one hand and decrees on the other; the first designed to levy tribute for the British Crown on all neutral trade with France, the second to deprive Great Britain of all trade with the continent of Europe. No neutral incapable of throwing a respectable military weight into the scale could expect much consideration from the great powers. What could be done with the pen to protect American rights Madison did. His diplomatic notes were able presentations of the legal arguments against the British and French practices. The ineffectiveness of such correspondence, however, was aptly summed up by John Randolph in his characterization of a treatise written by Madison against the Rule of 1756 as "a shilling pamphlet hurled against eight hundred ships of war" (Hill, "James Madison," in Bemis, *post*, III, 110). His contentions produced no modification of the belligerent practices. Nor can it be said that history has wholly vindicated Madison's position. Paper blockades and the confiscation of enemy non-contraband property on neutral ships were formally banned by international agreement in the Declaration of Paris (1856). Impressments went out of fashion when they ceased to be advantageous. But arbitrary extensions of the contraband lists, unreasonable and annoying searches and seizures, and the doctrine of "continuous voyage"—against all of which he protested—continued in use by the great naval powers including the United States itself. British policy, while morally no worse than French, came nearer home and was more widely felt in the United States, and hence produced a greater volume of diplomatic correspondence. Rufus King, James Monroe, and William Pinkney labored successively (the two last for a while together) in London in vain efforts to arrive at a settlement with the British government, and one British minister followed another every year or so in Washington with no better results. American exasperation was guided by Jefferson and Madison into the form of the Embargo Act of Dec. 22, 1807, which closed American ports and forbade American ships to go to sea. When this ineffectual measure was repealed, Mar. 1, 1809, the administration party desired measures of war against both Great Britain and France as a substitute, but proposals to that effect were defeated in Congress.

Jefferson had chosen Madison as his successor. There was little opposition to the choice, though James Monroe, offended by what he regarded as the failure of the administration to recognize the merit of his diplomatic service, allowed himself to be offered as a candidate by a group of Virginia malcontents. Monroe's support was feeble. Madison, elected over the Federalist candidate, Charles Cotesworth Pinckney, entered upon his new duties Mar. 4, 1809. Observers noted his careworn and aging appearance. At his inauguration he was "extremely pale and trembled excessively when he first began to speak, but soon gained confidence and spoke audibly." At the inauguration ball, where "poor Mrs. Madison was almost pressed to death," and "as the upper sashes of the windows could not let down, the glass was broken, to ventilate the room," Madison, though "he made some of his old kind of mischievous allusions," seemed "spiritless and exhausted" (Mrs. S. H. Smith, *The First Forty Years of Washington Society,* ed. by Gaillard Hunt, 1906, pp. 59–63). Washington Irving, another observer, thought him "but a withered little apple-John" (Hunt, *Madison,* p. 300). A small man, he was never impressive in person. Eight difficult years and considerable tragedy awaited him in the presidency. He made no change in Jefferson's cabinet, except to promote Robert Smith from the Navy to the State Department, making Paul Hamilton secretary of the navy. But an old feud between Smith and Gallatin, secretary of the treasury, produced so much trouble that Madison at length (April 1811) dismissed Smith and named Monroe to his place, thereby securing an abler secretary and a more harmonious cabinet, but adding strength to the Republican faction that already opposed his administration.

When Madison became president, the United States was under a régime of non-intercourse with the British and Napoleonic empires but unrestricted trade with the rest of the world. After holding out for a year a promise to trade with either belligerent which would repeal its obnoxious measures, Congress in May 1810 resolved to trade with both, authorizing the president, if either France or Great Britain should reform its practices, to revive non-intercourse against the other. Napoleon's pretense that the objectionable French decrees were revoked in so far as they affected the United States did not deceive Madison (Brant, *post*, V, 481–83). It suited his purposes, however, to assume that the revocation was genuine, and on Nov. 2, 1810, he issued a proclamation of non-intercourse against Great Britain. Privately, Madison had felt from the beginning of his presidency that refusal of Great Britain to repeal the Orders in Council would lead to war. When the pretense of French revocation, the renewal of non-intercourse, and the earnest efforts of Monroe, who became secretary of state in April 1811, failed to wring concessions from the British (until too late), the Orders in Council, with their injury to American commerce and their humiliating disregard of American nationality, became the principal cause of war. There were other contributing causes. The impressment issue, which had been relatively quiescent, was revived. Indian outbreaks in the Ohio Valley were ascribed to British intrigue, and the West raised the cry that the British must be driven from Canada and their allies, the Spanish, from Florida. Madison secretly encouraged revolution in Florida—a policy not in accord with his generally high principles—and when opportunity arose annexed to the United States as part of the Louisiana purchase the portions of West Florida which had declared their independence from Spain. The West shared the resentment at British maritime policy and harbored its own special grievances and ambitions. Thus it contributed to a disproportionate share of the "War Hawks" in the Congress that met in November 1811. In his message of Nov. 5, 1811, Madison warned Congress of the danger of hostilities and counseled preparation; in a special message of June 1, 1812, he advised a declaration of war against Great Britain, assigning as principal causes the impressment of American seamen, interference with American trade, and the incitement of the Indians to hostilities on the American frontier. The legend that Madison was coerced into recommending war by the threat that otherwise he would not be renominated for the presidency is unsupported by any reliable evidence (Hunt, *Madison*, pp. 316–19). Congress, which acted upon the advice of the June message and declared war June 18, had neglected to follow Madison's counsel of the previous November to put the United States "into an armor and an attitude demanded by the crisis," and the country was unprepared for war. All this he realized. Years later he told the historian Bancroft that "he knew the unprepared state of the country, but he esteemed it necessary to throw forward the flag of the country, sure that the people would press forward and defend it" (*Ibid.*, pp. 318–19) Unfortunately, Madison, despite his admirable qualities, was not the man to lead the country through such an ordeal. "Our President tho a man of amiable manners and great talents," wrote John C. Calhoun, "has not I fear those commanding talents, which are necessary to control those about him" (Pratt, *post*, p. 155). His martial efforts only amused; "he visited in person—a thing never known before—all the offices of the departments of war and the navy," wrote Richard Rush, "stimulating everything in a manner worthy of a little commander-in-chief, with his little round hat and huge cockade" (Henry Adams, *post*, VI, 229). Six months of failure went by before those same departments were cleared of their incompetent executives, and a year more before men of talent in the army could find their way to the top. The fact that Madison eventually found and promoted competent men and that he bore the early misfortunes of the war with fortitude and dignity (Brant, VI, 379–80) does not diminish his responsibility for the disastrous failures of his original appointees. Sectionalism and faction, furthermore, paralyzed the nation's energies. Federalists opposed the war *in toto.* Northern Republicans and Madison's personal enemies within the party thwarted the administration's efforts to seize what remained of the Floridas. Southern Republicans, including Monroe, secretary of state, felt little enthusiasm for conquering Canada and thus creating more northern states. Every thrust across the St. Lawrence or the Lakes before the summer of 1814 (except Harrison's brief campaign in 1813) was mismanaged and inexcusably bungled. In the remote struggle for the upper Mississippi valley, William Clark was so badly worsted by his Canadian opponents that, had peace been made on the basis of possession, the United States would have lost not only Wisconsin and Minnesota but also northern Illinois and Iowa. By the time the army became competent it was too late for victory, for Napoleon was on Elba and Great Britain could give undivided attention to the war in America. Efforts at peace had begun a few weeks after the declaration of war, when it was learned that Great Britain had repealed the Orders in Council—seemingly a tardy triumph for Jefferson's and Madison's policy of peaceful coercion. The war might have been halted then (August 1812) had the war-spirit in the West been less powerful. An offer of mediation from the Czar of Russia, precipitately accepted by Madison in March 1813, was declined by the British government, but an offer from the latter to negotiate directly with the United States led in time to the negotiations at Ghent from August to December 1814. At Madison's suggestion the American commissioners were instructed to drop the demand for the abandonment of impressments—formerly regarded as a *sine qua non* of peace—and to demand only the surrender of occupied territory. A treaty on this basis was signed Dec. 24, 1814. Though not a single aim of the war had been attained, though Washington had been captured and the President and his family forced to flee to the Virginia woods, a series of notable victories in the closing months—at Baltimore, Plattsburg, Fort Erie, and New Orleans—brought the struggle to an end in a blaze of glory and sent "Mr. Madison's war" down to posterity in the school-histories as an American triumph.

The war had been opposed throughout by the New England Federalists, who held the Hartford Convention in its closing months. Their conduct weighed heavily upon Madison. He was described in October 1814, as looking "miserably shattered and woe-begone . . . heart-broken. His mind . . . full of the New England sedition" (Henry Adams, VIII, 231). The outcome of the war marked the end of the Federalists as a party but the adoption of many of their principles by the Republicans. Madison shared partially in this conversion. He signed a bill providing for a new Bank of the United States. He signed the tariff act of 1816, the object of which was to protect American "infant industries" from British competition, and he allowed himself to be enrolled in a society for the encouragement of American manufactures, declaring his belief in "the policy of encouraging domestic manufactures, within certain limits, and in reference to certain articles" (Hunt, *Writings*, VIII, 392). He also approved measures strengthening the permanent military and naval establishments. Yet most of these changes on Madison's part were changes in policy rather than in constitutional interpretation, as was shown in his veto of a bill for internal improvements at federal expense. He approved the end sought in the measure, but found no express authorization for it in the Constitution and suggested the propriety of a constitutional amendment giving Congress the power in question (*Ibid.*, VIII, 386–88).

Madison retired from the presidency March 4, 1817, leaving the office to his and Jefferson's friend, Monroe. This brought to a close his political career, except for his participation in the Virginia constitutional convention of 1829. This participation, while unimportant, is interesting in that it gave occasion for a new approach to his favorite theme of the protection of rights of minorities in a democracy. The threatened minority interest in this instance was that of the slaveholders of eastern Virginia, and Madison's suggestion was for a representation of slaves in the Virginia legislature upon the "federal ratio," counting five slaves as three free men (*Ibid.*, IX, 358–64). He was a prominent supporter of Jefferson in the founding of the University of Virginia, of which he became rector after Jefferson's death in 1826. He was interested in the work of the American Colonization Society as the most eligible solution of the Negro problem, that "dreadful calamity which has so long afflicted our Country" (*Ibid.*, IX, 469), but declined to become its president. He was consulted by Monroe in regard to the British suggestion of joint action in defense of the independence of Spanish America and advised acceptance of the British proposal. This advice Monroe disregarded in favor of a lone declaration by the United States, the Monroe Doctrine. The controversy over nullification produced an occasion for Madison to review and reappraise his contributions to political thought and constitution making. The situation was precisely of the sort that he had warned against in *The Federalist* (No. 10); a majority in Congress representing the interests of certain economic groups was using its power in a fashion detrimental to the interests of the minority. This Madison saw, but he had slight sympathy with the injured minority, and he had no feasible plan for their relief, merely warning them that their interests would be no more secure outside the Union than in it. On the other hand, he denied the validity of the doctrines of nullification and peaceful secession and maintained stoutly the constitutionality of the tariff, the competence of the Supreme Court to decide questions of doubtful jurisdiction between the federal government and the states, and the general beneficence of the Constitution and Union which he had done so much to create (*Ibid.*, IX, 314–16, 480–82, 513). To the charge of inconsistency brought against him by advocates of the South Carolina doctrine Madison replied at length, maintaining (as has been said) that the nullification theory could not properly be derived from the Virginia Resolutions, and showing that upon all constitutional questions except the bank his position had been unchanged. That he had opposed Hamilton's bank as unconstitutional but had signed the law creating the Second Bank he explained by saying that on this point of interpretation he had yielded to an overwhelming "Public Judgment, necessarily superseding individual opinions" (*Ibid.*, IX, 477). Notably, in regard to the supremacy of the federal judiciary, he asserted that from the beginning he had regarded it as essential. "A supremacy of the Constitution & laws of the Union, without a supremacy in the exposition & execution of them, would be as much a mockery as a scabbard put into the hands of a Soldier without a sword in it" (*Ibid.*, IX, 476).

Apart from minor public service and controversial writing, Madison lived quietly with his wife, at "Montpellier," where he was under the necessity of reducing his scale of living and selling part of his farm because of straitened circumstances. Nevertheless, his hospitality to the many visitors who came his way was of the traditional Virginia kind, and his conversation and manner, at least to friends, were charming. Margaret Bayard Smith, who visited "Montpellier" in 1828, described his conversation as "a stream of history . . . so rich in sentiments and facts, so enlivened by anecdotes and epigramatic remarks, so frank and confidential as to opinions on men and measures, that it had an interest and charm, which the conversation of few men now living, could have. . . . His little blue eyes sparkled like stars from under his bushy grey eye-brows and amidst the deep wrinkles of his poor thin face." But she added that "this entertaining, interesting and communicative personage, had a single stranger or indifferent person been present, would have been mute, cold and repulsive" (*First Forty Years*, pp. 235–36). Harriet Martineau, who paid a similar visit to the Madisons in 1835, found him weakened by rheumatism but mentally agile, still given to gay conversation and anecdote, and full of "inexhaustible faith . . . that a well-founded commonwealth may . . . be immortal." Only on the slavery question was he pessimistic, "acknowledging, without limitation or hesitation, all the evils with which it has ever been charged" (Harriet Martineau, *Retrospect of Western Travel*, 1838, I, 191). The most important work of these later years was the arrangement and preparation for publication of his notes on the Federal Convention. Looking back over his busy life, he may have felt, as the historian must feel today, that his work as architect of the Constitution overshadowed in importance and success his labors as secretary of state or even as president. The direction of his political thinking in his last years may be inferred from a note found among his papers after his death under the caption "Advice to my Country." It concludes with the following: "The advice nearest to my heart and deepest in my convictions is, *that the Union of the states be cherished and perpetuated. Let the open enemy of it be regarded as a Pandora with her box opened, and the disguised one as the serpent creeping with his deadly wiles into paradise*" (Hunt, *Writings*, IX, facing p. 610). He died without issue in his eighty-seventh year at "Montpellier," and there he was buried.

[W. C. Rives, *Hist. of the Life and Times of James Madison* (3 vols., 1859–68), was never completed and ends with 1797. Briefer biographies are Gaillard Hunt, *The Life of James Madison* (1902); and S. H. Gay, *James Madison* (1884). Earlier editions of Madison's writings have been superseded by Gaillard Hunt, *Writings of James Madison* (9 vols., 1900–10), which, besides a large amount of private correspondence, includes his "Journal of the Constitutional Convention" (vols. III & IV), his speeches in the Virginia Convention of 1788, his speeches in Congress, and many of his official papers as secretary of state and president. Some letters not printed in this edition are in H. D. Gilpin, ed., *The Papers of James Madison* (3 vols., 1840); the Cong. ed., *Letters and Other Writings of James Madison* (4 vols., 1865); and E. C. Burnett, *Letters of Members of the Continental Cong.* (6 vols., 1921–33). The extensive collection of Madison papers in the Lib. of Cong. contains correspondence, largely covered by printed and manuscript calendars, together with miscellaneous MSS., his famous notes, and some printed matter. Henry Adams, *Hist. of the U. S. of America* (9 vols., 1889–91), is indispensable for the years of Madison's service as secretary of state and president. See also the sketches of Madison and Monroe by C. E. Hill and J. W. Pratt, respectively, in S. F. Bemis, ed., *The Am. Secretaries of State and Their Diplomacy*, vol. III (1927); and J. W. Pratt, *Expansionists of 1812* (1925). For portraits of Madison, see C. W. Bowen, *The Hist. of the Centennial Celebration of the Inauguration of George Washington* (1892).]

[SUPPLEMENTARY BIBLIOGRAPHY. A new and complete collection of *The Papers of James Madison*, including letters by and to Madison, his speeches and other writings, official and personal, is in process under the editorship of William T.

Hutchinson and William M. E. Rachal; the first two volumes were published in 1962. Saul K. Padover, ed., *The Complete Madison: His Basic Writings* (1953), affords a useful selection. Earlier biographies have been largely superseded by Irving Brant's comprehensive, laudatory *James Madison* (6 vols., 1941–61) and A. E. Smith's concise and judicious *James Madison, Builder* (1937). Special studies of value include Adrienne Koch, *Jefferson and Madison: The Great Collaboration* (1950), and Edward M. Burns, *James Madison, Philosopher of the Constitution* (1938). On Madison and foreign policy, see Bradford Perkins, *The First Rapprochement* (1955) and *Prologue to War* (1961). For other references consult John W. Cronin and W. Harvey Wise, Jr., *A Bibliography of James Madison and James Monroe* (1935).]

John Marshall

by

EDWARD S. CORWIN

MARSHALL, JOHN (Sept. 24, 1755–July 6, 1835), chief justice of the United States and principal founder of judicial review and of the American system of constitutional law, was born in a log cabin in the wilderness on the Virginia frontier. His birthplace, near Germantown, Va., lay in the western part of Prince William County, which in 1759 became Fauquier County. About 1765 the Marshall family, increasing steadily in size and prosperity, removed thirty miles westward to a small inlet of the Blue Ridge called "the Hollow," and a second removal some miles eastward occurred in 1773. The frame dwelling erected on the latter site, commodious and even elegant for the time and place, still stands as a wing of "Oak Hill," the residence which was built many years later by Marshall's eldest son Thomas. Until his twentieth year, "John Marshall was never out of the simple, crude environment of the near frontier" for more than a year (Beveridge, *post*, I, 33; autobiographical letter to Story, *post*). The circumstance necessarily rendered parental influence and immediate home environment factors of inestimable importance in his development.

Marshall on his father's side was of humble origin. The first American Marshall of the line appears to have been a Welsh immigrant. His descendant John, a small farmer of Westmoreland County, married Elizabeth Markham and became the father of Thomas Marshall and the grandfather of the Chief Justice. Little more is known of the family. On the side of his mother, Mary Randolph (Keith), the story is a very different one. Of the famous William Randolph of "Turkey Island" and his wife Mary Isham, ancestors also of Thomas Jefferson, of Robert E. Lee, and of many noted Randolphs, John Marshall was the great-great-grandson. Both the Randolphs and the Ishams traced their descent from English county gentry, while the Keiths, descended from hereditary earls marischal of Scotland, supported even greater pretensions in the motherland. Marshall's grandfather William Keith, a clergyman of the Church of England, owed his residence in Virginia to a youthful indiscretion in taking sides with the Pretender, and when he wed Mary Isham Randolph, he was already well past middle life. Surprisingly enough, Marshall's early biographers make no reference to his more distinguished lineage on his mother's side. The explanation, it may be surmised, is to be found in the tradition that Mary Isham Randolph had been married, following an elopement, before she met Keith, that the husband had disappeared, having been—as it was believed—slain by her brothers, but that late in life she received a letter purporting to come from him (Paxton, *post*, pp. 25–26). From these circumstances the validity of Mary's marriage with Keith and so the legitimacy of Marshall's mother have been challenged. Unfortunately, an assured evaluation of the tradition seems today impossible. Even Beveridge, in apparent despair, consigns the story virtually without comment to a footnote.

A portrait survives of each of Marshall's parents—testimonial again to the fact that this was a rising family. That of the mother shows an intelligent and winsome face with much sweetness and humor about the eyes and lips. The countenance of the father is of sterner mold; it is an unusually long face, and the compressed lips show stubbornness and determination; friendliness nevertheless, as well as shrewdness, light the dark eyes and intellectual brow. If one can read these portraits aright, Marshall's temperament was a happy combination of his mother's amiability and his father's resoluteness of purpose. For the rest, John appears to have been distinctly a father's boy. From the first the relations between the two were those not merely of natural affection but of entire congeniality, and the Chief Justice's most cherished memory was of his father's superior ability and force of character. "It was," says Story, "a theme, on which he broke out with a spontaneous eloquence," attributing to his father "the solid foundation" of all his own success in life (Joseph Story, *post*, p. 9; autobiographical letter). Nor was his son peculiar in appreciating the virtues of Thomas

Marshall. Between 1761 and 1776 at various times the latter represented Fauquier County in the House of Burgesses, exercised the
lucrative office of sheriff of the county, became principal vestryman
of his parish, and was made clerk of Dunmore (now Shenandoah)
County. These offices brought him, and through him in due course
his son, into touch with the great questions which were increasingly agitating the best minds of the colony and of America, a
tremendous stimulation to a boyish mind. Another consequence of
the elder Marshall's participation in public life was that he conceived an ever increasing admiration for his former neighbor and
employer, George Washington, which he duly shared with his son.
In young John's life this too was a formative influence of great
importance.

Of the more usual tools of education there was, naturally, in the
wilderness a considerable dearth. "The only book," says Beveridge,
"which positively is known to have been a literary companion of
John Marshall" in his early youth was a volume of Pope (Beveridge,
I, 44); and, according to Story, he had "at the age of twelve . . .
transcribed the whole of Pope's *Essay on Man*, and some of his
moral essays; and had committed to memory many of the most
interesting passages of that distinguished poet" (Joseph Story, p. 10;
autobiographical letter). The effect of so early and intensive cultiva-
tion of a single author was unavoidable. Pope's optimistic outlook
and his sententious style both affixed their hallmark on Marshall's
mind. The *Essay on Man* depicts the universe as a species of constitutional monarchy which is governed "not by partial, but by
gen'ral laws," and where, with reason to restrain it, "self-love" lies
at the basis of all human institutions, the state, government, laws.
Pope was, moreover, but the first of a succession of writers of similar
outlook with whom Marshall would later become acquainted—
Blackstone with his proprietarian legalism, Burke with his reasoned
abhorrence of revolution, Adam Smith with his philosophy of *laissez
faire*. For all these Pope's iambics had prepared receptive ground.

At the age of fourteen John was placed under the tuition of the
Rev. Archibald Campbell of Westmoreland County, where he remained one year. The following year he was taught at home by
a young Scotch clergyman, named Thompson, who during this
period lived in the Marshall household. Under him, John "com-
menced reading Horace and Livy," studies which he later continued "with no other aid than my Dictionary" (autobiographical
letter to Story). But his principal tutor was his father, who directed
his reading in English literature, thus inculcating in him his most

pronounced taste, the law aside, and one of his chief sources of pleasure in after life. Then in 1772 occurred the first American publication of Blackstone's *Commentaries,* one of the subscribers for which was "Captain Thomas Marshall, Clerk of Dunmore county, Virginia" (Beveridge, I, 56). As he had been "destined for the bar" from infancy ("Autobiography," Oster, *post,* p. 197), it is not unlikely that John now began his self-education in the law.

Though a child of the wilderness and reared amid its simple homespun conditions of life, Marshall was sheltered from the frontier's usual barbarism by parents who possessed uncommon gifts of character and entertained definite ideals for the advancement of their offspring. Frugality and helpfulness were watchwords of the small colony; for in time John's advent was followed by that of fourteen brothers and sisters, in whose daily upbringing he had a constant hand. All these children were reared to maturity and several of them attained distinction. From joyous youth spent largely out of doors Marshall derived that resiliency and health of body which he retained unimpaired till near the end of life itself, and a serenity of mind that never deserted him. To the same source are also to be traced his fondness for out-of-door relaxations, especially the primitive sport of tossing horseshoes, his love of wild nature, and his fondness for companionship—a much sought boon on the frontier. His "lax lounging manners," too, were not as Jefferson asserted, "affectations"; they were the habitual alertness at ease of the frontiersman which is stamped on all his portraits. Neither was his notorious carelessness of dress an artifice; it was due to the ingrained thrift of one of a family of seventeen most of whose apparel must have come from the family loom. With access to comparatively few books but living in a period of wide-flung and excited debate on the most profound topics of politics, he came naturally to fall into that category of mankind whose flow of mind is most readily started along the auditory nerve. His judicial opinions reveal this idiosyncrasy very strikingly. Marshall usually prepared these following hard upon the close of argument by counsel, sometimes even before it was concluded, and they betray the debater in every line, in the strength of their phrasing, in the sweep of their conclusions, and sometimes even in a point-by-point refutation of a rejected argument.

Further than this, Marshall was a leader of men. The group which he led was a small one, but its rôle in the country's government became of immense importance because of his leadership, and it was often exerted upon men of a divergent political faith, as well as upon men of professional attainments much surpassing his own. The raw stuff of leadership is, no doubt, a fact of nature rather than of nurture; yet nurture may give it shape. The distinctive feature of Marshall's leadership of the Supreme Court was its easy avoidance of anything suggestive of the strong hand. Its implement was not assertion but insinuation. In the words of a contemporary, John Marshall had the knack of "putting his own ideas into the minds of others, unconsciously to them" (George Gibbs, ed., *Memoirs of the Administrations of Washington and John Adams, . . . ,* 1846, vol. II, p. 350). Any competent nursemaid has the same knack and Marshall had been nurse to a whole squadron of younger brothers and sisters. Marshall's political creed, which embraced nationalism and individualism as twin values, combined with distrust of the too-immediate democracy of the state legislature and its proclivity to interference with anything not within its own narrow experience and comprehension, is sufficiently explicable by his own participation in and observation of events during and following the Revolution, and by his personal interests. Yet it also drew sustenance from his early reading, from reverence for Washington, from the sense of superiority that a rising, well-disciplined family like the Marshalls must inevitably have felt for the generality of their frontier neighbors.

Young Marshall was propelled from the family nest by "the shot heard round the world." His politics were those of his father, which were those of Henry, the dominant voice in the Virginia revolutionary convention of the same year. The news of Lexington and Concord found the two Marshalls already self-instructed in the manual of arms, and they now began putting their neighbors through the prescribed evolutions. John's own active service began at Greatbridge, Va., in the autumn of 1775. He then went to the siege of Norfolk, as a member of the Culpeper Minute Men; and on July 30, 1776, he was mustered into the Continental service in the 3rd Virginia Regiment. Successively as lieutenant, captain-lieutenant, and captain, he fought at the Brandywine, Germantown, and Monmouth, shared with characteristic cheerfulness the rigors of Valley Forge, and participated in the capture of Stony Point. What the import of his experience was for his subsequent career was stated by himself years later: "I was confirmed in the habit of considering America as my country and Congress as my government" (Joseph Story, p. 20; autobiographical letter). Like his great leader, on whose outlook the French and Indian War had affixed a like impress, he became an American before he ever had time to become a

Virginian. His regiment's term of enlistment running out in 1779, Marshall returned home to await a new command, and when this was not forthcoming he was mustered out of service in 1781. Meantime, in May–June 1780, he attended a course of lectures on the law given by Chancellor George Wythe at the College of William and Mary, on a foundation which his cousin Governor Jefferson had just created by converting to it funds which originally endowed a chair in theology. Altogether he must have spent at least a month under the learned Chancellor's tuition—his only institutional instruction of any sort; and during the same interval he contrived to fall in love with Mary Willis Ambler, the state treasurer's daughter. Nevertheless, on Aug. 28, 1780, he was admitted to the bar in Fauquier County.

In the autumn of 1782 Marshall was elected to the state Assembly from the family bailiwick, an event which transferred him to Richmond, Mary Ambler's home. On Jan. 3, 1783, they were married, and soon afterward he hung out his shingle in the new capital, thereby throwing down the gauntlet to the most brilliant bar in America. At the beginning things moved slowly, and during his first year he and Mary were glad to have his official salary. Perhaps his frontiersman's carelessness of attire hampered recognition fully as much as his exiguous professional equipment; to an even later period appears to belong the anecdote of an old farmer, who had at first engaged an empty-headed, showily powdered bigwig in preference to Marshall, but speedily repented his choice once he saw the two men in action (Beveridge, II, 166). At any rate, prosperity was not unduly delayed. Within two years, Marshall was recording considerable losses at whist and backgammon, generous contributions to churches, horse-races, festivals, card games, and balls, liberal purchases of wines and other drinkables, sundry entry fees to the Masons, "The Jockie Club," and "Farmicola's." He was also a frequent purchaser of books, though not often of law books; he bought an occasional slave, and in 1785 he made repeated purchases of "military certificates" which were redeemable in land. The same year he was presented with the Fauquier County estate by his father and was made city recorder (Beveridge, I, 148–99).

From this point Marshall's emergence both political and professional was swift. It is the latter which most demands explanation. One thing that greatly aided him in his struggle with his better-equipped competitors was the fact that following the Revolution English precedents were out of favor, while of American precedents there were as yet none. What was chiefly demanded of counsel was

consequently not acquired learning, but just what Marshall had
to a remarkable degree: a spider-like capacity, as it were, of rapidly
absorbing material suited to the immediate occasion and then of
spinning it out in his own silk—wrought, forsooth, into a web of
argumentation which his opponents would find exceedingly baffling.
Indeed, Marshall developed much ingenuity in making his daily
practice in open court educate him in the law. As Beveridge has
shown, he "preferred to close rather than open an argument," and
so "informed himself from the knowledge displayed by his adversaries" (Beveridge, II, 177). He cited few authorities, thus anticipat-
ing a striking feature of his judicial opinions.

Marshall's emergence into political prominence proceeded with
the crystallization of his political convictions. This was the period
when governmental power was concentrated in the state legislatures;
and they speedily forfeited the confidence of those elements of society whose views or interests transcended state lines, playing fast
and loose with the treaty obligations of the Confederation, starting
commercial wars among the states, and finally becoming in the
majority of instances the abject tools of the numerous but bankrupt
small-farmer class. To this course of policy in Virginia, Marshall
himself, as a member of the Assembly and of the Executive Council
from 1782 to 1784, was direct witness, and he did not hesitate to
announce his disgust for it, as well as for the body responsible. The
news from other states impelled him in the same direction, especially
that of Shays's Rebellion, which he thought drew into question man's
capacity to govern himself and so "cast a deep shade over that bright
prospect which the Revolution in America and the establishment
of our free governments had opened to the votaries of liberty
throughout the globe" (to James Wilkinson, Jan. 5, 1787, *American
Historical Review,* January 1907, p. 348). Accordingly, when Washington and Madison raised the banner of constitutional reform
looking to a strengthened Union, they found in Marshall an eager
recruit. In order to forward the ratification of the Constitution in
Virginia, Marshall again entered the Assembly in the autumn of
1787, and it was through his skill that that document was submitted
to the state ratifying convention without hampering instructions
with respect to amendments. Nor was his rôle in the ratifying convention, while comparatively inconspicuous, unimportant. Whether
by accident or preference, he gave his chief attention in the debate
to the judiciary article and in that connection championed the
idea of judicial review. Should Congress, said he, "make a law not
warranted by any of the powers enumerated . . . they [the judges]

would declare it void" (Jonathan Elliot, *The Debates . . . on the Adoption of the Federal Constitution*, II, 1828, p. 404). But he also expressed the opinion that Bills of Rights were "merely recommendatory. Were it otherwise . . . many laws which are found convenient, would be unconstitutional" (*Ibid.*, p. 409).

A champion of Washington's administration and of Hamilton's financial measures from the first, Marshall gradually became the recognized leader of the Federalist interest in Virginia. In 1795 Washington offered him the attorney-generalship, which he declined. In 1795–96 he won more than a local reputation by his vigorous defense of the Jay Treaty, so that when, in the latter year, he appeared in Philadelphia to argue *Ware* vs. *Hylton* (3 *Dallas*, 199), his first and only case before the Supreme Court, his effort drew interested auditors from other states. One of these was Rufus King of Massachusetts, whom a year later we find declaring that "his head" was "one of the best organized of anyone that I have known" (C. R. King, *The Life and Correspondence of Rufus King*, II, 1895, p. 235). In 1796 he again refused appointment under the federal government, as minister to France; but in 1797 he was finally induced by President John Adams to become one of the famous X. Y. Z. mission to the same government. His immediate motive, it is to be suspected, was largely mercenary. In 1793 or 1794 he had become one of a syndicate to purchase the remnant of the great Fairfax estate in the "Northern Neck," and this investment, owing to an act of confiscation which had overhung it from the days of the Revolution and to the bankruptcy of Robert Morris, who had financed the deal, was now in desperate case. At any rate, from this single year's employment Marshall as commissioner obtained nearly $20,000, which, says his biographer, "over and above his expense," was nearly "three times his annual earnings at the bar" (Beveridge, II, 211). The Fairfax investment was thus saved from its creditors. The act of confiscation, however, still remained to be reckoned with.

In 1798 Marshall was offered James Wilson's place on the Supreme Court but declined. The following year, nevertheless, at Washington's warm insistence, he stood for Congress and was elected. Here his most conspicuous act was his successful defense of Adams against the charge of having usurped a judicial function in surrendering, under the Jay Treaty, an alleged fugitive from the justice of Great Britain. Adams, who had now split with the Hamiltonian elements of his party and cabinet, needed defenders outside of Congress too; and he soon concluded that John Marshall was his best reliance. On May 7, 1800, without consulting him, Adams nominated him secretary of war, to succeed James McHenry, who had been forced to resign, and he promptly declined. Nothing daunted, the President a few days later asked him to become secretary of state (appointment May 12, 1800) in succession to Timothy Pickering, who had just been dismissed. After a fortnight's pondering Marshall accepted, and by so doing won the harassed President's eternal gratitude.

The actual circumstances of Adams's nomination of Marshall to the chief justiceship on Jan. 20, 1801, are recounted by Marshall himself in the autobiographical sketch which he prepared for Story in 1827, and which has only recently been recovered (see bibliography). "On the resignation of Chief Justice Ellsworth," Marshall there wrote, "I recommended Judge Patterson [William Paterson] as his successor. The President objected to him, and assigned as his ground of objection that the feelings of Judge Cushing would be wounded by passing him and selecting a junior member of the bench. I never heard him assign any other objection to Judge Patterson, though it was afterwards suspected by many that he was believed to be connected with the party which opposed the second attempt at negotiation with France. The President himself mentioned Mr. Jay, and he was nominated to the Senate. When I waited on the President with Mr. Jay's letter declining the appointment he said thoughtfully 'who shall I nominate now?' I replied that I could not tell, as I supposed that his objection to Judge Patterson remained. He said in a decided tone, 'I shall not nominate him.' After a moment's hesitation he said 'I believe I must nominate you.' I had never before heard myself named for the office and had not even thought of it. I was pleased as well as surprised, and bowed in silence."

The nomination, as Beveridge, with pardonable litotes, remarks, "was not greeted with applause from any quarter" (Beveridge, II, 554–55). The Republicans bitterly resented Ellsworth's too-opportune resignation, which had snatched from their very grasp the highest of appointive offices, while the more rabid Federalists, resenting Marshall's practice of kicking over the party traces, wanted Paterson. The President, however, was adamant; on Jan. 27 the Senate gave its consent; and on Feb. 4, Marshall, with customary lack of haste, accepted and took his seat, thereby opening court for the first time in the new Capital on the Potomac. He continued as secretary of state till the end of the administration, though he did not draw the salary of that office. He was thus able to lend a helpful hand in the so-called "midnight appointments," one of which went to a certain William Marbury.

For all the lack of enthusiasm attending his elevation, the new

Chief Justice possessed a personality to capture attention and then to captivate it. The contemporary pen of William Wirt pictures a man "tall, meagre, emaciated," loose-jointed, inelegant in "dress, attitudes, gesture," of swarthy complexion, and looking beyond his years, with a countenance "small in proportion to his height" but pervaded with "great good humour and hilarity; while his black eyes —that unerring index—possess an irradiating spirit, which proclaims the imperial powers of the mind that sits enthroned therein" (William Wirt, *The Letters of the British Spy*, 1803, p. 46). Marshall enjoyed, Wirt asserts, "one original, and, almost, supernatural faculty," that "of developing a subject by a single glance of his mind. . . . Nor does the exercise of it seem to cost him an effort." He determined immediately on which side a question was to be most advantageously assailed; and "his premises once admitted, the demonstration, however distant, follows as certainly, as cogently, as inevitably, as any demonstration in Euclid" (*Ibid.*, p. 47). In brief, he was a supreme debater. Another contemporary, Speaker Theodore Sedgwick, coming from the sterner atmosphere of Boston harbor, had previously been struck by his "very affectionate disposition," his "great simplicity of manners," his attachment to pleasures and "convivial habits strongly fixed." He was "indolent therefore" (King, *ante*, III, 1896, p. 237). The word is hardly the just one. Marshall led a leisurely life, but he did not permit his intellectual powers to corrode. On the contrary, the fresh energy of mind with which he usually met the larger occasions of his career is one of his most striking characteristics.

There being no causes to be heard in the February term of 1801, Marshall's first official duty as chief justice was to administer the presidential oath of office to Jefferson. In the August term, there was one case, *Talbot* vs. *Seeman* (1 *Cranch*, 1), and Marshall signalized the occasion to put into effect a significant reform. Hitherto the justices had frequently delivered *seriatim* opinions; henceforth for some years "the unanimous Court," or simply "the Court," was to speak generally through its Chief Justice. Of the reported opinions to the February 1805 term, Marshall delivered all except two, and those in causes over which he had presided on circuit. But one dissenting opinion was given, although the justices were not always agreed at other times. That the new procedure signified at this date Marshall's domination of his associates may be questioned; rather it betokened their appreciation of a common peril.

One of the last acts of the Federalists had been to enlarge the lower federal judicial establishment, and one of the early acts of the Jeffersonians was to abolish the new courts (Apr. 29, 1802). At the same time, in order to prevent a judicial test of the constitutionality of the repeal act, Congress postponed the next term of the Supreme Court to February 1803, by doing away permanently with all but the February term. Although Marshall was thus probably presented by his foes with several years of vigorous life, since in the warmer months Washington at this period was a malarial swamp, what he saw in their action was a dangerous challenge to the prestige of the Court, to the security of the lower federal judiciary, and to the principle, which had come to be generally accepted previous to the debate on the repealing act, that the Supreme Court was the final authoritative interpreter of the Constitution. It was, therefore, no wonder that he should make the most of the opportunity that soon offered to vindicate all these causes at one stroke. When the Court reconvened in February 1803, after its enforced vacation of fourteen months, the first case to claim its attention was that which appears in the *Reports* under the style of *Marbury* vs. *Madison* (1 *Cranch*, 137). Marbury and other "midnight appointees" to the office of justice of the peace in the District of Columbia were asking for a *mandamus* to the secretary of state, James Madison, to compel him to deliver their commissions, the basis of their application being section thirteen of the judiciary act of Sept. 24, 1789, which authorized the Court to issue this writ "to officers of the United States." Marshall, for "the unanimous Court," conceded that Marbury was entitled to the remedy he sought, but held that the Supreme Court could not award it, since to do so would be to assume original jurisdiction in a case not within the categories enumerated by the Constitution, and that section thirteen was unconstitutional and void.

A more cleverly contrived document for its purposes than Marshall's opinion in *Marbury* vs. *Madison* it would be impossible to imagine. By "backing into" the case, Marshall was able to read Jefferson a lecture on his legal duty, while by ultimately declining jurisdiction of it he avoided all danger of a direct clash with his antagonist. By holding the constitutional enumeration of cases in which the Supreme Court has original jurisdiction to be exclusive (wherein he had been anticipated by Ellsworth; 3 *Dallas*, 327), he put a spoke in Republican projects to abolish the lower federal judiciary and parcel out its jurisdiction between the Supreme Court and the state courts. Most important of all, by holding section thirteen unconstitutional, on the basis of an argument that Jefferson himself did not venture to traverse, he brought to the support

of the Union, while the memory of the Virginia and Kentucky Resolutions was still green, the ineffably important proposition that the
Constitution has one final interpreter, at the same time seizing for
the Court its greatest prerogative. Nor is this to say that, considered
as a judicial pronouncement, the opinion in *Marbury* vs. *Madison*
is flawless. Section thirteen, by the logic of later cases, was not intended to increase the Court's original jurisdiction, but only to give
it power to issue certain writs when it had jurisdiction; and in the
recent case of *Myers* vs. *United States,* Jefferson's claim that he had
removed Marbury, who was consequently not entitled to his commission, appears also to have been ratified by the Court. Besides,
it was Marshall who had countersigned and sealed that commission,
a circumstance which, by a nicer view of judicial propriety, should
have disqualified him from sitting in the case at all.

The Federalist Court had drawn first blood in its feud with the
Republican administration, but the decisive battle was still to be
fought. Not all the justices shared their Chief's "wise as serpents,
harmless as doves" disposition, least of all Justice Samuel Chase.
Early in May 1803, Chase, to whom the Republicans had already
succeeded in fastening something of the reputation of a "Bloody"
Jeffries, had the unwisdom to assail "our late reformers" in a
charge to a Baltimore grand jury, and on Mar. 12, 1804, the House
voted articles of impeachment against him. What was even more
alarming, the exponents of "judge-breaking" were now pressing the
theory that impeachment was historically not a punitive process at
all but "an inquest of office," talk which was at once interpreted by
contemporaries as indicating that the entire bench of the Supreme
Court was to be swept clean. For once in his life John Marshall was
obviously perturbed. This was shown not only by his timid manner
of testifying before the court of impeachment, ostensibly in Chase's
behalf, but also by a letter to his brother James at this time in which
he broached the remarkable suggestion that "the modern doctrine
of impeachment should yield to an appellate jurisdiction in the
legislature" (Beveridge, III, 177). In other words, if Congress would
only leave John Marshall in office they might reverse such of his
legal opinions as they "deemed unsound" to their heart's content,
and thereby consign both judicial review and the principle of the
separation of powers to the scrap-heap.

But Chase was not convicted, and in due course Marshall recovered his composure, so much so indeed that he was presently
ready to tilt against the administration all by himself. The opportunity offered when Aaron Burr was brought, early in 1807,

before his court at Richmond to be tried for treason. These proceedings began Mar. 30 and ended Sept. 15, and Marshall's conduct of them from start to finish was one prolonged baiting of the President, whose unholy zeal to see Burr hanged fairly exposed him to such treatment. In only one instance did Jefferson score, when he ignored a *sub poena duces tecum* which Marshall was incautious enough to send him. On the main point Marshall got his way: Burr's neck was saved, albeit in the process the whole common-law view of treason as a conspiracy, a view which the Constitution was undoubtedly intended to embody and which Marshall himself had accepted in the Bollman Case (4 *Cranch,* 75), was junked, with the "monstrous" result—as Wirt rightly urged—that it becomes impossible to convict the procurer of a treason who is canny enough to leave to his dupes the rest of the business—the "overt acts." Three years later Edward Livingston brought his famous "Batture Case" before Marshall at Richmond, in which he sued Jefferson for $100,000 damages on account of the latter's seizure when president of certain lands of Livingston in New Orleans. Fortunately a renewal of the vendetta between the two cousins was obviated when the case was dismissed on the point of jurisdiction (1 *Brockenbrough,* 203).

Meantime, Marshall had been busying himself for some years in hours off the bench with *The Life of George Washington* (5 vols., 1804-07). The work was doubly disappointing to its author. His hopes of large profits were blasted when Jefferson forbade the federal postmasters to take orders for it, and much of it was hastily written and badly proportioned. Yet it does not lack even to a present-day reader flashes of insight, especially in its treatment of the period immediately preceding the Convention of 1787. Furthermore, this part of the work stands in an important relation to Marshall's own later labors. Its preparation undoubtedly contributed not a little to that confidence which his famous constitutional opinions breathe of his knowledge of the intentions of the framers of the Constitution, as well as to his resolution that these should prevail. Indeed, the first half of his chief justiceship was largely a period of preparation for the greater achievement to follow. With the appointment of Duval and Story, in November 1811, the personnel of the Court became what it was to remain for twelve years and, with two changes, for eighteen years. As there was but one term of court annually and that, till 1827, rarely more than seven or eight weeks in length, none of the justices resided in Washington but they took lodgings, sometimes all in the same boardinghouse, living, as Story wrote, "in the most frank and unaffected intimacy" (W. W. Story, *Life and Letters of Joseph Story*, 1851, I, 215). "Our social hours when undisturbed with the labors of law, are passed in gay and frank conversation, which at once enlivens and instructs" (*Ibid.*, p. 217). Circumstances could not have been better contrived to enable Marshall to bring to bear upon his associates, all of them except Bushrod Washington Republican appointees and most of them his juniors, his charm of personality and his superiority in face-to-face discussion, or to win them with "the inevitability of gradualness" to his own constitutional faith. In the case of Story himself the process was not even gradual; he fell under the spell of "the Chief" at once. A uniquely fruitful friendship resulted. As Story testifies, Marshall's bias was "to general principles and comprehensive views, rather than to technical and recondite learning" (Joseph Story, *Discourse*, p. 70); while his own was that of the student and delver. The familiar legend that Marshall was accustomed to say to Story, "that, Story, is the law; now you find the precedents," is at least "well found." Nor should the Court under Marshall be thought of apart from the bar which practised before it. The membership of this body was almost as constant as that of the Court itself and included talent of the first order—William Pinkney, William Wirt, Luther Martin, Joseph Hopkinson, Daniel Webster, Jeremiah Mason, to mention only the most illustrious. Again Marshall's debt is discernible, even in the sphere in which he was supreme, although as regards Webster, this has been exaggerated. Indeed, one gains the impression that when it came to constitutional law, Marshall was often more grateful to counsel whose views he rejected than to their opponents, because of the stimulation they imparted to his own powers of analysis and statement.

His most important opinion during this early period, after that in *Marbury* vs. *Madison*, was in *Fletcher* vs. *Peck* (6 *Cranch*, 87), where he held that the "obligation of contracts" clause stood in the way of a state's rescinding a grant of public lands, although it had been induced by notorious bribery and corruption. The result is the more remarkable inasmuch as the "obligation" attributed to the fraudulent grant was manifestly not a legal but a moral one. The opinion indeed smacks of predetermination, and the case was probably a moot one. Could Marshall have been thinking of that act of confiscation which still overhung the Fairfax estate? Four years later this act too was before the Court (*Fairfax's Devisee* vs. *Hunter's Lessee*, 7 *Cranch*, 603). Quite properly Marshall declined to sit in the case, but his circumspection profited him little with his critics; if Story's opinion disallowing the measure was the voice of Esau, the hand that penned it was that of Jacob. Aside from those in *Marbury* vs. *Madison* and *Fletcher* vs. *Peck*, Marshall's foundational constitutional opinions are to be read in the following cases: *McCulloch* vs. *Maryland* (4 *Wheaton*, 316), *Sturges* vs. *Crowninshield* (17 *U. S.*, 122), and *Dartmouth College* vs. *Woodward* (17 *U. S.*, 518), all three delivered at the single term of 1819; *Cohens* vs. *Virginia* (6 *Wheaton*, 264), given in the 1821 term; *Gibbons* vs. *Ogden* (9 *Wheaton*, 1) and *Osborn* vs. *U. S. Bank* (22 *U. S.*, 738), rendered in 1825; *Brown* vs. *Maryland* (25 *U. S.*, 419) and *Ogden* vs. *Saunders* (25 *U. S.*, 213)—the latter Marshall's sole dissenting opinion in the constitutional field—rendered in 1827.

Herein is set forth a corpus of constitutional doctrine which possesses internal consistency to a notable extent, however open to attack some of its premises may have been on other grounds. The Constitution was the act of the people of the United States, although in bringing about its establishment they naturally made such use of existing governmental machinery as convenience dictated. It springs therefore from the ultimate source of authority in the country and possesses such characteristics as this authority chose to stamp upon it. By its own terms it is law and supreme law, wherefore its provisions control all governments and governmental agencies within the territory of the United States. Furthermore, being law, it is directly enforcible by courts in the decision of cases. Indeed, its clear intention is to designate the Supreme Court as the one final authoritative expositor of its terms; and while the Court has no will of its own apart from that of the law, it is none the less under obligation always to remember that "it is a constitution" which it is expounding, and that this Constitution was "intended to endure for ages to come" and hence to be "adapted to the various *crises* of human affairs." Especially should a narrow rendition of its terms be avoided when questions of the advancement of national unity and power or of the security of private, especially property rights, are involved. These were the interests which had suffered most acutely at the hands of the states during the period of the Confederation and concern for which had brought about the convention that framed the Constitution. By the same token must state power be sternly repressed whenever it entrenches upon the field of powers delegated by the Constitution to "the government of all" or when it menaces the principles on which public and private faith depends. The designated organ to effect these ends is the Supreme Court.

The immediate target, indeed, of all Marshall's great opinions following 1809 was furnished by the pretensions of the state legislature, the seat then as in 1787 of localizing and democratic tendencies. His system of constitutional doctrine thus becomes the vehicle to the present time both of his ingrained conservatism and of his love of the Union. But meantime a dilemma has arisen which, because of the then-particularistic outlook of democracy, Marshall did not have to face. Present-day American democracy is nationalistic, and at the same time it is more strongly inclined to regard government as an instrument of social betterment than ever before. By other preconceptions, too, his fellow citizens came to Marshall's assistance, even when perhaps they might have desired it otherwise. Natural science was still in its infancy, and intellectual method was deductive. Even the common law had not yet discovered that it was "inductive." Most intellectual enterprise set out accordingly from a safe base of agreed premises, and its chief weapon was the syllogism, of which Marshall was an acknowledged master. Furthermore, his age was willing to concede Marshall his three most vital premises. It acknowledged that the upright judge had no will of his own save that of the law. It acknowledged, too, that the meaning of the Constitution—like that of Scripture—was perfectly plain when the document was approached from the proper angle and with good intentions. Finally, it acknowledged that the proper angle in the case of the Constitution was furnished by the purposes of the framers.

Yet in the face of all this a constantly increasing consensus of his fellow countrymen found Marshall's reading of the Constitution less and less acceptable. The slogan of the day was "state rights" or "state sovereignty"—high-sounding phrases which not infrequently boiled down to a claim of right for some state legislature to foster "wild-cat" banking or to promote expedients of less than doubtful honesty for meeting public and private obligations. In Virginia, however, where the uprising started, it was based on grounds almost altogether personal and doctrinal. Here its spokesmen were Spencer Roane, chief judge of the court of appeals, and John Taylor of Caroline. The latter's *Construction Construed, and Constitutions Vindicated* (1820) applies to some of Marshall's great opinions a dialectic worthy of the Chief Justice's best steel; and what Roane, who would have been chief justice if Jefferson had had the naming of Ellsworth's successor, lacked in subtlety he more than made up for in vehemence. Nor was Jefferson himself at all averse to shying a missile now and then from the leafy boscage of his voluminous correspondence at the "subtle corps of sappers and miners" which

was "constantly working underground to undermine our con-
federated fabric" (P. L. Ford, Federal Edition, *The Works of
Thomas Jefferson*, XII, 1905, p. 177). To the standard hoisted by
Virginia soon repaired Ohio and Kentucky, whence the agitation
spread to Congress. From 1821 on, hardly a congressional session
intervened for some years which did not witness some proposal
for weakening the Court or at least Marshall's weight on it; and
by the act of Mar. 3, 1837, the Court was in fact enlarged by two
additional justices. Marshall himself was now dead, but the measure
guaranteed that the members who had survived him and whom he
had presumably indoctrinated should be in a safe minority.

These proceedings did not leave Marshall altogether unmoved.
Especially do his opinions in *Providence Bank* vs. *Billings* (4 *Peters*,
514) and in *Barron* vs. *Baltimore* (7 *Peters*, 243), in the latter of
which he rejected a most persuasive invitation to make the Bill of
Rights restrictive of state power, appear very like concessions to
the spirit of the hour, and his announcement in 8 *Peters* that decisions setting aside state laws must be supported by a majority of
the entire Court was unmistakably so. But to intellectual honesty
there is, after all, a limit to concession, and in *Craig* vs. *Missouri*
(4 *Peters*, 410) and *Worcester* vs. *Georgia* (6 *Peters*, 515) Marshall
quite justly felt that this limit had been reached and passed. Never
were state acts more palpably unconstitutional than those involved
in these cases. Yet in the former the Chief Justice's opinion divided
his associates three to three, and in the latter the Court's judgment
was defied openly, while the word ran round that President Jackson had declared "John Marshall has made his decision, now let
him enforce it" (Horace Greeley, *The American Conflict*, I, 1864,
p. 106).

With these developments and the contemporary Nullification
movement in South Carolina before him, Marshall saw the Union
crumbling: it had been "prolonged thus far by miracles" (Oster,
post, p. 143) and these could not continue. His hold upon the Court,
too, was weakening; a new generation was rising with "new aspirations of power" and bent on finding "new versions of the Constitution" to meet these; his life's achievement was seemingly being en-
gulfed before his eyes. One reassuring voice there was, however, for
in 1833 Story published his *Commentaries on the Constitution of
the United States* (1833). There Marshall saw his version of the
Constitution systematized and given its historical setting, and in
the dedication of the work to himself, he read: "Your expositions of
constitutional law enjoy a rare and extraordinary authority. They

constitute a monument of fame far beyond the ordinary memorials of political and military glory. They are destined to enlighten, instruct, and convince future generations; and can scarcely perish but with the memory of the constitution itself" *(Ibid.,* I, iii). That was it precisely—Marshall's fame was linked with that of the Constitution.

It has been observed that Marshall's judicial life was a somewhat leisurely one, although it became gradually less and less so. In his first three terms the Court decided, on the average, eight cases; in his last term of active service it decided sixty (8 *Peters,* 834). Meantime, beginning with 1827, the opening of Court had been moved up to the second Monday in January, with the result of lengthening the term from about nine weeks to twelve or thirteen. The Court's leisurely procedure, none the less, still continued, and in important cases counsel took their own time. In the argument of *Fletcher* vs. *Peck* the Court adjourned to enable Luther Martin to sober up; while on another occasion it permitted William Pinkney to go back and repeat part of an argument in order that some ladies who had just entered the courtroom might not miss some especially choice tropes. Marshall's own part in the labors of the Court were apparently considerably heavier than those of his associates. "Of a total of one thousand two hundred fifteen cases during that period [1801–1835], in ninety-four, no opinions were filed; in fifteen, the decision was by the Court; and in the remaining one thousand one hundred six cases, Marshall delivered the opinion in five hundred nineteen," of which thirty-six involved constitutional questions and eighty involved questions of international law or kindred questions (Warren, *post,* II, 273 note). The Chief Justice was free to lean on the learning of his associates, and doubtless often had their assistance in the preparation of opinions which he delivered, but the unmistakable *imprimatur* of his own style is on the opinions which support his fame.

In one respect Marshall had a distinct advantage over most of his brethren, in that he lived in his own circuit and near the seat of government. Altogether, his annual journeyings to and from court came to less than 900 miles, while the justice assigned to the seventh circuit had to travel more than 3,300 miles and over mountains. During the Burr trial Marshall was kept at Richmond continuously for nearly seven months, but usually his judicial labors on circuit both at Richmond and Raleigh could hardly have occupied more than three months. It thus appears that, except for opinion writing, Marshall had nearly half the year to devote to his duties and pleasures as householder, neighbor, and citizen. In all these capacities he appears in a singularly engaging light. For many years his wife was a nervous invalid, a fact which cut him off from society in the more formal sense, but far from repining he found in her conversation and their common fondness for good reading one of his chief satisfactions in life. When he eulogized to Story those qualities of womanhood which "make up the sum of human happiness and transform the domestic fireside into an elysium" (Oster, p. 125), he was voicing his own contentment. Bereavement, too, drew them together. Of the ten children born to them, four died early in life—"three of them," he informed Story, "bidding fairer for health and life than any that have survived them" (*Ibid.*, p. 135). Of the survivors five were sons—one of whom predeceased Marshall; his wife died Dec. 25, 1831. But with all his domesticity, Marshall never lost his intense delight in the companionship of men—in eating and drinking with them, frolicking with them, debating with them. A favorite resort of his when in Richmond was the famous Barbecue Club which had grounds just outside the city and was celebrated for its excellent repasts of roast pig and its generous supplies of choice drinks. The *raison d'être* of the organization, however, seems to have been furnished by the game of quoits, and more than one account remains of Marshall's boyish zest in this bucolic sport, in which he excelled. Besides the club, he had a farm nearby; while in summer he often retreated to his estate in the mountains out of the way of malaria—also, perhaps to refresh boyhood associations.

While official propriety forbade that Marshall should express himself publicly on political issues, in his correspondence he could be less reticent. A letter written in 1812 in criticism of the war with Great Britain suggests between the lines that he would not have regarded with aversion the Federalist nomination for president that year (Beveridge, IV, 35); and twenty years later he was hoping against hope for the election of Clay so that Jackson would not have the appointment of his successor, and when fate ruled otherwise, determining to stick it out to the end. Meanwhile, in 1829, he had accepted election, though with strong professions of reluctance, to the Virginia constitutional convention of that year. He at once took a leading rôle, and it was due in no small part to his and Madison's efforts that manhood suffrage was defeated and that the oligarchic system of county justices was fastened upon the state more tightly than ever.

Till his seventy-sixth year Marshall had scarcely known a day's illness. That year he underwent, at the hands of the celebrated Dr. Physick of Philadelphia, operation for stone. It proved successful and his health was restored. Three years later a more serious ailment appeared, an enlarged liver, and it was rendered critical by contusions received in a stage-coach upset. Again he went to Philadelphia, but this time surgery was impracticable. He died there with his sons about him July 6, 1835, in the thirty-fifth year of his chief justiceship and the eightieth of life.

[A. J. Beveridge, *The Life of John Marshall* (4 vols., 1916–19), reproducing the notable portraits by Chester Harding and Inman; L. C. Bell, "John Marshall: Albert J. Beveridge as a Biographer," *Va. Law Register*, March 1927; Edward S. Corwin, *John Marshall and the Constitution* (1919); R. E. Cushman, "Marshall and the Constitution," *Minn. Law Rev.*, Dec. 1920; W. M. Paxton, *The Marshall Family* (1885); E. J. Lee, *Lee of Virginia 1642–1892* (1895); Joseph Story, *A Discourse upon the Life, Character and Services of the Honorable John Marshall, LL.D.* (1835), republished with eulogy by Horace Binney in J. F. Dillon, *John Marshall, Life, Character and Judicial Services* (3 vols., 1903); U. S. Supreme Court *Reports* from 1 *Cranch* to 9 *Peters*, inclusive; J. M. Dillon, ed., *John Marshall: Complete Constitutional Decisions* (1903); J. P. Cotton, ed., *The Constitutional Decisions of John Marshall* (2 vols., 1905); J. W. Brockenbrough, ed., *Reports of Cases Decided by the Honourable John Marshall . . . in the Circuit Court of the U. S., for the Dist. of Va. and N. C., from 1802 to 1833 Inclusive* (2 vols., 1837); *Reports of the Trials of Col. Aaron Burr for Treason . . . and for a Misdemeanor*, by David Robertson, stenographer (2 vols., 1808); Charles Warren, *The Supreme Court in U. S. Hist.* (3 vols., 1922). Most of Marshall's published letters, as well as his will and a brief autobiography which he evidently prepared for Delaplaine's *Repository* in 1818, will be found in John E. Oster's absurdly entitled and still more absurdly arranged *The Political and Economic Doctrines of John Marshall* (1914). The *Repository* was discontinued before the Marshall sketch could be published (see Oster, pp. 197–99). In 1931 William Wetmore Story's widow died in Rome, and among her papers was found the "letter written long afterwards to a friend" which is referred to in Joseph Story's *Discourse*. Actually the letter was written to Story himself, at his request, in 1827 and is the principal source of the portion of the *Discourse* covering Marshall's early life. It concludes with the passage quoted above about the circumstances of Marshall's appointment to the chief justiceship—circumstances regarding which the *Discourse* maintains a discreet silence. The letter has been acquired by the William L. Clements Lib., at the Univ. of Mich., and the writer of this sketch was permitted to see a photostatic copy of the document through the courtesy of Dr. Randolph G. Adams.]

[SUPPLEMENTARY BIBLIOGRAPHY. A series of papers on different aspects of Marshall's judicial career may be found in W. Melville Jones, ed., *Chief Justice John Marshall: A Reappraisal* (1956). Marshall's role in the development of the nation is appraised in Edward S. Corwin, "John Marshall, Revolutionist *Malgré Lui*," *Univ. of Pa. Law Rev.*, Oct. 1955; in William B. Munro, "John Marshall and the Achievement of Nationalism," in *The Makers of the Unwritten Constitution* (1929); and in Charles G. Haines, *The Role of the Supreme Court in Am. Government and Politics, 1789–1835* (1945). Other aspects of Marshall's work are examined in Thomas S. Craigmyle, *John Marshall in Diplomacy and in Law* (1933); Benjamin M. Ziegler, *The International Law of John Marshall: A Study of First Principles* (1939); and William A. Foran, "John Marshall as a Historian," *Am. Hist. Rev.*, Oct. 1937. James A. Servies, *A Bibliography of John Marshall* (1956), is a comprehensive guide to writings by and about Marshall.]

Andrew Jackson

by

THOMAS P. ABERNETHY

JACKSON, ANDREW (Mar. 15, 1767–June 8, 1845), seventh president of the United States, was born in the lean backwoods settlement of the Waxhaw in South Carolina (Bassett, *Life*, 1911, pp. 5–7). His father, for whom he was named, his mother, Elizabeth Hutchinson, and two brothers had migrated from the neighborhood of Carrickfergus in the north of Ireland in 1765. Two years later, shortly before the birth of Andrew, the father died. Mrs. Jackson, being left a dependent widow, took up residence with relatives, and her little son started life under the most discouraging circumstances. He was sent to an old-field school, and developed into a tall, slender, sandy-haired, tempestuous stripling. When he had attained the age of nine years, the Revolution broke upon the country and its horrors later visited the Waxhaw settlement. His brother Hugh was killed in 1779; he and his brother Robert, though mere lads, took part in the battle of Hanging Rock, and afterward were captured by the British. The boy troopers were thrown in prison, where they contracted smallpox. Their mother secured their exchange and release, but Robert died from either the effects of the disease or neglected wounds. During 1781 Mrs. Jackson went to Charleston to nurse the sick, and here she died of prison fever. Bereaved of the last member of his family, Andrew at the age of fourteen was now alone in the world.

His mother's death at that place probably drew him to Charleston. Here he learned something of the great world, including the

racing of horses and the manners of "gentlemen." Returning to
his native settlement, he tried his hand at school-teaching and finally
decided to take up the study of law. This was a daring yet a
sagacious decision. Now seventeen years old, he apparently had no
funds with which to finance his studies, but he possessed a horse
and an abundance of courage; and the West was in need of young
lawyers who could endure the rigors of frontier practice. He began
the reading of law under Spruce Macay, at Salisbury, N. C., and
had as fellow student and companion John McNairy. The two
became close friends. Much of their time was spent in horse-racing,
cock-fighting, and carousing (Parton, *post,* 1860, I, 104, 108–09).
Certainly Jackson gained little knowledge of Blackstone, but after
two years of study, and a brief stay in Martinsville, N. C., he and
McNairy in 1788 packed their horses and moved along the slender
trail which led to the transmontane West. Tradition has it that
he arrived at Jonesboro (now Tenn.) riding a fine horse and leading
another mount, with saddle-bags, gun, pistols, and fox-hounds. This
was elaborate equipment for a struggling young lawyer, and within
the year he increased it by the purchase of a slave girl (John Allison, *Dropped Stitches in Tennessee History,* 1897, pp. 8, 10). Jackson and McNairy qualified to practise before the courts, but Jackson still found time to engage in his favorite sport of horse-racing,
and he fought a bloodless duel with Waightstill Avery, then the
most famous lawyer in western North Carolina. All this makes it
clear that the young man had set himself up in the world as a
"gentleman." Frontiersmen normally fought with their fists rather
than with pistols, and prided themselves more upon physical prow-
ess than upon manners. Though commonly looked upon as a typical
Westerner, Jackson was ever an aristocrat at heart.

In the fall of 1788 the first wagon road from the vicinity of
Jonesboro to the infant town of Nashville was opened by the militia,
and the two budding attorneys were of the first party to traverse
the new highway. McNairy had been appointed judge of the superior court of the new jurisdiction, and Jackson accompanied his
friend, doubtless hoping to profit from the association. On reaching
Nashville, then a stockaded village of log cabins, the young lawyer
found lodging with the widow of Col. John Donelson, a wealthy
and prominent land speculator from Virginia and one of the
founders of Nashville. In the home of his widow was another lawyer-
lodger, named John Overton, and the daughter of the house,
Rachel, who had made an unfortunate marriage to Lewis Robards.
Overton was a well-connected young man from Virginia, and he

and Jackson became lifelong friends. Jackson was also attracted to Rachel Robards, and their friendship led to divorce from her jealous husband. By reason of misapprehension they were married two years before the decree of divorce was granted, and a long-lived scandal was the result. A second marriage ceremony was, of course, necessary. Jackson had married into a family far superior to his own socially, and he reaped no small benefit from this tie. Though of good birth, Rachel had been reared in the wilderness and consequently was almost illiterate and without training in the niceties of social usage. Jackson was attached to her with romantic devotion throughout his life. They had no children, but he adopted his wife's nephew, who in his foster father's will was called Andrew Jackson, Jr.

While establishing himself in such personal ways, Jackson was also engaged in establishing himself in business. He secured a ready practice in the collection of debts, and McNairy appointed him prosecuting attorney for the district. In 1790 North Carolina ceded her western country to the United States, and William Blount, powerful in North Carolina politics, was appointed governor. Blount was wealthy and prominent; Jackson was an unknown backwoods lawyer. But the two became acquainted shortly after Blount's appointment. A man situated as was the Governor needed energetic young lawyers in his administration, and Jackson probably facilitated his own introduction. In 1791 he was given the same appointment under the territorial government that he had held under North Carolina, and soon was also appointed judge-advocate of the Davidson County militia regiment ("Governor Blount's Journal," *American Historical Magazine*, Nashville, July 1897, pp. 234, 247). Strangely enough, this was the only military office which Jackson held until he became a major-general of Tennessee militia in 1802. Land was the great commodity of the West and land speculation the most obvious avenue to riches. Being an enterprising, ambitious young man, Jackson bought and sold many thousand acres. His transactions in two instances at least were extremely equivocal, one of them gaining him an airing before the United States Senate (T. P. Abernethy, *From Frontier to Plantation in Tennessee*, 1932, pp. 262–76). Among other purchases was that of the "Hermitage" tract, where he made his home and lived the life of a cotton planter after 1795. He established a store nearby where he exchanged manufactured articles from Philadelphia for cotton and peltry, which he shipped to New Orleans.

When Tennessee was admitted as a state in 1796, Jackson sat as a delegate in the convention which framed its first constitution. The fact that he was placed upon the committee which was appointed to draw up a frame of government was a recognition of his professional qualifications. The constitution of North Carolina was followed as a model, but the drafting committee omitted from the new instrument the clause in the older document requiring all officials under the state to believe in God, in a future state of rewards and punishments, and in the divine authority of the Old and New Testaments. A motion from the floor proposed to insert it. The future leader of Democracy here made his début as a liberal. Jackson, along with most of the prominent men of the convention, opposed the motion, though it passed with modifications (*Journal of the Proceedings of a Convention . . . at Knoxville . . . for the Purpose of Forming a Constitution,* ed. 1852, pp. 23–24, 29).

Under the new state government Jackson was elected without opposition to the one seat which Tennessee was allotted in the federal House of Representatives. This might be taken as an indication of his outstanding popularity, but it does not appear that he was notable in that respect. All the evidence tends to indicate that the plans of William Blount, who was now sent to the federal Senate, were responsible for the elevation of Jackson. As protégé of the powerful Blount, Jackson was given many a lift along the highroad to success. Though he did not win laurels in Congress as an orator, he did make himself conspicuous by voting against resolutions approving Washington's administration, and by securing compensation for militiamen who had marched under Sevier on an Indian raid not only unauthorized by the government but actually contrary to its orders. The latter accomplishment, which must have required some ability, won him a secure place in the favor of his constituency.

In 1797 Blount was expelled from the Senate. He and John Sevier were the leaders of rival factions in state politics, and this reverse threatened to injure not only Blount but also his entire following. Jackson occupied an important position in this group, and the responsibility for retrieving the situation devolved upon him. It was under these circumstances that he resigned his seat in the House and sought and secured a place in the Senate ("Correspondence of Gen. James Robertson," *American Historical Magazine,* Nashville, Oct. 1899, pp. 343–45). Jackson now returned to Philadelphia, but, being greatly involved in business difficulties, in April 1798 he resigned for a second time a seat in the federal legislature. He was not the kind of man to take an interest in wordy debates and the subtleties of political intrigue. He had a certain shrewdness, but it was not of a complex type. He was restless and vigorous and he loved action rather than words.

In 1798, at the instance of William Blount, he received the support of Governor Sevier and was elected one of the superior judges of Tennessee (Tennessee Historical Society MSS., Blount to Sevier, July 6, 1798). Jackson was not a learned judge, but he was a fearless and energetic one and no criticism has ever come upon him in connection with his work in this capacity. The conventional picture of the irascible soldier and self-willed president should be tempered by recalling this phase of his career. He seems to have had no plans other than to live out his life as a gentleman of the western border. He rode the circuit, planted cotton at "The Hermitage," raced horses at Clover Bottom, and talked with his friends at the taverns in Nashville. While political office apparently held no great attraction for him, he was keenly interested in the major-generalship of the militia of Tennessee. This office, filled by the vote of the field officers of the division, was, next to the governorship, the most important in the gift of the state. In those days militia offices were no sinecures. All able-bodied men were liable to serve, and they were not infrequently called upon for active duty. Even in times of peace, musters were often held, and the belted and plumed officers drilled their men in hunting shirts with much éclat. In 1801 Governor Sevier, being ineligible for a fourth successive term, gave way to Archibald Roane, a young lawyer who had come out to the wilderness with Jackson in the early days and was of the Blount faction. Sevier now ran against Jackson for the generalship, and when the vote was found to be tied, Roane cast his deciding ballot for his friend, Jackson, who was thus elected (1802). Upon such slender threads does the destiny of even the greatest men sometimes depend. In 1803 Jackson supported Roane for the governorship against Sevier, who was now eligible. The quarrel between Sevier and Jackson, which had begun earlier (A. V. Goodpasture, "Genesis of the Jackson-Sevier Feud," *American Historical Magazine,* Nashville, Apr. 1900, pp. 115–23), developed into bitter enmity and all but led to a serious personal encounter. Sevier, however, was successful in the election and Jackson gained no advantage. The next year he resigned his judgeship and retired to private life except for his military commission. But the fates were still unkind. When Aaron Burr visited Nashville in 1806 in the interest of his well-known expedition down the Mississippi, Jackson entertained him at "The Hermitage" and undertook a contract to build boats for him. When Burr was discredited, Jackson's connection with him was used to his disadvantage by his enemies. During the same year he fought his famous duel with Charles Dickinson. While severely wounded himself, he brought down his man. Since Dickinson had powerful connections, Jackson was further weakened politically by the affair.

Jackson lived the life of a country gentleman from 1806 until 1812. Then the second war with Great Britain broke upon the country and gave him his chance for fame. The massacre by the Creeks of the inmates of Fort Mims in the Mississippi Territory was followed by a call upon Tennessee for assistance. Willie Blount, half-brother to William, was then in the gubernatorial chair, and he gave to his friend Jackson the command of the forces sent by Tennessee to subdue the hostile natives. The country through which the latter had to march was naturally difficult, and without roads of any kind. The troops under his command were militiamen and volunteers enlisted for short tours of duty. His supplies had to be shipped down the river from East Tennessee. The enemy gave him far less trouble than his "friends," but he overcame all obstacles and accomplished the seemingly impossible by defeating the Indians at Horseshoe Bend (Mar. 27, 1814). It was perhaps not a great feat of generalship, but it was a supreme feat of will. The victory established his military reputation and brought him a commission as major-general in the army of the United States. It was in this capacity that he was called upon to defend New Orleans against the veterans of Wellington whom the British sent against that city. The military problem was a relatively simple one, for the enemy had to approach the city along a narrow strip of land lying between the river and the marsh, and Jackson selected for his main line of defense an old canal lying athwart this passage. Again his main problem was tactical rather than strategic, for his troops were motley and undisciplined. Collecting his militiamen from Kentucky and Tennessee, his creoles, his Negroes, and his pirates, he threw up a palisade and manned the canal. Thrice the British attacked with desperate bravery, and three of their generals were left lying upon the bloody field of Chalmette. Finally the thin red line recoiled, and New Orleans was saved. Jackson's victory (Jan. 8, 1815) came, as it developed, after the treaty of peace had already been signed at Ghent. But the treaty was not to go into effect until ratified, and had the British taken New Orleans they might well have sought, as there is reason to believe they planned, to detach all of the Louisiana Purchase from the United States. Jackson's victory was thus of more moment than is generally realized.

The battle made Jackson the major hero of the war, and a national figure of the first magnitude. He was now forty-eight years of age. Tall and slender even to the point of emaciation, his frail body supported a head of great strength. His face was long and narrow, with a high forehead and hair which stood stiffly erect. His eyes were small and blue and kindled with a burning fire. His nose was straight and his mouth generous and strong, but the teeth were too long and the upper lip too heavy. The jaw was thin and lantern, but the chin was firm and clear-cut. It was an impressive countenance, and one altogether distinctive (H. A. Wise, *Seven Decades of the Union,* 1872, p. 80). The character of his mind was even more distinctive than was his appearance. His temper was hot and his spirit high, yet he could restrain emotions or play them up for the sake of effect. He spoke volubly, in a vehement and somewhat declamatory manner, but with perfect self-possession. He was tender and gentle with those whom he loved, and loyal to those whom he considered his friends. He hated his enemies with unabated fervor, and all who opposed him were his foes. He was strong-willed and impetuous in action, yet he reflected carefully before coming to a decision. In political matters he sometimes deferred to the advice of others, but as often acted upon his own initiative. The course which he followed in such cases depended primarily upon whether the subject were one which touched him personally, or whether it were one upon which he could look objectively.

Shortly after the battle, it occurred to several keen politicians, including Aaron Burr, Edward Livingston, and William Carroll, that the victorious general had become a presidential possibility. But Monroe was the incumbent and he was scheduled for reëlection in 1820. Jackson was his friend and had no intention of competing with him. Though the General denied that he sought office, it is clear that his thoughts began to turn toward Washington. His prospects were disturbed by the Seminole affair of 1818. In this year Jackson was sent to chastise some Florida Indians who were making trouble along the Alabama-Georgia border. Believing that he was acting in accord with the wishes of the administration, but without official authorization, he followed the natives across the international line and captured the Spanish town of Pensacola. In addition to this, he hanged two British subjects who had been exercising hostile influence among the red men. The government was thus brought face to face with the possibility of war with both Great

Britain and Spain, and it was left for Monroe and his advisers to find a way out of the difficulty in which the over-zealous Jackson had involved them. The President and every member of the cabinet save John Quincy Adams felt that Jackson had exceeded his authority and that his acts should be disavowed, but the Secretary of State advised that the blame be put upon Spain for her lax administration, and his counsel prevailed. It was a happy solution, for Jackson's conduct was pleasing to the majority of the Western people, and a reprimand might have made him president before his time. Monroe's position had been a delicate one. He wished Jackson to believe that he was friendly, but he refused to assume responsibility for the attack on Pensacola, and he did not come openly to the defense of the General. After the excitement had blown over and the United States had acquired Florida, the President made amends of a kind by appointing Jackson to be the first governor of the new territory. Resigning his military commission on June 1, 1821, Jackson accepted the position because its tender was looked upon as a public vindication of his conduct and because he thought it would enable him to furnish offices to some of his friends (Bassett, *Correspondence*, III, 1928, p. 65). In the latter expectation he was largely disappointed, and his experiences as governor were otherwise embarrassing. Tact rather than courage was the qualification which the position required, and he was never noted for this virtue. Before the end of the year he gave up the post in disgust and retired to "The Hermitage" to become once more a private citizen.

Meanwhile, Monroe had been elected president for a second term in 1820. The time had come when men might turn their attention to the election of 1824, and it was with an unwonted interest that they did so. The great panic of 1819 had left the West economically prostrate and the hordes of debtors sent up a cry for relief. In many states the legislatures passed various measures for their benefit, including, in some cases, the establishment of state-owned, state-operated banks whose paper money was to be used for the succor of the needy (T. H. Benton, *Thirty Years' View*, I, 1854, p. 5). In Tennessee, as well as Kentucky and Alabama, such institutions were established. Ambitious politicians saw the opportunity offered by the situation and demagoguery was rife. Jackson was one of the few who opposed the state bank in Tennessee. It was also opposed by the two candidates for the governorship of the state in 1821. Of these, Edward Ward, wealthy and educated, was looked upon as the aristocratic candidate, and William Carroll as representing the democracy. Jackson supported Ward, who was overwhelmingly de-feated (T. P. Abernethy, "Andrew Jackson and the Rise of South-western Democracy," *American Historical Review*, Oct. 1927, pp. 67–68). Thus the hero of New Orleans aligned himself with the conservative interests in his state at the time the great popular movement which bears his name was getting under way. Though his presidential campaign was already on foot, he made no attempt to conceal his views.

When he returned to "The Hermitage" in 1821, a group of three old friends who resided in or near Nashville constituted themselves a confidential committee for political purposes. Of these, William B. Lewis was a neighbor who had married a ward of Jackson; John H. Eaton was a satellite who had defended the General when the Seminole affair was before the Senate in 1819; and John Overton had lodged with Jackson at the widow Donelson's in frontier days and had remained a loyal friend and business associate during all the intervening years. He furnished most of the initiative, Eaton contributed diplomatic ability, and Lewis was the informal secre-tary and general busybody. Together they supplied the press with favorable material, formed connections in other states, and secured Jackson's nomination by the Tennessee legislature in 1822. There were similar groups elsewhere who saw the opportunity to organize the masses, so lately stirred to political consciousness by the panic, and thrust the old-time politicians from the seats of power. Thus the Jackson movement was launched as a popular cause in spite of the unpopular stand which he took at the same time in the politics of his own state. The explanation is that he was known as a successful general and Indian fighter, a son of the frontier with the romance of the pioneer about him, and an expansionist, and that few people outside the state knew or cared anything about Tennessee politics. In the state all factions were anxious to see the favorite son become president of the nation. The presidential move-ment developed smoothly until 1823, when it became necessary for Tennessee to elect a new senator. The incumbent, Col. John Wil-liams, had fought Jackson bitterly during the Seminole controversy of 1818–19, and the friends of the latter did not think that they could afford to permit the return of such an enemy. But no man could be found with sufficient strength to defeat him, and· the only recourse was to put forward Jackson himself. He objected, for he had been in the Senate once before. His friends insisted, however, and he finally gave way. The result was that, in 1823, for a second time Jackson occupied a seat in the Senate of the United States. Just as in 1798, he accepted the place in order to prevent the election of an opponent, and held it only long enough to secure the succession of a friend. This time he took a more active part in the proceedings of the body and registered his vote on the leading measures. It is notable that he favored bills providing for the construction of internal improvements at federal expense, and supported the protective tariff (Bassett, *Life,* pp. 344–45). He was a true representative of the West, favoring an expansionist policy which would result in the development of the newer states.

It was, therefore, with a political as well as a military record that Jackson stood before the country as a presidential candidate in 1824. His opponents were Henry Clay and John Quincy Adams, both nationalists. John C. Calhoun, once a rival, now occupied the second place on the Jackson ticket. William H. Crawford, the anointed of the "Virginia Dynasty" and the only strict constructionist of the five, was strong with the politicians of Washington and greatly feared by his opponents. Jackson had quarreled with him in 1816 over an Indian treaty, and this animosity added zest to the General's ambition. In the election, Jackson received the highest popular vote, but, as compared with the votes in succeeding elections, it was an exceedingly small one. The military hero had not yet conquered the nation. In the Southwest, where the memory of Indian wars was still fresh, his strength was overwhelming except in the vicinity of New Orleans and among the commercial elements elsewhere. The movement for him was in the nature of a popular uprising in this section, and the conservative elements in the population, though numerically weak, were inclined to be hostile. Clay divided the Northwest with him and Crawford split the Southeast. In the East, where Indian wars were long forgotten, Jackson's strength was due more to the work of local politicians than to any direct appeal which his personality made to the masses. His support here came partly from the rural democracy, and partly from the nationalists. Political power was still commonly wielded by the few, who were able to shape public opinion among a people accustomed to leadership.

When the Clay supporters combined with those of Adams to elect the latter, the Jackson following sent up a cry of "bargain and corruption" in which they fully believed, and which furnished the motive power for a campaign of renewed intensity to elect their favorite in 1828. It was during this period that the campaigners were able to arouse the masses throughout the country to an active interest in politics and to a pitch of enthusiasm which was more general than anything that had previously affected the people. The Jackson movement became a personal matter, the vindication of a hero who had been wronged, and the campaigners conjured with the name of "Old Hickory." No definite program of reform was proposed; no political ideals were set forth; the sole aim was the election of Jackson. Men who could not understand principles of any sort could understand this issue. Before the year 1828 came around, the political situation had changed radically. Clay withdrew from the race, and ill health forced the retirement of Crawford. This left the Jackson-Calhoun ticket to face Adams alone. Martin Van Buren of New York had supported Crawford in 1824. Now he turned to Jackson and carried with him a strong Crawford following in Virginia and Georgia (C. H. Ambler, *Thomas Ritchie,* 1913, pp. 107–08). Thus a state-rights element had joined a nationalist group. The question of the Bank of the United States had not been before the people in 1824, and Jackson, in spite of later utterances, had not previously manifested hostility toward that institution. He began to show a hostile spirit, however, at about the time of his coalition with Van Buren, and the fact that some of the branches of the bank opposed him during the campaign fixed his animosity (R. C. H. Catterall, *The Second Bank of the United States,* 1903, pp. 183–84; R. C. McGrane, ed., *The Correspondence of Nicholas Biddle,* 1919, pp. 87–88). This was Jackson's first commitment to the strict-constructionist faction and it is highly probable that Van Buren was responsible for the change. Since Adams was a nationalist of strong convictions, it was natural that his opponent should take the other side, and the vote in the election of 1828 shows that he was understood to have done so. The combination between Jackson and Van Buren was certain to bring on a struggle between Calhoun and Van Buren for the succession. When the hero of New Orleans journeyed to the scene of his great victory to participate in an anniversary celebration on Jan. 8, 1828, James A. Hamilton, a trusted friend of Van Buren, went along to sound him on a reconciliation with Crawford and to suggest to him the disloyalty of Calhoun. But Jackson would not believe that Calhoun had been disloyal, and was not enthusiastic over reconciliation with Crawford (Jackson Papers, Library of Congress, J. A. Hamilton to Jackson, Feb. 17, 1828; *American Historical Magazine,* Nashville, Jan. 1904, pp. 93–98, R. G. Dunlap to Jackson, Aug. 10, 1831). Thus the first move failed, but Van Buren bided his time. When the election occurred, Jackson carried both New York and Pennsylvania with a solid West and South except for Maryland. His popular vote was four times what it had been in 1824.

The popular campaign had succeeded. The masses had been aroused for the first time to an active interest in politics. At the inauguration they stormed the White House and their leaders busied themselves in demanding a share of the spoils of victory. The new administration satisfied this demand, removing many old employees of the government and putting new men in their places. This process was facilitated by the adoption of the principle of rotation in office, under which tenure was usually limited to four years instead of during good behavior. All this was in keeping with Jackson's personal views, for he looked upon politics as a very personal matter, and he had always believed that his friends should be rewarded by public preferment. No abstract principle of equal rights actuated him in this stand. Van Buren became secretary of state and John H. Eaton became secretary of war, but Calhoun's friends had to be rewarded with several cabinet posts. It was clear from the first that harmony could not prevail between the factions thus represented. It was Eaton who first introduced discord by marrying the notorious Peggy O'Neill, daughter of a Washington tavern-keeper. The ladies of the cabinet refused to receive her and Mrs. Calhoun took a leading part in the work of exclusion. Jackson, ever gallant, defended Peggy; and Van Buren, being a widower, aided his chief. The President took the matter personally, and the Secretary of State was much strengthened by the incident. Thus a social issue all but wrecked the Cabinet of the arch-Democrat. Van Buren's cause was also promoted by the nullification controversy. Calhoun had been a strong advocate of internal improvements while a member of Monroe's cabinet, and was known as a decided nationalist in 1824. The tariff measure of that year, however, was opposed by South Carolina, and that of 1828 drove her into strenuous resistance to the policy of protection (C. S. Boucher, *The Nullification Controversy in South Carolina*, 1916). State-rights ideas were revived and strengthened, and Calhoun joined the movement without openly avowing the fact when he drew up his "Exposition" of 1828. There was much reason to look upon Jackson at that time as a state-rights man, and the difference of opinion was not revealed until the famous Jefferson birthday dinner of 1830, when the President gave his toast, "Our Union, it must be preserved!" (Bassett, *Life,* p. 555). The breach which thus developed was widened and made irreparable by Crawford's publication of the facts in regard to the cabinet meeting of 1818, when Calhoun had wished to see Jackson censured for his conduct in the Seminole campaign. Thus everything worked into the hands of Van Buren, and he supplanted the great Carolinian in the councils of the administration. In 1831 the cabinet was reorganized so as to force the friends of Calhoun out, and Van Buren, on being rejected by the Senate as minister to the Court of St. James's, became Jackson's choice to replace Calhoun in the vice-presidency.

While this struggle was in progress, the administration faced an equally important issue involving the Bank of the United States. The charter was to expire in 1836, but so important was the matter that it could not be ignored until that time. Jackson failed to mention it in his inaugural address, but in his first annual message to Congress brought up the question. Here he expressed himself as opposed to the existing charter, but as favoring one which would establish a government-owned bank so limited in its operations as to avoid all constitutional difficulties (Richardson, *post,* II, 1896, p. 462). In 1820 Jackson had opposed a government-owned bank in Tennessee, and time had justified his opposition. He knew, or should have known, that the notes issued by the Bank of the United States were almost the only paper currency which would circulate without depreciation in all parts of the Union, and that there was not enough gold and silver to serve the needs of trade (T. P. Abernethy, "Early Development of Commerce and Banking in Tennessee," *Mississippi Valley Historical Review,* Dec. 1927, pp. 318–25). The ideas expressed in his message therefore seem unnecessarily crude, and are hard to account for. There is much reason to suspect that they were inspired by Van Buren and that they represent New York's opposition to the Philadelphia bank. It was his opponents, however, rather than Jackson, who forced the issue. Clay together with Nicholas Biddle, president of the Bank, decided that the recharter should be demanded before the election of 1832 so that, if Jackson should veto it, it would become the issue in the campaign. As they anticipated, the measure was passed and vetoed, and the bank question became the leading issue in the election which followed.

Van Buren's hand could be seen even more clearly in another issue which confronted the people at the time. The Western states were greatly in need of improved transportation facilities, and macadamized roads were just coming into use. When Congress in 1830 passed an act for the improvement of the road from Maysville to Lexington, Ky., Jackson vetoed the measure. His message explain-

ing his act stated that works of national importance might be coun-
tenanced, but that the road in question was of local interest only.
He thus did not argue on strict-constructionist grounds, but on
grounds of expediency (Richardson, *post,* II, 1896, p. 487). His position was badly taken, however, for the highway from Wheeling to
Maysville was one of the most important in the whole West, and
the great southwestern mail was being carried along it at the time.

In 1832 the Democratic party held its first national nominating
convention for the purpose of naming Van Buren for the vice-
presidency. Since the congressional caucus had favored Crawford in
1824, Jackson and his following opposed it as an undemocratic
institution and succeeded in killing it. The nominating convention
grew up to take its place. This device was advocated as giving a
more direct expression to the will of the people, but Jackson was
not interested in the will of the people unless it coincided with his
own, as his attitude toward this and the succeeding convention well
proves. In the election of 1832 Jackson stood before the country
with his policy well developed. The theorist would have found it
difficult to determine whether he was a strict or a liberal constructionist, an advocate of state rights or of nationalism; but such
abstract questions did not enter much into consideration. The bank
question was the paramount issue, and the President's stand was
immensely popular. The back-country people correctly regarded
the banks as privileged institutions, and they looked upon the losses
which they themselves sustained because of a fluctuating paper currency as amounting to sheer robbery. Jackson's position appeared
to them to be a manifestation of pure democracy, and they supported it with utmost enthusiasm. The result was that the President was reëlected over Clay by a popular vote which slightly exceeded that of 1828 and broke the opposition even in New England. Shortly after this election, the nullification controversy came
to a head. A new protective tariff measure was passed in 1832 and
South Carolina called a convention which forbade the collection
of the duties within the state. Jackson countered with a proclamation threatening to use force if necessary in the execution of the
law. In this crisis Clay secured the passage of the compromise
tariff of 1833 and the danger was averted, each side claiming victory. Jackson's attitude in this matter was characteristic of his
temperament, and he doubtless acted upon his own initiative. While
nullification received little support outside South Carolina, the
state-rights school in the South was offended by the President's

assumption of the right to coerce a state, and some of the leaders of this wing of the party deserted to the opposition.

Having prevented the recharter of the Bank of the United States, Jackson feared that it would retaliate by trying to bring on a panic. In order to curb its dangerous power, he decided that the federal deposits should be withdrawn from its vaults. After he had experienced some difficulty in finding a secretary of the treasury who would cooperate in the work, the object was accomplished. The Senate passed resolutions condemning the action of the President, and an important group of leaders in the Southern wing of the party was alienated. But the Bank was dead, and the government funds were distributed among state banks. Neither the credit nor the currency of the country was improved by these measures, which were in effect inflationist, but the "money power," once so arrogant, had been humbled and the masses who were not interested in commerce applauded the policy. His "specie circular" (July 11, 1836) later added to the difficulties of sound banks and served in part to precipitate the panic of 1837.

Jackson's record as an expansionist was all that should have been expected. His policy of removing the Indians west of the Mississippi quieted a dangerous situation in Georgia, where he had upheld state aggression in defiance of John Marshall and the Supreme Court, but met with less success in Alabama. His desire to take advantage of the Texas revolution in order to secure the annexation of that province to the United States was not gratified. It seems probable that he hoped, through the instrumentality of his friend Samuel Houston, to find an excuse for intervention, but the plan did not succeed and prudence did not permit it to be pushed (H. A. Wise, *Seven Decades of the Union*, 1872, p. 149). In diplomatic affairs the administration succeeded signally. The trade of the British West Indies was opened to the United States for the first time since the Revolution, and a claim against France for Napoleonic spoliations was settled by strong-handed methods. The last great struggle of Jackson's career was over the selection of his successor. He had chosen Van Buren for this honor, and the nomination of the latter by the convention of 1836 was secured by forceful action. Jackson apparently did not realize that it was inconsistent with the principles of democracy for a president to select his successor by manipulating a convention, but many of his followers saw it and deserted his cause. Thus Jackson, at different times, alienated several groups of his earlier supporters, and these joined the Clay-Adams opposition to form the Whig party. The new organization adopted Clay's nationalist policy. Jackson on the other hand, had disappointed the West in regard to internal improvements, and the commercial interests, including a large proportion of the planters of the South, on the bank question. Thus he left his party with a strict-constructionist heritage. He had entered politics as a member of a school which looked upon public office as a fit subject for personal exploitation; he had always considered himself a strict constructionist, but he had grown up in the spirit of Western nationalism and had represented that school as late as 1824. Under the influence of Van Buren he veered toward the opposite stand. The partisan alignment established in his day persisted for many years, and the Democratic party retains until the present time some of the principles which he adopted.

The nation and the executive office grew stronger because of Jackson, and his administration ranks as one of the most important in American history. With his practical mind and aggressive spirit, he was never a theorist. He met issues as they arose, sometimes acting on his own initiative and sometimes on the suggestions of others. He was doubtless unconscious of his inconsistency, and his advisers must share with him the credit for his extraordinary political success. He had little understanding of the democratic movement which bears his name and he came to support it primarily because it supported him. Yet the common man believed implicitly in him and remained his faithful follower. While he yet lived a tradition grew up around his name which has made him one of the greatest of American heroes, and the glamor of his colorful personality will never fade from the pages of American history.

After seeing Van Buren elected and inaugurated he retired once more to "The Hermitage," where his strength gradually failed and in 1845 he died. He was buried in the garden by his beloved Rachel, who by seventeen years had preceded him.

[The principal biographies are: J. S. Bassett, *The Life of Andrew Jackson* (1911); Jas. Parton, *Life of Andrew Jackson* (3 vols., 1860); and W. G. Sumner, *Andrew Jackson* (1882). From the Jackson MSS. in the Lib. of Cong., 5 vols. of the *Correspondence of Andrew Jackson* (1926–31), edited by the late J. S. Bassett, have been published. For state papers see J. D. Richardson, *A Compilation of the Messages and Papers of the Presidents*, vol. II (1896). Several collections of

Jackson letters have been published in *Am. Hist. Mag.* (Nashville, Tenn.), Apr. 1899, pp. 99–104; July 1899, pp. 229–46; Apr. 1900, pp. 132–44; Jan. 1904, pp. 83–104. Among works dealing with the Jackson period may be cited: Wm. McDonald, *Jacksonian Democracy* (1906); F. A. Ogg, *The Reign of Andrew Jackson* (1919); C. G. Bowers, *The Party Battles of the Jackson Period* (1922); S. G. Heiskell, *Andrew Jackson and Early Tenn. Hist.* (2nd ed., 2 vols., 1920); T. P. Abernethy, *From Frontier to Plantation in Tenn.* (1932). Among articles on Jackson as distinguished from Jacksonism are: J. S. Bassett, "Maj. Lewis on the Nomination of Andrew Jackson," *Proc. Am. Antiquarian Soc.*, XXXIII (1924), 12–33; and T. P. Abernethy, "Andrew Jackson and the Rise of Southwestern Democracy," *Am. Hist. Rev.*, Oct. 1927, pp. 64–77. For his military activities, see H. S. Halbert and T. H. Ball, *The Creek War* (1895); G. R. Gleig, *Narrative of the Campaigns of the British Army at Washington and New Orleans* (1821); G. C. Moore Smith, *The Autobiog. of Lieut.-Gen. Sir Harry Smith* (1901), vol. I; A. L. Latour, *Hist. Memoir of the War in W. Fla.* (1816). Information on Jackson's early career is to be found in the letters of Gen. Jas. Robertson in the library of George Peabody College for Teachers; on his later career in the papers of Jas. K. Polk in the Lib. of Cong.; and the John Overton Papers in the library of the Tenn. Hist. Soc.]

[SUPPLEMENTARY BIBLIOGRAPHY. An important biography, not mentioned above, is Augustus C. Buell, *Hist. of Andrew Jackson* (1904), and a more recent one is Marquis James, *Andrew Jackson, the Border Captain* (1933) and *Andrew Jackson, Portrait of a President* (1937)—reissued together in 1938 as *The Life of Andrew Jackson*. Important phases of Jackson's career are discussed in two books by Thomas P. Abernethy, *The Burr Conspiracy* (1954) and *The South in the New Nation, 1789–1819* (1961); the latter has a chapter on the battle of New Orleans and its significance. Glyndon G. Van Deusen, *The Jacksonian Era, 1828–1848* (1959), includes a useful bibliography. See also Leonard D. White, *The Jacksonians: A Study in Administrative Hist., 1829–1861* (1954). A vast literature on Jacksonian Democracy has followed in the wake of Arthur M. Schlesinger, Jr.'s *The Age of Jackson* (1945), much of it taking issue with or qualifying that author's interpretations. For an incisive consideration of this and the earlier literature on Jacksonian Democracy, see Charles G. Sellers, Jr., "Andrew Jackson versus the Historians," *Miss. Valley Hist. Rev.*, Mar. 1958. For recent analyses of the Jacksonian temper in general, see Marvin Meyers, *The Jacksonian Persuasion: Politics and Belief* (1957), and John W. Ward, *Andrew Jackson, Symbol for an Age* (1955). Harold C. Syrett, *Andrew Jackson: His Contribution to the Am. Tradition* (1953), combines a selection of Jackson's writings with an interpretation of his career. A recent highly technical study is Lee Benson, *The Concept of Jacksonian Democracy, N. Y. as a Test Case* (1961).]

Henry Clay

by

E. MERTON COULTER

CLAY, HENRY (Apr. 12, 1777–June 29, 1852), congressman, senator, secretary of state, was descended from English ancestors who came to Virginia shortly after the founding of Jamestown but did not rise to any position of importance in the colony. His father, John Clay, was a Baptist minister who moved from Henrico County to the frontiers of Hanover County in search of a district more hospitable to the practise of his religion. His mother was Elizabeth Hudson, who came of a family of no greater prominence than the Clays. Henry Clay was born in the midst of the Revolution in a region overrun by war, in that part of Hanover County generally referred to as The Slashes. He was the fourth son, and next to the youngest child, in a family of eight—three daughters and five sons. Of these children only two sons besides Henry lived far beyond the age of maturity. His father died in 1781 leaving the family little more than the respectability of his name. As Henry was only four years old at the time the influence of his father could have affected him very little. To his mother he owed much. He always held her in affectionate remembrance. His formal education consisted of three years before the master of The Slashes log school, Peter Deacon, whom Clay always pleasantly recalled. In 1791 Clay's mother married Henry Watkins, a man who came to regard his step-children kindly and who took a particular interest in Henry. He moved the family to Richmond, where he was a resident, and soon secured for Henry a position in a retail store kept by Richard

Denny, where the young clerk remained for a year. Feeling that Henry's capacities recommended him for a higher position, his step-father secured work for him in the office of the clerk of the High Court of Chancery, and here Clay remained for the next four years, until 1796. Though somewhat ungainly in appearance, he attracted attention by his open countenance and industry, and thereby recommended himself to Chancellor George Wythe, who made him his amanuensis to copy the court's decisions when not busied in the clerk's office. In his contact with Wythe, Clay secured good counsel and intelligent direction of the reading which he had begun in Denny's store. All his surroundings and his proclivities suggested to him the study of law. This he began in 1796 in the office of Attorney-General Robert Brooke, and within a year he secured his license to practise. During this time he lived in the home of the Attorney-General and had unusual opportunities to meet the people of prominence in the Virginia capital.

While his introduction to Richmond had been far more fortunate than he could have had reason to expect, he felt that conditions were settled there and competition too keen. The same lure that had drawn so many others to the new state of Kentucky also tempted him. Added to this was the fact that his mother was now living there, having left Virginia the year Kentucky became a state. In 1797 Clay moved to Lexington, the outstanding city of all the West in culture and influence. His reputation as an attorney-at-law was soon made and his clients became numerous. As a criminal lawyer, he came by common consent to have no equal in Kentucky. It has been repeatedly stated that no person was ever hanged in a trial where Clay appeared for the defense. He used every trick in argument and procedure in addition to his great skill as an orator. Infrequently he appeared as prosecutor for the state, once serving under protest for a short time as attorney for Fayette County, but by preference he usually acted for the defense. It was not long before the law became to him the means to a much more important end, the regulation of the political and constitutional relations of Kentucky. His first appearance in a political capacity was in 1798, when he followed George Nicholas in a denunciation of the sedition law before a great throng in Lexington. This speech, which was never forgotten by those who heard it, was a fitting introduction to his new constituents. In 1803, in a contest against Felix Grundy, he was elected to the legislature, where he continued until 1806. He had by this time become typically Western in his point of view, and when it seemed that the United States might at the last moment be cheated by Spain out of the prize of Louisiana, he became as greatly excited as any other Kentuckian over the possibility of marching on New Orleans.

In this new community, so little acquainted with the sanctity of law and of established usages, Clay generally took a conservative stand. In 1804 when a fight was made to repeal the charter of the Kentucky Insurance Company in which banking powers had been secured by a stratagem, he championed the cause of the corporation by arguing that a contract was involved and could not be broken except by the agreement of both parties; and in 1807 when the animosity against England was so bitter that the legislature was about to exclude from Kentucky courts the citation of English precedents, he was able to limit the application of the law to the period after July 4, 1776. While Clay was still completely identified with Kentucky affairs, Aaron Burr made his second visit to the West (1806) and came violently into conflict with Joseph Hamilton Daveiss, a Federalist and the federal district attorney for Kentucky. When Daveiss sought an indictment against Burr, Clay agreed to come to the defense of the latter, who appeared to be the object of persecution. Clay was also moved to take this course because he did not like Daveiss, with whom he had come near fighting a duel in 1803. Before the first hearing was held, Clay had been elected to the United States Senate to fill the unexpired term of John Adair and now felt that he should have double assurance of Burr's innocence in the form of a written statement. This Burr gave him. Later when, on going to Washington, he was persuaded by Jefferson of Burr's guilt, he felt that he had been tricked, and never afterward spoke to Burr. In the meantime, when Burr's associate, Harman Blennerhassett, came through Lexington and was proceeded against in a civil matter, Clay defended him. Although Clay's enemies later attempted to implicate him in the Burr schemes, he never suffered in the eyes of the people on account of these charges.

Clay spent the short session of 1806–07 in the United States Senate, where he appeared on the floor as a supporter of internal improvements. When he returned to Kentucky, it was with a pleasant feeling toward national politics. The importance which the legislature had attached to him in 1806 had by this time been increased; and when the next year Fayette County returned him to the legislature he was elected speaker. He remained in this body until he was reëlected in 1809 to fill out another unexpired term in the United States Senate. His interests were unmistakably becoming national; and when in 1809 he introduced in the Kentucky House a set of resolutions praising Jefferson's embargo measures and the general accomplishments of the President, Humphrey Marshall brought in a substitute set and started a debate which soon became acrimonious. Later, when Clay introduced a resolution in favor of home manufactures, Marshall's language became so obnoxious that Clay challenged him to a duel, which was fought in Indiana, across the river from Louisville. Both were wounded.

In 1809 Clay returned to Washington, never again to serve his state officially in any other than a national capacity, except in 1822 when he went to Richmond in company with George M. Bibb to secure an agreement with Virginia on the occupying claimants' law, and in the following year when again with Bibb he appeared for Kentucky before the Supreme Court in Washington in the case of *Green* vs. *Biddle* and lost. From the beginning he took an active part in the discussion in the Senate, here supporting some policies from which he never after swerved and others upon which he completely changed his views. He laid the beginnings of the foundations of his celebrated American system in 1810 when he spoke in favor of promoting home manufactures; also, following the instructions of the Kentucky legislature as well as carrying out his own views, he opposed the re-chartering of the United States Bank, charging it with being a money power dangerous to free institutions and holding it to be unconstitutional. These doctrines he later entirely abandoned. He made his first entry into matters of foreign policy when he upheld the Perdido River as the eastern boundary of the Louisiana Purchase. Much of his enthusiasm and inspiration in official life came from his feeling that he was a direct agent and defender of the people; hence it was only natural that in 1810 he should decide to exchange the Senate for the House of Representatives and should make the following announcement: "In presenting myself to your notice, I conform to sentiments I have invariably felt, in favor of the station of an immediate representative of the people" (*Lexington Gazette,* May 15, 1810). He was elected from the district of which Fayette County was a part, and which came to be known as the Ashland district, from the name of his home near Lexington. His strong nationalism was by this time unmistakable and was by no means incompatible with his equally strong advocacy of Western interests. He entered the Twelfth Congress as the leader of the young, unterrified "war hawks," determined to uphold the national honor against Great Britain whether on the high seas or west of the Alleghanies. He was elected speaker, and intrenched in this position he proceeded to prepare for war by appointing "war hawks" to prominent committees, urging President Madison on to a stern course, advocating military preparation, and arousing general enthusiasm with such flourishes as the assertion that the Kentucky militia alone could take Montreal and Upper Canada. He pushed Madison into war and stood valiantly behind him. When in 1814 it seemed that Great Britain might be willing to engage in peace parleys, Madison added Clay and then Gallatin to the commission composed of Adams, Russell, and Bayard, and the negotiations at Ghent were started. As Clay had had Western interests in mind in getting into war, he was not now going to forget them in getting out of the war, especially when it came to trading them for Eastern benefits. The conference almost collapsed when Adams insisted on giving England the free navigation of the Mississippi in exchange for the Newfoundland fisheries. Clay saved the Mississippi, won a certain secret contempt in the mind of Adams, and after visiting Paris and London, returned in 1815, convinced that the United States was now one of the powerful nations of the earth. He was reëlected to his position in Congress, which he had abandoned the year before, and was again made speaker, to both of which positions he was reëlected until 1821, resigning the latter in October 1820, and refusing to stand for election to the former after Mar. 4, 1821.

Unquestionably Clay had been greatly broadened by his European experiences, and his power and influence were much increased. Madison sought to reward him by offers of the Russian post and the secretaryship of war, both of which he refused, largely because he was now intent on consolidating his position of leadership in Congress. He hoped to receive the secretaryship of state from Monroe, who became president in 1817, but this had been reserved for Adams, who thereby became, according to the custom of the times, the designated successor to the presidency. Instead, Monroe successively offered Clay the ministry to England and the secretaryship of war, both of which he declined. He soon found easy means to become a critic of the national administration and with one exception maintained this rôle for the rest of his life. His position in Kentucky being now paramount, his confidence in himself and in his country awakened in him an ambition for the presidency which haunted him to his dying day, making of his life an unending series of disappointments. He developed and set forth a program of nationalism, including surveys for canals and highways and the building of them, the re-chartering of the United States Bank, protection for American industries, and a policy of national defense in keeping with the grandeur and glory of his country. The Bank was re-chartered and the protective principle was incorporated in the tariff of 1816, but Clay was never to see his program of internal improvements carried out.

His impetuosity soon precipitated him into conflicts with the President and various other prominent leaders. He incurred the most momentous and bitter enmity of his life when in 1819 he left the speaker's chair to attack Andrew Jackson for his invasion of Florida. Jackson never forgave him for his offense. Already critical of Monroe's administration and impelled by a sympathy for the South American revolutionists, Clay began in 1818 his campaign for the recognition of this independence, and by his eloquence and persistency made himself a hero in South America second only to Simon Bolivar. Not being a part of Monroe's administration, he was unconcerned with the effect his speeches were having on the Florida treaty which was then being negotiated with Spain, and when this document came up for ratification he attacked it for its failure to include Texas. His sympathy for the Greeks struggling against Turkey for their independence he strongly expressed in 1824, regardless of the fact that American interference in European affairs was incompatible with the position his country had taken in the recently announced Monroe Doctrine.

In the Missouri Compromise debate the dangers of a divided country first rudely shocked the nation, and propelled Clay into a new rôle, which he was to play thereafter. The essence of the struggle to him was not the extension or restriction of slavery, but the continuance of the Union of equal states. If Congress could lay restrictions on slavery in Missouri, its power might extend to any subject. Herein lay the fundamental danger to the Union. Through the compromise suggested by Senator Thomas, Clay saw the question practically settled, and in 1820 he returned to Kentucky to look after his private affairs, and to be absent from much of the session beginning in the fall. Trouble broke out anew when Missouri sought to exclude free Negroes from her boundaries. Clay hastened back to Washington in January 1821 and succeeded in pushing through the House a compromise plan, substantially the same as that which Senator Eaton had introduced in the Senate. He returned to Kentucky at the end of the session, in March 1821, not to reappear in Congress until he should come as an avowed candidate for the presidency. His private affairs in Kentucky engaged his attention for the next two years, during which time he enjoyed the almost universal acclaim of Kentuckians. In 1822 a joint meeting of the legislature nominated him for the presidency, and other states soon followed. He was also reëlected to Congress, where he served from 1823 to 1825, being again the choice of that body for speaker. He now set about consolidating a national program calculated to secure his election. It was during this period that he developed fully his American system of protective tariffs and internal improvements. The tariff bill of 1820 had failed, but in 1824 he secured the passage of the highest protective tariff enacted up to that time. In the presidential election of 1824 he received the smallest number of votes cast for any of the four candidates and was thereby eliminated by the Constitution from those to be voted upon by the House, which body chooses the president when no one receives a majority of the electoral college. Clay had carried Kentucky by an overwhelming vote against Jackson, his nearest competitor, who had received a plurality in the nation. Jackson had grievously wounded the feelings of Kentucky in 1815 when he had accused the Kentucky troops at New Orleans of cowardice, but even so he was much more attractive to Kentuckians than Adams, whose enmity shown at Ghent was well known. The legislature instructed Clay to vote for Jackson when the House should take up the election of the president, instructions which Clay ignored by voting for Adams and effecting his election. For this rebellious conduct Clay suffered his first eclipse in Kentucky, temporary though it was. Jackson and his friends were furious, charged Clay with making a bargain with Adams, and when Clay accepted the secretaryship of state were irretrievably convinced of his duplicity. Clay and his friends labored throughout the rest of their lives to disprove this slander, but it dogged his tracks in every subsequent campaign. When he returned to Kentucky he found considerable hostility, but the warmth of the welcome extended by his friends soon convinced him of the solidarity of his position. He bitterly attacked Jackson, and repeatedly asked how the winning of a military victory and the possession of an imperious and dictatorial spirit could possibly be a recommendation for the civil leadership of the nation. Yet many of Clay's friends could never shake off the feeling that the alliance with Adams was a most unnatural one.

As secretary of state, Clay was thoroughly loyal throughout to the Administration. He served the full term and perhaps never spent a more miserable and uninteresting four years in all his life. He was by nature opposed to the routine of administrative work, finding his chief delight in the excitement of debate and parliamentary maneuvers. Much of the time he was ill, and but for his loyalty would have resigned. No problems of great importance in foreign affairs arose, though he made a host of minor commercial treaties. The best-known incident of his incumbency was the Pan-American Congress, in which he sought to have the United States participate. The enemies of the Administration started an acrimonious debate in Congress over the instructions to the delegates, which delayed their departure so long that they arrived too late. Out of this controversy grew a harmless duel between Clay and John Randolph of Roanoke, precipitated by the cutting sarcasm of the latter.

In the election of 1828 Clay supported Adams, though he was unable to convince his own Kentucky of the New Englander's worth. Jackson carried the state and the nation, and Clay was temporarily disheartened when he saw the government handed over to a military chieftain. He refused to accept a position on the Supreme Court, and returned wearily over muddy roads to Kentucky, with his simple faith in the good sense of the people much shaken. The ardor of his reception, however, soon brought a return of the warm glow and enthusiasm that were characteristic of him. In company with his friend John J. Crittenden he toured western Kentucky, where he was received with unexpected acclaim. He also visited New Orleans twice within the next two years, his progress up and down the Mississippi reaching the proportions of a triumphal procession. Yet with all this manifestation of support, he was tempted to become a quiet country gentleman. At this time he wrote a friend, "My attachment to rural occupation every day acquires more strength, and if it continues to increase another year as it has the last, I shall be fully prepared to renounce forever the strifes of public life" (Calvin Colton, ed., *Private Correspondence of Henry Clay*, 1856, p. 261). But in 1830 the legislature again nominated him for the presidency and in order to place him in a more strategic position sent him to the Senate in 1831. Crittenden resigned to make a place for him. Clay now began to weld together all the elements of protest against Jackson and to develop his program. In the debate leading to the tariff of 1832 Clay restated at great length the protectionist argument. He presented to Jackson a bill which to his amazement the President signed. As another move in his campaign he decided that the Second United States Bank should be re-chartered. He pushed the bill through Congress, and Jackson vetoed it. Finally, he wished to settle the question of public lands and the problem of the surplus by distributing the proceeds of land sales among all the states according to population. The bill was finally passed (1833), but Jackson met it with a pocket veto, and at the beginning of the next Congress gave the reasons for his action. Clay then attacked Jackson from every angle and harassed him by leading the Senate to reject the President's nominations, the most conspicuous example being that of Van Buren as minister to London. Clay was nominated by the anti-Jackson men in Baltimore in December 1831, but in the election the next year he was disastrously defeated. The popular appeal of the vigorous Jackson and the activities of the anti-Masons combined to bring about his discomfiture. Again Clay almost despaired of the popular good sense, but he soon found a menacing problem that required his best thought and efforts. South Carolina had assumed a threatening attitude toward the tariff, and when the law of 1832 was passed, nullified it. Jackson's threats disturbed Clay almost as much as did Calhoun's nullification, for he feared lest Jackson should precipitate a civil war. He soon had ready the compromise tariff of 1833, which gradually reduced the rates. Substituting it for the administration bill, he secured its passage with the aid of Calhoun and his friends. Again he had effected a compromise in a menacing situation and perhaps saved the Union from disruption.

Throughout the rest of Jackson's official life Clay battled against him, as an overwhelming threat to the liberties of the people. For the purpose of curtailing Jackson's power, he advocated amendments to the Constitution which if adopted would have been of lasting harm to the country. When the President sought to hurry the destruction of the bank by the removal of the deposits, Clay in 1834 introduced and secured the passage of resolutions of censure. In January 1837, however, these were expunged from the record, an event which so unstrung Clay that he gloomily declared, "The Senate is no longer a place for a decent man." When Jackson's brusque language angered the French and came near precipitating war, Clay as chairman of the Committee on Foreign Relations in the Senate smoothed out the affair satisfactorily. In 1836, however, he felt that no one could stop the headlong course of the Jackson party, and looked upon the election of Van Buren as so inevitable that he did not offer himself to the Whigs as a candidate. He chose to remain in the Senate, to which the Kentucky legislature elected him for another term.

Following the panic of 1837, which soon burst upon the country, Van Buren brought forward the sub-treasury system to take the place of Jackson's "pet banks." Clay opposed the measure, here parting company with Calhoun, who supported it and rejoined the Democrats. Thereafter Clay and the South Carolinian engaged in many tilts on the floor of the Senate. Van Buren's administration

proved so unsatisfactory to the country that the Whigs felt certain of
victory in 1840 and Clay fully expected the nomination. But a new
schemer with new tricks now appeared prominently in American
politics. Thurlow Weed, by his astute maneuvers in the Whig convention at Harrisburg, threw the nomination to William Henry
Harrison, a questionable military hero thirty years removed from
his exploits and an incomparably less able leader than Clay. John
Tyler, a Democrat of the old school and an admirer of Clay, became
the vice-presidential candidate. Though Clay was enraged when he
learned of Weed's trickery he campaigned vigorously for the ticket.
The Whigs won and Clay rejected the offer of the secretaryship of
state in order better to assume the leadership of the new administration. He introduced in the Senate a set of resolutions which he
expected to be accepted as the party program, consisting of the repeal of the sub-treasury system, the re-chartering of the United
States Bank, the distribution among the states of the proceeds from
the public lands sales, and the passage of a new tariff. But when
Tyler succeeded to the presidency on the death of Harrison exactly
one month after assuming office, he soon showed the Whigs how
completely they had been cheated out of their victory. Clay, indeed,
succeeded in getting the sub-treasury system repealed, but when he
sought to have the United States Bank re-chartered he found Tyler
unsympathetic. He so amended his measure that he thought it
would secure the President's approval, and after putting it through
Congress was almost stupefied to see Tyler veto it. He had no better
success with the tariff, and in 1842 resigned his position in the
Senate, making on Mar. 31 a farewell address which created a profound effect on his auditors.

If Clay had revived the idea of retiring to Ashland and settling
down to the stock farming which he so much enjoyed, he was soon
dispossessed of the thought, for his reception in Kentucky was so
vigorous as to constitute a mandate for the presidency in 1844. Enthusiasm for him was equally marked throughout the rest of the
country. The year he retired from the Senate, two years before the
election, various states began to nominate him. He made a few trips
out of Kentucky, notably one to the states north of the Ohio. In
Dayton it was estimated that 100,000 people gathered to hear him.
Long before 1844 it was conceded that Clay would be the Whig
nominee, and it was no less an accepted fact in Clay's mind that
Van Buren would receive the Democratic nomination. When Van
Buren chanced to visit Ashland, the two prospective candidates

appear to have agreed to eliminate the question of Texas from the campaign. Accordingly, on the same day in the latter part of April, after Clay had made a trip through the lower South, both he and Van Buren issued statements opposing immediate annexation (for Clay's letter, see *Niles' Register*, LXVI, 152–53). A few days later Clay was nominated by acclamation in the Whig national convention. Van Buren, however, lost the Democratic nomination to Polk, as the Democrats were determined on expansion. The apparent enthusiasm of the country for annexation, and the widespread impression that he was favoring the abolitionists, led Clay to restate his position in what came to be called the "Alabama letters." In these he declared that slavery was not involved one way or the other in the Texas question, and that he would be glad to see Texas annexed, if it could be done "without dishonor, without war, with the common consent of the Union, and upon just and fair terms" (*Ibid.*, LXVI, 439). Owing to this ill-advised maneuver, Clay lost New York, and thereby the election, to Polk. "Never before or since has the defeat of any man in this country brought forth such an exhibition of heartfelt grief from the educated and respectable classes of society as did this defeat of Clay" (James Ford Rhodes, *History of the United States*, 1902, I, 84).

Polk's success brought annexation, at the hands of Tyler, and war with Mexico. Clay felt that the declaration of war was an outrage, yet after war was declared he supported it. His favorite son, Henry, was killed at Buena Vista. Much concerned over the ultimate outcome of the war, Clay made a speech in Lexington on Nov. 13, 1847, in which he called upon Congress to disclaim any intention of annexing Mexico and to announce the purposes of the war. During this period of retirement he made two trips to the East and was received with almost unbounded enthusiasm in New York, Philadelphia, and other cities. Again the clamor began to arise for his nomination in 1848. Convinced of support, he announced his candidacy in April 1848. But there were many Whigs who felt that he could not be elected, and some of these were in Kentucky. A Kentucky Whig wrote John J. Crittenden, Jan. 2, 1847, that "the Whig party cannot exist, or with any hope of success, so long as Mr. Clay continues his political aspirations" (Mrs. C. Coleman, *Life of John J. Crittenden*, 1871, I, 266). Crittenden's desertion brought to an end a long-standing friendship. Gen. Zachary Taylor was nominated, and Clay, disconsolate because he did not control even the Kentucky delegation, felt that the Whig party had destroyed itself by its own act. The folly of nominating a military hero who had no qualifications for civil leadership had been repeated. Clay definitely refused to take part in the campaign.

After Taylor's election, when the problems growing out of the war and the sectional struggle had nearly driven the country to disunion, he returned to the Senate (1849) in a last effort to ward off disaster. Spurning Taylor's weak course, he set forth in detail his plan for gradual emancipation in the Pindell letter of 1849 and introduced in the Senate his well-known series of resolutions. In the debate in the Senate he made his greatest and last effort to save the Union, begging the radicals, in both North and South, to abandon a course which could mean only disruption. He particularly warned the South against secession, declaring that no such right existed and that he would advocate force in opposing it. Clay hoped that the compromise measures would definitely settle the sectional struggle; but to make doubly sure he with forty-four other members of Congress signed a pledge to oppose for public office any one who did not accept the settlement. In the summer of 1851 he returned to Kentucky by way of Cuba, hoping the Southern climate would help a racking cough with which he was now afflicted, but he found no relief. In the fall he was back in Washington, determined, it seemed, to die in the service of his country. On the following June 29, death closed his career. His remains were taken to Lexington by way of Baltimore, Philadelphia, New York, Albany, Buffalo, Cleveland, and Cincinnati, amid national mourning. He was buried in the Lexington cemetery.

No man in American public life has had more ardent supporters or more bitter enemies than Clay, and no one has depended more for his happiness on the friendship of the people. His mastery of Kentucky's emotions and reason was complete and lasting on every public question except that of slavery. Kentucky absorbed his strong Unionism but refused to adopt his plan of emancipation. Clay obtained much pleasure from his Ashland home with its six hundred acres and fifty slaves; but however often he might resolve to abandon public life, the importunities of his friends and his love of debate changed his mind. When his home was in danger of being sold for his debts, unknown friends throughout the country raised $50,000 with which they settled his obligations. He was not by nature a religious man, though he joined the Episcopal Church in later life (1847). He fought duels, but he afterward came strongly to oppose that method of vindicating honor. In common with his contemporaries, he played cards, was fond of horse-racing, and liked good liquors, though he did not drink to excess. In appearance he was tall, with a high forehead, gray eyes, and a large mouth. His voice was engaging, and in debate he employed every movement of his body with grace and skill, even using his snuff box to great advantage. His personal magnetism was remarkable; he seemed never to be without a proper word or expression, and always seemed to be perfectly at ease. Enthusiasm and warmth characterized his speaking, getting the best of his reason at times and leading him into untenable positions. His knowledge was not characterized by the profundity of Webster's, nor did he have the philosophical powers of Calhoun or the acquaintance with the classics which Adams and Sumner possessed. But in his understanding of human nature, in his ability to appeal to the common reason, and in his absolute fearlessness in stating his convictions, he was unexcelled by any of his contemporaries. He was married in 1799 to Lucretia Hart, a daughter of Col. Thomas Hart of Henderson's Transylvania Company, by whom he had eleven children—six daughters and five sons. All his daughters and one son died before him. Another son became insane from an accident. Of the others, Thomas H. Clay was minister to Guatemala under Lincoln and died in 1871; James B. Clay was chargé d'affaires at Lisbon under an appointment from Taylor, was later elected to Congress, and died in 1863; and John M. Clay became a farmer and was the last surviving member of the family, dying in 1887.

[The letters and papers of Henry Clay are voluminous. Many of them have been scattered among his descendants, but the largest single collection is in the Lib. of Cong. Among his published letters and speeches are the following: Richard Chambers, ed., *Speeches of the Hon. Henry Clay, in the Cong. of the U. S.* (1842); Daniel Mallory, ed., *Life and Speeches of Henry Clay* (2 vols., 1843); Calvin Colton, ed., *Private Correspondence of Henry Clay* (1856); *Works of Henry Clay* (6 vols., 1856, repub., with additional matter, in 7 vols., 1896); and *Monument to the Memory of Henry Clay* (1857). The principal biographies of Clay are: Geo. D. Prentice, *Biog. of Henry Clay* (1831); Epes Sargent, *Life and Public Service of Henry Clay* (1842, repub. with additions, 1848); Calvin Colton, *Life and Times of Henry Clay* (2 vols., 1846); Calvin Colton, *The Last Seven Years of the Life of Henry Clay* (1856); Carl Schurz, *Henry Clay* (2 vols., 1887); Thos. H. Clay and E. P. Oberholtzer, *Henry Clay* (1910); Jos. M. Rogers, *The True Henry Clay* (1902). An estimate of Clay's service as speaker of the House of Representatives is in M. P. Follett,

The Speaker of the House of Representatives (1909), and H. B. Fuller, *Speakers of the House* (1909). The ancestry of Clay has been most fully set forth by Zachary F. Smith and Mrs. Mary Rogers Clay in *The Clay Family* (1899), being no. 14 of the Filson Club Publications.]

[SUPPLEMENTARY BIBLIOGRAPHY. The most recent biography of Clay is Clement Eaton, *Henry Clay and the Art of Am. Politics* (1957). Two additional biographies appeared in 1937: Glyndon G. Van Deusen, *The Life of Henry Clay*, and Bernard Mayo, *Henry Clay, Spokesman of the New West*. Two works in which the personality and career of Clay are assessed are: Gamaliel Bradford, *As God Made Them, Portraits of Some Nineteenth-Century Americans* (1929), and Holmes Moss Alexander, *The Famous Five* (1958). A special study is George Rawlings Poage, *Henry Clay and the Whig Party* (1936). A comprehensive collection of letters by and to Clay and of his speeches and public papers is in the process of publication under the title *The Papers of Henry Clay*, ed. by James F. Hopkins and Mary W. M. Hargreaves; of the projected ten volumes, two have appeared (1959, 1961). Besides the Clay papers in the Lib. of Cong., other depositories having more than 100 items are: Henry E. Huntington Lib. and Art Gallery; Ind. Univ. Lib.; Transylvania College Lib.; Buffalo Hist. Soc.; and N.-Y. Hist. Soc.]

John Caldwell Calhoun

by

ULRICH BONNELL PHILLIPS

CALHOUN, JOHN CALDWELL (Mar. 18, 1782–Mar. 31, 1850), was secretary of war, vice-president, senator, secretary of state, and political philosopher. Three Scotch-Irish brothers Colquhoun, Colhoun or Calhoun, in the unstable spelling of the time, entered Pennsylvania about 1733, and moved southward by stages. By 1746 one of them, James, was dwelling with Catherine his wife, four sons and a daughter in Bath County on the Virginia frontier. Driven thence by the Indian disorders after Braddock's defeat, this family and some of its kinsfolk founded the "Calhoun settlement" in the South Carolina uplands near the Savannah River. James appears to have died in peace, but Catherine was killed by a party of Cherokees in 1760 at a spot which her youngest son Patrick marked with a slab. The four sons clung to their steadings through foul times and fair, supporting the American cause against Great Britain and attaining considerable repute. Patrick in particular was for many years a member of the South Carolina legislature. As a pronounced individualist in political philosophy, he opposed the ratification of the Federal Constitution. Having lost a first wife without surviving issue, he married Martha Caldwell and by her had a daughter and four sons, of whom the youngest but one was named for an uncle whom Tories had murdered, John Caldwell.

After a normal childhood in a family prosperous enough to possess a score or two of slaves when slaves were few in that primitive region, the youth went in his fourteenth year to become a pupil of his brother-in-law, the talented Moses Waddel, in Columbia County, Ga. But Mrs. Waddel's death soon caused the academy to suspend, and young Calhoun returned home, where his father's death in the same year, 1796, cast some of the burdens of the farm upon him. Here he continued at work and at play till the turn of the century. Then an elder brother, who was in business at Charleston, prompted him to prepare for a profession. John returned for a time to Waddel's academy, then entered the junior class at Yale College, graduated in 1804, studied law in Tapping Reeve's school at Litchfield, Conn., and in Henry W. DeSaussure's office at Charleston, was admitted to the bar, and opened an office at Abbeville near his native home. Though quickly acquiring a substantial practice he found the pursuit uncongenial and resolved to abandon it as soon as opportunity should permit. This came within a few years through his marriage and his entrance into public life.

John Ewing Colhoun, cousin of Patrick, had attained wealth and distinction in the South Carolina lowlands, partly through his marriage to Floride Bonneau, who inherited from her Huguenot family a plantation on Cooper River. After her husband's death in 1802, the widow continued a practice, fairly common among grandees of the "rice coast," of spending the summers at Newport and the winters at Charleston or on the plantation. John C. Calhoun became a protégé of hers and an intimate of her household. Friendship with her daughter Floride, who was ten years his junior, ripened into love which led to a happy marriage in January 1811. His bride brought him a modest fortune, which, because of his objection to the lowland custom of marriage settlements, was put under his control. This property when added to his own patrimony and savings made Calhoun financially independent, though the increase of his family (nine children all told) kept a degree of frugality expedient. Calhoun enlarged his landholdings and in 1825 established a commodious plantation homestead in his native district. Later named "Fort Hill" from its having been a fortified spot in days of Indian warfare, the dwelling still stands on what is now the campus of Clemson College.

Calhoun's interest in public affairs doubtless began at his father's knee, and his Republicanism was intensified by his encounters with Federalists during his years at New Haven and Litchfield. His own political career began in 1807 with a speech at a public meeting in Abbeville denouncing British aggressions upon American maritime rights. In the next year he was elected to the South Carolina legislature, in time to share in the revision of representation to give numerical preponderance in the lower house to the uplands of the state while the control of the Senate was left with the lowlands. This device of "concurrent majorities" or mutual checks was one which he was eventually to propose for the relief of sectional apprehensions in the United States. But at the time of his election to Congress in 1810, and for long thereafter, his federal program had quite another direction.

Calhoun's service in national halls began with the convening of the Twelfth Congress which the "war hawks" were to make famous. Regardless of consequences in Europe and impatient of opposition from New England, these young men were resolute for war with Britain. Clay as speaker made the most effective use of the copious talent available in committee assignments, and Calhoun soon became acting chairman of the committee on foreign affairs. After months of labor to gain a favorable majority in the House, he presented on June 3, 1812, a report in ringing phrase recommending a declaration of war. Since James Monroe's authorship of this (*American Historical Review*, XIII, 309, 310) was kept secret, the episode spread Calhoun's fame afar.

As long as the war continued he wrought constantly to raise troops, to provide funds, to speed the service of supply, to improve the currency, to regulate commerce, to do everything in short which he thought conducive to military success. Disasters to American arms made him double his legislative efforts to wring victory from defeat. He was in the thick of every important debate, laboring to overcome the obstructionism of Randolph and Webster alike but occasionally separating himself from the bulk of his customary associates to find other allies wherever he might. A. J. Dallas called him, in happy phrase, "the young Hercules who carried the war on his shoulders."

Calhoun was sufficiently a supporter of the administration to indorse the treaty of Ghent; but its inconclusive character as concerned the issues which had provoked the war gave him an expectation that the peace would prove but a truce and left him with a continued zeal for promoting American strength. In a speech of Jan. 31, 1816, he advocated as the first consideration an effective navy, including steam frigates, and in the second place a standing army of adequate size; and as further preparation for emergency "great permanent roads," "a certain encouragement" to manufactures, and a system of internal taxation which would not be subject like customs duties to collapse by a war-time shrinkage of maritime trade (*Works*, II, 135–53). In the further course of the session he spoke for a national bank and again for internal improvements and protective tariff, deprecating sectional spirit and "refined arguments on the constitution" (*Works*, II, 191, 192), and asserting his own preference for "that erectness of mind which in all cases is disposed to embrace what is in itself just and wise." There can be no doubt that in this period Calhoun's early Republicanism in so far as it connoted allegiance to state rights was in eclipse. The word "nation" was often on his lips, and his conscious aim was to enhance national unity which he identified with national power.

Calhoun was at this time described as "the most elegant speaker that sits in the House. . . . His gestures are easy and graceful, his manner forcible, and language elegant; but above all, he confines himself closely to the subject, which he always understands, and enlightens everyone within hearing; having said all that a statesman should say, he is done" (letter of J. C. Jewett, in *William and Mary Quarterly*, XVII, 143). His talent for public speaking seems to have been acquired by systematic effort. A later critic, remarking the sharp contrast between his talking and speaking tones, said that Calhoun "had so carefully cultivated his naturally poor voice as to make his utterance clear, full, and distinct in speaking and while not at all musical it yet fell pleasantly on the ear" (H. S. Fulkerson, *Random Recollections of Early Days in Mississippi*, 1885, p. 63).

But his power in debate did not incline Calhoun to remain always in legislative halls. Before the end of his third term in Congress he accepted appointment as secretary of war in Monroe's cabinet. His conspicuous concern with military affairs made him an obvious choice for this post; and during the seven and a half years of his tenure he discharged its functions with marked capacity, improving the organization of the army in general and establishing in particular the useful bureaux of the surgeon-general, commissary-general of subsistence, and quartermaster-general.

In the cabinet Crawford and Calhoun were in habitual disagreement, but Adams and he were for some years in close accord. As late as the fall of 1821 Adams wrote in his diary: "Calhoun is a man of fair and candid mind, of honorable principles, of clear and quick understanding, of cool self-possession, of enlarged philosophical views, and of ardent patriotism. He is above all sectional and factious prejudices, more than any other statesman of this Union with whom I have ever acted" (Adams, *Memoirs*, V, 361). But with the Federalist party dead and Monroe reëlected for a final term in the presidency there now began a free-for-all race for the succession. Crawford was the candidate of the reviving state-rights school now styled Radicals; Adams and Clay, Lowndes and Calhoun became rivals for the leadership of the nationalists; while Jackson turned from military to civilian campaigning as the candidate of those who were more interested in popular power than with details of policy. The homes of these candidates lay in an arc reaching from Massachusetts through Kentucky and Tennessee to Georgia and South Carolina. The choice among them must needs lie with the states of the middle seaboard. Lowndes's death left Calhoun the favorite son of his state; Pennsylvania for a while gave promise of support because of his advocacy of tariff protection, and he had hopes also of New York and some lesser states. But the nominating convention in Pennsylvania gave its indorsement to Jackson for the first office and to Calhoun for the second. Thereupon Calhoun lowered his ambition for the time being and was elected vice-president in 1824 by a large majority. For the presidency Jackson had a plurality in the electoral college, but Clay's influence gave Adams the victory at the hands of the House of Representatives. Adams's appointment of Clay as secretary of state in sequel to this gave Jackson a mighty grudge, spurred Randolph to seek new epithets, and caused Calhoun to remark that it created a most dangerous precedent which the people would presumably reprove at the next election (*Correspondence*, p. 231).

In presiding over the Senate Calhoun was meticulous, attending assiduously but confining his participation within the positive specifications of the Constitution. His abstinence from interrupting Randolph's vituperations of Adams and Clay, except when a senator raised a point of order, involved him in a newspaper controversy in which the president himself was his putative opponent. Another episode of some salience arose from a journalist's charge that Calhoun while secretary of war had participated in the profits of a fortification contract. Calhoun asked the House of Representatives to investigate the matter as a "grand inquest of the nation," and he discontinued his attendance upon the Senate until a House committee had cleared him. Conspicuously cherishing his repute, he was shaping his course for the White House, though the Adams-Jackson battle clearly postponed the goal for him for another quadrennium. For the time being he chose the Jackson alliance and was elected in 1828 on the Jackson ticket for a second term as vice-president. His hope now was to succeed to the presidency after a single term of Jackson.

But the next four years brought events great and small which impinged heavily upon Calhoun's career and upon the course of

American history. Jackson's predilection for Van Buren whom he put at the head of the cabinet was itself ominous; and Eaton's appointment as secretary of war, followed by his indiscreet marriage and Mrs. Calhoun's exclusion of his wife from social recognition, brought a strain between the President and Vice-President. Close upon this came Crawford's betrayal of the fact that in Monroe's cabinet in 1818 Calhoun had censured the capture of Spanish posts by Jackson during his campaign against the Seminoles. Jackson's egotistic sense of outrage now produced a breach which Calhoun found irreparable.

Meanwhile developments in South Carolina, which for some years had followed an ominous course, were producing a national crisis. Successive measures in Congress enhancing and proposing further enhancement of protection to favored industries caused increasingly stringent opposition, coming as they did in a decade of declining cotton prices. By the middle of the twenties this opposition movement was spreading widely in the South and was becoming linked with a denial of the constitutional power of Congress in the premises. Calhoun was an object of censure in anti-tariff publications because of his formerly conspicuous and still unrecanted protectionism. He confronted a grave dilemma. If he held his course South Carolina would repudiate him, and if he changed it he would lose his following in Pennsylvania. But his personal fortunes, whether as a cotton planter or a presidential aspirant were of smaller concern than the national prospect. Early in 1827 he defeated the Woollens Bill by his casting vote in the Senate; and before the end of the year he was deprecating the project of a higher-tariff convention as tending to place the great geographical interests in hostile array, to promote political plundering, and eventually "to make two of one nation." He was now finding it "a great defect of our system; that the separate geographical interests are not sufficiently guarded." But these reflections were expressed only in a confidential letter (*Correspondence,* pp. 250, 251). At the beginning of the next year he joined in a jockeying project to divide the eastern and western groups of protectionists to the defeat of both; but the plan was thwarted by Van Buren and the result was the "tariff of abominations" (*Works,* III, 48–51).

During the congressional recess of 1828, which Calhoun spent as usual at his plantation home, he painstakingly informed himself of the South Carolina situation. He was already acquainted with the legislature's resolutions of 1825 and 1827 denying the constitutionality of protective tariffs and with the turbulent writings of Thomas

Cooper, R. J. Turnbull, and sundry others. Reading now the conviction that without mitigation of grievances desperate resources were in train, he complied with a request of W. C. Preston and wrote a report for a committee of the legislature. The result, modified by the committee, was the "South Carolina Exposition" (*Works*, VI, 1–57), embodying the doctrine which was to become famous as nullification. After asserting the unconstitutionality of the protective tariff and maintaining the power of a state within its own area to estop the enforcement of an unconstitutional act, the document concluded by recommending that decisive steps be deferred in the hope that reflection by the people and Congress might bring abandonment of the obnoxious policy. The legislature ordered the report printed in a large edition, and it adopted resolutions asking the sister states to express their sentiments in the premises. The Exposition was a warning of what might be done should the protectionist program be pursued. Its promulgation did not commit the state to a course of action; and in particular it committed Calhoun to nothing, for he kept his authorship confidential until the middle of 1831.

Having thus devised a plan for use in a contingency, Calhoun sought in various ways to prevent the contingency from coming. For a while he pinned his faith to Jackson; then he nursed a project for a complete intersectional accord. The West, by a constitutional amendment, was to be given a great public-land fund for internal improvements; the South was to procure a reduction of the tariff in the main to a revenue basis; but the North was to be placated by sundry special tariff concessions (*American Historical Review*, VI, 741–45, conversation reported by J. H. Hammond). But events proceeded otherwise. The systematically protective tariff of 1832 was enacted by Congress and approved by Jackson in July, whereupon Calhoun hastened home to guide proceedings there.

In August he published his famous letter to Gov. Hamilton (*Works*, VI, 144–93), containing the final embodiment of nullification doctrine. This is a superb piece of rigorous reasoning. Premising the possession of sovereignty by the people and the trustee character of all governments, and asserting that in the American federal system the central and state governments alike are mere organs of popular power, it argued, on the basis of the records of the Federal Convention, that "with us *the people* mean *the people of the several states*," whose delegates and conventions framed and ratified the Constitution creating the general government as their common agent. The ratification by any state bound all its citizens to obey the Constitution although some of them might individually have opposed it. The purpose of any constitution is at once to empower and to restrain the government; and if the general government should exceed its powers against the will of the people of a state it is within their legitimate power, by means of a convention though not by act of the legislature, to declare the congressional act null and to require the state government to prohibit enforcement within the limits of the state. "It is the constitution that annuls an unconstitutional act. Such an act is itself void and of no effect." Any court may proclaim such nullity, but the people of a state retain a similar power which no federal agency may override. Indeed, the general government in all its branches must acquiesce in such declaration of nullity, so far as enforcement within the state is concerned; or, as an escape, it may apply to the states to obtain a grant of the disputed power in the form of an amendment to the Constitution. But if the amendment should fail of ratification, "no alternative would remain for the general government but a compromise or its permanent abandonment." Nullification would give no ground for clash of arms; it would be "a conflict of moral, and not physical force," a trial before courts and juries. The rights of nullification and secession inhere in the sovereign states; but the two programs are poles apart in their purposes and effects. The object of secession is to withdraw a member from the Union; while the object of nullification is to confine the general government within its prescribed limits of power in order to perpetuate the Union on an equable basis. Nullification may indeed be followed by secession in case a proposed amendment should be ratified by the sister states to such effect as to defeat the object of the Union so far as the nullifying member is concerned. The power of nullification, it is true, tends to weaken the general government; but the power of amendment is an adequate offset. The two powers establish a system of mutual checks, in effect a system of government requiring agreement by concurrent majorities in critical issues, and as such it is in the line which genuinely free institutions have followed ever since the Tribunate in ancient Rome. Such a system, which inheres in the Federal Constitution as thus interpreted, maintains "the ascendency of the constitution-making authority over the law-making—the concurring over the absolute majority." It maintains a power, essential for liberty and the general welfare, "to compel the parts of society to be just to one another by compelling them to consult the interest of one another."

Affairs now marched rapidly. A legislature was elected in South

Carolina with an overwhelming majority favorable to nullification; this was called into special session and in turn it ordered the election of delegates to a convention of the state; the convention adopted an ordinance nullifying the tariff acts of 1828 and 1832; and the legislature thereupon enacted sundry laws to make the ordinance effective. Thus by the beginning of December 1832 the schedule was complete, though by its own terms the ordinance was not to take effect until the first day of February following.

December brought a battle of proclamations between President Jackson and the governor of South Carolina, and a mustering of military forces. But these things had somewhat of a sham character, for the concrete issue was the tariff, which could only be handled by Congress. In the Senate R. Y. Hayne had proved not letter-perfect in the nullification doctrine, and he was now shifted to the governor's chair to make room for Calhoun who resigned the vice-presidency and appeared on the floor of the Senate at the turn of the year. Jackson soon sent a message to Congress asking to be empowered in case of need to use armed force to execute the laws. A bill introduced in response, commonly known as the Force Bill, brought Calhoun into debate with Webster in which he opposed argument to eloquence with better effect than Hayne had done two years before. Meanwhile Calhoun joined hands with Clay in support of a tariff bill to reduce duties by degrees and put the customs on a revenue basis at the end of a decade. This bill, which repealed the tariff act of 1832, was passed and became law on the same day as the Force Bill.

In South Carolina an informal meeting of the leading nullifiers had postponed the effectuation of the ordinance, and Gov. Hayne had called a second meeting of the convention for Mar. 11, 1833. Calhoun hastened to Columbia to persuade the members to accept the compromise tariff as a settlement of the essential issue. B. W. Leigh as commissioner from Virginia to South Carolina aided these efforts; and the convention repealed the ordinance nullifying the tariff but adopted another nullifying the Force Bill. Thus every one saved his face. The result of the contretemps as a whole was in South Carolina the virtual destruction of Calhoun's opponents and an eclipse of his own lieutenants; in the United States an alignment of new parties with Calhoun holding himself and South Carolina somewhat aloof from both.

For some years the advocates of Clay's "American system" had maintained a rudimentary organization as National Republicans to oppose the administration. And now state-rights adherents in many

Southern states reacted so strongly against Jackson's proclamation and the Force Bill that they were disposed to embrace an alliance against the President. Hence the coalition in the middle thirties to form the Whig party opposing the Democratic. It was under this régime that the final phase of Calhoun's career took form. In sequel to the recent clash he retained his repugnance toward Jackson and his favorites. At the same time he distrusted Clay and held Webster in low esteem except for oratory, and he was not disposed to make a "choice of evils" (*Correspondence,* p. 330). He revived his presidential ambitions ere long and acted as an auxiliary of the Whigs. But no sooner was Jackson succeeded in the White House by the mild-mannered Van Buren than Calhoun began to shift to the Democratic side. In the Senate he was constantly attentive to the public business; and whatever were his views upon banking, public lands, or foreign relations, he voiced them in a manner which proved his concern with sound government for the whole country. The growth of his prestige gave him a following in all parts of the South and rehabilitated him in many Northern quarters. But the rise of the abolition agitation made impossible for him any return to nationalistic paths.

In the premises of Negro slavery the South was more conspicuously marked as a distinct community with a minority status than in regard to the tariff; and the menace of a hostile domination was reckoned to involve not mere shrinkage of income but destruction of capital and a precipitation of social chaos. Organization and strategy were widely demanded in Southern defense, and Calhoun came to be regarded as the main source of plans, arguments, and inspiration. His devices were manifold: to suppress agitation, to praise the slaveholding system; to promote Southern prosperity and expansion; to procure a Western alliance; to frame a fresh plan of government by concurrent majorities; to form a Southern bloc; to warn the North of the dangers of Southern desperation; to appeal for Northern magnanimity as indispensable for the saving of the Union. A devoted lieutenant, Dixon H. Lewis of Alabama, wrote in 1840: "Calhoun is now my principal associate, and he is too intellectual, too industrious, too intent in the struggle of politics to suit me except as an occasional companion. There is no relaxation in him. On the contrary, when I seek relaxation in him, he screws me only the higher in some sort of excitement" (Hunt, *Calhoun,* p. 228).

Was the conflict irrepressible? Calhoun feared it might prove so, but he hoped and labored unceasingly to find means for its avoidance. If he turned again and again to formulæ, that was the in-

grained bent of his mind. He could never consent to mere "muddling through."

Reluctantly he faced the slavery issue. In 1815 he had expressed
shame at the record of South Carolina in having caused the Constitution to forbid for twenty years any congressional prohibition of
the foreign slave trade (*Works*, II, 133). In 1820 the stringency of
debate on the Missouri question caused him to remark that he could
"scarcely conceive of a cause of sufficient power to divide this
Union, unless a belief in the slave-holding states, that it is the intention of the other states gradually to undermine their property in
their slaves and that a disunion is the only means to avert the evil.
Should so dangerous a mode of believing once take root, no one can
calculate the consequences" (Hunt, *Calhoun*, p. 54). In the next
year he expressed relief at the prospect "that a question which has
so deeply agitated this country will be settled forever" (*Correspondence*, p. 181). But Garrison's work revived his apprehensions and
set his feet upon their final path. At the close of his debate with
Webster in February 1833, he said that slavery might give the South
greater reason than the tariff to cherish state-rights.

Within the next two years the increase of anti-slavery activities
and a turbulent counter-agitation in the South determined him to
meet the issue "on the frontier"; and he became the most thorough-
going advocate of the exclusion of incendiary publications from the
mails and of anti-slavery petitions from Congress. His own devices
in these premises were too technical to procure much indorsement,
though the essential purposes were attained for the time being by
other means. There was virtually no Southern dissent from his
declaration in 1836 that abolition "strikes directly and fatally, not
only at our prosperity, but our existence as a people. . . . The door
must be closed against all interference on the part of the general
government in any form, whether in the District of Columbia, or in
the states or territories. The highest grounds are the safest" (*Niles'
Weekly Register*, L, 432).

By the next year he had followed Governors Miller and McDuffie
of South Carolina and the Rev. James Smylie of Mississippi toward
asserting that slavery was a positive good: "Our fate, as a people,
is bound up in the question. If we yield we will be extirpated; but if
we successfully resist, we will be the greatest and most flourishing
people of modern time. It is the best substratum of population in
the world; and one on which great and flourishing Commonwealths
may be most easily and safely reared" (*Correspondence*, p. 369; see
also *Works*, III, 179, 180). And by 1838 he was even contemplating

a separation of the Union, though resolved still to labor for less drastic programs (*Correspondence,* p. 391).

The issue, ramifying endlessly, involved the mathematics of equilibrium in the Senate, the admission of new states, the organization of territories as prospective states, and the cherishing of sectional prestige for the sake of morale. In premises which he considered unessential Calhoun deprecated controversy. Thus he suppressed a movement in South Carolina to nullify the tariff of 1842; and on sundry other matters he was conciliatory in this period when his hopes were high for the presidency through a Democratic nomination. But in the main, and upon every issue which he thought vital, he was disposed to force the fighting, to lead a campaign of aggressive defense of "Southern rights."

He had spoken in favor of the annexation of Texas immediately after the battle of San Jacinto in 1836. But his assertions from the outset that the slaveholding states had a special interest in the question operated rather to delay than to speed the achievement. At length A. P. Upshur, secretary of state under Tyler, negotiated a treaty; and upon Upshur's death a maneuver by H. A. Wise carried Calhoun into that office to complete the proceedings. In the department Calhoun found a note from Mr. Pakenham communicating a dispatch from Lord Aberdeen to the effect that the British government desired to see slavery abolished in Texas and throughout the world, but that it had no purpose to disturb the domestic tranquillity of the slaveholding states of the Union. Calhoun seized the occasion to write and publish a reply to Pakenham saying that abolition in Texas would necessarily impinge upon the domestic security of the states adjacent, and proceeding to praise Negro slavery in terms even stronger than he had previously used (*Works,* II, 333–39). This again was bad strategy. The treaty was defeated in the Senate by anti-slavery votes; and only after months of further delay was annexation accomplished by joint resolution of Congress.

Where Calhoun sat in cabinet, there was the head of the table. In this Tyler acquiesced; but Polk, wishing to be chief of his own administration, did not invite Calhoun to continue in office. Most of the year 1845 was accordingly spent by the latter in private life, though not without participation in public projects. He had long desired to see a system of railroads linking the West with the South, preferably a connection from Charleston across Georgia as against Hayne's plan of piercing the Blue Ridge in a line to Cincinnati. As a culmination of similar meetings, a large railroad and waterway convention was held at Memphis in November which Calhoun was persuaded to attend as a delegate from South Carolina. After a journey signalized by thronged public entertainment at every stopping-place, he was chosen to preside over the sessions. The address he delivered urged his railroad program and in addition argued that Congress had constitutional power to improve the navigation of the Mississippi because the Father of Waters, washing the shores of many states, was virtually an inland sea. The splitting of a logical hair seemed expedient in behalf of the desired alliance of sections.

This interlude was abbreviated by a summons once more into the public service. With war clouds lowering on two horizons, Calhoun was urgently needed in the national councils. D. E. Huger willingly resigned his seat in the Senate, and the legislature elected Calhoun unanimously to fill the vacancy. Arrived in Washington, his positions on the Oregon and Texas boundary questions proved much alike, for he advocated conciliation toward both Great Britain and Mexico. The Oregon issue resulted as he wished; but to his dismay and against his vehement opposition, the war with Mexico was precipitated.

Wilmot's proposal to prohibit slavery in all areas to be acquired by this war set Calhoun to spinning his last fine theory and involved him in the most desperate of his struggles. Aware as he was that the region was unsuited to plantation industry and slave labor (*The Diary of James K. Polk,* 1910, II, 283–84), he took the Proviso to be a gratuitous affront to the South, an index of aggressive disposition by Northern Democrats, and a culminating ground of Southern apprehension. To make state sovereignty applicable he framed a new series of syllogisms: that all territories were an estate owned by the states in common, to be administered by the central government only as a trustee for them; that any citizen of any state had full right to emigrate to any territory, carrying with him whatever property he possessed in his own state, and was entitled to Federal protection in the enjoyment of that property in his new home until the community should itself become a state. Therefore, whether his migration be to California, New Mexico, or Oregon, no slaveholder could be debarred from the transport and continued use of his slaves (*Works,* IV, 344–49). In short, notwithstanding the precedents of the ordinance of 1787 and the Missouri Compromise act, which he now considered erroneous, Congress was estopped from restricting the spread of slaveholding. He was perhaps willing to be outvoted in the organization of Oregon if he could carry his point as concerned the more southerly regions; but a sense that this hope was forlorn drove him to two devices which he had held somewhat in reserve. For permanent purposes he sped his pen to complete his treatises on government in general and the Federal Constitution in particular; and to meet the present exigency he strove to rouse and organize the South with a view to its issue of an ultimatum.

His treatises, destined to have only a posthumous publication, embodied his final philosophy. In the "Disquisition on Government" (*Works*, I, 1–107) he declares that society is essential to mankind, and government necessary to preserve and perfect society by curbing individual selfishness. But government itself must be held in check by constitutions in order that public agents may be prevented from abusing their power whether by self-aggrandizement or by promoting majority interests through the spoliation of minorities. The problem here, he said, is extremely difficult. No plan devised abstractly can suffice, but a satisfactory system can arise only as the product of an intelligent community seeking in the light of experience to meet its own conscious needs. On the one hand authority must be adequate to meet external emergencies by summoning the whole strength of the community. In domestic affairs, on the other hand, apparatus must be available by which minorities may compel majorities to compromise issues between them. That the two requirements are not mutually exclusive is shown by the common success of the jury system in forcing unanimous verdicts and by the long duration of the Polish Kingdom despite the possession of a veto by every member of its Diet. Far better designed, however, and therefore more lasting, were the constitutions of ancient Rome and modern England embodying less extreme examples of automatic check upon authority. The elements of aristocracy and monarchy embodied in them were wholesome in correcting the tendency of numerical majorities to tyrannize; but such elements are not indispensable, for a democracy may combine equity with efficiency if it avoid the "great and dangerous error" of considering all people equally entitled to liberty and if at the same time it maintain government by concurrent majorities and avoid the demagogic tendency and the despotic proclivities inherent in control by mere numbers.

In the "Discourse on the Constitution and Government of the United States" these lessons are given specific application, but in a tone of argument rather than of exposition. With elaborate citation of eighteenth-century records he contends that the American system is in no sense national, but purely federal. The people of the several states ordained alike their separate state governments and the general government. "Deriving their respective powers . . . from the same source, . . . the two governments, State and Federal, must, of necessity be equal in their respective spheres" (*Works*, I, 167). Sovereignty, which is indivisible, remains in the people of the several states; but the exercise of "the powers of sovereignty" may be distributed and has actually been divided between the two agencies. To make it efficient, the central government was clothed with the attribute of deciding, in the first instance, on the extent of its power (*Works*, I, 168); but the people of any state may challenge any assumption of undelegated authority in order to preserve the equilibrium of the complex system. The sectionalizing of interests or policies in the Union has made it imperative upon the South as the minority to oppose the concentration of despotic force. Calhoun's contentions of 1832, though he repeats them, now seem to him inefficacious in view of the progress of unconstitutional centralization in the interim. He, therefore, concludes that the domestic tranquillity of the South can be secured and the Union perpetuated only by a new device. To this end he advocates an amendment to the Constitution to replace the single president by a dual executive, each of the two chief magistrates to be chosen by one of the great sections of the country, and the assent of both to be requisite for the validation of acts of Congress (*Works*, I, 392–95).

These writings had influence upon political thought and projects not only at home but in the German Confederation (C. E. Merriam in *Studies in Southern History and Politics*, 1914, p. 336). The North in one case and Prussia in the other were quite unconvinced; but Lord Acton echoed Calhoun by saying that liberty can only be safeguarded by a multiplicity of checks—and the conversion of the British Empire into a "commonwealth of nations" has given practical embodiment to the precepts of decentralization.

But the current crisis could not be solved by a dissertation even if it had been ready for the press. Convinced as he was that the existing political parties were so constituted that the control of both must lie in the North and be used for Southern injury, Calhoun summoned a meeting, in January 1849, of the Southern senators and congressmen to consider an address which he had written for their adoption. This reviewed the history of the slavery issue, foretold disaster from the continuance of the existing scheme of politics, and called for unity in holding Southern rights paramount over party allegiance. The prophecy in this document was amazingly corroborated within two decades; abolition by a dominant North against Southern resistance; hatred between the whites of the two sections; enfranchisement of the Negroes and a party union between them and the North to hold the Southern whites in subjection; a carnival of profligacy and a bottomless degradation (*Works,* VI, 310–11). But most of the members attending were unconvinced, and a mere minority signed the address for issue to their constituents. Calhoun next turned to local committees and newspaper agitation to procure a call from some commonwealth for a convention of the slaveholding states, and was rejoiced when Mississippi responded and the convention was scheduled to meet at Nashville (*Correspondence,* pp. 765–79).

Before the end of the year an irregular convention in California applied for statehood with a constitution excluding slavery. This met Calhoun's trenchant opposition on the grounds that the proceedings had not been authorized by an enabling act, and that their validation would at once and forever destroy the Senate equilibrium. Nearing the allotted span of three score and ten, his life was drawing to a close in baffled zeal and unrelaxed strain. His tall frame emaciated by half a decade of intermittent illness, his voice failing but his piercing eyes undimmed, he tottered from his lodgings to the Senate chamber day by day to save the Union if it might be saved upon a basis of comity and to preach Southern resistance to the point of independence if that should prove essential for social security.

The California demand, which put his territorial theorizing to scorn, was clearly not to be denied nor long delayed in its granting. A crisis was at hand, and the South, or its lower half at least, was at length girding its loins. Demonstrations became too vigorous to be longer disregarded. Clay framed the celebrated Omnibus Bill to settle the many pending issues on a give-and-take basis. Calhoun approved the purpose but criticized the text as failing to provide adequate guarantees for the South. To express these views he wrote his last formal speech, which was read to the Senate on Mar. 4, 1850, by Senator Mason while its author sat voiceless in his chair. A few days later he expressed praise of Webster's great speech of Mar. 7, but still thought it "difficult to see how two peoples so different and hostile can exist together in one common Union" (*Correspondence,* p. 784). At the end of this, one of his last letters, he wrote: "Kiss the children for their grandfather"; but virtually his last spoken words were "The South, the poor South." Fading out of life, he died at the end of the month. His body was carried in state to Charleston and interred with an outpouring praise and lamentation, for he was first in the hearts of his Carolina countrymen. His course was run, but his work was to have a mighty sequel.

———

[To promote his presidential prospects, there was published in 1843 a volume of Calhoun's *Speeches,* including sundry public papers; and simultaneously a *Life of John C. Calhoun.* The latter, unusually substantial for a campaign biography, was currently attributed to R. M. T. Hunter, but latterly Calhoun himself has been proved to have been its principal author (*Am. Hist. Rev.,* XIII, 310–13). Just after Calhoun's death R. K. Crallé edited his *Works* (1851–57), including the "Disquisition on Government" and the unfinished "Discourse on the Constitution" in the first volume, the speeches in the next three, and reports and public papers in the fifth and sixth. In 1857 was published *The Carolina Tribute to Calhoun,* J. P. Thomas, ed., containing the record of obsequies along with the text of many eulogies; and in 1888 *A Hist. of the Calhoun Monument* at Charleston, S. C., with its chief item the notable commemorative address by L. Q. C. Lamar. Biographies have been written by John S. Jenkins (1851), a perfunctory product; Hermann von Holst (1882), censorious and homiletic; Gustavus M. Pinckney (1903), eulogistic; Gaillard Hunt (1908), discriminatingly sympathetic; and William M. Meigs (2 vols., 1917), elaborate and painstaking. A stout volume of Calhoun's correspondence, J. F. Jameson, ed., has been published in the *Ann. Report of the Am. Hist. Asso. for the Year 1899,* vol. II, being *House Doc. No. 733,* 56 Cong., 1 Sess.]

[SUPPLEMENTARY BIBLIOGRAPHY. The Jameson edition of Calhoun's letters was supplemented in 1930 by Chauncey S. Boucher and Robert P. Brooks, ed., *Correspondence Addressed to John C. Calhoun, 1837–1849.* These and other earlier collections will eventually be superseded by *The Papers of John C. Calhoun,* now in process under the editorship of W. Edwin Hemphill; the first volume (ed. by Robert L. Meriwether) appeared in 1959, the second in 1963. For selected writings of Calhoun see *Basic Documents* (1952), ed. by J. M. Anderson. Recent biographies include the full-scale *John C. Calhoun* by Charles M. Wiltse (3 vols., 1944–51); Margaret L. Coit, *John C. Calhoun, Am. Portrait* (1950); Arthur Styron, *The Cast-iron Man: John C. Calhoun and Am. Democracy* (1935); and Gerald M. Capers, *John C. Calhoun, Opportunist: A Reappraisal* (1960). For recent treatments of Calhoun as political philosopher see August O. Spain, *The Political Theory of John C. Calhoun* (1951); Richard N. Current, "John C. Calhoun, Philosopher of Reaction," *Antioch Rev.,* Summer 1943; and Richard Hofstadter, "John C. Calhoun: The Marx of the Master Class," in *The Am. Political Tradition* (1948).]

Jefferson Davis

by

NATHANIEL WRIGHT STEPHENSON

DAVIS, JEFFERSON (June 3, 1808–Dec. 6, 1889), president of the Confederate States of America, was born in Christian (now Todd) County, Ky., the tenth child of Samuel and Jane (Cook) Davis, who had moved westward from Georgia. Samuel Davis commanded a troop of irregular horse in the Revolutionary War. His father, Evan Davis, was a Welsh emigrant who had entered America through Philadelphia and had followed the drift of emigration southward into the new lands of Georgia. In Kentucky the Davis family do not appear to have thriven. When Jefferson was a mere child they wandered on to Mississippi, where they found their anchorage on a small plantation near Woodville, Wilkinson County. Though Samuel Davis does not appear to have done much by way of lifting his middle-class family in the social scale, that result was achieved by his eldest son, Joseph Emory Davis, who rapidly acquired a fortune, an education, and a prominent position in the new community of the Southwest. While Samuel Davis lapses into the background of the picture, Joseph becomes the real head of the family and the patron of his younger brother, many years his junior. Eventually Joseph Davis was considered one of the wealthiest men in the South.

Jefferson Davis was an extremely sensitive, a highly imaginative child and boy. At the age of seven he rode northward nearly a thousand miles to become a pupil of the Roman Catholic seminary, St. Thomas's College, in Washington County, Ky. What induced his

Baptist parents to place him there is not known. They very nearly had a reward that doubtless would have appalled them. The impressionable lad became so fond of the priests who were his teachers that he wished for a time to adopt their religion (Davis, *Memoir, post,* I, 13–14). The incident in its fullness has a reminder of Henry Esmond and Father Holt. Indeed, one may find a sort of clue to Davis, to his strength and his weakness, his loftiness, his sensibility, his egoism and his illusions, in Thackeray's famous character. Nothing came of the juvenile Roman enthusiasm, and at nine he was back in Mississippi. After several years in local schools he was entered at Transylvania University, in 1821. Very little is known of his college life. The early records of Transylvania have been destroyed and the traditions are few. Davis himself has said, "There I completed my studies in Greek and Latin, and learned a little of algebra, geometry, trigonometry, surveying, profane and sacred history, and natural philosophy" (*Memoir,* I, 27). He did not finish the course at Transylvania. A Mississippi congressman nominated him to West Point. It is safe to attribute this to the growing influence, social and political, of his brother Joseph. On Sept. 1, 1824, Jefferson Davis matriculated at West Point. In 1828 he was graduated and became a second lieutenant in the United States army. Among the other distinguished Southerners who were cadets when he was, and who were destined to have fateful relations with him in after time, were both the Johnstons and Robert E. Lee. Of the youth of Davis, anecdote has preserved a good deal, and if most of it may be trusted, we may think of him as a very engaging young man, fearless, generous, modest, with personal charm, and in friendship rashly loyal.

His military apprenticeship of nearly seven years was spent in Wisconsin and in the unsettled portions of Illinois, in little, remote posts, garrisoned by mere handfuls of men, in as lonely regions as the world possessed. The Black Hawk Indian war in 1832 was like a brief interlude of relieving storm that blew across this dreary period. Nobody did anything distinguished in that war. But both Jefferson Davis, as a minor officer of the regular army, and Abraham Lincoln, as an inconspicuous officer of volunteers, took part in it. They did not meet. In 1833 Lieutenant Davis was stationed much of the time at Fort Crawford, Wis., where the commandant was Col. Zachary Taylor. He had a daughter, Sarah Knox. The young people fell in love. Colonel Taylor disapproved. But they would have their way. Davis resigned June 30, 1835; Miss Taylor sought a friendly aunt in Kentucky; Davis followed; they were speedily married and set out for Mississippi.

During the next ten years, 1835–45, from the age of twenty-seven to the age of thirty-seven, Davis was a planter, absorbing the mental atmosphere of the distinctive new state, which had been peopled by emigrants from so many regions and where his family was now entering the upper rank. The outward story of these years was lacking in drama except for one event. His early romance closed suddenly, tragically within three months of his marriage. Mrs. Davis died of malarial fever Sept. 15, 1835. Except for a little travel in Cuba while convalescing from the same malady that had killed his wife, followed by a brief visit to New York and Washington, where he made a short sojourn among important politicians at a senatorial boarding-house, the remainder of the ten years was spent quietly on his plantation or at nearby cities. The period closed with two events which took place close together, his election to the national House of Representatives and his second marriage. Varina Howell, who on Feb. 26, 1845, became the second Mrs. Davis, was a local beauty, a member of the upmost social rank, a high-spirited and accomplished woman. This marriage identified him conclusively with the local aristocracy.

It was during these long, quiet years as a country gentleman that Davis's mind was formed politically. His father, who had died several years before, had bequeathed him a little money. His brother Joseph added to it. Not far from Joseph's plantation, "Hurricane," the plantation "Brierfield" became the seat of the younger brother. It was rough new land overlooking the Mississippi. Much of it was "cleared" for the first time by its new owner. He was a hard worker, taking the most intense interest in his estate, and often sharing field work with his slaves. Nevertheless, he now became an extensive, even omnivorous, reader, especially in the fields of politics and history. Joseph was also a natural student. He had been bred to the law and never lost his delight in close argument. Frequently the brothers would spend the night at the same plantation and there would be long evenings of discussion of books and politics. Hitherto the younger Davis had lived since childhood away from home; he had been a student or a soldier in distant lands; he had lacked the sense of soil. This he now acquired. He was permeated by that peculiar atmosphere which belonged to the Mississippi environment. Like those others whom it had drawn to itself from such great distances, he became devoted to its social system.

The quietude of life at Brierfield in the late thirties was a sharp contrast with the stormy life of the nation at large. The Abolitionists had begun their crusade. The country rang with their denunciation of the Southern social system. As was often pointed out, they made no distinction between slavery and slaveholders, cursing both in the same breath. The relation of Davis to his slaves was peculiarly gentle and patriarchal. He resented bitterly the Abolitionist attack, and, like practically all the members of the planter class, met it with state-rights arguments. These were destined to be turned against him when he was chief executive of the Confederacy.

It is more than likely that a temperamental influence throughout these quiet years was his deep-seated love of the army and of the military life. He had renounced it for sentimental reasons; he was destined to renounce it twice again for other reasons; but he never lost his zeal for it. Nor did he ever lose his faith in himself as a soldier. A rooted egoism was thus revealed. Though he never did anything of first importance in a military way, he was capable, in the heat of the Civil War, of regarding himself as the equal of the greatest generals of the time. Another quality of his mind, his lack of humor, was brought out eventually by this invincible delusion. Mrs. Davis, with Olympian indiscretion, has preserved one of the most unfortunate of the slips in speech that have been made by men of genius. In the darkest hour of the Confederacy, Davis said to his wife, "If I could take one wing and Lee the other, I think we could between us wrest a victory from those people" (*Memoir*, II, 392).

This extraordinary self-confidence rested on nothing but a brief, creditable service in the year 1846, and on one very gallant action in the year 1847. He had gone to Congress as a Democrat in December 1845; the outbreak of the Mexican War was the cause of his resignation the following June. He accepted command of a volunteer regiment known as the "Mississippi Rifles," swiftly whipped it into shape, and joined General Taylor in time to participate in the attack upon Monterey. What had passed between himself and his former father-in-law since the death of his first wife is not known, but apparently they were again friends. Taylor appointed him one of the commissioners to negotiate the surrender of Monterey. The next year, in the strangely jumbled battle at Buena Vista, Davis won his reputation as a soldier. Very probably the stand made by the Mississippi Rifles at a crucial moment saved Taylor from defeat. The action was praised extravagantly, far and wide. There came a time when the effect of its applause upon Davis's mind formed the basis of sneers. Long afterward, a Confederate newspaper, bitter against Davis's military policy, alluded to the form in which he disposed his men at Buena Vista, and said "If the Confederacy perishes, it will have died of a V."

The course of the authorities at Washington caused Davis's second renunciation of the military life. Taylor was side-tracked in favor of Scott, and the Mississippi Rifles were left with the minor force that plainly was to have no more chances. The "Rifles" had enlisted for a short period. At its expiration in the summer of 1847 Davis withdrew from the army. Mississippi made him a national senator. He took his seat in December 1847. He was a conspicuous figure; in the popular eye, he was a "hero" of Buena Vista. But popular heroes are not always the heroes of the Senate. His first period as a senator, closing with his resignation in the autumn of 1851, lasted nearly three years, and while it gave him for the first time a national reputation politically, it ended without his having attained a commanding position in his party. In 1848 he steadily supported President Polk and opposed Calhoun, approving the great seizure of Mexican territory on which the President had set his heart. He went so far as to advocate the occupation of Yucatan by the United States, expressing the fear that otherwise it might be taken by Great Britain (*Congressional Globe,* 30 Cong., 1 Sess., p. 729, May 5, 1848). When it was proposed to organize the territory of Oregon without provision for slavery he "denied that there was any power in Congress or in the people of the Territory to interrupt the slave system" by forbidding a slaveholder to take his slaves thither (*Ibid.,* 30 Cong., 1 Sess., p. 927, July 12, 1848). In the debate over the admission of California he reiterated this position but was willing to compromise on the extension of the line of the Missouri Compromise to the Pacific (*Ibid.,* 31 Cong., 1 Sess., App., p. 286, Mar. 8, 1850). He was one of ten senators who opposed to the last the admission of California and who signed a "Protest against the California Bill."

In his course with regard to California, Davis was opposed by his colleague from Mississippi, Senator Henry S. Foote, a politician of great boldness. Though the legislature of Mississippi passed resolutions instructing their senators to resist the admission of California "by all honorable and constitutional means," Foote refused to be bound by them. It turned out that he had gauged the conditions at home with deep shrewdness. He was nominated for governor on a "Union" ticket, supported by Whigs and dissatisfied

Democrats, and in September 1851 seemed about to carry the election. The political situation in the South in 1851 was extremely complex and Davis's relation to it is not altogether clear. The struggle against the admission of California and the failure to extend the Missouri Compromise line had produced a general movement for secession. A convention of the whole South which held two meetings at Nashville, one in June 1850, the other in November, had secession in view. The desire to secede was practically universal, but there were two policies on the subject. Extreme state-rights men such as R. B. Rhett of South Carolina and W. L. Yancey of Alabama wanted their states to rush ahead irrespective of what other states might do. The course followed by another group revealed a point of view that may be labeled Southern nationalism. Between the first and second meetings of the Nashville convention these others concluded that it was impossible to effect an immediate secession of the whole South. Thereupon they threw themselves into an attempt to arrest the secession movement, to postpone it until the whole South could be persuaded to leave the Union together. Rhett, who refused to accept this view, was eventually defeated in a popular campaign, on the issue of secession, by the South Carolina "co-operationists."

A third Southern part was for accepting the compromise measures of 1850 as the start of a satisfactory new chapter in the history of the Union. With this group Foote was associated. His opponent was Gov. John A. Quitman, who was in Mississippi pretty much what Rhett was in South Carolina. By September 1851 it was plain that the tide had turned. The genuine Unionists and the "co-operationists" between them were going to prevent an immediate movement for secession. The Democratic leaders in Mississippi appear to have concluded that the game was up. They looked around for a way out. Quitman was persuaded to resign; Davis was persuaded to leave the Senate and take his place. Though there is no positive evidence upon his motives, a safe guess would fix upon two. He was instinctively a party man; all his military predisposition, his *esprit de corps,* tended that way. The desire to save the party, to perform a strategic retreat with as much credit as possible, must have influenced him. But it is fair to assume a deeper motive. In him, even more thoroughly than in the anti-Rhett men of South Carolina, the vision of the South as a nation was a real thing. We may conclude that Davis took the place of the secessionist Quitman with a view to relieving his party of its hasty commitment to immediate secession and for the purpose of aligning it, tacitly at least, with "cooperation." His strategic retreat was a success. A vote for a convention that was to decide the issue of secession or "submission" had given Foote a majority of 8,000, but when the vote was cast for governor, his majority was less than 1,000.

Davis resumed his life as a planter, only to reënter politics on Mar. 7, 1853, when he became secretary of war in the cabinet of his friend Franklin Pierce. His tenure of the war office was perhaps the peak of his career; certainly no chapter of his life was more to his taste. His health, which both before and after was delicate, was during most of this period robust. The Davises were the center of a delightful coterie in Washington; Mrs. Davis, witty and charming, drew all sorts of people into her drawing-room. Despite political differences, men as unlike her husband as Seward were his close personal friends. The most brilliant portrait of him is contained in a passage from Carl Schurz: "I had in my imagination formed a high idea of what a grand personage the War Minister of this great Republic must be. I was not disappointed. He received me graciously. His slender, tall, and erect figure, his spare face, keen eyes, and fine forehead, not broad, but high and well-shaped, presented the well-known strong American type. There was in his bearing a dignity which seemed entirely natural and unaffected—that kind of dignity which does not invite familiar approach, but will not render one uneasy by lofty assumption. His courtesy was without any condescending air. . . . His conversation ran in easy . . . well-chosen and sometimes even elegant phrase, and the timbre of his voice had something peculiarly agreeable. . . . I heard him deliver a speech in the Senate, and again I was struck by the dignity of his bearing, the grace of his diction, and the rare charm of his voice—things which greatly distinguished him from many of his colleagues" (*The Reminiscences of Carl Schurz*, II, 1907, p. 21).

Apparently, the idea of secession was allowed to lapse in Davis's mind during several years. But the idea of the South as a social and economic unit, a nation within the Union, was constant. His policies were governed by the steadfast hope of so enlarging the South territorially and of so developing it economically that it would prove the equal in political power of the opposite section. Consequently he was eager for expansion southward, and was frequently in opposition to the secretary of state, William L. Marcy, whose eyes were on the Northern, not the Southern, wing of the party. In their general attitudes toward Spain and Mexico, Davis may be described as belligerent, Marcy as conciliatory. In the case of the ship *Black Warrior*, seized by the Spanish authorities at Havana on a legal technicality, and in connection with the Ostend Manifesto, issued by three American ambassadors as a statement of our Spanish policy, Davis failed to control the foreign policy of the administration. With all the more zeal he turned to the advancement of Southern economic interests at home. Asia had become of first importance in the minds of most Americans who thought about trade. To obtain a window upon the Pacific was a great part of the inspiration of the Southern nationalists in 1850. Davis, still hoping for Southern expansion to the Pacific, took the liveliest interest in promoting a great scheme for a transcontinental railway that should be close to the Mexican border and terminate in that part of California which the Southerners in 1850 had attempted to obtain. To make such a railroad possible he induced Pierce and Marcy to acquire from Mexico the region now known as the Gadsden Purchase. To demonstrate the practicability of such a road he dispatched an expedition comprising engineers, artists, and scientists who prepared a monumental report on the Southwest which the government published in ten large volumes.

The close of his term as secretary of war (1857) was followed immediately by his reëntry into the Senate. During the period in which he had been withdrawn from obvious participation in congressional politics one main chapter in American history had closed and another had opened. He had had a part in the conclave of party leaders that met at the White House on Sunday, Jan. 22, 1854, from which emerged the Kansas-Nebraska Bill. Just how much he contributed to this epoch-making bill must remain a matter of conjecture. Promptly after his return to the Senate he became again a conspicuous defender of the South. During the three years and more of his second period as senator his arguments are much the same as in the first period; but they are presented with more heat. He defends slavery because it "bears to capital as kind a relation as can exist between them anywhere" and assures the South that the election of an Abolitionist as president "would be a species of revolution by which the purposes of the Government would be destroyed and the observance of its mere forms entitled to no respect" (Speech before the Mississippi Legislature, Nov. 16, 1858; Rowland, *post,* III, 356). It seems probable that he had already passed the summit of his career both mentally and physically. The splendid manifestation of energy that so impressed Schurz is now pathetically absent from the picture. Ill health returned. He suffered intensely from neuralgia, from nervous indigestion, and from a very painful disease of the eyes that came near wrecking his sight.

The frequency of the heated tone in his speeches may be a significant symptom. Intellectually, he does not stand forth from the group of Southerners who opposed a firm but desperate front to the growing power of the North. He had a place in their first rank and in all their councils, but his contribution to their battle was mainly oratorical and emotional. He was still a brilliant figure in the public eye, and the intensity of his convictions, the patent honesty of his purpose, gave great weight to all his utterances.

In the bitterly furious internal history of the Democratic party from the day of the Dred Scott decision of 1857 to the breakup of the Charleston convention in 1860, Davis and Douglas fought each other to the death. Ostensibly the issue was between "popular sovereignty," as defended by Douglas, and the doctrine of the Dred Scott decision, which affirmed Davis's constant position that neither Congress nor local law could interfere with slavery in a territory. Behind this ostensible issue was something else that is not quite apparent. Davis joined with Yancey and Rhett in their successful effort to prevent the nomination of Douglas at Charleston, and therefore it has been assumed rashly that he shared their hope for secession as a result of the events of 1860. On the other hand, when the party had been split in two and both Douglas and Breckinridge were "Democratic" nominees, Davis, though a supporter of Breckinridge, wrote to Rhett discouraging secession and reviving exactly the "cooperationist" reasoning of 1851. Perhaps one may assume that what Davis really wanted was a confessed duality within the Union—the South to have substantially what was afterward known as "dominion status," like that of Canada or Ireland in the British Empire today—and that he did not share Rhett's enthusiasm for secession in itself.

He was relatively passive during the anxious weeks that followed the election of Lincoln. The one issue of the moment which seemed to him vital was whether the South was to continue to have an open frontier with the possibility to expand. Lincoln settled this by his declaration that while he would concede almost every other point at issue between the sections, there should be no more slave states. Thereafter Davis's course was predestined. When Mississippi seceded he acquiesced. In one of his most noted speeches he announced to the Senate the secession of his state and himself formally withdrew, Jan. 21, 1861.

Unlike most of the Southern leaders, Davis expected war. There can be no doubt that he hoped to be the chief commander of the Southern armies. Mississippi promptly appointed him major-general of the state troops. Meanwhile, a general convention of the seceding states had made one of those compromise choices so common in American conventions and had agreed upon a provisional President of the Confederacy who was nobody's first choice. It was Davis. "The messenger with the notification . . . found him in our garden [at Brierfield] assisting to make rose cuttings; when reading the telegram he looked so grieved that I feared some evil had befallen our family" (*Memoir*, II, 18). It was the summons of circumstance to make the third, the final renunciation of his own unconquerable ambition, the desire for military fame. He accepted his destiny. On Feb. 18, 1861, at Montgomery, he was inaugurated president.

A tired man in very delicate health attempted an almost impossible task. The South was unprepared for war and based its hopes of independence mainly upon the idea that "Cotton was King." Foreign affairs at once became the master key to the situation. But neither Davis nor his successive secretaries of state were able to exert much influence upon the policies of Europe. Those were determined by circumstances beyond their control which are part of Federal rather than Confederate history. The successful blockade of the Confederate coast quickly shut off the outflow of cotton and also prevented the inflow of munitions.

Davis found himself unable to control the course of events except in two respects, both of which brought into clear view convictions and qualities of mind that had been taking form during many years. First of all he kept a close hand upon the management of the army. In doing so he gave rein to his delusion that he was the equal of any one as a strategist. To Lee, alone, does he appear to have conceded preëminence. With other generals, he permitted his egoism and his irritability frequently to assert themselves. He was not always wise in his choice of men to trust. He would not listen to any one who belittled either Gen. Braxton Bragg or that brilliant but unpopular Jew who served both as secretary of war and as secretary of state, Judah P. Benjamin. He did not hesitate to set public opinion at defiance. When Congress was about to vote a condemnation of Benjamin because of the disaster of Roanoke Island in 1862, Davis showed his haughty contempt for it by promoting Benjamin from the War Department to the State Department. His animosities were as uncompromising as his friendships. He had a relentless quarrel with Joseph Johnston, whom he removed from command in Georgia at a critical moment in 1864. When Congress compelled the reinstatement of Johnston in high command, Davis evaded making the necessary appointment and contrived to have it made by Lee. Another assertion of his autocratic will was the letter he wrote to J. A. Seddon, secretary of war, deploring the resignation that had been wrung from him by the hostility of Congress.

His imperious temper aggravated by ill health—his wife speaks of his coming home from his office "fasting, a mere mass of throbbing nerves"—did not help him in the difficult political problems which rapidly developed. As soon as it became apparent that Davis's loyalty was given to the South as a whole, that he would sacrifice the interest of any Southern state if thus he could create a Southern nation committed to the preservation of the Southern social order, excessively theoretical advocates of state rights like Rhett and Yancey became his bitter political enemies. An anti-Davis party was quickly formed which was rallied, ostensibly at least, around the central idea of state sovereignty. Governor Brown of Georgia and such powerful politicians as Robert Toombs and Alexander H. Stephens were drawn into the opposition. It controlled some of the most influential Southern newspapers, including the most influential of all, the *Richmond Examiner*. The *Charleston Mercury*, owned by the Rhett family, was Davis's uncompromising enemy throughout the war (see Owsley, *post*).

The active beginning of opposition to his government very nearly coincided with his formal inauguration as regular president. He had been elected in October 1861 and was inaugurated Feb. 22, 1862. Even before this he had stirred antagonism by his veto of a bill that would have permitted the officering of a Texas regiment by the governor of the state. The *Mercury* was very sharp in its comments on this veto. Within a month of the inauguration he had defied Congress by transferring Benjamin to the State Department. About the same time he proposed a general conscription law which, though enacted, was at once taken up by the state-rights apologists and denounced as unconstitutional. This was the beginning of a desultory quarrel between state and Confederate authorities over control of enlistments that did not cease until the Confederacy collapsed (see Moore, *post*). Incidental to this controversy were the repeated attempts of the administration party to vest in the President large powers through the suspension of the writ of *habeas corpus*. Though, of course, the usual complex of political interests informed the two parties, it is fair to impute to them a real antagonism over ideas—centralization upon the one hand, local autonomy upon the other. The controversy was quieted briefly by the brilliant military events of 1862, but broke out with renewed vigor after the failure of the great triple offensive—in Maryland, in Kentucky, in Mississippi—of the autumn of that year.

Among the tremendous military events of the following year the political issues seem almost to escape from view, but, in fact, the hostility of the two parties raged with increasing violence. Confederate money had ceased to have value worth talking about. Financial taxation was an unreality. To meet this difficult situation the government revived the ancient system of tithes through a statute known as the Tax in Kind. Being all but unable to support itself, the government was also empowered, by means of an Impressment Act, to seize supplies and to pay for them at prices fixed by official commissioners. A third measure inspired the *Mercury* to publish an attack upon the government entitled "A Despotism over the Confederate States Proposed in Congress." It referred to a renewed attempt to suspend the writ of *habeas corpus*. The argument in favor of suspension was chiefly the flagrant obstruction of the conscription acts, connived at, if not encouraged, by many state officials, especially in North Carolina and Georgia. The leader of the opposition in Congress was the same Henry S. Foote who had defeated Davis for governor in 1851. His furious denunciations of the administration ended in the defeat of the bill.

Despite a great deal of spasmodic opposition, the administration had been able on most questions to obtain adequate support hitherto in Congress. The general elections of the autumn of 1863 made a change. The resulting Congress was composed very largely of men who were new to legislation; and it contained a majority hostile to Davis. The constitutional issue had melted into a less definite but even more dangerous one. There was a real though vague belief widely spread that the President was a despot, that some sort of *coup d'état* might be expected at any moment. An atmosphere of dread, created by unlimited denunciation of Davis's motives, was darkened by a series of difficulties with regard to labor. Early in the war it was tacitly agreed that the government should not be allowed to own slaves. The imaginary vision of a government owning an army of obedient barbarians—a hundred thousand, two hundred thousand—gave point to the cries against despotism and a *coup d'état*. The government had to rent slaves from their owners and used them as army laborers. At the same time it exempted one white man for every plantation of fifteen slaves or more to serve as overseer. This "Fifteen Slave Law" produced envy in men of small property. They were further embittered by a law which permitted the hiring of substitutes by men drafted for the army. They vented their anger in the saying that the Confederacy was waging "a rich man's war and a poor man's fight." There was no end of complaint against impressment commissioners; also charges of profiteering by government officials, some of which seem to have been justified.

Against this background of discontent three passages in Davis's annual message, November 1864, took on, in the popular mind, menacing significance. He urged Congress to authorize the government to purchase outright 40,000 slaves. He suggested that when the government was through with them these slaves should be set free. He recognized the existence of a disturbing popular controversy by saying that he dissented "from those who advise a general levy and arming of the slaves for the duty of soldiers" (Journal, post, IV, 258; Rowland, post, VI, 396). This was the beginning of the last important controversy of Confederate history. The army, worn and wasted by three and a half years of dreary valor, had to be reinforced. Negroes were the only remaining source of supply. The message was doubtless a "feeler" to take the sense of the country upon a policy which originated probably with Secretary Benjamin. Incidentally it carried with it the policy of emancipation. The administration party at once introduced both subjects into Congressional debate. During the terrible winter of 1864–65, while the military power of the Confederacy was visibly crumbling on every hand, the fanatical slaveholders in Congress kept the discussion in suspense. Eventually a bill was passed permitting a fresh levy of 300,000 men, but making no mention of emancipation, and providing that these new troops were "to be raised from such classes of the population irrespective of color, in each State as the proper authorities thereof may determine" (Journal, VII, 611–12). Virtually, it was a defeat for the administration. But Davis refused to admit that it was a defeat. He had become infatuated with the idea of emancipation as the last trump in his hand. He believed that by means of it he could yet win over the British government, induce it to enter the war, and at the eleventh hour save the Confederacy. A secret agent, Duncan F. Kenner, was sent to London, only to be told that the offer came too late.

The frame of mind of Davis this concluding winter was strangely deluded. He appears to have had no doubt of a successful outcome of the war. In the preceding autumn with Sherman entrenched at Atlanta he had gone South on a tour of inspiration. His aim was to stir up a "people's war" by giving to popular audiences a true picture of the soldier's task. But he was not happy in his way of doing it. In describing General Beauregard, whom he had placed in command in Georgia, he attempted to give an impression of soldierly self-effacement. He said that this brave general would do whatever the President told him to do. His enemies seized upon the words. Here was further evidence that he was planning a *coup d'état*. Davis's last effective reinforcement of the army was accomplished by a general order this autumn revoking all exemptions, stripping the plantations of the overseers, and calling to the colors all soldiers furloughed or in hospital "except those unable to travel." Davis returned to Richmond, and Sherman began his march to the sea. While a wide swath of desolation was sweeping over the lower South, Davis confronted a crisis the seriousness of which he did not in the least appreciate. There were "peace movements" agitating the South, and here and there something like a clamor for negotiations with Washington. The advocates of these movements had no clear notion of what they were trying to do, and had they not inspired overtures from the North would have little historical significance. They contributed indirectly to bring about a series of attempts to negotiate. In the summer of 1864 two Northerners came to Richmond unofficially for the purpose of catching Davis in a trap. They believed that he would refuse to treat for peace on any terms except the recognition of Southern independence, and they wanted to use the fact to hearten the North for the reëlection of Lincoln. As they had no official credentials, Davis refused to discuss public affairs with them (Rowland, X, 32). A notable, but informal, attempt to induce Davis to consent to reunion was made by Francis P. Blair in January 1865. Napoleon III, defying the Monroe Doctrine, had recently established Maximilian as Emperor of Mexico. Blair proposed to Davis a plan of reconciliation involving the complete abandonment of slavery, the reunion of all the states, and an expedition against Mexico in which Davis was to play the leading rôle. Davis cautiously refrained from committing himself, though he gave Blair a letter in which he expressed his willingness to enter into negotiations for peace between "the two countries." The visit of Blair gave new impetus to the peace movements. The Committee on Foreign Affairs of the Confederate House reported resolutions favoring an attempt to negotiate with the United States so as to "bring into view" the possibility of coöperation between the United States and the Confederacy to maintain the Monroe Doctrine. Before the end of the month Davis appointed commissioners to confer with the Northern authorities with regard to peace. There followed the famous Hampton Roads Conference, Feb. 3, 1865, at which Lincoln was present and Stephens was the chief spokesman for the Confederacy. Whether it is true, as tradition has it, that Lincoln told Stephens to write Union at the top of a page and anything he pleased under it, there is no doubt that the tradition fairly represents the situation of the moment. But Davis, though now committed in his own mind to emancipation, was determined to accept nothing short of independence. His delusion of power could not be shaken. Three days after the conference he made his last public oration as President of the Confederacy. He spoke in the precincts of the African Church in Richmond. Snow lay thick on the ground. A man in a dream, he talked with the passion of a seer and for the moment swept his audience before him. "Let us then unite our hands and our hearts, lock our shields together, and we may well believe that before another summer solstice falls upon us, it will be the enemy who will be asking us for conferences and occasions in which to make known our demands" (see Dodd, *post*, p. 353). Two months later Richmond had fallen and Davis was a fugitive.

The President's party left the city on Apr. 3. The next day he was at Danville, where he waited five days. On Apr. 4 he issued his last proclamation, calling on his people to resist to the last and promising them that Richmond would soon be recovered. The news of Lee's surrender caused him to turn southward. At Greensboro, Apr. 12, a cabinet council was held which Johnston and Beauregard attended. Reluctantly, Davis gave Johnston permission to negotiate for the surrender of his army to Sherman. Twelve days later, at Charlotte, Davis held his last council with his cabinet, approved Johnston's surrender, and finally admitted that the Confederacy had been overthrown. The party broke up. Davis continued southward, hoping to escape out of the country. At Irwinville, Ga., he was captured by Federal cavalry, May 10.

During two years he was a state prisoner in Fortress Monroe. The commandant, Gen. Nelson A. Miles, acting upon instructions from General Halleck and Assistant Secretary of War Charles A. Dana, ordered him put in irons (*A Statement of the Facts concerning the Imprisonment and Treatment of Jefferson Davis*, etc., 1902). He was later accorded different treatment. His health failed. At length he was assigned comfortable quarters which his family were permitted to share. He was never brought to trial. The lawyers of the government saw technical danger in every charge that was suggested. He was released on bond, May 13, 1867 (Nichols, *post*). Horace Greeley and Gerrit Smith, once the bitter enemies of everything Southern, were among his bondsmen.

He was not yet an old man, and twenty-two years of life remained to him. They were valiant but sad years. His fortune was wrecked, his home a ruin, and his health impaired. Though these years, with the exception of three, contain no remarkable achievement, they have a moral distinction second to nothing in his career. Health was recovered gradually, partly through European travel but more through sheer resolution and strength of will. In his seventieth year Davis was probably a more vigorous man than at any time since the great days when he was secretary of war. He embarked in a succession of business ventures, but as he had no predilection for business and no business experience, they were all unsuccessful. Though a portion of the Brierfield estate was saved, he was in his later years a poor man. A home was provided for his old age through the bequest of Mrs. Sarah A. Dorsey, a friend of Mrs. Davis. This was "Beauvoir" on the Gulf of Mexico. There he prepared his own version of his stormy career by writing *The Rise and Fall of the Confederate Government,* devoting to it the three years 1878–81. Though Mississippi would have sent him to the Senate, he refused to ask for the Federal pardon without which it was impossible for him to take his seat. He died at New Orleans in his eighty-second year.

[The most important biography is Wm. E. Dodd, *Jefferson Davis* (1907). *Jefferson Davis, Ex-President of the Confederate States of America: A Memoir,* by his wife (2 vols., 1890), is an invaluable but rambling and fragmentary collection of details. *Jefferson Davis, Constitutionalist, His Letters, Papers, and Speeches* (10 vols., 1923), ed. by Dunbar Rowland, though voluminous, does not contain all the known private letters, omits all the dispatches in the *Official Records,* and is not complete in its selections from the *Cong. Globe.* For the mind of Davis, previous to secession, the *Globe,* after all, is the true record. His own apologia is *The Rise and Fall of the Confed. Govt.* (2 vols., 1881). J. P. Richardson, *A Compilation of the Messages and Papers of the Confederacy* (2 vols., 1905), contains some of the state papers; others are embedded in *Jour. of the Cong. of the Confed. States of America* (7 vols., 1904–05), being *Sen. Doc. No. 234,* 58 Cong., 2 Sess., and in the Fourth Series of the *Official Records.* Three newspapers may be regarded as government organs: the *Richmond Enquirer,* the Richmond *Sentinel,* and the *Charleston Courier.* The official gazette of the government abroad was the *Index* published in London. As Davis was engaged in many controversies, all the writings of Confederate leaders contain Davis matter, but as a rule it is sharply partisan. Important recent studies are: A. B. Moore, *Conscription and Conflict in the Confederacy* (1924); F. L. Owsley, *State Rights in the Confederacy* (1925); R. F. Nichols, "United States vs. Jefferson Davis," *Am. Hist. Rev.*, Jan. 1926. A number of excellent essays on Davis have been written by Walter L. Fleming but have not been collected. For his military career, see G. W. Cullum, *Biog. Reg. Officers and Grads. U. S. Mil. Acad.* (3rd ed., 1891), I, 416.]

[SUPPLEMENTARY BIBLIOGRAPHY. The most recent biography is Hudson Strode, *Jefferson Davis* (2 vols., 1955–59). See also the earlier and comprehensive Robert M. McElroy, *Jefferson Davis, the Unreal and the Real* (2 vols., 1937). Allan Nevins, *The Statesmanship of the Civil War* (1951), compares the leadership of Davis and Lincoln. See also Rembert W. Patrick, *Jefferson Davis and his Cabinet* (1944).]

Abraham Lincoln

by

JAMES G. RANDALL

LINCOLN, ABRAHAM (Feb. 12, 1809--Apr. 15, 1865), sixteenth president of the United States, was, to use his own words, born "in the most humble walks of life" (*Works,* I, 8). His birthplace was a log cabin about three miles south of Hodgen's mill on what was known as the "Sinking Spring Farm" in Hardin (now Larue) County, Ky. Lincoln himself could trace his line no farther back than to certain ancestors in Berks County, Pa., whom he vaguely described as Quakers; but research has disclosed a lineage reaching back to Samuel Lincoln who came from Hingham, England, and settled in Hingham, Mass., in 1637. On the Lincoln side the descent was as follows: Samuel Lincoln (d. 1690); Mordecai Lincoln of Hingham and Scituate, Mass. (d. 1727); Mordecai Lincoln of Berks County, Pa. (d. 1736); John Lincoln of Berks County, Pa., and Rockingham County, Va. (d. 1788); Abraham Lincoln of Rockingham County, Va., and later of Kentucky; Thomas Lincoln, father of the President. The merging of the Lincolns with the migratory streams of pioneer America is illustrated by the progeny of John Lincoln mentioned above—"Virginia John" as he was called. Of his five sons, whose names were reminiscent of ancient Israel, Jacob alone remained in Virginia, while Abraham, Isaac, John, and Thomas removed to Kentucky, eastern Tennessee, or Ohio. Abraham Lincoln, grandfather of the President, emigrated from Rockingham County, Va., to Green River, Lincoln County, Ky., about 1782; but was killed about 1786 by Indians while opening a farm in the forest (Beveridge, *post,* I, 11, note 2).

Thomas Lincoln (1778–1851) was large, powerful and compactly built. According to his distinguished son, he was "a wandering laboring-boy," and "grew up literally without education" (*Works,* VI, 25), and in mature life was barely able to write his name. Born in Rockingham County, Va., he went with his father to Lincoln County, Ky., roved about for some years, married and settled in Elizabethtown, Hardin County, after which he pursued the occupations of carpenter and farmer, changing his residence frequently, making nothing of his poorly chosen farms, avoiding contacts with "society" in town, and bequeathing little beside life itself to his son. Thomas's first wife, Nancy Hanks, was the mother of Abraham. According to the best available authority, she was the natural child of Lucy Hanks; and her paternity is unknown, the date of her birth being a matter of conjecture. Some years after the birth of Nancy, Lucy Hanks married Henry Sparrow in Mercer County, Ky.; and Nancy was reared by her aunt, Betsy Hanks (Mrs. Thomas Sparrow). Though many tender eulogies of Lincoln's mother have been written, there is little reliable evidence concerning her. She seems to have been superior to the general Hanks level in intellectual vigor, and was described as spiritually inclined, affectionate, amiable, cool, and heroic (Herndon and Weik, *post,* I, 10). Whatever her natural endowments, she was "absolutely illiterate" (Beveridge, I, 16) and was throughout life identified with lowly people. Her marriage to Thomas Lincoln occurred on June 12, 1806, the backwoods ceremony being performed in the cabin of a friend in Washington County, Ky., by Jesse Head, a Methodist parson. On the Hanks side the ancestry of Lincoln is beclouded in a maze of misinformation; and much of the data presented by earlier biographers on this subject must be rejected, including unreliable accounts of a mythical Nancy Shipley Hanks, sometimes erroneously mentioned as Lincoln's maternal grandmother, and of various alleged Hankses whose real name was Hawks. According to W. E. Barton (*Lineage of Lincoln,* pp. 186, 210), the parents of Lincoln's grandmother, Lucy, were Joseph and Ann (Lee) Hanks of Hampshire County, Va., and Nelson County, Ky.; and one finds Hankses in the seventeenth and eighteenth centuries living on the Rappahannock as close neighbors of various Lees with whom at times they intermarried. It is only by conjecture as to several links, however, that Barton argues a connection between Lincoln's line and that of Robert E. Lee (*Ibid.,* pp. 208–11).

Without following all the migrations of "Thomas the unstable," it may be noted that during the years of Abraham's early boyhood the family lived in a picturesque spot on Knob Creek about eight miles from his birthplace—a spot of natural beauty, of peace and grandeur, in a region of rocky cliffs, noble trees, and clear streams. Throughout life Lincoln carried fresh recollections of his Kentucky home—of the backwoods school where he was taught to read, write, and "cipher to the rule of three," of fishing and hunting adventures, of boyish escapades, of the old stone house on Nolin Creek where the young people gathered for dances, and of the mill to which as a child he carried the family grist. When the boy was seven the family was again on the move, this time for the Indiana woods. With their sorry stock of household goods they "packed through" to the Ohio River, ferried across, and followed a newly blazed trail to the nearby home in the brush which Thomas had selected. This home, in which the Lincolns were at first but squatters, was located in the Pigeon Creek neighborhood in what is now Spencer County, Ind. The first winter they had not even a cabin—merely a rude shelter of poles, brush, and leaves enclosed on three sides and called a "half-faced camp." Their cabin, when Thomas got round to building it, had at first neither floor, door, nor window; and the family fare was a matter of game animals, honey, birds, nuts, and wild fruit. The family of Thomas and Nancy Lincoln, with their two children, Sarah and Abraham, was soon joined by Nancy's foster parents, Betsy and Thomas Sparrow, with the colorful Dennis Hanks, who was as essential a part of this backwoods picture as "that Darne Little half face camp," as Dennis called it, which the Sparrows used after the Lincolns had discarded it. Tragedy soon descended upon Pigeon Creek. Thomas Sparrow and Betsy his wife were stricken with what the settlers called the "milk sick," and were laid away in coffins fashioned by Thomas Lincoln. To these and other sufferers Nancy Lincoln had generously ministered. She soon fell ill, lingered without medical help for a week, and died (October 1818) with words of pious admonition for her children. In life and death her brief story was that of the American pioneer woman.

Thomas Lincoln soon found another wife in Sarah (Bush) Johnston of Elizabethtown, Ky., widow of Daniel Johnston, who came with her three children to the Indiana cabin; and with the addition in 1823 of John Hanks there were nine persons in this narrow abode. The household equipment was now improved; and the stepmother became an important factor in the boy's rearing. From the Weik manuscripts—memories of Lincoln's early associates recorded after many years—we may reconstruct, through Beveridge's pages, a fairly definite picture of Lincoln as an easy-going backwoods youth who did his stint of hard labor on the homestead, performed odd jobs for neighbors, shunned the vociferous camp-meetings of the time, avoided membership in the church, and used his leisure for self-improvement by the reading of a few good books. The Bible, *Robinson Crusoe, Pilgrim's Progress,* Aesop's *Fables,* William Grimshaw's *History of the United States,* the *Kentucky Preceptor,* Weems's *Life of Washington,* and various other biographies and books of verse were the principal works known to have been used by Lincoln at this period. As to formal schooling, there was very little. While living in the Knob Creek home in Kentucky, Abraham and his sister Sarah had attended country schools for some weeks; now in Indiana he sat for brief periods under several schoolmasters (Andrew Crawford, Azel W. Dorsey, and William Sweeney by name) to whose log schools he had to walk long distances; but, in all, his attendance at school did not exceed one year. Out of school his vigor for reading and study was probably less a matter of ambition than of healthy intellectual interest. It was his stepmother who told the familiar story of his ciphering on boards which he shaved off with a drawing-knife to prepare for fresh efforts. His readiness to walk many miles for books is well attested, as is also his fondness for speech-making and for mimicking the preachers and orators who penetrated to the rough creekside. He somehow grew up without the frontier vices, avoiding liquor and being wholly free from dissoluteness and profanity. Though avoiding girls, he was uncommonly sociable; and the nearby country store at Gentryville held for him an unfailing fascination. The river attracted him powerfully and entered largely into his early life. He earned a few dollars by rowing passengers from the shore to passing steamers; and in the year 1828 he made the trip from Gentry's landing on the Ohio to New Orleans. Though stirred with the ambition to become "a steamboat man," he returned to the monotony of Pigeon Creek, where his father had a claim upon his labor. As the boy emerged from his teens he was tall, powerful, muscular, ungainly, tender toward animals, a recounter of robust stories, mighty with the axe, and not without a certain latent poetry in his nature. His relations with his father seem not to have been happy, and he welcomed the day when he could shift for himself.

In the year of Abraham's coming of age (1830) the Lincolns were again on the move. Having sold his Indiana holdings, Thomas set out with his family to Macon County, Ill., whither John Hanks had preceded them. With ox-drawn wagons they trekked through forest and prairie, crossed the Wabash, and settled on the Sangamon River not far from Decatur. At first Abraham remained with the family, helping to build the new cabin, splitting fence rails, planting corn, and assisting in the rough tasks of the following winter. In the service of one Denton Offutt he assisted in building and navigating a flatboat from a point on the Sangamon River near Springfield to New Orleans; but the story that "the iron entered his soul" on seeing the New Orleans slave auction, and that he vowed if he ever had a chance to "hit that thing" he would "hit it hard," is untrustworthy (Beveridge, I, 107). Returning from the southern mart on a steamer, Lincoln, then only a drifter, selected as his home the village of New Salem, about twenty miles northwest of Springfield—a remote hamlet set high on a bluff overlooking the Sangamon.

Here he spent six picturesque and formative years (1831–37), working in the store of Denton Offutt till it "petered out"; managing a mill; conducting a store with W. F. Berry, who died leaving a heavy debt ($1,100) all of which Lincoln finally paid; splitting rails and doing odd jobs to earn a scant living; acting as village postmaster; traversing the county as deputy surveyor; and all the while reading law, studying grammar, widening his acquaintance, following the trends of national politics, and laying the foundations for a wide personal influence. It was during this period that he served in the Black Hawk War, being unanimously elected captain by the men of his company. Another gauge to measure his stature is the devotion of the "Clary Grove Boys"—stalwart rowdies to whom hero worship was as natural as swearing, drinking, and fighting. This tribute to Lincoln's manhood, which came in spite of his freedom from the vices of the gang, seems to have been in part a recognition of his prowess in competitive sport, especially wrestling, and in part a pure matter of personal attachment.

In 1834 Lincoln was chosen to the state legislature; and he served during four successive terms (1834–41), first at Vandalia, the old capital, and later at Springfield. It was a frontier legislature, but its party maneuvers were spirited, and it offered Lincoln his first political training. Being a Clay Whig in a Democratic body, he belonged to the minority; but he became Whig floor leader and directed the fortunes of his party in the lower house, receiving in several sessions the full party vote for the speakership. On national issues, which were necessarily of concern to him as a prominent party worker, he acted as a regular Whig, supporting the Bank of the United States, opposing the leading measures of Jackson and Van Buren, and attacking the independent treasury. He studiously avoided association with abolitionists, but he did not want this attitude construed as positive support of slavery. Consequently, when the legislature in 1837 passed resolutions severely condemning abolition societies, Lincoln and his colleague Dan Stone from Sangamon County entered a protest, asserting that slavery was "founded on both injustice and bad policy, but that the promulgation of abolition doctrines tends rather to increase than abate its evils" (*Works*, I, 52).

In 1837 Lincoln left New Salem, which was soon thereafter abandoned, later to be rebuilt as a memorial to him, and made his home in Springfield. So poor was he at this time that his surveying instruments had been attached to pay a debt; he rode into town on a borrowed horse carrying his possessions in two saddle-bags, and was glad to make arrangements with friends for free lodging and board. He was now a practising lawyer, having been licensed as an attorney Sept. 9, 1836; and he formed a partnership with J. T. Stuart, a man of influential family, able in the law, and prominent in Whig circles. While in New Salem, Lincoln had paid court to Ann Rutledge whose father kept the rude inn where he boarded. Though the girl's attractions and tragic death have inspired an extravagant amount of sentimental fiction, actual evidence on the matter is scant. She was engaged to a man named John McNamar, but his long absence suggested desertion. Her engagement to Lincoln seems to have been conditional upon honorable release from her absent lover. That Ann preferred Lincoln in case her lover should return and renew his suit seems doubtful; and on both sides there were reasons for deferring marriage. With matters in this unsettled state, Ann died of "brain fever," Aug. 25, 1835. Lincoln's proposal to Mary Owens, whom he met through the kindness of her sister at New Salem, need not be treated here; nor is there room to analyze the confused testimony that surrounds his troubled courtship of Mary Todd.

Herndon's sensational story of Lincoln's failure to appear at his wedding, said to have been set for Jan. 1, 1841, has produced a mass of contradictory discussion. In the best treatment of the subject (Sandburg and Angle, *Mary Lincoln, Wife and Widow*, 1932, pp. 40–60, 174–85, 330), the conclusion is reached that there was no defaulting bridegroom at a wedding, but that some violent emotional disturbance did occur; indeed, no one can read Lincoln's correspondence of the period without being impressed with his excessive morbidity. After a series of breaks and reconciliations, complicated by Mary's rumored flirtations with other men, the disturbed lovers were finally brought together; and they were married in some haste on Nov. 4, 1842. As to the degree of happiness that attended their married life it is equally difficult to reach a fully rounded conclusion. On Lincoln's side there was indifference to domestic niceties and a certain untidiness and lack of dignity that grated upon the sensibilities of a proudly reared woman; on the other hand, the domestic atmosphere was not improved by Mary's bursts of temper. Their first son, Robert Todd, was born Aug. 1, 1843; he alone grew to manhood. The other children were: Edward Baker (Mar. 10, 1846–Feb. 1, 1850), William Wallace (Dec. 21, 1850–Feb. 20, 1862), and Thomas or "Tad" (Apr. 4, 1853–July 15, 1871).

In the years 1847–49 Lincoln served one term in Congress, where he had the distinction of being the only Whig from Illinois. His election with more than 1,500 majority over the doughty backwoods preacher Peter Cartwright was a significant personal triumph, for Cartwright was himself a man of great popularity. In his undistinguished career as congressman the matters most worthy of comment are those which pertain to the Mexican War and to slavery. Lincoln had not opposed the war while campaigning as a candidate; but when his party sought political advantage by denouncing the conflict as a Democratic war unjustly begun by Polk, Lincoln joined aggressively in this party attack. He voted (Jan. 3, 1848) that the war was "unnecessarily . . . begun by the President"; and on Dec. 22, 1847, he introduced his "spot resolutions" (*Congressional Globe*, 30 Cong., 1 Sess., p. 64), which were so worded as to imply that the "spot" on which had occurred the shedding of American blood, which Polk had interpreted as Mexican aggression, was in fact an unoffending settlement of Mexican people, outside American jurisdiction, against which an American force had been unnecessarily sent contrary to General Taylor's advice. On Jan. 12, 1848, he made a striking speech on his resolutions—a Whig speech in which he subjected the President's evidence to cold analysis, accused him of befogging the issue, and questioned the purposes of the administration as to the duration of the war and the terms of peace (*Ibid.*, pp. 154–56). In this speech Lincoln made a declaration which hardly comported with his later declarations against Southern secession; for he asserted the right of "any people," or of "a majority of any portion of such people," to "shake off the existing government, and form a new one" (*Works*, I, 338–39). Though Lincoln had voted to grant supplies to sustain the war, and though his anti-war speech made but slight impression generally, he had deeply offended the people of his state. His attitude was denounced in Illinois as unpatriotic; he was described as a "second Benedict Arnold," and was accused of having plead the cause of the enemy (Beveridge, I, 432). On various occasions Lincoln voted for the Wilmot proviso; and on

Jan. 10, 1849, he read a proposal to abolish slavery in the national capital (*Congressional Globe,* 30 Cong., 2 Sess., p. 212). It is characteristic of his conservatism that he proposed such abolition only in case three conditions should be met: emancipation was to be gradual; compensation was to be made to slaveholders; and the proposed act was not to go into force unless approved by the citizens of the District at a special election.

Lincoln did not move among the great in Washington, nor did he rise above the obscurity of the average congressman. He amused a small circle by his camaraderie and droll stories, but the more brilliant social life of the capital was closed to him. Vigorous anti-slavery men were not his associates, but he formed a real friendship with Alexander H. Stephens of Georgia. Party affairs took much of his energy. He spent weary hours addressing documents to voters; wrote numerous letters; served as the Illinois member of the Whig national committee; delivered a rollicking speech against Cass which was essentially a campaign document (July 27, 1848, *Works,* II, 59–88); and participated in the Whig convention at Philadelphia in 1848, laboring hard for the inexperienced Zachary Taylor and against his former hero, Henry Clay. In the campaign of 1848 his services on the stump were not eagerly sought, least of all in Illinois; but he visited Massachusetts, speaking at Worcester, Chelsea, Dedham, Cambridge, Lowell, and Boston. One misses in these speeches the resonant tone of Lincoln's later declarations. Anti-slavery as he was at heart, he counseled against voting for the Free-Soil candidate, Van Buren, since such action would help to elect Cass. Though the Whigs were nationally successful in this election, Lincoln had the humiliation of seeing his party lose his own district, where the defeat of S. T. Logan for Congress might be interpreted as a repudiation of Lincoln's record by his neighbors. With a sense of futility he bade goodbye to Washington; and, while the thunders of the mid-century slavery crisis were shaking the country, he renounced politics, returned to the obscurity of Springfield, and sadly resumed his law practice.

As a lawyer Lincoln rose to front rank in his own state. He was associated with capable partners—at first John Todd Stuart, then Stephen T. Logan, and finally William H. Herndon. His practice was important and extensive in the state supreme court and also in the federal courts. After Illinois was divided into two federal judicial districts, Lincoln attended the sessions of the United States courts in Chicago with increasing frequency. In his circuit practice, where cases had to be quickly whipped into shape, he was not more than ordinarily successful; but in the higher courts, where careful study served to bring into play the sureness of his matured judgments, his record was outstanding (Paul M. Angle, in *Lincoln Centennial Association Papers*, 1928, esp. pp. 38–41). It is true that Lincoln is chiefly remembered as a luminous figure among the circuit-riding lawyers who traveled the judicial circuit presided over by Judge David Davis. He thoroughly enjoyed this picturesque life, jogging over the prairies in his rickety buggy, meeting the country folk on their own level, and joining the happy migratory life of judge and attorneys as they lodged two in a bed and eight in a room, swapped stories, and made the taverns resound with hilarity. During court week the lawyers were in demand for political speeches, and Lincoln's popularity was enhanced by his aptness on these occasions. It was here that his humor and story telling showed at their best; and to the stories themselves must be added the wizardry of Lincoln's quaint manner and the charm of his smile. Some of the specific cases of this circuit-riding phase have received undue emphasis, such as the Wright case in which Lincoln represented the widow of a Revolutionary soldier and recovered an exorbitant fee which a grasping pension agent had charged, and that of "Duff" Armstrong whom Lincoln successfully defended on a murder charge, making use of an almanac to refute testimony as to moonlight on the night of the murder. The human interest of these smaller cases has served to obscure the really important litigation with which Lincoln was connected. His services were enlisted in determining such important matters as the right of a county to tax the Illinois Central Railroad (17 *Illinois*, 291–99), the right to bridge a navigable stream (the *Effie Afton* case, Beveridge, I, 598–605), and the protection of the McCormick Reaper Company against infringement of its patents (*Ibid.*, I, 575–83). In this McCormick case, which was tried before a federal court at Cincinnati, Lincoln suppressed his feelings when snubbed by eastern attorneys; and later as president he appointed one of these lawyers, Stanton, to his cabinet. A study of his whole legal career shows that he was more than a country lawyer; and to those factors which gave him fair success in the rural county seats— his common sense, his shrewdness, his effectiveness before a jury, his strong invective, and his reputation for honesty—one must add further qualities that mark the outstanding attorney: a searching thoroughness of investigation (Beveridge, I, 573–74), a familiarity with pertinent judicial doctrines, and a knack of so stating a legal question as to brush away its technicalities and get at the core of the controversy. There are instances of his declining to receive excessive fees, refusing questionable cases, and even withdrawing from a case on discovering during the trial that his client's cause was unjust. In fragmentary notes for a law lecture he stated his conception of professional standards (*Works,* II, 140–43). A successful lawyer, he said, must stress diligence, attend promptly to the preparation of documents, and cultivate extemporaneous speaking as the "lawyer's avenue to the public." He should discourage litigation and choose honesty above professional success. "Work, work, work," he said, "is the main thing" (*Ibid.,* VI, 59).

The Lincoln of the prairies was a man of marked individuality. Standing six feet four, with uncommon length of arms and legs, his figure loomed in any crowd, while the rugged face bespoke a pioneer origin and an early life of toil and poverty. In a head not over-large each feature was rough and prominent. In contrast to the round, full-cheeked Douglas, Lincoln's face showed deep hollows and heavy shadows. The craggy brow, tousled hair, drooping eyelids, melancholy gray eyes, large nose and chin, heavy lips, and sunken, wrinkled cheeks produced an effect not easily forgotten. A wide variety of qualities is revealed in his portraits, which give the impression of a character whose depth is not readily sounded—a personality in which conflicting hereditary strains were peculiarly blended. Those who have described him from life dwell upon the contrast between the seeming listlessness of the face in repose and the warmth of the countenance when animated with conversation or public speech. The trappings of the man intensified the effect of crudeness. In a day of grandiloquent male adornment Lincoln's habiliments departed as far from the Godey fashion plate as did his midwestern speech from the sophisticated accent of the East. The battered stovepipe hat stuffed with papers, the rusty ill-fitting coat, the ready-made trousers too short for the legs, the unpolished boots, the soiled stock at the neck, the circular cloak in winter or linen duster in summer, the bulging umbrella and hard-used carpet-bag, gave an entirely unpremeditated effect of oddity, the man's appearance being apparently of no more concern to him than the food which he seemed to eat without tasting.

Few men could match Lincoln as a stump-speaker. Beginning with apparent diffidence he gained composure and assurance as he proceeded, speaking with freedom, naturalness, and convincing power. In impassioned periods the gaunt figure, despite the sunken chest, became "splendid and imposing" (Herndon and Weik, II, 77); and in the directness of his intense passages the tall form seemed to gain in height. His mind had that tenacity and steadfastness of logic that goes with slowness in forming conclusions. There is a clarity and compactness in his writings which is in pleasing contrast to the verbosity so common in his day. Never descending to triteness or banality, his papers show careful composition and abound in epigrams and pithy phrases. This power of written and spoken utterance must be reckoned high among his qualities as a statesman. His political philosophy revealed a democratic liberalism closely resembling the creed of Thomas Jefferson. Anglo-Saxon principles of civil liberty were fundamental in his thinking (A. C. Cole, in *Journal of the Illinois State Historical Society,* Oct. 1926–Jan. 1927, pp. 102–14); he advocated the broadening of political rights, even favoring woman suffrage far ahead of his time; and the leveling doctrines of the Declaration of Independence became a kind of religion with him. Laborers and the less favored classes generally found in him an earnest champion. Though never identifying himself with any ecclesiastical denomination, he was not lacking in the religious sense; and in his public papers he expressed with sincerity the spiritual aspirations of his people.

In the agitation that swept the country with the repeal of the Missouri Compromise Lincoln emerged from political inactivity and launched upon the larger career which occupied the coming years. From 1854 on there appeared a new tone in his speeches, a notable earnestness combined with adroitness in narrowing the contest to one phase of the slavery question, thus making it a suitable party issue. In a speech at Springfield, Oct. 4, 1854, repeated at Peoria on Oct. 16 (*Works*, II, 190–262), Lincoln answered Douglas, who had spoken in the same hall the previous day. His reasoned appeals to the Declaration of Independence, his sarcasm, his searching questions, and his shrewdness in avoiding pitfalls, indicated that he had now struck his stride as a leader. Still calling himself a Whig, though events were drawing him toward the new Republican party, he worked hard for the senatorship from Illinois in 1855; but, after successive ballots in the legislature indicated his dwindling strength, he aided the cause of the Anti-Nebraska fusionists against the Democrats by throwing his support to Trumbull.

The next year Lincoln became definitely identified with the new party; and at the Republican state convention at Bloomington he delivered, on May 29, 1856, what some have called his greatest speech (*Works*, II, 308 note). In a time of high excitement over the Kansas struggle, when radicals were trying to capture the Republican party, Lincoln's task was to make a fighting speech which would have enough boldness to inspire the crusading abolitionists and yet so define the issue as to keep the support of moderates. Herndon exhausted his adjectives in describing the speech and declared that on that occasion his partner was seven feet tall. Lincoln soon became active in the new party, attending every meeting he could reach, speaking frequently, managing the details of party machinery, and carrying on an extensive correspondence with voters. He was now the leading Republican as he had been the leading Whig of Illinois. At the time of Frémont's nomination for the presidency at Philadelphia in 1856 he received 110 votes for the vice-presidential nomination; and in this way his name was widely advertised in the North. He campaigned for Frémont in this election, though McLean had been his choice; but he had only partial success in winning Whig support for the Republican cause.

Successfully seeking the Republican senatorial nomination in 1858, Lincoln delivered a carefully prepared speech on June 16 before the state Republican convention at Springfield. "A house divided against itself cannot stand," said he. "I believe this government cannot endure permanently, half slave and half free. I do not expect the Union to be dissolved—I do not expect the house to fall —but I do expect it will cease to be divided. It will become all one thing, or all the other" (*Works,* III, 2). In this speech, as elsewhere, Lincoln denounced the Dred Scott decision of 1857 as part of a proslavery conspiracy which, unless thwarted, would one day legalize slavery even in the free states. In the campaign with Douglas for the senatorship, Lincoln at first trailed his opponent, speaking at Chicago on July 10 just after his antagonist had spoken at the same place, and repeating the performance at Bloomington and elsewhere. On July 24, 1858, he challenged Douglas to a series of debates; and the acceptance of the challenge gave Lincoln the advantage of being matched against the outstanding leader of the Democratic party. Beginning at Ottawa, Aug. 21, reaching an early climax at Freeport, Aug. 27, and closing at Alton on Oct. 15, the seven "joint debates" were but the most striking incident of a long duel between Lincoln and Douglas. It was indeed a memorable contest. The emotion of cheering crowds, the clack and rattle of western campaigning, the sporting spectacle of contestants facing each other in successive forensic rounds, the physical disparity between the candidates, the contrast between Douglas's private railroad car and the crowded coach or freight caboose in which Lincoln, not without an eye to political effect, lumbered into town to be fetched to his lodging in a hay wagon—these features lent a picturesque interest to a contest in which the importance of the stakes far exceeded the realization of participants or spectators. Each candidate showed respect for the other, and the discussions were conducted on a high plane, albeit with a deadly earnestness. In the speeches there were few elements that were new. Lincoln shrewdly capitalized the growing split in the Democratic ranks; he denounced Douglas's indifference as to the right or wrong of slavery; and he used with telling effect the inconsistency between "popular sovereignty" and the doctrine of the Dred Scott decision, both of which Douglas favored. At Freeport, by a question as to whether the people of a territory could exclude slavery, he forced Douglas to compromise himself as presidential candidate in 1860 by taking a position which offended the South, though gaining votes for the senatorial contest in Illinois.

Once and again in the debates Lincoln disavowed abolitionist doctrines and stressed the conservative note. He did not advocate the unconditional repeal of fugitive-slave laws nor oppose the admission of states in which slavery might be established by constitutions honestly adopted. Negro citizenship did not receive his indorsement, nor did he urge political or social equality for the races. His advocacy of abolition in the District of Columbia was again qualified by those safeguarding conditions which he had previously proposed as congressman. With the politician's eye for vote-getting and for uniting the incongruous elements of his nascent party, he avoided the language of the anti-slavery crusader and narrowed the issue to the clear-cut doctrine of freedom in the territories. The effectiveness of his campaign was shown in the election returns. His party carried districts containing a larger population than those carried by the Democrats, but inequitable apportionment gave Douglas a majority in the legislature, insuring his election. The contest lifted Lincoln into national prominence; and in 1859 he made many speeches in Ohio, Indiana, Iowa, Wisconsin, and Kansas, impressing his ideas upon the people of important doubtful states.

His name was now being mentioned for the presidency, and it was as a presidential possibility that he delivered on Feb. 27, 1860, his Cooper Institute (Cooper Union) speech in New York (*Works*, V, 293-328). This was a notable formulation of the issues on which the new party could do battle. Exclusion of slavery from the territories as the doctrine of the fathers was the keynote of the address, which was delivered in Lincoln's best style and with a dignity in keeping with the occasion. Decrying the efforts to discredit the Republican party by identifying it with the radicalism of John Brown or the abusiveness of Helper's *Impending Crisis*, he spoke for an attitude of understanding and friendliness toward the Southern people. He urged his party to "yield to them if . . . we possibly can," doing "nothing through passion and ill temper"; and he denounced efforts to destroy the Union.

Lincoln was named in state convention as the choice of Illinois Republicans for the presidency; and a combination of factors led to his success in the national convention at Chicago. Seward was considered too radical and was injured by the powerful opposition of Greeley. Other candidates had weak points; Bates could not carry the Germans; Chase could not muster his own state. The moderate element was growing in the new party, and in certain "battle-ground states"—Illinois, Indiana, Pennsylvania, and New Jersey, which had supported Buchanan in 1856—it was vitally important to nominate a conservative candidate. Lincoln had steadily counseled moderation; he had avoided connection with the Know-Nothings, had pleased the Germans by his opposition to measures directed against foreigners, and had made himself highly acceptable as a second choice in case Seward could not be named. In short, Lincoln was so free from radicalism, so careful to avoid offense, and yet withal so skillful in inspiring enthusiasts that he proved to be precisely the type of candidate to which a convention turns after the luminous stars of the pre-convention canvass have proved unavailable. The atmosphere of the Wigwam at Chicago was favorable to the "rail splitter," opposition within the state having been skillfully sidetracked. O. H. Browning, for instance, who favored Bates because of his strength with the old Whigs, was a member of the Illinois delegation pledged to Lincoln; and he labored loyally for him at the convention. David Davis, in charge of the Lincoln forces at Chicago, worked tirelessly and did his part well, though his bargaining in cabinet positions was contrary to Lincoln's instructions. With 465 delegates present and 233 necessary to a choice, the first ballot stood: Seward 173½, Lincoln 102, Cameron 50½, Chase 49, Bates 48, the rest scattered. On the second ballot Cameron's name was withdrawn to Lincoln's advantage, Seward receiving 184½ votes, Lincoln 181, Chase 42½, Bates 35. On the third ballot the change of four Ohio votes during the count precipitated a stampede to Lincoln, who became the convention's choice amid scenes of wild excitement.

In the fury of the ensuing campaign, with the Democratic party split between North and South and disunion threatened in case of Republican success, Lincoln remained quietly at Springfield. He conferred with leaders, received delegations, wrote letters, and prepared a short autobiography for campaign purposes; but he avoided political speeches. While the people of the South were expecting the worst from him, he did but little to reassure them. In the election of Nov. 6, 1860, he was chosen president by pluralities in enough states to give him a considerable electoral majority; but as regards the whole popular vote he was a minority president. There were ten Southern states in which not a single popular vote had been cast for him; and, strangely enough, his own county in Illinois voted against him. Lincoln carried every Northern free state except New Jersey. His vote in New England was nearly three times that of Douglas; elsewhere in the East his vote stood to that of Douglas as 7 to 4; in the Western states the contest was closer, the ratio being 8 to 7. Lincoln's total in the popular vote was 1,866,452 as compared to 1,376,957 for Douglas, 849,781 for Breckinridge, and 588,879 for Bell (Edward Stanwood, *A History of the Presidency*, 1924, I, 297). The electoral vote stood: Lincoln 180, Breckinridge 72, Bell 39, Douglas 12.

In the critical interval between his election and his inauguration Lincoln continued his policy of silence, making no speeches and avoiding public statements as to his policy. While events were moving rapidly in the lower South and disunion was consummated by the formation of a Southern Confederacy without hindrance from Washington, the President-elect, though never doubting that the government possessed the authority to maintain itself, remained passive and quiet at Springfield. Matters of patronage, cabinet making, the preparation of his inaugural address, conferences, and correspondence occupied his attention. He found time for a trip to Coles County where he visited his aged stepmother, directing that the grave of his father be suitably marked, and for one to Chicago to meet Hannibal Hamlin, Nov. 21–26, 1860. To the measures of compromise proposed in Congress he gave scant encouragement. The Crittenden proposal to avert disunion was shattered by Lincoln's inflexible refusal to countenance the territorial extension of slavery. He requested General Scott to be ready to "hold or retake" the forts in the South as the case might require; and he did little to allay Southern fears as to his policy. He assured John A. Gilmer of North Carolina (Dec. 15, 1860, *Works*, VI, 81) that he would not discriminate against the South in appointments and that the only substantial difference between the Southern people and himself was in the matter of slavery extension. To another Southerner, Samuel Haycraft, he wrote that the "good people of the South" would find in him "no cause to complain" (Nov. 13, 1860, *Ibid.*, VI, 69–70). These and other similar letters, however, were confidential, and the pacific nature of his intentions was not appreciated. The pliable Seward, during these days, was more prominent as Republican spokesman than the President-elect. A survey of the Southern press in this crisis shows a division of sentiment between those who recognized Lincoln's election as legal and would await an "overt act" before embarking upon disunion and those who asserted that abolition had swept the North and that the "cause of the South" had no future except by separation. (See D. L. Dumond, *Southern Editorials on Secession,* 1931, esp. pp. 221–23, 304–06; see also A. C. Cole in *American Historical Review,* July 1931, pp. 740–67.) It was not long before the men who held the latter view seized the reins in the lower South; and fast-moving events made theirs the controlling policy for the South in general. (Much light is thrown on Lincoln as president-elect by the colorful letters of Henry Villard to the *New York Herald,* November 1860 to February 1861.) In the matter of cabinet making, the inclusion of Seward, Chase, and Bates was a recognition of rivals, while Welles was chosen as a New Englander and a former Democrat who had turned Republican. Lincoln had wished to include some representative of the South (as distinguished from the border states) and had approached John A. Gilmer of North Carolina on this subject, but his efforts to this end proved unsuccessful. Bargains in the nominating convention were kept by the appointment of Caleb B. Smith of Indiana and Simon Cameron of Pennsylvania.

On Feb. 11, 1861, with words of restrained emotion, Lincoln left Springfield for Washington. His speeches en route did little to reassure the skeptical East, but they made it clear that the government would resist secession. The effect of these speeches in the South was distinctly unfavorable (D. L. Dumond, *The Secession Movement,* 1931, pp. 258–60). Newspapers carried full accounts of the journey, and unfortunate publicity was given to trivial incidents, as when Lincoln, whose chin was now marred by a new-grown beard, publicly kissed a little girl for whom he inquired as his train stopped at her town, and explained that the facial adornment had been assumed at her request. His secret night ride to Washington, occasioned by detective reports of assassination plots, was a humiliation to his friends and a subject of ridicule by his opponents. In a conciliatory inaugural address Lincoln again disclaimed any intention to interfere with slavery in the states, counseled observance of all federal laws (not excepting the Fugitive-slave Law), and plead earnestly for the preservation of the Union, which he declared to be perpetual (*Works,* VI, 169–85). Denouncing secession as anarchy, he announced that the national power would be used to "hold, occupy, and possess" (he did not say "repossess") federal "property and places." Declaring that "physically speaking, we cannot separate," he asked his countrymen "one and all" to "think calmly," pledging that the government would not assail them, and closed with a poetic reminder of those "mystic chords of memory" which he hoped would yet "swell the chorus of the Union."

Inexperienced as he was in the management of great affairs, untrained in executive functions requiring vigorous action, the new President found himself borne down by a cruel pressure of miscellaneous duties, overwhelmed by a horde of office seekers, and embarrassed by unfamiliar social exactions, while through it all the Sumter crisis, involving the momentous issue of civil war, was pressing for a solution. With the eyes of the nation on the fort at Charleston as a test of the new administration, with Major Anderson reporting that in a few weeks the garrison must surrender unless provisioned, and with informal negotiations in progress between Union leaders and Southern commissioners concerning the relation of the Washington government to the Confederacy, events were pushing the new executive to a decision. Meanwhile his very position as leader was at stake. Seward had begun by supposing that he would be premier, and had fatuously proposed a startling program of foreign aggression as a means of reuniting the country. Lincoln's answer to his secretary left no doubt as to who was president, but his words left no sting. If a certain thing must be done, said he simply, "I must do it" (*Works*, VI, 237). As to Sumter, Lincoln took advice but made his own decision, not, however, without a certain laxness in his control of the situation which unfortunately gave Southern leaders the impression of bad faith; for Seward, without Lincoln's authority, had made virtual promises which the administration could not keep. Lincoln asked his cabinet to submit written advice as to provisioning Sumter. Only two members, Chase hesitatingly and Blair emphatically, favored it. Seward, Cameron, Wells, Smith, and Bates counseled evacuation, though some of the secretaries later changed their positions. Having already committed himself to the general policy of holding federal property, and feeling that evacuation would be tantamount to surrender, Lincoln ultimately decided to provision the fort. Yet Seward assured the Confederate commissioners that the fort would be evacuated; and Lincoln himself was willing to evacuate it if by this means the secession of Virginia could be averted. "A State for a fort," he is reported to have said, "is no bad business" (*Annual Report of the American Historical Association for the*

Year 1915, 1917, p. 211). Late in March he sent Ward H. Lamon to Charleston, primarily to investigate and report; but Lamon unfortunately gave Anderson, Beauregard, and Governor Pickens the impression that the garrison would be withdrawn (*War of the Rebellion: Official Records*, ser. I, vol. I, 1880, pp. 222, 230, 237, 294). In all this there was considerable muddling, though without bad faith on Lincoln's part; and the confusion was increased by a bungling of orders due to Seward's interference with arrangements made by Lincoln and Welles, as a result of which the Sumter expedition was crippled by the detachment of the powerful *Powhatan*. The pacific attitude of the President was manifest in the purpose of the expedition (to convey food to the garrison and to land reënforcements only in case of attack), and also in the care which he took to notify the governor of South Carolina of his action, thus removing the element of hostile surprise.

Diverse interpretations have been placed upon Lincoln's action, and the whole subject has occasioned a flood of controversy. There are many threads to the story; and to the perplexities of conflicting evidence must be added the difficulties of reading thoughts and assessing motives in a field where violent misunderstandings were inevitable. Under the onslaught of opposing forces, with the border states and upper South on the brink of secession and the war clouds gathering, Lincoln himself seems to have vacillated, to have pondered evacuation, meanwhile testing its possible consequences and even giving hints that such a course was under consideration without committing himself to it (a process to which statesmen must often resort), and in the end to have concluded that, in view of the uncertainty of compensating benefits accruing to the cause of union, the fort should not be surrendered. As the exhaustion of supplies made some change inevitable, the closest approximation to the preservation of the status quo was what Lincoln decided to do—to feed the garrison without aggressively strengthening it.

When the war came, Lincoln met the issue with a series of purely executive measures, for Congress was not convened until July 1861. He treated the conflict as a huge "insurrection"; and before Congress, on July 13, 1861, recognized a state of war, he had summoned the militia, proclaimed a blockade, expanded the regular army beyond the legal limit, suspended the *habeas corpus* privilege, directed governmental expenditures in advance of congressional appropriation, and in cooperation with his cabinet and the state governments had launched a multifold series of military measures. In a masterly message to Congress on July 4, 1861, he explained his Sumter policy, recounted the steps that led to war, stated the issue as between separation and union, commented on the world significance of the struggle, and appealed for ratification of previous acts as well as for future cooperation (*Works*, VI, 297–325). This legislative ratification of the president's irregular acts was soon given (*United States Statutes at Large*, XII, 326); and the Supreme Court added its sanction by deciding in the Prize Cases (67 *U. S.*, 635–99), though not without vigorous dissent, that executive proclamations were adequate for the inauguration of maritime war.

As the war progressed, Lincoln extended his executive powers until, man of peace that he was, he was called a dictator. In dealing with disloyal activities—a serious problem because of pro-Southern activity in the North—he urged no special laws against treason, he but slightly used such laws as existed, and he had no system of nationwide prosecutions; but, under his suspension of the *habeas corpus* privilege, thousands of persons were arrested on suspicion, after which, usually without trial, they were kept in prison for a time and then released. In this his purpose was precautionary and preventive, not punitive or vindictive. When confronted with anti-war or anti-administration agitation in speech or press, Lincoln usually showed toleration; and throughout the war "Copperhead" meetings were common and opposition newspapers persisted in their attacks upon the President and his party. The case of C. L. Vallandigham, arrested for an anti-war speech of May 1, 1863, by order of General Burnside, was a familiar theme of denunciation by Lincoln's opponents; but the facts show leniency and tact in him rather than severity. He and all the cabinet regretted the arrest; and when a military commission condemned the agitator to imprisonment during the war, Lincoln commuted the sentence to banishment within the Confederate lines. Later, when Vallandigham escaped from the South and conducted a violent agitation in Ohio, Lincoln left him unmolested. There were, it is true, instances of newspaper suppression, as in the case of the *Chicago Times* in June 1863 (in which case Burnside's suspension order was promptly revoked); but in general Lincoln advised military restraint and counseled the suppression of assemblies or newspapers only when they were working "palpable injury" to the military (*Works*, IX, 148).

Looking broadly at his administration, one is impressed with the many difficulties that beset Lincoln's path. He had a rival for the presidency (Chase) in his cabinet. Within his own party the "Jacobins," a group which seemed at times a cabal of congressional leaders but which became the dominant element, tried his patience with their radicalism, their defiant opposition, and their interference in the conduct of the war. Abolition demands required his utmost tact; for the outcries of such men as Wendell Phillips reached at times an almost hysterical pitch. Always he had the activities of anti-war leaders to deal with. Though bringing Democrats within his cabinet and appointing many of them to civil and military positions, he was unable to carry through his "all parties program"; and he found it necessary to function as leader of one party, the Republican or "Union" party. Scheming men imposed on his generosity and a constant stream of people clamored at his doors. He had the defeatists to deal with—men who demanded peace first and union afterward; while he had the equally hard problem of keeping the Union cause clear of abuse, so that victory, when achieved, would not itself become a curse. The maladjustment of governmental activities, state and federal, military and civil, made his tasks needlessly hard; while the profiteering, plunder, and graft that came in the wake of war wounded his honest soul. A group of senators, partisans of Chase, descended upon him in December 1862, demanding the removal of Seward and threatening to take important matters of policy out of his hands. Though inwardly suffering bitter distress (*Diary of O. H. Browning*, I, 601), Lincoln received the intriguing senators with calm, rode the storm by shrewd steering, kept both Seward and Chase in his cabinet, silenced his critics, and reassured the public. Often he faced a hostile and meddling Congress, and at times he seemed almost deserted. Favoring a war policy with as little of vengeance as possible, always remembering that the people of the South were to be respected, he encountered the opposition of the vindictive element which ultimately seized the Republican party and overthrew his policy in reconstruction days. It is in his reaction to these difficult circumstances that we find the measure of Lincoln's qualities as president: his unaffected kindness, his poise, his humor, his largeness of soul, his fairness toward opponents, his refusal to get angry, his steadiness, his ability to maintain that well-tempered morale which is so indispensable in a desperate war. There was also the notable trait of selflessness; for if Lincoln suffered when his pride was pierced, such was the temper of his self-control (which must not be misunderstood as mere humility) that no outward reaction of irascibility, peevishness, or ungenerous conduct resulted.

In his cabinet Lincoln found an ill-assorted group. Welles inwardly denounced Seward; Bates distrusted Stanton, Seward, and Chase; Stanton and Seward were uncongenial; and Chase, though never actually disloyal to Lincoln, was a constant source of discord.

Yet Lincoln, lax as he was in administrative methods, maintained an attitude of cooperation in his official family. Such changes as occurred in his cabinet were of a sort to strengthen the President's position, the vigorous Stanton displacing the incompetent Cameron, Chase being shrewdly kept in the cabinet until after the renomination of Lincoln when he gave way to the more pliable Fessenden, Speed and Dennison serving as acceptable substitutes for Bates and Blair.

In the military phases of his task Lincoln was sorely beset. Governmental organization for war purposes was ill suited to the emergency and seemed at times formless. Some of the state governors embarrassed him by over-activity that trenched upon the duties of the secretary of war; others caused trouble by sheer recalcitrancy. Military efficiency was subordinated to personal ambition; there was a superfluity of political generals; and there was confusion and experimentation in the central control of the army. Troops when brought into the field were often unreliable; "some of the brigadier-generals," wrote Halleck (*Works of Lincoln*, VII, 77), were "entirely ignorant of their duties and unfit for any command." The war machine suffered from an ill-advised system of conscription, from undue state control of military matters, from widespread desertion and "bounty jumping," and from harmful newspaper activity, which betrayed military secrets, discredited the government, defamed generals, fomented antagonism among officers, and weakened the morale of soldier and citizen. Congressional interference was evident in the Committee on the Conduct of the War (W. W. Pierson, in *American Historical Review*, April 1918, pp. 550–76), which investigated Union disasters, held protracted conferences with the President, and considered themselves "a sort of Aulic Council clothed with authority to supervise the plans of commanders in the field, to make military suggestions, and to dictate military appointments" (*Ibid.*, p. 566, citing W. H. Hurlbert, *General McClellan and the Conduct of the War*, 1864, p. 160). That Lincoln listened patiently to the committee and yet never permitted them to take the wheel from his hand, is evidence at once of his tact and his shrewdness.

With his burning sense of the issues at stake and his pathetic eagerness for one battle to end it all, Lincoln was subjected to repeated humiliation in the defeat of Union arms. His reaction to defeat is illustrated in his memorandum of July 23, 1861, following the first Bull Run, in which he outlined a comprehensive plan for pushing the blockade, drilling the forces, discharging "three-months men" who would not reënlist, bringing forward new volunteer units, protecting Washington against attack, and formulating a joint forward movement in the West (*Works,* VI, 331–32). The pressure of military duties upon Lincoln was more than any president of a republic should bear. He pored over books on strategy; scanned the military map; prepared orders for the army; gave counsel concerning such details as the acquisition of horses and the price of guns; outlined plans of campaign, not forgetting, however, the hazard of binding a distant commander to specific lines and operations; directed the allocation of supplies; attended war councils; and devoted constant attention to military appointments. He assumed a special degree of military responsibility at the time of McClellan's illness in January 1862; and he had to make those repeated calls for troops which intensified the depression of the country. In his experimentation with men he expressed a whimsical wish for a "school of events"—mimic situations in which men might be tried (F. B. Carpenter, *Six Months at the White House,* p. 225); and he even contemplated taking the field himself (*Diary of O. H. Browning,* I, 523).

Kindness and forbearance, mingled at times with fatherly admonition, characterized his attitude toward his generals. When Frémont issued impossible orders in the West without consulting the President, Lincoln sent him a word of "caution, and not of censure," directed that certain orders be "modified," sent Blair from his cabinet for a friendly conference, and finally removed the General only when his insubordinate conduct left no alternative. Lincoln's search for a winning general is a painful story. McClellan snubbed him, differed with him as to plans, wrote complaining letters, and fell short in the business of fighting. Lincoln ignored the snubs with the remark that it were better "not to be making points of . . . personal dignity" (*Letters of John Hay and Extracts from Diary,* I, 53); and on the retirement of Scott in November 1861 he made McClellan general-in-chief of all the armies. The President's plans, beset as he was by boards, senators, councils, military "experts," and clamoring editors, proved hopelessly at variance with McClellan's performance. In January 1862 the perplexed President issued a peremptory "war order" directing a "general movement of all the land and naval forces of the United States against the insurgent forces" for Feb. 22 (*Works,* VII, 89). This order was ignored, and Lincoln acquiesced in McClellan's oblique movement against Richmond via the peninsula. At the outset of the peninsular campaign, however, Lincoln relieved McClellan of supreme command; and he modified the latter's plan for the concentration of Union forces against Richmond by retaining McDowell's corps near Washington, while he also decreased Mc-

Clellan's importance by reorganizing the army under corps commanders. McClellan's ineffectiveness caused Lincoln to put Pope in command of a separate Army of Virginia; but on Pope's failure at the second battle of Bull Run the President dropped him and ordered a reconsolidation of forces under McClellan, who was thus given a new opportunity. Then came McClellan's failure to pursue Lee after Antietam, upon which Lincoln finally removed him from command. The failure of McClellan's successors—of Burnside at Fredericksburg and Hooker at Chancellorsville—added to Lincoln's perplexity and tended to discredit his ability in military matters; while Meade's success at Gettysburg was marred by another failure to pursue and crush Lee's army, and even under Grant, whom Lincoln brought to the East in 1864, there were months of sanguinary fighting with hope deferred. Lincoln's blunders in military matters, which are not to be denied, were largely attributable to political pressure or to unsatisfactory human material, and were partly offset by constructive factors such as his guarding of Washington, his attention to the western phases of the war, and his final support of Grant in the face of bitter criticism.

Cautious in his dealings with Congress, Lincoln seldom seized the initiative in the framing of legislation. He went his own way by a remarkable assumption of executive authority; and on the few occasions when he sought to direct important legislation he was usually unsuccessful. The congressional election of 1862 was unfavorable to him; and elements out of sympathy with Lincoln were often dominant in Congress, which sought to curb the president's power of arrest, passed measures which he disapproved, and came to an impasse with him as to reconstruction. Though the reconstruction issue is a notable exception, Lincoln usually yielded when Congress enacted measures distasteful to him, as in the case of the West Virginia bill and the second confiscation act. Moderates were disappointed in this pliancy, which they described as "going over to the radicals"; yet the radicals themselves were far from capturing Lincoln, and at the time of his death in office an open break such as that which occurred under Johnson seemed probable.

Though the issuing of the Emancipation Proclamation is the most memorable of Lincoln's acts, the stereotyped picture of the emancipator suddenly striking the shackles from millions of slaves by a stroke of the pen is unhistorical. Lincoln's policy touching slavery was a matter of slow development. Throughout the struggle he held that Congress did not have the power to abolish slavery in the South; and in keeping with his "border-state policy" he resisted for many months the clamors of abolitionists. When Union generals, notably Frémont in Missouri and Hunter in the lower South, attempted emancipation by military edict, Lincoln overruled them; and he said to a religious group: "I do not want to issue a document that . . . must . . . be inoperative, like the Pope's bull against the comet" (*Works*, VIII, 30). Answering Greeley's anti-slavery appeal on Aug. 22, 1862, he wrote, though with the proclamation already in his drawer, that his "paramount object" was to "save the Union," and was not "either to save or to destroy slavery" (*Ibid.*, VIII, 16). It was found, however, that war over a vastly extended front with a slave-holding power forced the government either to take steps toward emancipation or to become both its own enemy and a promoter of slavery. By July 1862, therefore, Congress had, at least on paper, pro-vided as much as the Emancipation Proclamation involved, by free-ing slaves coming within Union military lines, emancipating slave-soldiers, and decreeing liberation generally as to all "rebel-owned" slaves in the sweeping though ineffectual confiscation act of July 17, 1862. In addition, Congress had by this time prohibited slavery in the territories and in the District of Columbia.

Meanwhile, from Lincoln's pondering of the slavery problem there had emerged a plan of constructive statesmanship. Recognizing state authority in the premises, mindful of Southern property rights, and moved by the conviction that the North ought equitably to share the financial burden of emancipation, since it must share the guilt of slavery, Lincoln had urged Congress to launch a scheme of gradual emancipation by voluntary action of the states, with federal com-pensation to slave-holders. This plan, however, as well as the scheme of deportation and colonization in Africa, had broken down; and in July 1862 Lincoln reached the decision to issue his edict of liberation. By this time the increasing radicalism of the war mind, the indif-ference of the border states to his compensation scheme, and the realization that foreign sympathy could not be obtained for a gov-ernment which "sought to put down the rebellion with the left hand, while supporting slavery with the right hand" (Chase Manuscripts, Library of Congress, vol. LXII, no. 1989) had done their work. On July 22, 1862, Lincoln summoned his cabinet and read aloud the first draft of the Emancipation Proclamation. His decision was now made; he was not asking advice "about the main matter." Rather he was announcing his course and taking counsel about incidental ques-tions pertaining to its execution. Accepting Seward's suggestion that the measure would gain force if issued on the morrow of victory, he waited until Lee had been fought off at Antietam and gave out his preliminary proclamation on Sept. 22, 1862 (*Works*, VIII, 36–41). In this edict he gave warning that on Jan. 1, 1863, all slaves in rebellious districts would be made free; but the proclamation was far from an abolition document, for the President emphasized the restoration of the Union as the object of the war, and pledged further efforts to provide compensation to slaveholders. By common usage, the term "Emancipation Proclamation" applies to the edict of Jan. 1, 1863, that of Sept 22, 1862, being but a warning. The Proclamation of Jan. 1, 1863, contained no general declaration against slavery as an evil (*Ibid.*, VIII, 161–64). The Union slave states were naturally not affected; and important districts of the South (the whole state of Tennessee as well as portions of Virginia and Louisiana) were excluded from the terms of the proclamation. The most curious fact about the whole matter was that the proclamation applied only to regions under Confederate control; and Lincoln was denounced for freeing slaves only on paper in districts where his power could not extend. It is hard to put in a word the actual effect of the Proclamation. Preservation of slavery in non-rebellious districts was clearly implied; and if the Southern states had done all Lincoln asked in September 1862, thus obviating the necessity of the final proclamation, there was nothing in the preliminary document to prevent the war from ending with slavery still maintained. Yet the President's stroke at slavery did somehow change the character of the war; and its moral effect was great, albeit somewhat offset by the displeasure of those who opposed a "war to free the Negroes." Military emancipation extended as the armies advanced in the South; but as to the legal potency of the Proclamation Lincoln himself had grave doubts. Effective liberation, in fact, came through state action in the border states and more notably through the anti-slavery amendment to the Constitution. Perhaps the chief importance of the Proclamation was in paving the way for these final measures. Lincoln's part in the whole matter was necessarily central. It was he who determined the time, circumstances, and manner of the proclamation; and it was his conviction that, had it been issued six months earlier, public sentiment would not have sustained it (F. B. Carpenter, *Six Months at the White House*, p. 77).

In spite of serious complications with France and Great Britain, Lincoln gave little direct attention to foreign affairs. He brushed aside Seward's bellicose foreign program of Apr. 1, 1861; and he materially assisted in the preservation of peace by softening Seward's instructions of May 21, 1861, to Charles Francis Adams on the general question of Great Britain's attitude toward the war and by directing that Adams treat the whole dispatch as confidential. In the *Trent* affair the influence of Sumner, Seward, and Bright contributed powerfully toward peace with Great Britain, the threads being in Seward's hands; but Lincoln's moderation, though at first he seems to have supposed that Mason and Slidell ought not to be released (Frederic Bancroft, *The Life of W. H. Seward*, 1900, II, 234), was an important factor. His restraint in international dealings is shown by a "paper" which he prepared, advocating that the *Trent* case be arbitrated *(Diary of O. H. Browning*, I, 517). On such questions as the French proposal for mediation, French intervention in Mexico, and the protests against British aid in the building and equipment of Confederate warships, the course of the administration was successfully directed by Seward, to whom Lincoln wisely delegated foreign affairs with the minimum of presidential interference.

While preserving the dignity of his high position, Lincoln's manners as president were unconventional and his habits irregular. Often his meals, when carried upstairs, would be left untouched for hours. He took no regular exercise, his chief relaxation being found in the summer evenings at the Soldiers' Home. During the first week of the battle of the Wilderness, says Carpenter *(Six Months at the White House*, p. 30), he "scarcely slept at all"; and the black rings under his eyes bespoke the strain under which he labored. In his last year his friends all noted his mental weariness; as he expressed it, the remedy "seemed never to reach the *tired* spot" *(Ibid.*, p. 217). Despite this strain there was always a readiness to shake hands with a casual visitor and to receive the humblest citizen or soldier. In reviewing the death penalty for desertion or sleeping on sentinel duty, he eagerly sought excuses for clemency; yet his mercy was not mere weakness, and at times he did confirm the death sentence. He read the newspapers but little, for news reached him through more direct channels. Day and night his familiar form was seen in the telegraph office of the War Department across from the White House. In humorous stories and the repetition of favorite literary passages he found mental relaxation. The poem "Oh Why Should the Spirit of Mortal Be Proud" had a peculiar fascination for him, and his familiarity with Shakespeare was often a matter of surprise. Laughter was an absolute need of his harassed mind and he habitually thought in terms of parable, his anecdotes usually having a backwoods flavor and a tang of the pioneer West. His enjoyment of rough jest is shown in his fondness for such humorists as Nasby and Artemus Ward; his matter-of-fact secretaries had to endure a chapter from Ward as a preface to his reading of the Emancipation Proclamation in cabinet meeting. The melancholy of the earlier Lincoln deepened under the pressure of war. Not alone did the nation's woes bear heavily upon him, but the death of his son Willie in February 1862, following nightly vigils at the bedside, added a personal bereavement which would have come nigh to prostration but for the pressure of public duties.

Though a ready speech-maker, Lincoln as president made very few public addresses, the chief examples being his inaugurals, his Gettysburg address, and his last speech, Apr. 11, 1865, which dealt with reconstruction (*Works,* XI, 84–92). In lieu of the "White House publicity" of later presidents, he made use of the art of correspondence. When answering criticism or appealing to the people, he would prepare a careful letter which, while addressed to an individual or delegation, would be intended for the nation's ear. When a meeting of citizens protested against the arrest of an agitator, Lincoln wrote an elaborate letter (to E. Corning and others, June 12, 1863) explaining his policy of arbitrary arrests and pointing out the inability of the courts to deal with rebellion. Referring to the death penalty for desertion he asked, "Must I shoot a simple-minded soldier boy who deserts, while I must not touch a hair of a wily agitator who induces him to desert?" (*Works,* VIII, 308). Writing to Cuthbert Bullitt, July 28, 1862, he raised the question whether Southern unionists should be "merely passengers . . . to be carried snug and dry throughout the storm, and safely landed right side up" (*Ibid.,* VII, 296). On finding it impossible to attend a meeting of "unconditional Union men," at Springfield, Ill., he wrote an important letter to J. C. Conkling (*Works,* IX, 95–102) in which he defended the Emancipation Proclamation as a measure for saving the Union. In this letter he paid tribute to the men of Antietam, Murfreesboro, and Gettysburg, not forgetting "Uncle Sam's web-feet," for whose noble work "at all the watery margins" he expressed deep thanks. Of like importance were his letter to Greeley on the slavery question (Aug. 22, 1862), to Raymond of the *Times* regarding compensated emancipation, to Governor Seymour concerning the opposition of New York to the conscription law, and to Mrs. Bixby, whom he beautifully consoled for the loss of her sons in battle. On Nov. 19, 1863, in dedicating a soldiers' cemetery at Gettysburg, Lincoln lifted the nation's thoughts from the hatreds and imminent horrors of war in a brief address which is recognized as his most famous speech (*Works,* IX, 209–10). In his few simple words of dedication the factor of enmity toward the South was notably lacking; and the prevailing note was Lincoln's central idea of the broad significance of the Civil War as a vindication of popular rule.

The story of the campaign and election of 1864 has never been fully told. In an atmosphere of national depression and war-weariness, with prominent men denouncing the "imbecility" of the administration at Washington, with victory deferred after three years of terrible losses, with financial credit at low ebb, and with defeatists demanding peace on the ground that the war was a failure, the President faced the hazard of a popular election. Though the presidential boom of Salmon P. Chase, to which Lincoln closed his ears, soon collapsed, Frémont accepted nomination from an anti-Lincoln group; and the Democrats ominously gathered their forces while at the same time postponing their nomination until August. Such Republicans as Greeley, H. W. Davis, Beecher, Bryant, Whitelaw Reid, and many others, were minded to drop Lincoln; but Republican managers set an early date for the party convention (June 7), Lincoln meanwhile keeping Chase in the cabinet, and there was little difficulty in obtaining the President's renomination when the convention met at Baltimore. The renomination was in fact unanimous; but in the months that followed, the military outlook became still gloomier; and when McClellan was nominated by the Democrats in August on a peace platform his strength seemed truly formidable. At this juncture a surprising movement developed—nothing less than an effort to supplant Lincoln with a "more vigorous leader" and force his withdrawal (New York *Sun,* June 30, 1889, p. 3). A plan was laid for a convention to meet at Cincinnati, Ohio, on Sept. 28 "to concentrate the union strength on some one candidate, who commands the confidence of the country, even by a new nomination if necessary" (*Ibid.*). At this time Greeley wrote that Lincoln was "already beaten," and that only "another ticket" could save the party from "utter overthrow." As late as Aug. 25, H. W. Davis wrote: "My letters from Maryland say Lincoln can do nothing there, even where the Union party is most vigorous, and everybody is looking for a new candidate from somewhere." These extracts will serve to suggest the active opposition to Lincoln within his own party, which was due to such factors as the lack of Union success in battle, the conservatism of Lincoln, his leniency toward the South which ran counter to the radical plan of reconstruction, his call of July 18, 1864, for 500,000 volunteers, and the feeling that the President under Seward's influence was an opportunist and compromiser rather than a vigorous executive. The real strength of the anti-Lincoln movement is difficult to gauge because a favorable turn in the administration's fortunes occurred in September with the fall of Atlanta and Republican electoral successes in Vermont and Maine, after which, for the sake of party harmony, various anti-Lincoln men such as Wade and Greeley gave him their support. With this turn of the tide the demand for Lincoln's withdrawal lost its point and the Cincinnati convention was never held. Efforts were put forth to include certain states of the Confederacy in the election, and the President carried Louisiana and Tennessee where reorganized "loyal" governments had been set up; but the votes of these states, being unnecessary, were not recognized by Congress in the electoral count. Thus only the Union states were counted; and all of them except Kentucky, Delaware, and New Jersey gave Lincoln their electoral vote. This electoral sweep, together with Lincoln's popular majority of more than 400,000 over McClellan, gave the election somewhat the appearance of a Lincoln landslide; there were, however, powerful McClellan minorities in Illinois, Indiana, Ohio, New York, and Pennsylvania. (H. M. Dudley, "The Election of 1864," *Mississippi Valley Historical Review,* March 1932). In the event of McClellan's election Lincoln had resolved "to so cooperate with the President-elect as to save the Union between the election and the inauguration." As his secretaries record, it was the President's intention to "talk matters over" with McClellan and say to him: "Now let us together, you with your influence and I with all the executive power of the Government, try to save the country." At the time when this patriotic resolve to cooperate with a victorious opponent was made (Aug. 23, 1864), the President considered his own defeat "exceedingly probable" (Nicolay and Hay, *Lincoln,* IX, 251–52).

At his second inauguration, Mar. 4, 1865, Lincoln made no effort to review the events of his administration, but delivered a brief address which, for loftiness of tone, ranks among his greatest state papers (*Works,* XI, 44–47). Breathing a spirit of friendliness toward the enemy, he refused to blame the South for the war, and counseled his countrymen to "judge not, that we be not judged." "With malice toward none; with charity for all," he concluded, "let us strive on to finish the work we are in; to bind up the nation's wounds; . . . to do all which may achieve and cherish a just and lasting peace. . . ." There were few Northern leaders who manifested as fair an understanding of the Southern people as Lincoln (A. C. Cole, in *Lincoln Centennial Association Papers,* 1928, pp. 47–78); and he devoted careful thought and labor to the restoration of the Southern states to the Union. In his proclamation of Dec. 8, 1863, he pardoned (with certain exceptions) those Confederates who would swear allegiance to the Union; and he vigorously promoted the organization of "loyal" governments in the Southern states, requiring that they abolish slavery, and standing ready to welcome them into the Union though the loyal nucleus be no more than ten per cent of the voters of 1860. When Congress, on July 2, 1864, passed the Wade-Davis bill providing a severe plan that would hinder reconstruction, Lincoln applied the "pocket" veto, and announced his reasons in a "proclamation" of July 8 (*Works*, X, 152–54), upon which the authors of the bill, with an eye to the President's embarrassment in the campaign for reëlection, severely attacked him in an address to the people known as the Wade-Davis manifesto. The details of Lincoln's further efforts toward reconstruction are too elaborate to be recounted here. His scheme was carried through to his own satisfaction in Tennessee, Louisiana, Arkansas, and Virginia; but Congress never recognized any of these "Lincoln governments" of the South.

As to peace negotiations with the Confederacy, Lincoln insisted upon reunion and the abolition of slavery, but manifested a generous disposition on collateral issues. This was his attitude in connection with the peace efforts of Horace Greeley in 1864; and the same moderate attitude was manifested in connection with the elder Francis P. Blair's mission to Richmond in 1864 and in the Hampton Roads Conference of February 1865. In this conference Lincoln, in company with Seward, conferred on board a warship with three Confederate commissioners (J. A. Campbell, A. H. Stephens, and R. M. T. Hunter); and accounts agree that, while the President again insisted upon reunion and emancipation, he showed willingness to use the pardoning power freely in the South, to allow self-government to the returning states, and even to recommend liberal compensation to slave-holders. On the fall of Richmond Lincoln visited the Confederate capital, where he walked the streets unmolested, and advised with Southern leaders, notably J. A. Campbell. He expressed a desire to permit the "rebel" legislature of Virginia to return and reorganize the state; but this purpose, as well as his other plans for the South, was defeated.

He gave the closest attention to the final military phase of the war, visiting the army and remaining with Grant at City Point from Mar. 24 until Apr. 9, except for his two-day visit to Richmond on the 4th and 5th. His return to Washington coincided with Lee's surrender, an event which gave added significance to the President's last speech, which was a statesmanlike paper read to a cheering crowd at the White House on the night of Apr. 11. Returning to the subject of reconstruction, he appealed to a divided North to let the South come back to the Union. Casting theories aside, he said: "We all agree that the seceded States . . . are out of their proper practical relation with the Union, and that the . . . object of the government . . . is to again get them into that proper practical relation" (*Works*, XI, 88). "Concede," he said, "that the new government of Louisiana is . . . as the egg is to the fowl, we shall sooner have the fowl by hatching the egg than by smashing it" (*Ibid.*, XI, 91). On the last day of Lincoln's life the subject of reconstruction was discussed at length in cabinet meeting; and a project was considered which resembled the plan later announced by President Johnson on May 29, 1865 (40 Cong., 1 sess., *Report of Committees of the House of Representatives*, no, 7, pp. 78–79). Again Lincoln expressed the wish that all vindictiveness be laid aside and that the Southern people be leniently treated (F. W. Seward, *Reminiscences*, 1916, p. 254). With opposition growing within his own party and threatening the ruin of his generous plans had he lived, he was removed by assassination, which silenced criticism and conferred the martyr's crown. At Ford's Theatre on the night of Apr. 14, 1865, he was shot by John Wilkes Booth. After lying unconscious through the night he died the following morning. The state rites over, the funeral train moved west with frequent stops; and amid fulminations of vindictive oratory, with people and soldiers mourning their beloved Chief, the body was laid to rest at Springfield.

The early crystallization of the enduring Lincoln tradition was illustrated by Stanton's comment, "Now he belongs to the ages." That he was among the "consummate masters of statecraft" may be disputed, but such was the impression he left that this distinction has been accorded him. In the shortest list of American liberal leaders he takes eminent place: liberalism with him was no garment; it was of the fiber of his mind. His hold upon the affection of his own people has not been due merely to the fact that he, a backwoods lad, rose to the highest office in the land. It is doubtful whether any other leader of the North could have matched him in dramatizing the war to the popular mind, in shaping language to his purpose, in smoothing personal difficulties by a magnanimous touch or a tactful gesture, in avoiding domestic and international complications, in courageously persisting in the face of almost unendurable discouragements, in maintaining war morale while refusing to harbor personal malice against the South. Not inappropriately, he has become a symbol both of American democracy and of the Union.

[REVISED BIBLIOGRAPHY, by David Donald. The voluminous Robert Todd Lincoln Collection in the Lib. of Cong. is the largest and most valuable collection of manuscripts dealing with Abraham Lincoln. For a selection from this material see David C. Mearns, ed., *The Lincoln Papers* (2 vols., 1948). The Herndon-Weik Collection, also in the Lib. of Cong., contains manuscripts of great value on Lincoln's pre-presidential years; for an extensive but uncritical selection see Emanuel Hertz, ed., *The Hidden Lincoln* (1938). The definitive edition of Lincoln's writings is *The Collected Works of Abraham Lincoln* (9 vols., 1953–55), ed. by Roy P. Basler with the assistance of Marion Dolores Pratt and Lloyd A. Dunlap. The preceding biographical sketch, however, was prepared before the publication of the Basler collection, and citations to Lincoln's own statements are from John G. Nicolay and John Hay, eds., *Complete Works of Abraham Lincoln* (Gettysburg ed., 12 vols., 1905). Selections from Lincoln's writings are numerous, the best being Paul M. Angle and Earl S. Miers, eds., *The Living Lincoln* (1955). Though containing some spurious entries, Archer H. Shaw, ed., *The Lincoln Encyclopedia* (1950), is a convenient index to Lincoln's own words. Earl S. Miers, ed., *Lincoln Day by Day* (3 vols., 1960), offers a full chronology of his career; it is an invaluable tool. The standard bibliography is Jay Monaghan, ed., *Lincoln Bibliography, 1839–1939* (2 vols., 1945), which is, however, all-inclusive and therefore uncritical. For a mere selective, annotated list see Paul M. Angle, *A Shelf of Lincoln Books* (1946). Many important articles about Lincoln are contained in the Lincoln Centennial Asso. *Bull.*, the *Bull.* and *Papers* of the Abraham Lincoln Asso., and, especially, the *Abraham Lincoln Quart.* Also valuable are the periodicals *Lincoln Lore*, *Lincoln Kinsman*, and the *Lincoln Herald*.

Biographies of Lincoln begin as early as 1860, when campaign lives were issued by J. L. Scripps, J. H. Barrett, and J. Q. Howard; others by H. J. Raymond, W. M. Thayer, and, again, J. H. Barrett followed in 1864. After Lincoln's death there appeared a number of biographies by men who had known him more or less closely. Ward H. Lamon brought out *The Life of Abraham Lincoln from his Birth to his Inauguration as President* (1872). This work, which gives a realistic and partly unfavorable picture of Lincoln, was written not by Lamon but by Chauncey F. Black. Isaac N. Arnold of Chicago, from years of association with Lincoln, published studies in 1866 and 1869, and *The Life of Abraham Lincoln* (1885). J. G. Holland, *Life of Abraham Lincoln* (1866), though produced too soon to permit of historical perspective, was a work of merit, compiled with discrimination and attractively written. In 1889 appeared *Herndon's Lincoln: The True Story of a Great Life,* by William H. Herndon and Jesse W. Weik, which should be used in the edition by Paul M. Angle (1930). With all its limitations, this biography is a classic. It presents Lincoln without the halo, giving a view of the everyday life of the man with a wealth of anecdote and a power of portrayal which has caused it to be extensively used by later biographers. It is, however, the Lincoln of the prairies whom Herndon and Weik present; their account of the presidency is wholly inadequate. For a critical study of this most influential of Lincoln biographies, see David

Donald, *Lincoln's Herndon* (1948). Many years later Weik returned over the same trail and published *The Real Lincoln* (1922). The monumental work by Lincoln's secretaries, John G. Nicolay and John Hay, *Abraham Lincoln: A History* (10 vols., 1890), inaugurated a new era of Lincoln historiography. It is a voluminous history as well as a biography, for the authors attempted to include everything. Approved by Robert Lincoln, it possesses both the advantages and the defects of an authorized biography. From their daily contact with the President, Nicolay and Hay had an inside acquaintance with his administration; and they made use of a vast range of material, including the President's own papers, which have only recently become available to other scholars. Their uniform tendency, however, to treat everything from the point of view of Lincoln, their unsympathetic attitude toward his opponents, and their partiality for the Republican party, made it impossible for them to produce the definitive biography.

Since Nicolay and Hay, the Lincoln bibliography has reached tremendous dimensions, and a full list would comprise thousands of items. The activity of collectors and dealers in Lincolniana has magnified the importance of every trivial item; and the yearly output of Lincoln addresses and articles, tinctured with the political or social predilections of the authors, is of staggering proportions. Only a few outstanding titles can be mentioned here. Once highly popular but little used today is Ida M. Tarbell, *The Life of Abraham Lincoln* (2 vols., 1900), based on material collected by the author in the service of *McClure's Mag.* and first published serially in that periodical in 1895–96. Nor are the works of that most tireless of Lincoln students, W. E. Barton, now frequently read: *Life of Abraham Lincoln* (2 vols., 1925); *The Paternity of Abraham Lincoln* (1920); *The Soul of Abraham Lincoln* (1920); *The Women Lincoln Loved* (1927); *The Lineage of Lincoln* (1929); *Lincoln at Gettysburg* (1930). Emanuel Hertz is another most prolific Lincoln author whose works, too numerous to list here, are now infrequently consulted. For many years Lord Charnwood's *Abraham Lincoln* (1917), an excellently proportioned narrative based on but little original research, was considered the best one-volume biography, but with the publication of lives by B. P. Thomas and R. H. Luthin (see below) it is today little read. Other short biographies which have fallen into disuse include: Emil Ludwig, *Lincoln* (1930); Carl Schurz, *Abraham Lincoln* (1891); E. P. Oberholtzer, *Abraham Lincoln* (1904); J. T. Morse, *Abraham Lincoln* (2 vols., 1893); J. G. Nicolay, *A Short Life of Abraham Lincoln* (1902).

A major revision in Lincoln historiography may be dated from the publication of Albert J. Beveridge, *Abraham Lincoln, 1809–1858* (2 vols., 1928), a massive but incomplete work which for the first time made full, if occasionally uncritical, use of the Herndon-Weik MSS. Revisionist scholarship has combined a warm admiration for Lincoln's personality and character with a cool, critical attitude toward his political objectives and career. As applied to Lincoln's pre-presidential years, revisionism has "tended to question the ultimate wisdom of his antislavery stand, to minimize his sympathy for the Negro, to underscore his social and political conservatism, to stress his political opportunism at the expense of his idealism, and, above all, to reduce his stature in the 1850's"

(Fehrenbacher, *post,* 169–70). The fullest revisionist treatment of the presidential years is J. G. Randall, *Lincoln the President* (4 vols., 1945–55; vol. IV completed by Richard N. Current), which stresses Lincoln's blundering in the secession crisis (while denying that he plotted to start a war with the South), his weakness in bowing before political pressure from the Radicals within his own party, his failure properly to support Gen. George B. McClellan or to find an able replacement for that commander until 1864, his suppression, albeit reluctant and necessary, of civil rights, and his inefficient administrative techniques; these deficiencies, however, Randall and Current find largely redeemed through Lincoln's personal greatness, his political astuteness, and his statesmanlike program of reconstruction. The best one-volume statement of this revisionist attitude is Reinhard H. Luthin, *The Real Lincoln* (1960). It is important to distinguish between this scholarly revisionist attitude and the devastating denigration of Edgar Lee Masters, *Lincoln the Man* (1931), which is almost the only hostile biography.

Not all writers, of course, were affected by revisionist ideas. Carl Sandburg's *Abraham Lincoln: The Prairie Years* (2 vols., 1926) and *Abraham Lincoln: The War Years* (4 vols., 1939) largely ignored these critical attitudes toward Lincoln and recreated with great vividness the President as a personality of deep poetic insight. Similarly Benjamin P. Thomas's *Abraham Lincoln* (1952), probably the best one-volume biography, stood aloof from the revisionist trend. There are indications in recent years that revisionism has spent its force, and the works of Allan Nevins, Harry V. Jaffa, and Don E. Fehrenbacher (all cited below) take a much more positive view of Lincoln's ideas and accomplishments. Two useful anthologies which give extracts from these and other Lincoln biographies are Paul M. Angle, ed., *The Lincoln Reader* (1947), and Courtland Canby, ed., *Lincoln and the Civil War* (1960). Four books of essays which deal with important and controversial aspects of Lincoln's career are: Richard N. Current, *The Lincoln Nobody Knows* (1958); David Donald, *Lincoln Reconsidered* (1956); Norman A. Graebner, ed., *The Enduring Lincoln* (1959); and J. G. Randall, *Lincoln the Liberal Statesman* (1947).

On Lincoln's ancestry, in addition to the works of W. E. Barton listed above, see Marion D. Learned, *Abraham Lincoln: An American Migration* (1909); Waldo Lincoln, *Hist. of the Lincoln Family* (1923); and Louis A. Warren, *Lincoln's Parentage and Childhood* (1926). Material on Lincoln's childhood is sparse and generally unreliable. For reminiscences on this and other subjects, see Hertz, *The Hidden Lincoln,* cited above. Louis A. Warren, *Lincoln's Youth . . . 1816–1830* (1960), is uncritical. Lincoln's Illinois phase is much more elaborately documented. Benjamin P. Thomas's *Lincoln's New Salem* (rev. ed., 1954) is a charming book. Paul M. Angle's *"Here I Have Lived"* (1935) is a valuable history of Springfield in Lincoln's time. Lincoln's early career in the state legislature can be traced in William E. Baringer, *Lincoln's Vandalia* (1949). Harry E. Pratt, *The Personal Finances of Abraham Lincoln* (1943), is a mine of information. Lincoln's legal career is elaborately treated in John J. Duff, *A. Lincoln, Prairie Lawyer* (1960); John P. Frank, *Lincoln as a Lawyer* (1961); and Albert Woldman,

Lawyer Lincoln (1936). See also Willard L. King, *Lincoln's Manager, David Davis* (1960).

On Lincoln's pre-presidential political activities David Donald, *Lincoln's Herndon* (previously cited), is full. Donald W. Riddle's *Lincoln Runs for Congress* (1948) and *Congressman Abraham Lincoln* (1957) adequately cover their subject. William E. Baringer, *Lincoln's Rise to Power* (1937), and Don E. Fehrenbacher, *Prelude to Greatness: Lincoln in the 1850's* (1962), are important for Lincoln's re-emergence as a politician. For the general national setting of Lincoln's political activities see Allan Nevins, *The Emergence of Lincoln* (2 vols., 1950). On the Lincoln-Douglas debates one should read the full texts of the speeches in Edwin E. Sparks, ed., *The Lincoln-Douglas Debates of 1858* (1909), or in Paul M. Angle, ed., *Created Equal?* (1958). The best analysis of the debates is Harry V. Jaffa, *Crisis of the House Divided* (1959). For Lincoln's almost forgotten political activities in 1859, see Harry V. Jaffa and Robert W. Johannsen, eds., *In the Name of the People* (1959). The best monograph on Lincoln's role in the 1860 election is Reinhard H. Luthin, *The First Lincoln Campaign* (1944). William E. Baringer, *A House Dividing* (1945), is sprightly and informative on Lincoln as President-elect. On Lincoln in the months after his election, see David M. Potter, *Lincoln and his Party in the Secession Crisis* (1942), and Kenneth M. Stampp, *And the War Came* (1950). The President's inaugural trip to Washington is chronicled in Victor Searcher, *Lincoln's Journey into Greatness* (1960). His rather ignominious entry into the capital can be followed in Norma B. Cuthbert, ed., *Lincoln and the Baltimore Plot* (1949). John S. Tilley, *Lincoln Takes Command* (1941), is an unfriendly and unfair view of Lincoln's course in the Sumter crisis.

After 1861 Lincoln's career tends to become identical with the history of the Union cause, and there is much information to be found in such general histories as James Ford Rhodes, *Hist. of the U. S. from the Compromise of 1850* (7 vols., 1893–1900); Edward Channing, *Hist. of the U. S.*, vol. VI (1925); John B. McMaster, *Hist. of the People of the U. S. during Lincoln's Administration* (1927); and, especially, Allan Nevins, *The War for the Union* (2 vols., 1959–60). Of course the major Lincoln biographies by Luthin, Nicolay and Hay, Randall and Current, Sandburg, and Thomas give full coverage to the war years. Note also the biographies of Lincoln's leading contemporaries and, especially, of his cabinet members. The following Civil War diaries cast an invaluable first-hand light on the President: Howard K. Beale, ed., *The Diary of Edward Bates, 1859–1866* (1933); Theodore C. Pease and J. G. Randall, eds., *The Diary of Orville Hickman Browning* (2 vols., 1927–33); David Donald, ed., *Inside Lincoln's Cabinet: The Civil War Diaries of Salmon P. Chase* (1954); Adam Gurowski, *Diary* (3 vols., 1862–66); Tyler Dennett, ed., *Lincoln and the Civil War in the Diaries and Letters of John Hay* (1939); Allan Nevins and Milton H. Thomas, eds., *The Diary of George Templeton Strong, 1835–1875* (4 vols., 1952); and Howard K. Beale, ed., *Diary of Gideon Welles, Secretary of the Navy under Lincoln and Johnson* (3 vols., 1960). Lincoln's relations with his cabinet are traced in Burton J. Hendrick, *Lincoln's War Cabinet* (1946), and in Clarence

E. Macartney, *Lincoln and his Cabinet* (1931). Harry J. Carman and Reinhard H. Luthin, *Lincoln and the Patronage* (1943), shows the President as an adroit political manager. On Lincoln's struggle to achieve and maintain supremacy within his own party, three books are invaluable: William B. Hesseltine, *Lincoln and the War Governors* (1948); T. Harry Williams, *Lincoln and the Radicals* (1941); and William F. Zornow, *Lincoln and the Party Divided* (1954). For Lincoln's efforts to shape military strategy Colin R. Ballard, *The Military Genius of Abraham Lincoln* (rev. ed., 1952), and T. Harry Williams, *Lincoln and his Generals* (1952), are excellent. Clarence E. Macartney, *Lincoln and his Generals* (1925), is still useful. Kenneth P. Williams, *Lincoln Finds a General* (5 vols., 1949–59), is a comprehensive and masterful study of the Northern armies and their commanders to 1864. Robert V. Bruce, *Lincoln and the Tools of War* (1956), breaks new ground in showing Lincoln's minute attention to the details of Northern armament.

On Lincoln's conception of his war powers and his relation to the Constitution the definitive work is J. G. Randall, *Constitutional Problems under Lincoln* (rev. ed., 1951). Also useful is David M. Silver, *Lincoln's Supreme Court* (1956). Jay Monaghan, *Diplomat in Carpet Slippers* (1945), is a vivid but somewhat overstated account of Lincoln's role in foreign policy. A. R. Tyrner-Tyrnauer, *Lincoln and the Emperors* (1962), discusses American relations with France, Austria, and Mexico. Albert A. Woldman, *Lincoln and the Russians* (1952), fully covers that topic. Some idea of the abuse to which the President was subjected can be gained from Robert S. Harper, *Lincoln and the Press* (1951). Herbert Mitgang, ed., *Lincoln as They Saw Him* (1956), is an extensive anthology of newspaper comments upon the President. George F. Milton, *Abraham Lincoln and the Fifth Column* (1942), shows how Lincoln dealt with subversives. For Lincoln's personal life in the White House, in addition to John Hay's sprightly diary one should read David H. Bates, *Lincoln in the Telegraph Office* (1907); Noah Brooks, *Washington in Lincoln's Time* (1895); Francis B. Carpenter, *Six Months at the White House* (1866); Elizabeth Keckley, *Behind the Scenes* (1868); A. K. McClure, *Abraham Lincoln and Men of War-Times* (1892); A. T. Rice, ed., *Reminiscences of Abraham Lincoln* (1886); and W. O. Stoddard, *Inside the White House in War Times* (1890). F. Lauriston Bullard, *Abraham Lincoln and the Widow Bixby* (1946), and John H. Cramer, *Lincoln under Enemy Fire* (1948), deal adequately with two small but controversial subjects. For Lincoln's Gettysburg address, see W. E. Barton, *Lincoln at Gettysburg* (previously cited). Lincoln's attitude toward his enemies is treated with sympathy and insight in J. G. Randall, *Lincoln and the South* (1946). For two widely variant views of his plans for the postwar South, see Charles H. McCarthy, *Lincoln's Plan of Reconstruction* (1901), and William B. Hesseltine, *Lincoln's Plan of Reconstruction* (1960). Jonathan T. Dorris, *Pardon and Amnesty under Lincoln and Johnson* (1953), is a full treatment of a difficult subject.

For interpretations of Lincoln's political philosophy, see David Donald, *Lincoln Reconsidered*, pp. 123–43; Richard Hofstadter, *The Am. Political Tradition* (1948), pp. 92–134; Stanley Pargellis, "Lincoln's Political Philosophy," *Abraham Lincoln Quart.*, June 1945; Vernon L. Parrington, *Main Currents in Am.*

Thought, II (1930), 152–60; J. G. Randall, *Lincoln the Liberal Statesman,* pp. 175–206; T. Harry Williams, "Abraham Lincoln: Principle and Pragmatism in Politics," *Miss. Valley Hist. Rev.,* June 1953; and Edmund Wilson, "Abraham Lincoln: The Union as Religious Mysticism," in *Eight Essays* (1954). For Lincoln's religious views see, in addition to W. E. Barton, *The Soul of Abraham Lincoln* (previously cited), Edgar D. Jones, *Lincoln and the Preachers* (1948), and William J. Wolf, *The Almost Chosen People* (1959). On Lincoln's family the authoritative works are *Mary Lincoln: Biography of a Marriage* (1953) and *Lincoln's Sons* (1956), both by Ruth Painter Randall. William A. Evans, *Mrs. Abraham Lincoln* (1932), and Carl Sandburg and Paul M. Angle, *Mary Lincoln: Wife and Widow* (1949), are still useful. Rather too much has been written about Lincoln's assassination. The best work is still David M. DeWitt, *The Assassination of Abraham Lincoln* (1909), but Jim Bishop, *The Day Lincoln Was Shot* (1955), and George S. Bryan, *The Great American Myth* (1940), are also valuable. Otto Eisenschiml's *Why Was Lincoln Murdered?* (1937) and *In the Shadow of Lincoln's Death* (1940) contain much new data but are marred by an attempt to implicate Stanton in the assassination plot. The same can be said of Theodore Roscoe, *The Web of Conspiracy* (1960). Lloyd Lewis, *Myths after Lincoln* (1929), is a remarkable book.

The best guides to Lincoln historiography are David Donald, *Lincoln's Herndon* (previously cited); David M. Potter, *The Lincoln Theme and Am. National Historiography* (1948); J. G. Randall, "Has the Lincoln Theme Been Exhausted?" *Am. Hist. Rev.,* Jan. 1936; and, especially, Benjamin P. Thomas, *Portrait for Posterity* (1947). Roy P. Basler, *The Lincoln Legend* (1935), deals mostly with literary interpretations of Lincoln. For pictures of Lincoln, Frederick H. Meserve and Carl Sandburg, *The Photographs of Abraham Lincoln* (1944), is the most scholarly work, but Stephen Lorant, *Lincoln: A Picture Story of his Life* (1952), is more handsome. Rufus R. Wilson, *Lincoln in Caricature* (1945), and F. Lauriston Bullard, *Lincoln in Marble and Bronze* (1952), also deserve mention.]

Robert Edward Lee

by

DOUGLAS S. FREEMAN

LEE, ROBERT EDWARD (Jan. 19, 1807–Oct. 12, 1870), soldier, the fifth child and third son of Henry, "Light-Horse Harry," Lee and Anne Hill (Carter) Lee, was born at "Stratford," Westmoreland County, Va. His father, a member of a famous Virginia family, a distinguished cavalry officer of the Revolution, and a former governor of the state, had married as his second wife a daughter of the wealthy and religious planter, Charles Carter of "Shirley." His brilliant political prospects were wrecked by a mania for speculation, and in 1811 he was forced to leave "Stratford," which belonged to Henry Lee, a son by his first marriage. Moving to Alexandria, Va., which offered inexpensive educational facilities, the family lived modestly on the income from a trust estate left Mrs. Lee by her father. The fortunes of "Light-Horse Harry" continued to decline, and in 1813, having been badly injured in the Baltimore riot, he went to the West Indies. He died at Cumberland Island, Ga., on his way home, Mar. 25, 1818.

Diligent in his studies at the Alexandria schools and displaying marked aptitude for mathematics, Robert led a normal, outdoor life, but from boyhood he had the care of an ill mother. In 1824 the inspiration of his father's military career and the opportunity of procuring a professional education without draining the limited financial resources of the family led him to seek appointment to West Point. Entering in 1825, much more mature and better prepared than the average boy of his age, he distinguished himself alike by his scholarship and by his proficiency in military exercises, was adjutant of the corps, and was graduated number two in the class of 1829 without a demerit.

The seventeen years that followed his commission as brevet second lieutenant of engineers were such as might have been spent by any young officer of that service who combined a fine presence with social graces, exemplary conduct, energy, and ability. After seventeen months of work on Fort Pulaski, Cockspur Island, Ga., he served as assistant engineer at Fort Monroe, Va., from May 1831 to November 1834. While stationed there, he married at "Arlington," June 30, 1831, Mary Ann Randolph Custis, only daughter of George Washington Parke Custis, grandson of Martha Washington. Association with Custis and with the Washington traditions at "Arlington" made his father's old commander Lee's ideal, whom he seems consciously to have emulated in his bearing and in his conception of duty. His marriage was happy. Mrs. Lee was not a housekeeper, and by her tardiness habitually offended his sense of punctuality, but she was intelligent and appreciative, though strong and outspoken in her political likes and dislikes. A constant reader, she had a deeply religious nature. She held his love, without a suggestion of wavering, through nearly forty years of married life. She bore him seven children, George Washington Custis, Mary, William H. Fitzhugh, Agnes, Annie, Robert Edward, and Mildred, who were reared chiefly at "Arlington." Only William H. Fitzhugh and Robert left issue. The others died unmarried.

After leaving Fort Monroe, Lee was an assistant in the chief engineer's office in Washington during the years 1834–37, and in the summer of 1835 aided in running the Ohio-Michigan boundary line. His first important independent assignment came in July 1837, as superintending engineer for St. Louis harbor and the upper Mississippi and Missouri rivers. When this work, which he performed with much success, was suspended for lack of funds in October 1841, he was transferred to Fort Hamilton, New York harbor, where he remained, with one brief stay at headquarters in Washington (1844), until Aug. 19, 1846. Then he was sent, via Washington, to San Antonio, Tex., as assistant engineer to the army under Gen. John E. Wool. He followed Wool's futile marches until the column reached Buena Vista, and won much praise by a very bold reconnaissance in front of that place. Transferred then to the Vera Cruz expedition, he immediately captivated its commander, Gen. Winfield Scott, by his diligence and capacity, and had every opportunity of winning a name for himself. At Vera Cruz, he was charged with locating the heavy land-batteries. The strategy of Cerro Gordo was largely based on reconnaissance made by him. In the advance on Mexico City he distinguished himself by two crossings of the lava field between San Augustin and Padierna in the dark, and during the battle of Churubusco he conducted the column of General Shields to the left of Scott's line. His exhausting work in placing batteries in front of Chapultepec and a slight wound received in the battle of Sept. 13, 1847, forced him to retire from the field, but he rejoined Scott in Mexico City the next day and was promptly set to work preparing maps for future operations.

Lee had been made first lieutenant of engineers in 1836 and captain in 1838; when he returned to the United States in 1848 and was placed in charge of the construction of Fort Carroll, Baltimore harbor, he had been promoted for gallantry to the rank of brevet colonel. After three years and nine months at Fort Carroll (November 1848–August 1852), he was made superintendent at West Point, much against his wishes. His term there was distinguished by a number of improvements in the plant, by changes in the curriculum, and by close attention to the individual cadets, among whom were individuals as different in taste and sympathies as James Abbott McNeill Whistler, the artist, and "Jeb" Stuart, the Confederate trooper. The social life of the academy was pleasant, but Lee was glad, with the assistance of Jefferson Davis, secretary of war, to change from the staff to the line as lieutenant-colonel of the 2nd Cavalry in March 1855. The transfer hardly fulfilled his expectations. His long absences from home became increasingly burdensome as he grew older, and were rendered more tedious by repeated details for court-martial duty. In October 1857 his father-in-law died. He was named one of the executors and had to hasten home and procure a succession of furloughs to settle a large property under a confusing testament. Mrs. Lee, meantime, had developed chronic arthritis and was fast becoming an invalid, to her husband's great distress. These circumstances kept him from active duty and made 1857–59 a dark period in his life. At one time he contemplated resigning from the army. During the time his regiment was on frontier duty in Texas, Lee was actually with it only from March 1856 to October 1857, and from February 1860 to the same month of the next year. During the last period he was in command of the Department of Texas. Prior to 1861, he had never commanded more troops in the field than four squadrons of horse, and that number only for a forty-day scout in

June–July 1856. Chancing to be in Washington at the time of the John Brown raid in 1859, he was sent to Harpers Ferry to put down the "insurrection." He did so with little waste of time and life.

During the later months of his second period of duty in Texas, the secession movement began. Lee had no sympathy with it. With him, a Whig, warmly devoted to the Union, the political and economic arguments for Southern independence did not weigh. He knew little of constitutional law, and the few slaves he had owned in earlier years had died or been manumitted. The question with him—a question he hoped he would never see brought to an issue —was simply whether his first allegiance was due his state or the Union. He answered it without mental debate: in case Virginia seceded, the traditions of his family and its long association with Virginia instinctively determined him to cast in his lot with her. He stated this repeatedly before he left Texas, and said at the same time that he regarded secession as revolution. It was not until the discussions of wartime camp-fires had acquainted him more fully with its constitutional basis that he accepted the doctrine of secession.

Recalled to Washington in February 1861, and placed by General Scott on waiting orders, probably with an eye to promoting him quickly in case of war, Lee watched the crisis approach, but his natural optimism led him to believe that some solution would be found before extremists, Northern and Southern, could destroy the Union. On Mar. 16, he was made colonel of the 1st Cavalry and accepted the commission without hesitation. On Mar. 15, the Confederate secretary of war wrote him offering him rank as brigadier-general in the Confederate States army, but if he ever received the letter, which shows plainly that he had not been consulted, he ignored it. Virginia, meantime, had called a constitutional convention to decide on secession. While waiting on the action of his state, Lee realized that, regardless of her decision, his conscience would not permit him to bear arms against the South. Therefore, when Francis P. Blair on Apr. 18, 1861, told him that he was authorized to offer him the field command of the United States army (Lee to Reverdy Johnson, Feb. 25, 1868, R. E. Lee, *Recollections and Letters of General Lee,* pp. 27–28), Lee declined the offer and stated his reasons for doing so. He then called on General Scott and recounted what had happened. Scott, his frank friend and admirer, told him that his position was anomalous and that he should either resign or be ready to accept any duty assigned him. Lee felt that this was true, but his affection for the army and the Union was so deep that he still hoped his honor would not compel him to dissociate himself from either. The next day he learned that the Virginia convention had voted in favor of secession. He had thereupon to decide whether he should resign immediately or await the action of the voters of the state on the ordinance of secession, which had to be submitted for their approval. The events of that single day, however, convinced him that war would not wait on a referendum. Accordingly, he submitted his resignation on Apr. 20, intending that it be effective immediately. As it was not accepted until his accounts had been checked in the routine manner, the formal date of resignation appears in official records as Apr. 25.

Lee had not communicated with the Virginia authorities, and had hoped that he would not have to participate in a war he deplored; but he considered that his sword was at the command of his native state, and when Virginia chose him as commander of her forces he accepted on Apr. 23 and threw all his energies into her defense. After making an extraordinary record in fortifying the rivers and mobilizing the volunteers of the state, he was informally designated as military adviser to President Davis, with the rank of general (confirmed Aug. 31, 1861, to rank as of June 14, 1861). Dispatched on July 28 to the vicinity of Monterey, Va., he succeeded in halting a threatened invasion from western Virginia; but military jealousies, lack of supplies, bad weather, and over-elaborate strategy robbed him of larger results, and when he was recalled to serve again as the president's consultant his popular reputation had declined greatly. Despite some clamor against him, Davis's confidence in Lee was undiminished and he sent him, early in November, to organize the defenses of the South Atlantic seaboard. This work occupied Lee until March 1862, when he was summoned back to Richmond for a third time to assist the president, with the honorific but empty title of general in charge of military operations under the direction of the president.

The assignment was unpleasant, the duties were vague, and the difficulties immense, but Lee steered a courageous course between President Davis and Gen. Joseph E. Johnston, both of them hypersensitive, and with the help of "Stonewall" Jackson, then commanding in the Shenandoah Valley, he worked out a plan to keep the Federals in northern Virginia from reënforcing General McClellan, who was then preparing to besiege Richmond. Johnston having been wounded May 31, 1862, Lee was assigned next day to the command of the troops he promptly named "The Army of Northern Virginia." At this time, when his career as a field-commander really began, he was fifty-five years old, physically magnificent and in full vigor, five feet, ten and a half inches tall, weighing around 170 pounds, with powerful shoulders and chest, a large neck and well-moulded head, dark-brown eyes, a florid complexion, and hair that was rapidly turning gray. A short beard, which he had not worn until that spring, covered a powerful jaw, and thin, straight lips. He had never commanded in a battle. During the thirty-four months that followed he at no time had a force comparable in numbers, in artillery, or in equipment to the opposing armies. This is the fact that must constantly be remembered in any study of his campaigns. The odds against him were always three to two and sometimes three to one.

He inherited a crisis. McClellan, with nearly 100,000 men, was within seven miles of Richmond. Three separate forces were threatening Jackson in the Valley of Virginia. A large Federal army was on the Rappahannock, preparing to support McClellan. If McClellan were reënforced or permitted to bring his siege guns within range, Richmond would certainly fall. Lee hurriedly fortified the city and collected such troops as he could from the South. His problem was greatly simplified when Jackson, acting under the plan he and Lee had jointly formulated, defeated two Federal columns at Cross Keys and Port Republic, June 8–9. Lee brought Jackson's troops to Ashland, sixteen miles from Richmond, and, with the combined forces, took the offensive in what were destined to be the Seven Days' battles. At Mechanicsville, on June 26, the slowness of a turning-movement that Lee entrusted to Jackson led A. P. Hill to a costly and futile attempt to storm Beaver Dam Creek; the next day, at Gaines's Mill, Lee drove Fitz John Porter's corps from the north side of the Chickahominy River and forced McClellan to change his base to the James. The rearguard action at Savage Station on the 29th did little more than expedite and somewhat confuse the Federal retreat; on June 30 a mistake as to the line of the enemy's withdrawal and the non-arrival of two of the converging columns led to an indecisive battle at Frayser's Farm, where Lee had hoped to envelop and destroy McClellan; on July 1, at Malvern Hill, the inexperience of the staff prevented the massing of the whole army in a tangled terrain for a simultaneous attack on the strong Federal positions. Isolated attacks, though gallantly pressed, failed to dislodge McClellan, who withdrew that night unchallenged and took refuge under cover of his gunboats at Harrison's Landing. This campaign was the most important period in Lee's military education. Strategically sound in principle, though demanding too much of untrained officers, the campaign was tactically bad on the Southern side. It taught Lee the necessity of simpler methods and organization. It served its immediate purpose, however, in relieving the threat against Richmond, and it supplied a large part of his army with superior small-arms. Similarly it raised greatly the morale of the army and inspired confidence in Lee.

Quietly and quickly ridding himself of incompetent division commanders, Lee soon detached Jackson to the vicinity of Orange Court House to confront a new "Army of Virginia" under Maj.-Gen. John Pope. Lee had to watch both Pope and McClellan, not knowing which might strike first, but he carefully fed troops from the James to the Rapidan, and, at the first sure sign of the impending departure of McClellan to join Pope, he anticipated the actual Federal movement and soon confronted Pope with the greater part of his army. This was Lee's first display of skill in the difficult military art of troop-movement. Arriving at Gordonsville on Aug. 15, Lee determined on an immediate campaign of maneuver, in order to increase the distance between Pope and McClellan and to subsist his army in territory that otherwise would be occupied by the enemy. His initial plan of surprising Pope between the Rapidan and Rappahannock rivers was thwarted, but he crossed the Rapidan, shifted his line as far up the Rappahannock as possible, and then, boldly dividing his army, sent Jackson by roundabout roads to attack Pope's line of communication. Jackson chose to strike at Manassas Junction, Pope's advance base. Knowing that Jackson's move would force Pope to retreat at once, Lee followed Jackson's route with Longstreet's command and before noon on Aug. 29, when Jackson was fighting a defensive battle against part of the Union army, Lee concentrated his entire command in front of Pope. He encountered great unwillingness on the part of Maj.-Gen. James Longstreet to attack that afternoon, because Longstreet believed delay until the next morning would offer greater advantage. Lee held to the view that it was the duty of the commanding general to bring the forces together at the right moment on the chosen ground of action and to leave actual combat to the divisional and brigade commanders, and he usually contented himself with "suggestions" to competent officers. In this instance, he yielded to Longstreet's stubbornness and disclosed for the first time his one great weakness as field commander —his inability to work with unwilling tools. The general assault, thus delayed, was delivered on Aug. 30 and routed Pope in the battle of Second Manassas (Second Bull Run), but Aug. 31 was lost in reconcentrating the weary and scattered army, and a rainstorm at

Chantilly (Ox Hill) on the afternoon of Sept. 1 kept Lee from over-taking his adversary.

Lee could not feed his army where it then stood. Neither could he attack the Washington fortifications, whither Pope had fled. A with-drawal would impair the morale of his army and raise that of the Federals. Accordingly, Lee determined to move into Maryland and to renew the campaign of maneuver there. Reaching Frederick on Sept. 7, he soon found that the Federals were not evacuating Harpers Ferry as he had anticipated they would be. His line of communica-tions through the Shenandoah Valley lay close to that strongly gar-risoned post, so he was forced to detach five divisions under Jackson to reduce it. After their departure, a false rumor of a Federal ad-vance on Hagerstown led him to direct Longstreet thither. He did so the more readily as he now planned to destroy the Baltimore & Ohio and then to advance on Harrisburg and cut the other main railway line that linked East and West. While Longstreet was on the road to Hagerstown, McClellan suddenly undertook a swift west-ward advance on Frederick, having received a copy of Lee's general order that had been carelessly dropped by a courier or staff-officer. Lee was caught with his forces badly divided. Hurrying Longstreet back on Sept. 14 to support the rearguard under D. H. Hill, he vainly attempted to check McClellan on South Mountain (Boons-boro) that day. Finding this impossible, he ordered a retreat to Virginia, but learning that Harpers Ferry would certainly be cap-tured by Jackson the next day, he retreated to Sharpsburg. He mis-calculated the time required for the troop-movements, his only serious blunder in logistics, and on Sept. 17, the bloodiest single day of the war, the slow arrival of troops from Harpers Ferry nearly cost him a serious defeat in the battle of Sharpsburg (Antietam). He held his ground on the 18th and then returned to Virginia, hoping soon to reënter Maryland. Including the troops captured at Harpers Ferry, he had inflicted a loss of 27,000 on his adversary during the Maryland expedition, but he had lost 13,000 himself, and his army was so badly shaken by straggling that he had to forego a further offensive.

Lee at once reorganized the army into two corps under Long-street and Jackson, refitted it and restored its morale, and awaited the next move of the Army of the Potomac, which was now placed under command of Maj-Gen. A. E. Burnside. Nearly two months passed. Then, on Nov. 14, Lee interpreted certain Federal troop-movements as indicating that Burnside was marching toward Fred-ericksburg. Lee would have preferred to fight on the North Anna, where he could have followed up a victory, but he could not afford to sacrifice the supplies of the lower Rappahannock valley, so he followed Burnside, accepted battle at Fredericksburg, and on Dec 13 repulsed repeated Federal assaults with bloody losses. He could not pursue the enemy because the Union artillery on the north side of the Rappahannock dominated the plain.

Food was scarce and forage almost unprocurable during the winter that followed. Most of the cavalry had to be sent to the rear, and two divisions of Longstreet's corps were dispatched to the south side of the James to meet a threatened advance against the railroad leading southward from Richmond. Lee hoped for the speedy return of these troops, but Longstreet did not take the offensive and dispersed his troops so widely, while collecting supplies in eastern North Carolina, that he could not reconcentrate quickly on receipt of orders to rejoin Lee. The Army of Northern Virginia had, therefore, been reduced to 62,500 men when, on Apr. 29, a new Federal commander, Maj-Gen. Joseph Hooker, launched a well-planned offensive across the Rappahannock above and below Fredericksburg. Lee was just recovering at the time from a severe illness, but he did not hesitate. Reasoning that the main attack would be west of the town, he left 9,000 troops under Early at Fredericksburg, marched with the rest to meet Hooker, and, on May 1, found his adversary withdrawing to a strong line around Chancellorsville. Lee decided to turn the Federal position from the west and directed Jackson to undertake this movement. Jackson early the next morning countered with a proposal to employ all his infantry, 28,000, with part of Stuart's cavalry, so as to roll up the whole right wing of the Federal army. Lee consented, and with 14,000 men faced the enemy's main force at Chancellorsville while Jackson marched beyond Hooker's right. Late in the day Jackson routed the XI Corps in one of the most spectacular operations of modern war. The next morning the two wings of the Army of Northern Virginia attacked the Federals, forced them into the country between Chancellorsville and the Rappahannock, and were about to deliver another assault when Lee was forced to detach troops to cope with Maj.-Gen. John Sedgwick, who had forced Early from the heights around Fredericksburg and was advancing on Lee's rear. Owing to the hesitant tactics of Maj.-Gen. Lafayette McLaws at Salem Church, it took Lee two days to dispose of Sedgwick and to reconcentrate in front of Hooker. When Lee prepared to attack again on the morning of May 6, he found that Hooker had retreated to the north bank of the Rappahannock. This, the battle of Chancellorsville, was the most brilliant of Lee's victories, but it was one of the greatest of Southern tragedies because it cost him the services of Jackson, who was wounded on May 2 and died May 10. Lee had worked in complete understanding with Jackson, whom he regarded as a perfect executive officer, and he never was able to replace him.

In the reorganization of the army that Jackson's death necessitated, Lee decided to increase the number of corps to three and to reduce their size, because he considered the old corps too large for one man to handle to the fullest advantage in a wooded country. Esteeming A. P. Hill the best division commander in the army, he named him to head the new III Corps, and for Jackson's II Corps he selected the latter's senior division commmander, R. S. Ewell. This choice was dictated by sentiment, for Ewell had been associated with Jackson's most famous battles, but it placed one-third of the Army of Northern Virginia under an officer who had served only a few weeks with Lee and was unaccustomed to exercise the discretion that Lee always gave his corps commanders. The staff, of course, was reorganized at the same time, and many new officers were assigned to direct troops of whom they knew little. The result of all this was to create a new machinery of command for two-thirds of the army. Lee does not seem to have realized the dangers this change of command involved, but his decision to resume the offensive immediately and to carry the war into the enemy's country, before the new officers became familiar with their troops and their duties, must be accounted the major mistake of his entire career. It explains, more fully than anything else, the fatal lack of coördination at Gettysburg.

He was prompted to invade the North again for three reasons: first, to supply his army; secondly, to strengthen peace sentiment in the North by showing the futility of the effort to force the South into submission; and, thirdly, in the hope that he could compel Lincoln to detach troops from the far South and thereby relieve the pressure on Vicksburg. Leaving A. P. Hill with 20,000 to hold the line of the Rappahannock temporarily, he skillfully moved into the Shenandoah Valley and reëntered Maryland, with Harrisburg again his objective. On June 23 Stuart's fondness for raids around the enemy led him to exceed his orders and to separate the largest and most proficient part of the cavalry from the rest of the army at a time when Lee needed every mounted unit to watch Hooker, who was now between him and Stuart. Finding on June 28 that Hooker had crossed into Maryland on the 25th, Lee had to concentrate quickly his columns, which had been widely scattered for the collection of supplies. The advance of A. P. Hill discovered a force of unknown strength at Gettysburg on June 30. Ewell advanced promptly from the north to support him and the two, on July 1, won a stiff fight, capturing 5,000 men. Lee arrived during the afternoon and, in the language he usually employed in dealing with his corps commanders, suggested to Ewell that the advantage be pushed south of Gettysburg. In the absence of peremptory orders, Ewell delayed the attack and gave the Federals time in which to strengthen their forces on Cemetery Hill and Culp's Hill. Lee's one chance of victory lay in striking before the Federals could concentrate all their force on the strong ground of Cemetery Ridge, but on the morning of July 2 he encountered an unexpected difficulty. Before the army had left Virginia, Longstreet had urged Lee to employ offensive strategy but defensive tactics in Pennsylvania, and he had persuaded himself that Lee had promised to do this. When he discovered that Lee was determined to attack Meade, who had now succeeded Hooker in command, Longstreet felt that Lee was courting ruin. All his pride of opinion asserted itself. He was chagrined and humiliated at the rejection of his plan, and if he did not deliberately delay in the hope of keeping Lee from what he believed would be a slaughter, he at least acted so slowly and unwillingly that Cemetery Ridge was heavily manned and its capture was almost impossible when the I Corps assaulted late in the afternoon of July 2. The movement was just successful enough to make a renewal of the attack the next morning a virtual necessity. Pickett's and Pettigrew's (Heth's) divisions charged with a valor worthy of the finest achievements of the army, but they were hurled back with dismal slaughter, and the battle was lost. Lee was forced to retreat the next day in order to reëstablish his line of communications. On the night of July 13–14 he crossed the Potomac to Virginia soil. Gettysburg was the great defeat of his military career. The caution of Ewell and the defective staff work on the two newly formed corps were responsible for some serious tactical blunders. The absence of Stuart's cavalry during the preliminaries of the battle, the strength of the Union position, and the obduracy of Longstreet explained the rest. Lee assumed full responsibility for all that had happened and sought to resign the command of the army. It was no mere gesture of humility, for however culpable Longstreet was for his behavior, Lee was to be blamed for not dealing effectively with that stubborn officer. Yet, for all of Longstreet's defects, Lee had no one in the army whom he felt justified in substituting for him. He was compelled to make the best of the personnel he had.

Despite his 20,000 casualties, Lee was anxious to resume the offensive after Gettysburg, but the detachment of two divisions of Longstreet's corps to Tennessee, the condition of the commissary, and the scarcity of replacements rendered this impossible. Only two abortive operations, one by him against Bristoe Station and one by Meade to Mine Run, occurred until May 4, 1864, when Grant crossed the Rapidan, headed for Richmond. Lee then had somewhat more than 60,000 men. Grant's force was almost precisely twice that. Grant's cavalry and artillery were better than they had ever been; the horses of the Army of Northern Virginia had been so close to starvation in the winter of 1863–64 that they could scarcely drag the guns or carry the men. The quartermasters' and commissary stores of the Army of the Potomac were ample and flawlessly organized; Lee's men had been subsisting on a daily ration of a pint of cornmeal and a quarter of a pound of bacon, and they had scarcely any equipment or supplies except their arms and ammunition. It was impossible from the outset, therefore, for Lee to assume the offensive against Grant on open ground where the artillery of the enemy could be used and the full Union strength be employed. He did not attempt to dispute the crossing of the Rapidan, but hurried forward to the Wilderness of Spotsylvania, in the hope of catching Grant on the move in that tangled terrain, the American counterpart of the Meuse-Argonne. On May 5 and 6 Lee repulsed Grant's attacks with heavy slaughter, and on the 6th was in the midst of a turning movement when the serious wounding of Longstreet threw the Confederate right into disorder. On May 7, Lee concluded that Grant was swinging southward, and by the dispatch of Longstreet's corps (now under R. H. Anderson) to Spotsylvania Court House, he blocked Grant's road to Richmond. Two weeks' fighting and maneuvering followed at Spotsylvania (May 8–21). Longstreet was *hors de combat*. A. P. Hill was ill and Ewell was scarcely able to keep the field. Lee had to give the closest attention to the tactical dispositions as well as to the strategy, but he constructed admirable field fortifications and beat off all Grant's assaults except that of May 12 on a salient in Ewell's front ("The Bloody Angle"). In that day's action Grant gained an early advantage because Lee, on mistaken reports from his scouts, had withdrawn the artillery supporting Edward Johnson's division; but a new line was drawn in rear of the salient and the enemy, on May 14, abandoned the captured position. Sensing on May 21 that Grant was starting another flank movement, Lee made a forced marched to the North Anna and again confronted him when he arrived on May 23. The

Army of Northern Virginia took up the strongest position it had yet occupied, diverted Grant's line of advance on Richmond, and effectively covered the Virginia Central railroad, though part of its track was temporarily torn up. Had Lee been able to strike either the Federal right, under Warren, or the left, under Hancock, immediately after the Union forces had crossed the river, he might have inflicted a severe defeat on one or the other of Grant's exposed wings; but after the Federals were entrenched, Lee's opportunity was lost. Moreover, he was stricken with a debilitating intestinal malady, and before he recovered, Grant (May 27) had moved again by Lee's right, this time down the Pamunkey River. Lee marched swiftly, faced Grant on the Totopotomoy (May 28–30), and forced him to maneuver to the Confederate right for the fourth time. During the whole of this period, from the time he engaged Grant on May 4, Lee was constantly seeking an opportunity to catch Grant on the move, or to attack the Federals in detail, but he found no opening. At Cold Harbor, on June 3, Grant was repulsed with such heavy casualties that he abandoned his bludgeoning tactics. During the month that had then elapsed since Grant had crossed the Rapidan, his losses had been about 50,000, a number equal to approximately 90 per cent of the strength of the infantry of Lee's army at the opening of the campaign. The record of Lee's losses, if ever filed, was destroyed in the evacuation of Richmond. The number was approximately half that of Grant's.

Beginning on the night of June 12–13, Grant withdrew from Cold Harbor, marched to Wilcox's Landing, and crossed the James River to destroy Lee's communications and to invest Richmond by way of Petersburg. Lee had anticipated such a move, but since the absence of his cavalry kept him from penetrating the screen Grant threw about the Army of the Potomac, and Beauregard on the south side of the river could not ascertain what part of Grant's army confronted him there, Lee was uncertain of the position of his adversary and therefore hesitated to uncover Richmond. He had been compelled to detach Breckinridge and later the II Corps (now Early's) to meet new threats in western Virginia and in the Shenandoah Valley, and for that reason, his ability to reënforce Beauregard was limited. He fed troops to the south side, however, as fast as he had assurance of a Federal concentration there, and with the help of Hoke's division, which Lee sent him promptly, Beauregard saved Petersburg. The investment of that city, which formally began on June 18, was essentially a campaign of attrition. With headquarters in or near the city, Lee had to defend a line of thirty miles, slowly lengthened to thirty-six. At the same time, he had to protect the railroads connecting Richmond with the South. He sent Early into Maryland in the hope that Grant would detach troops heavily to defend Washington, or else would be tempted to attack the strong lines in front of Petersburg. Early reached the outskirts of Washington, but the diversion failed of its larger purpose. Lee's forces steadily declined through casualties and, after the winter began, through desertion, chiefly on the part of new conscripts. Every day brought starvation nearer; the exhaustion of the horse supply threatened to render the army immobile; Lee could only hold on by fortifying heavily and by using as a reserve the troops on the extreme right of the Petersburg front, where the lines of the opposing forces were not close together. The principal actions of the siege were the Crater, July 30, 1864, the battles of the Weldon railroad and Reams's Station, Aug. 19–25, 1864, and the capture of Fort Harrison, on the north side of the James, Sept. 29, 1864.

On Feb. 6, 1865, orders were issued designating Lee general-in-chief of all the Confederate armies, but the condition of his own command and the plight of operations elsewhere made it impossible for him to give more than a general strategic direction to the last-ditch battles of the exhausted Confederacy. In March the advance of Sherman's army into North Carolina made it certain that Lee would be overwhelmed if he remained at Petersburg. On the 25th he made a desperate attempt to divide the Federals by an assault on Fort Stedman, and when the repulse of this was followed by an extension of the Federal left and by a general assault on the Petersburg lines, he was forced to evacuate Petersburg and Richmond on the night of Apr. 2–3 and to begin a retreat toward the small army of Gen. Joseph E. Johnston in western North Carolina. Failure to receive supplies at Amelia Court House on Apr. 4 lost him a day and compelled him, when the Federals arrived in his front, to turn toward Lynchburg up the Southside railroad. On Apr. 6, his retreating line was struck at Sailor's Creek, and on the 9th, finding himself blocked by Sheridan, and almost surrounded at Appomattox Court House, he was forced to surrender to General Grant. Of the 35,000 troops with which he started from the Richmond-Petersburg line, only 7,800 remained with arms in their hands. When he appeared among his men after the surrender, mounted on his famous war horse, "Traveller," the veterans of the Army of Northern Virginia overwhelmed him with their regard and sympathy.

As a paroled prisoner of war, treated with great consideration by the Federal army, Lee returned to Richmond and remained there or in the vicinity until the autumn. He had no home, for "Arlington" had been sold in 1863 for non-payment of taxes, but in September, having accepted the presidency of Washington College, he moved to Lexington, Va. He was profoundly interested in the education of the young men of the South, and, with the help of an enthusiastic faculty, he soon raised a discouraged college to a high level of scholarship and attendance, though it is not certain that all of the interesting educational innovations at the school originated with him. His supreme interest after the war was in restoring the economic, cultural, and political life of the South. Shunning all discussion of politics, and reading little about the war, though he at one time planned to write a history of the campaigns of his army, he set an example of obedience to civil authority. He applied for a pardon on June 13, 1865, and consistently urged his former soldiers to work hard, to keep the peace, and to accept the outcome of the war. Indicted for treason, he was never brought to trial. On his few lengthy journeys, especially on a tour of the South Atlantic seaboard for his health in the spring of 1870, he was welcomed with a measure of affection no other Southerner since Washington has received. His mail, which was immense, was crowded with offers of business proposals, all of which he rejected. In the midst of peaceful activities, he was stricken on Sept. 28 and died on Oct. 12, 1870, in Lexington, where he was buried. He probably had angina pectoris, and his final illness was due to some atherosclerotic process. The news of his death put every Southern community in mourning. Admiration for him, which had been almost universal in the South after 1862, found new expression in biographies, in monuments, and in countless memorial addresses. Washington College changed its name to Washington and Lee University in his honor. After sixty years, the affection and reverence of the South for him are, if anything, higher than in 1870. No American has ever had an influence on the people of the old Confederate states comparable to his. In all matters on which he expressed himself, he is still regarded as the final authority. In him the South still sees the embodiment of all its best ideals.

While Lee was distinguished as an educator, his place in American history is that of a notable Christian gentleman and a great soldier. He was confirmed in the Episcopal church in 1853, and the fundamentals of the Christian religion—humility, prayer, faith, and kindness—were his code of daily conduct. His equanimity was religious, rather than philosophical, and, though he was not a fatalist, he believed that God directed the daily affairs of man and ordered even man's adversities to his good. It was for this reason that he accepted defeat without repining. His unique relations with his soldiers, his affection for children, his dignified courtesy, and his love of animals are illustrated by a thousand anecdotes that are part of the spiritual treasury of Americans. His temper and patience seldom failed him. Self-control was second nature. His rare outbursts of wrath, usually attended by a reddening of the neck and a curious jerk of the head, were generally followed by some particularly gracious act to the object of his displeasure.

Both absolutely and in the light of the odds he faced in men and resources, Lee has been adjudged one of the greatest of modern soldiers and probably the most eminent American strategist. His achievements did not owe their brilliance to contrasted mediocrity, for most of his adversaries were able. Neither was he a great soldier because he had a great lieutenant in Jackson. Lee devised and Jackson executed. If Lee won fewer victories after Jackson's death it was not because he lacked strategical ability when acting alone but because his resources were diminished and because he found no successor to "Stonewall." His one great weakness was his inability to shape contrary minds to his purpose. Stubborn incompetents he courteously disregarded, but in dealing with Longstreet he thrice yielded to the latter's obstinacy and sought victory by assiduous pursuit of the second-best plan. Excessive consideration for the feelings of others explained this weakness. His strategical powers sprang from his extraordinary brain-power, his ability to put himself in the place of his opponents, his analysis of military intelligence, his masterful logistics, and his capacity for gauging accurately the offensive and defensive strength of given bodies of troops. These qualities and the long odds with which he had to contend in all his campaigns explain a daring that would have been rashness in a less capable leader. A desperate cause demanded desperate risks. His power to inspire confidence and to create morale was due to his record of victories, his inflexible justice, his attention to detail, his great aptitude for organization, his imperturbable presence in battle, his regard for his men, and the quality of his military material. He was less renowned as a tactician than as a strategist, because of his theory of the duties of a commanding general (outlined in the references to Second Manassas); but his facility in tactics increased steadily, especially in the employment of field fortification, which some consider his greatest contribution to the science of war. Where possible, he always reconnoitered in person, and with an unusual eye for terrain. He was wont to say that he had to see for himself. If he failed to follow up his successes, it was not for slowness or lack of dash but because the margin of superiority in combat was always so narrow that his army was usually exhausted after a victory.

Almost alone among the principal Confederate commanders he was consistently on good terms with the administration. Only on some three occasions, and these at times when President Davis was suffering to an unusual degree from the facial neuralgia that dogged him throughout the war, did he ever receive sharp messages from the chief executive. One of these he tore into bits; the others he ignored. The first reason for his success in dealing with as difficult a man as the Confederate President was his unfailing, deferential respect for constituted authority, a respect equaling that displayed by General Washington himself. The second reason was his willingness at all times to subordinate his operations to the general strategy of the administration and to explain his plans to the President. He knew Davis thoroughly, and in the urgent matter of reënforcements, which was always a subject of delicate and difficult correspondence, he usually got troops, if they were to be had, by stating frankly that if he did not receive them he might be compelled to retreat on Richmond. That never failed to arouse the President to action. Davis consulted him often regarding the enlistment and organization of the troops and about the strategy of campaigns on other fronts. Lee was prompt to answer and frank in his advice, but he was slow to impose his views on other commanders, especially on Gen. Joseph E. Johnston, whose capacities he perhaps over-valued. In nearly all his dispatches to the President, when operations elsewhere were under discussion, he explained that it was impossible to judge at a distance, when he did not know the special difficulties that had to be encountered. Consequently his influence on the "grand strategy" of the South was not great. To him, however, more than to any other military official, was due the enactment of the conscript laws.

———

[The major manuscript sources are as follows: private papers, in the possession of the daughters of Capt. Robert E. Lee; engineering papers, Army Engineers' archives, Washington; educational papers, at West Point and Washington and Lee Univ.; military papers, War Dept., Washington, and in the care of a committee of trustees for U. C. V., Richmond, Va.; field-telegrams on operations of June–Aug. 1864, Confederate Museum, Richmond, Va. His maps and military library are at the Va. Military Inst., Lexington, Va. The greater part of his printed letters and dispatches appear in: *War of the Rebellion: Official Records (Army)*; *Lee's Dispatches* (1915); J. W. Jones, *Personal Reminiscences, Anecdotes and Letters of Gen. Robert E. Lee* (1874); J. W. Jones, *Life and Letters of Robert Edward Lee* (1906); and the invaluable *Recollections and Letters of Gen. Robert E. Lee, by his son Capt. Robert E. Lee* (2nd ed., 1924). Other important books on his life or campaigns are: E. P. Alexander, *Military Memoirs of a Confederate* (1907); Gamaliel Bradford, *Lee the American* (1912); E. J. Lee, *Lee of Va., 1642–1892* (1895); A. L. Long, *Memoirs of Robert E. Lee* (1886); James Longstreet, *From Manassas to Appomattox* (1896); Sir Frederick Maurice, *Robert E. Lee, the Soldier* (1925); Sir Frederick Maurice, ed., *An Aide-de-Camp of Lee* (1927); Walter H. Taylor, *General Lee, His Campaigns in Virginia, 1861–65* (1906). To these may be added: *Memoirs of Lieut.-Gen. Scott* (1864); Jefferson Davis, *The Rise and Fall of the Confederate Government* (2 vols., 1881); *Battles and Leaders of the Civil War* (4 vols., 1887–88); Fitzhugh Lee, *General Lee* (1894); John Bigelow, Jr., *The Campaign of Chancellorsville* (1910). The best of the one-volume biographies, which number twenty or more, is H. A. White, *Robert E. Lee and the Southern Confederacy* (1897).]

[SUPPLEMENTARY BIBLIOGRAPHY. Douglas S. Freeman's definitive *R. E. Lee, A Biography* appeared in four volumes in 1934-35; there is a one-volume abridgment by Richard Harwell under the title *Lee* (1961). A recent collection is *The Wartime Papers of R. E. Lee* (1961), ed. by Clifford Dowdey and Louis H. Manarin. Stanley F. Horn's *The Robert E. Lee Reader* (1949), which seeks to present a "full-length portrait" of the man, contains primary as well as secondary material. Other recent biographies include Robert W. Winston, *Robert E. Lee, A Biography* (1934), and Earl S. Miers, *Robert E. Lee: A Great Life in Brief* (1956). Among the numerous works on the military aspect of Lee's career Carl C. Rister, *Robert E. Lee in Texas* (1946), treats his early military experience. Books on the Civil War include Burke Davis, *Gray Fox: Robert E. Lee and the Civil War* (1956), and Clifford Dowdey's *Death of a Nation: The Story of Lee and his Men at Gettysburg* (1958) and *Lee's Last Campaign: The Story of Lee and his Men Against Grant–1864* (1960). Two comparative studies are John F. C. Fuller, *Grant and Lee: A Study in Personality and Generalship* (1933), and Alfred H. Burne, *Lee, Grant, and Sherman: A Study in Leadership in the 1864–65 Campaign* (1939). Indispensable for Lee's experience in the Civil War is Douglas S. Freeman's *Lee's Lieutenants* (3 vols., 1942–44). Marshall W. Fishwick, *Virginians on Olympus: A Cultural Analysis of Four Great Men* (1951), contains an interesting chapter on the Lee myth and its meaning for Virginian (and American) self-knowledge. See also Roy Meredith, *The Face of Robert E. Lee in Life and in Legend* (1947). For a more complete bibliography of works published before 1951, see Marshall W. Fishwick and William M. Hollis, *Preliminary Checklist of Writings about R. E. Lee* (1951). Other important manuscript holdings are at the Lib. of Cong. and the Va. Hist. Soc.]

Ulysses Simpson Grant

by

CHRISTIAN A. BACH
FREDERIC LOGAN PAXSON

GRANT, ULYSSES SIMPSON (Apr. 27, 1822–July 23, 1885), general of the armies, president of the United States, was the descendant of a long line of hard-working, undistinguished Grants, of whom the earliest in America, Matthew Grant, landed in Massachusetts with his wife, Priscilla, in 1630. The progeny of this Puritan clung to New England until Capt. Noah Grant, having served throughout the Revolution, emigrated to Pennsylvania in 1790 and later to Ohio. The Captain's second son, Jesse Root Grant, learned the trade of tanner and established himself at Point Pleasant, Ohio, where in 1821 he married Hannah Simpson, the daughter of a farmer. She had youth, strength, and health, and stood in need of them during the years of hard work and meager comforts that followed. In their little two-roomed frame cabin the future president was born. He was baptized Hiram Ulysses Grant. His youth was spent at Georgetown, Ohio, whither the family moved when he was a year old.

From his mother he seems to have inherited many of the traits that distinguished him. She was a silent, undemonstrative, religious woman, of great common sense and good judgment. The father, Jesse Grant, was an aggressive, hard-working person whose shrewdness and thrift were rewarded, in the passage of time, by business successes. Almost entirely self-taught, he desired for his children the educational opportunities that had been denied him. From the time he was six years old until he was seventeen, young Ulysses regularly attended school, but this did not exempt him from labor. Detesting the tannery, he was set to work on his father's farm. Like many silent people, the boy had no difficulty in understanding and in securing the obedience of dumb animals. His love of horses amounted to a passion. At seven he was hauling wood with a team; at eleven he was strong enough to hold a plow; thereafter, until seventeen, he writes, "I did all the work done with horses" *(Personal Memoirs,* I, 26). During these years he developed the qualities that later marked him—fearlessness, self-reliance, resourcefulness, determination. In person he was rather short but sturdy and well-muscled; he was modest, reticent, clean-minded, and did not use profanity; he abhorred hunting and the taking of animal life.

In the winter of 1838–39, Jesse Grant applied for and received for his son an appointment to the United States Military Academy. The information roused no enthusiasm in the boy. In due time, however, he departed and, after several wonderful days in Philadelphia and New York, registered at West Point as Ulysses Hiram Grant. He had transposed his given names, fearing that his initials "H. U. G." would make him an object of ridicule. At West Point he was informed that his congressman had reported his name as Ulysses Simpson Grant. Failing to obtain a correction from the authorities, he accepted uncomplainingly the designation bestowed upon him (Edmonds, *post,* pp. 35–37; Wilson, *post,* pp. 7, 21–22). No highlights marked Grant's four years at West Point. Throughout this time he held a place near the middle of his class, though his work in mathematics was above average. As a rider he had no peer among the cadets, but in other respects he was colorless. Quiet, unobtrusive, as tidy as necessary, "Sam" Grant sought neither honors nor popularity. He had no intention of remaining in the army.

Upon graduation in June 1843, the best rider at West Point requested a commission in the cavalry, but as there was no vacancy in that arm, he reported for duty with the 4th Infantry. He served two years in Missouri and Louisiana, and in September 1845 joined General Taylor's small but efficient army at Corpus Christi, Tex. Later it moved to the Rio Grande River where a conflict with the Mexicans occurred. With the Mexican War, Grant was never in sympathy *(Personal Memoirs,* I, 53). Nevertheless, he took part actively in all of Taylor's battles except the last, Buena Vista. At Monterey he participated, as the only mounted man, in the charge of his regiment and repeatedly distinguished himself, making at one time a dash, mounted, through the city held by the enemy to obtain ammunition for the troops. For Taylor, Grant conceived a great admiration (*Ibid.*, I, 100). He saw this rough and ready Indian fighter, individualized by bluntness, lack of ostentation, and by the uniform success of his operations, advance from a seat in the saddle to the president's chair. Unconsciously perhaps, he seems to have patterned his own habits and dress on those of Taylor (Coolidge, *post*, p. 30). After Monterey, Grant, with his regiment, was transferred to General Scott's army, and as regimental quartermaster made the long march from Vera Cruz to Mexico City. He took part in the hand-to-hand fighting at Molino del Rey and in the attack on the gates of the capital city, receiving mention in division orders and in brigade and regimental reports for bravery. From the war Grant emerged a first lieutenant and brevet captain, but no less averse to a military life than he had always been.

As soon as his regiment was settled in its new station in Mississippi he obtained leave and, on Aug 22, 1848, married Julia Dent, to whom he had become engaged shortly after graduation. The wedding journey ended at his new station, Sackett's Harbor, N. Y., where the southern bride with unimpaired cheerfulness made the best of a northern winter. The year 1852 witnessed his departure with his regiment for the Pacific coast by way of the Isthmus of Panama, a region so infested with disease that Mrs. Grant, who in 1850 had given birth to a son, did not make the journey. The transit of the Isthmus was a nightmare. Mules could not be obtained. Delays occurred. Cholera broke out and many died. Grant, the quartermaster, buried the dead, cheered the living, and by his energy and resourcefulness prevented a greater loss of life. From the mushroom city of San Francisco, the regiment was ordered to Fort Vancouver, near the present city of Portland. Here Grant remained until September 1853, when promotion to a captaincy took him to Humboldt Bay, Cal. No place more dreary than this tiny frontier settlement can be imagined. With little to do, lonely as only the inarticulate can be lonely, hungry for his wife and children whom he saw no prospect of supporting on his pay, Grant at times drank more than he should have done (Coolidge, p. 35; Edmonds, p. 74; Meade, *post*, II, 162–63; W. C. Church, in *Army & Navy Journal*, June 6, 1908). A warning from his commanding officer was followed by his resignation, which was promptly accepted by Jefferson Davis, then secretary of war (Old Records Section, Adjutant General's Office).

In July 1854, after eleven years of service, Grant was out of the army, out of money, without an occupation, and a long way from home. Late in August he joined his family in St. Louis. In the six years that followed he was successively farmer, real-estate agent, candidate for county engineer, and clerk in a custom house. In none of these occupations was he successful. Finally, after a visit to his father, he was given a clerkship in a leather store conducted by two of his brothers at Galena, Ill. He did not, however, remain very long. The turn in the tide had arrived. Following the bombardment of Fort Sumter in April 1861 and Lincoln's call for volunteers, Grant presided at a mass-meeting in Galena. He declined the captaincy of a company but announced that a war would find him in the service.

There followed a period of about six weeks during which he strove without success to find in the military hierarchy a place that befitted his training and experience. He was successively drill-master of the Galena company, clerk in the state adjutant-general's office, and mustering officer. He wrote to the adjutant-general at Washington requesting the command of a regiment but never received a reply. He spent two futile days in Cincinnati cooling his heels in the outer office of George B. McClellan, then considered the coming man. Finally, in June, Governor Yates appointed him colonel of the 21st Illinois Volunteers. In a few days Grant had the regiment in camp at Springfield, hard at work. In a month it was ordered to Mexico, Mo., where, in August, much to Grant's surprise, he was appointed brigadier-general (*Personal Memoirs*, I, 254; Wilson, p. 86; Woodward, *post*, p. 189).

In 1861 Illinois and the states west of the Mississippi constituted what was known as the Western Department, under the command of Maj.-Gen. John C. Frémont. The latter, in September, placed the new brigadier in charge of a district with headquarters at Cairo, Ill. Throughout the next two months recruits poured in until Grant had nearly 20,000 men. The Confederate General Polk had converted Columbus, Ky., about twenty miles south of Cairo, into a strong fortification which controlled the traffic on the Mississippi. Across the river lay Belmont, a Confederate camp. Early in November, Frémont directed Grant to make a demonstration down the river toward Columbus. By converting this demonstration into an attack on Belmont, Grant nearly ruined a promising career. Having defeated the enemy on landing, his 3,100 boisterous recruits got out of hand and began to loot the captured camp. Meanwhile the Belmont garrison, reënforced from Columbus, had been rallied and interposed between the Union troops and their boats. Grant fired the tents to regain the attention of his men. They reformed, forced their way through the enemy, and, under heavy Confederate fire, piled pell-mell into the boats which hastily pulled out. Their commander was the last to embark (Badeau, *post,* pp. 17–18; *Personal Memoirs,* I, 273, 279; *Battles and Leaders,* I, 351).

At this time the Confederates under Gen. Albert Sidney Johnston held the West Tennessee border and protected their great supply depot at Nashville by a line from Bowling Green, Ky., westward to Columbus. The flanks were strongly held, but the center was lightly guarded by Fort Donelson on the Cumberland River and Fort Henry on the Tennessee. Grant proposed to Gen. Henry W. Halleck, who had succeeded Frémont, the capture of Fort Henry (*Personal Memoirs,* I, 287). He purposed to penetrate Johnston's vulnerable center, capture the forts, and cut in two the enemy's forces. In making this proposal, he was probably unaware that, since November 1861, General Buell at Louisville had repeatedly urged upon both McClellan and Halleck, without success, a similar movement in connection with a land movement against Nashville (*Official Records, Army,* 1 ser., VII, 451, 457, 487, 520, 527, 531). The recurrence of these recommendations caused Halleck to study the situation. Appreciating that the capture of the forts would cause the abandonment of Columbus, a place too strong to attack, he acceded to Grant's second request of Jan. 28, in which Commodore A. H. Foote joined (*Official Records, Army,* 1 ser., VII, 121; Badeau, p. 27; Wilson, pp. 103–04; Woodward, p. 215).

Preceded by gunboats, the expedition of 17,000 men started up the Tennessee five days later. Fort Henry surrendered to the gunboats, whereupon two of them steamed twelve miles upstream and destroyed the Memphis and Ohio bridge. Donelson, twelve miles eastward, was Grant's next objective. Heavy rains delayed his start until Feb. 12, but by the 13th his army had invested the fort, then held by about 17,000 men. Foote attacked with the gunboats on the 14th, but was so roughly handled that he withdrew. In the freezing dawn of Feb. 15, Grant, at the request of the wounded Foote, boarded the flagship for a conference. While this was in progress the Confederates attacked heavily and by 9:00 A. M. had driven back and broken the Union right and most of the center. The road was open for their escape.

While returning to his headquarters from the flagship, Grant was informed of the situation. A gallop along the line determined his conduct. With his right and center in confusion, he decided, with rare courage, to attack with his left. His order to Gen. C. F. Smith to assault at once was magnificently executed. By nightfall the Union troops had possession of the entire outer line of Confederate trenches. The fate of the garrison was sealed. Gen. Simon B. Buckner on the following morning requested an armistice. Grant replied: "No terms except an unconditional and immediate surrender can be accepted. I propose to move immediately upon your works" (Badeau, p. 48). So Buckner, who in 1854 had loaned Grant the money to rejoin his family (Wilson, pp. 77–78; Coolidge, p. 37; Edmonds, p. 78), surrendered over 14,000 men to his former classmate. When the telegraph announced this victory, the North became frantic with joy. President Lincoln at once named Grant a major-general of volunteers and the Senate promptly confirmed the nomination.

Buell's advance into Tennessee with about 37,000 effectives and Grant's control of the Tennessee determined the Confederates to seek a union of their forces south of that river. About 40,000 effectives were concentrated at Corinth, Miss., to crush Grant's army before it could be reënforced by Buell. A brief misunderstanding between Halleck and Grant, early in March, resulted in the replacement of the latter by Gen. C. F. Smith. On Mar. 17, Grant was reinstated (*Personal Memoirs*, I, 327; Badeau, I, 60, 65; *Official Records, Army*, 1 ser., X, pt. 2, pp. 3, 5, 6, 15, 17, 32; Woodward, pp. 225–27). While Smith commanded, he took the army up the Tennessee River, established headquarters at Savannah, and began operations for the capture of Corinth. When Grant rejoined, he retained the headquarters at Savannah, for no apparent good reason, and ordered the concentration at Pittsburg Landing of all his forces (about 38,000 men), except Gen. Lew Wallace's division of 5,000 which was left at Crump's Landing, five miles below Pittsburg.

Although both Grant and his chief lieutenant, Sherman, were aware that the numerically superior Confederate army was only twenty-two miles distant, no intrenchments were constructed about the Union camp, no line of defense was established, no adequate system of reconnaissance instituted, no plan of action prepared. From Mar. 17, when Grant reassumed command, to Apr. 6, when Johnston's army attacked, the Union commander was in ignorance of the movements of his foe. Grant says: "When all reinforcements should have arrived I expected to take the initiative by marching on Corinth. . . . I regarded the campaign . . . as an offensive one and had no idea that the enemy would leave strong intrenchments to take the initiative" (*Personal Memoirs*, I, 332). Less than one and a half miles from Sherman's headquarters, Johnston's soldiers formed line of battle on the afternoon of Apr. 5, and, without discovery, slept all night on their arms. That afternoon Grant had said: "There will be no fight at Pittsburg Landing; we will have to go to Corinth" (*Official Records, Army*, 1 ser., X, pt. 1, p. 331).

That evening he had sent a telegram to Halleck: "I have scarcely the faintest idea of an attack (general one) being made upon us, but will be prepared should such a thing take place" (*Ibid.*, X, pt. 1, p. 89). Before 6:00 A. M. on the 6th, the Confederates attacked. Notwithstanding desperate efforts, the Union lines were forced steadily back.

Grant, breakfasting at Savannah nine miles from the battlefield, heard the roar of the guns and hastened to Pittsburg Landing. On the battlefield he rode from division to division, encouraging officers and men, but otherwise exercising no influence on the combat (*Personal Memoirs*, I, 343). He sent an urgent appeal to Buell and ordered Lew Wallace to march to the battle. Johnston was killed about 2:30 in the afternoon. Beauregard, his successor, issued an order at 5:30, suspending the attack. At this time the leading regiments of Buell's army were moving into position on the heights above the landing to repel Confederate attacks. Grant spent the stormy night of Apr. 6 on the river bank, nursing a swollen ankle. Lew Wallace arrived about 7:00 P. M. on his extreme right. Three divisions of Buell's army took position on the left. With 25,000 fresh men in line, there was no question as to the outcome of the struggle when it opened on the following morning. Resisting stubbornly, the Confederates were driven back all day and by nightfall were in full retreat toward Corinth. There was no pursuit.

No battle fought in the West ranks with Shiloh in severity. No major battle displayed less generalship, and none more courage on the part of the enlisted men. Doubtless, on the night of Apr. 6, Grant, sitting under a tree in the rain, reviewed in his mind the things he had left undone. The results of this mental castigation became evident in the next campaign. In the storm of denunciation that followed, the captor of Donelson offered no excuses. Lincoln refused to relieve him, saying: "I can't spare this man—he fights."

During the remainder of 1862, Grant, at Corinth, devised plans for taking Vicksburg, the capture of which would give the Union army control, not only of the Mississippi, but also of the Confederacy's only remaining railroad leading east from that river. In November, Grant with 30,000 men marched south from Memphis in his first effort to take Vicksburg. Sherman's force was to cooperate by moving down the Mississippi. Sherman was defeated. Grant's movement was halted when the enemy cut his railroad line of communications and burned his supply depot at Holly Springs, Miss. Back again in Memphis, he began on Jan. 20, 1863, the formation of the second expedition. In this, several projects were attempted, all of which contemplated the cutting of waterways for placing the troops, by boats, south of Vicksburg, without encountering the Confederate river batteries.

Convinced, by the end of March, of the impracticability of these schemes, Grant decided to march the army, west of the river, to a point below the fortifications and then transport it by steamers to the eastern bank. Rear Admiral David D. Porter undertook to run the batteries with his iron-clad gunboats and transports and then place them at Grant's disposal. The plan was successfully carried out. On Apr. 30 the invading force, consisting of 20,000 men, landed at Bruinsburg. It was one of the boldest movements in modern warfare (Wilson, p. 169). Abandoning his communications, Grant had placed his numerically inferior force in the heart of a hostile country. Behind him was a wide river controlled above and below his landing place by the enemy; between him and Memphis, his base, were Johnston's and Pemberton's armies. Knowing that he must live off the country he immediately sent out foraging parties. Before the three days' rations carried by his men had been consumed, ample supplies were on hand, and the army did not thereafter lack food.

Shiloh showed Grant at his worst; Vicksburg showed him at his flawless best. He skillfully interposed his army between the forces of Johnston and Pemberton and struck quickly and vigorously. With his right he defeated Johnston and drove him out of Jackson; with his left he defeated Pemberton at Champion's Hill. Pemberton withdrew to the fortifications of Vicksburg on May 20, to emerge therefrom as a prisoner of war. The garrison never had a chance. The surrender took place on July 4, 1863. When, ten days thereafter, Port Hudson fell, the Mississippi was Unionist from source to mouth. The Confederacy was cut in two.

During the months of the campaign, Grant had been denounced by the newspapers and would perhaps have lost the confidence of Lincoln but for the favorable reports of Charles A. Dana, who "probably saved Grant's career" (Woodward, pp. 291–93; J. H. Wilson, *The Life of Charles A. Dana*, 1907, p. 193). Now, after the completion of one of the most brilliant military operations in American history, he was again acclaimed and promoted, this time to major-general in the regular army; and again, as at Corinth, his army was scattered. In September, by Halleck's direction, he ordered four divisions, under Sherman, eastward to cooperate with Rosecrans in the relief of Chattanooga. Before these started, Rosecrans had been badly defeated at Chickamauga and penned in Chattanooga while

Bragg, perched on Missionary Ridge and Lookout Mountain, in control of all approaches, waited for the Union army to starve into surrender.

In this plight the Administration turned to Grant. Secretary of War Stanton met him en route to Louisville in October, conferred on him command of all the territory from the Alleghanies to the Mississippi except the southwestern section, and enabled him to replace Rosecrans by Thomas (*Personal Memoirs*, II, 17–19; Wilson, pp. 184–85). Grant proceeded to Chattanooga, where he found the Union army not only perilously close to starvation but almost without shoes and clothing for the coming winter. Acting on plans that had been prepared before his arrival (Coppée, *post,* pp. 165–68; Edmonds, p. 197, note; *Battles and Leaders,* III, 717–18), Grant, within five days, had opened communications with his base at Nashville. The army was soon reclothed, well fed, and supplied with ammunition.

As soon as Sherman arrived at Bridgeport on Nov. 14, Grant fixed Nov. 23 for the execution of his plan for attacking Bragg. Accordingly, Thomas on that day took Orchard Knob, the right of the Confederate outpost line. On the 24th, Hooker captured the point of Lookout Mountain and Sherman seized the extreme right of Missionary Ridge. When, the following morning, Thomas attacked the Confederate center, his men, as directed, captured the first line of rifle pits; then, without orders, in a tremendous burst of patriotic fervor, swept up Missionary Ridge to its summit and drove their enemies from the field. Pursuit begun by Sherman was halted by Grant when Bragg's defeated army, the only obstacle between the Union forces and Atlanta, intrenched at Dalton, Ga.

A gold medal, the thanks of Congress, and the grade of lieutenant-general, the latter to carry with it the command of the armies of the United States, were bestowed on Grant, together with the adulation of a grateful nation. He was undeniably the man of the hour. Repeatedly urged to become a candidate for the presidency, he invariably refused, stating that he had but one desire—to end the war (Woodward, pp. 307–08; Coolidge, p. 142). Lincoln sent for him, wanting to judge for himself what manner of man Grant was. He saw a short, round-shouldered, rather scrubby-looking man in a tarnished major-general's uniform, with clear, resolute blue eyes, a heavy jaw, and an inscrutable face partially covered by rough light-brown whiskers which served to conceal its strength (Badeau, II, 20; Coolidge, p. 146). Lincoln liked him, believed in him, and remained his steadfast friend.

When Grant became general-in-chief, the Union forces stood in need of nothing so much as unity of plan and coordination of effort. The new leader supplied both. For the first time since the beginning of the war a plan of action was prepared that covered the concerted movements of all the Union forces. In his letter of Apr. 4, 1864, to Sherman (*Personal Memoirs*, II, 130), Grant proposed three simultaneous major movements: that of Meade's Army of the Potomac against Lee's army; that of Butler's Army of the James against Lee's communications and Richmond; that of Sherman's Army of the Tennessee against Johnston's army and Atlanta (Wilson, p. 223). For these he had available about 253,000 men. Grant's policy, to which he consistently adhered, was to use the greatest number of troops practicable against the armed forces of the enemy; to hammer those forces and their resources until by mere attrition, if in no other way, there should be nothing left to them but submission. On May 4 all the armies moved. Throughout the campaigns that followed, Grant, from his headquarters with the Army of the Potomac, kept in touch with them, directing and coordinating their operations toward the common end.

Meade's army crossed the Rapidan and bivouacked the night of May 4 in the Wilderness. Meade hoped to pass its tangled depths before Lee could intercept him, but that alert foe had decided that the Union army should fight in a locale where the terrain compensated for his weakness. He had 65,000 men to Meade's 118,000. When Meade, early on May 5, moved southward, he was struck in flank by Lee. For two days the opponents, in the desperate battle that ensued, swayed back and forth through the dense forest, without material advantage to either. Undeterred by his appalling losses (17,666, *Battles and Leaders*, IV, 248), Grant then determined to march by Lee's right flank and interpose between him and Richmond. Sherman called this decision "the supreme moment of his [Grant's] life" (*Battles and Leaders*, IV, 248). But Lee, informed of the movement, beat his opponent to the objective—Spotsylvania Court House.

At Spotsylvania, after another bloody conflict, and again after North Anna, Grant repeated successfully his tactics of passing by Lee's right. When Lee, however, only twenty miles from Richmond, assumed an intrenched position past Cold Harbor to the Chickahominy, Grant realized that his former tactics would no longer avail, that he must attack Lee in front or abandon the the campaign north of the James. A break through Lee's center would probably result in the capture of Richmond and possibly in the disintegration of

Lee's army. So Grant attacked at Cold Harbor and lost nearly 6,000 men in an hour (Steele, p. 502; *Battles and Leaders,* IV, 148). Satisfied that he could not drive Lee from his intrenched position, he called off the attack and, on the night of June 12, withdrew from Lee's front to cross the James River. The Wilderness campaign was ended. The terrific losses of the Army of the Potomac were made up by heavy reënforcements, but in the public mind Grant's prestige was lowered (Woodward, p. 325). He had not defeated Lee during the entire campaign and had been regularly outmaneuvered (Meade, II, 202), yet his policy of attrition had worn down his enemy and robbed him of the initiative. After the battle of the Wilderness, Lee did not again assume the offensive.

In conception and execution, the withdrawal from Lee's front and the movement across the James was a brilliant military achievement. The army began its silent march after dark on June 12. By midnight of the 16th it was south of the river. Lee was completely deceived and for four days lost his foe (*Battles and Leaders,* IV, 541; Lee, *post,* p. 348). Finally realizing what had occurred, he brought his army south of Richmond. The long-drawn-out siege of Petersburg was on—a siege made necessary by the failure of the left wing, under Butler, to capture Petersburg and invest Richmond during the progress of the Wilderness campaign (Adams, *post,* pp. 269–75; Coolidge, p. 170; Wilson, p. 223; Woodward, pp. 318–19, 346–48). From June 18, 1864, to Apr. 2, 1865, the Army of the Potomac invested Petersburg, sapping, mining, assaulting, cutting Lee's avenues of supply and sending out flanking expeditions far to the west. In this long siege the Confederate commander, having the advantage of interior lines, was able to meet every attack that Grant made with a force large enough to stop it. But the siege was doing its work. The Confederate army stood desperately in need of food and transportation. Sherman's men, marching through Georgia, found it a land of plenty while Lee's heroic army was starving in the trenches.

Sheridan's victory at Five Forks on Apr. 1, 1865, marked the beginning of the end. On the following day Grant assaulted the Confederate right, breaking it and forcing it back. That night Lee's army abandoned Petersburg and Richmond and marched westward, hoping to join Gen. Joseph E. Johnston's army. Grant paralleled the march and sent Sheridan's cavalry far ahead to carry on a running fight and cut off Lee's retreat. At Appomattox Court House, Sheridan stood across Lee's path. The end was at hand. On Apr. 9, 1865, Lee surrendered the Army of Northern Virginia on Grant's terms, which were so considerate and magnanimous that they were

never questioned by the Confederate chieftain (*Personal Memoirs,*
II, 483–94). Seventeen days later Johnston surrendered his army
to Sherman. The Civil War was over.

Grant's greatness lay in his ability to visualize the war in its essentials. He saw that as long as the Confederacy was an undivided
unit its military forces and resources could be shifted to any point
where they were needed. He saw, furthermore, that no great success could result from the capture of localities, that success could
come only by the destruction of armies. As general-in-chief his
strategy was sound: to cut the Confederacy into fragments; to engage
all its armies at the same time so that one could not reënforce another; to destroy those armies by following them wherever they might
go and by pounding them to pieces. To these principles he adhered
and by them he won.

[*Personal Memoirs of U. S. Grant* (2 vols., 1885–86); *Official Records (Army)*;
Old Records Section, Adjutant-General's Office; A. Badeau, *Mil. Hist. of Ulysses
S. Grant* (3 vols., 1868–81); Jas. G. Wilson, *General Grant* (1897); W. C. Church,
"The Truth about Grant," *Army and Navy Jour.*, June 6, 1908; F. S. Edmonds,
Ulysses S. Grant (1915); L. A. Coolidge, *The Life of Ulysses S. Grant* (1922); W.
E. Woodward, *Meet General Grant* (1928); J. F. C. Fuller, *The Generalship of
Ulysses S. Grant* (1929); J. H. Smith, *The War with Mexico* (2 vols., 1919);
Battles and Leaders of the Civil War (4 vols., 1887–88); J. C. Ropes, *The Story
of the Civil War* (4 vols., 1894–1913); J. F. Rhodes, *Hist. of the U. S.*, vols. III–V
(1893); C. F. Adams, "Some Phases of the Civil War," in *Studies Military and
Diplomatic* (1911); M. F. Steele, *Am. Campaigns* (1922); H. Coppée, *General
Thomas* (1893); Fitzhugh Lee, *General Lee* (1894); Jas. Longstreet, *From
Manassas to Appomattox* (1896); George Meade, *Life and Letters of George
Gordon Meade* (1913).]   C.A.B.

The subsidence of conflict left Grant in command of the army of
the United States, in a position under the President and the Secretary of War which was never clearly defined. He had been transferred rapidly from volunteer and temporary status to a commission
in the permanent establishment; and in 1866 Congress revived the
rank of general, unused since 1799, in the certainty that President
Johnson would nominate Grant for the post. Trusting Grant more
completely than it did the President, the radical Congress in the
following year blocked removals from office by the Tenure of Office
Act and required that all army orders must pass through the office

of the commanding general. Johnson was as ready to give as Grant was to accept the position, for he was at the moment courting Grant. He forced him, in the month after the appointment, to join the presidential party in the memorable "swing round the circle," hoping to gain popularity from citizens who saw Grant on the same platform with himself. Grant declined to be ordered on a mission to Mexico for the President, and tried, but without skill, to avoid giving the prestige of his own name to Johnson's plans.

Demobilization, a shapeless affair, took place under Grant. The policing of the western border and the protection of the construction camps of the continental railroads came under his control; yet he was convinced that the whole Indian policy of the United States was corrupt and wrong. His most delicate duty, however, was in connection with the administration of the Reconstruction acts, passed over Johnson's veto and enforced by the army until such time as Congress was ready to declare the Confederate states restored. Grant had toured the South for the President, and thought the "mass of thinking men of the south" were willing to accept the result of the war (*Senate Executive Document No. 2*, p. 106, 39 Cong., 1 Sess.); but he supported Stanton who had become anathema to Johnson. Protesting the suspension of Stanton, Grant assumed the duties of secretary of war *ad interim*, Aug. 12, 1867. For the next five months he was his own superior officer, for he retained the actual command as general. But he enraged Johnson by surrendering the secretaryship to Stanton after the Senate had declined to concur in the latter's dismissal. Johnson raised an issue of personal veracity (R. W. Winston, *Andrew Johnson*, 1928, p. 418), asserting that Grant had promised not to surrender the office but to force a case for judicial interpretation of the Tenure of Office Act. The merit of the issue seems beyond historical determination, but it ended the relations of the two men. Grant never forgave the President, and upon the occasion of his own inauguration in 1869 declined to ride in the same carriage with his predecessor (H. Garland, *Ulysses S. Grant*, 1920, p. 385).

The course of events of the spring of 1868 made Grant the inevitable nominee of the Republican party for the presidency. He had become the rallying figure for the opponents of Andrew Johnson, and was already the outstanding character in American life. He had no real party affiliation. Only once had he voted for president, and that time for James Buchanan, "because I knew Frémont" (L. A. Coolidge, *Ulysses S. Grant*, 1917, p. 270). But he embodied the forces that maintained the Union. Without enthusiasm he allowed himself to be nominated by the Republicans. He disliked politics as he disliked war; he had no vindictive spirit toward the soldiers who had sustained the Confederacy, but he had no intention of permitting the defeated leaders to direct the policy of the United States. He was aware that election would mean retirement from the comfortable salary and allowances of the general of the army (nearly $25,000 a year) and an exchange of a life post for the presidency, which meant eight years at most. He accepted the nomination in a brief note, four words of which have constituted his contribution to American opinion: "Let us have peace." His companion on the ticket was a popular Indiana politician, Schuyler Colfax.

Grant was elected president in 1868, losing the electoral votes of only eight states, though the popular majority was much smaller than these figures would indicate. He had taken no active part in the canvass and he admitted no one, not even his wife, to his confidence after election. The official family that he set up in the Executive Mansion was like an army headquarters, where work was done with military aides and orders were expected to receive in time of peace the same respect that they had commanded in time of war. Grant was in no sense a militarist, but the only way he knew how to work was the way of a commanding general. He picked his cabinet officers to suit himself, and so clumsily that the group had to be reorganized before it could function. The state department he gave to a personal friend, Elihu B. Washburne, to gratify his pride; he allowed a military aide, John A. Rawlins, to appropriate the war department to reward himself (J. H. Wilson, *The Life of John A. Rawlins*, 1916, p. 351); he picked a great merchant with whom he had dined well, Alexander T. Stewart, to fill the treasury post, only to discover that his appointee was legally incompetent. The other places he passed around with no reference to the existence of a party that fancied it had a right to rule, or to popular sense of fitness in appointment; and he could not understand or forgive criticism of himself because of this.

He and his family enjoyed life in the White House. All four of the children were there part of the time, though Frederick Dent Grant graduated at West Point in 1871, went to Europe, and was then on active duty. The military guard that had remained on duty since Lincoln's time was dispensed with, and the mansion was opened to family and friends. A former mess sergeant became the butler until Mrs. Grant rebelled. There was a "spare room" for the casual guest. Mrs. Grant's father, Col. Frederick Dent, still an unreconstructed Southerner but meticulously polite, was commonly much in evidence. The correspondents around the offices led him on to tell them how the General was a good Democrat but did not know it. Grant's own old father, Jesse, was sometimes there, though more often he was at his post-office at Covington, Ky., where Grant found him and left him. The vacations were likely to be spent in a cottage at Long Branch, where Grant kept out of ballrooms and took his keenest pleasure in driving in a light carriage behind a span of spirited horses. He did not care who gave him the horses. The old rumors about his excessive drinking hovered about him periodically, but most of the testimony is unreliable and none suggests that any of his official acts was ever affected by intoxication.

The financial status of the government was at the front among the problems of the Grant administrations. The Democratic party, in the preceding canvass, had made an appeal to the debtor farmers of the West and South, with an offer of greenbacks as a painless way of paying off the war debt. Earliest of the important bills to receive Grant's signature was one to establish the public credit by declaring a policy of ultimate redemption of legal-tender notes in coin. Steps were taken promptly to fund the confused mass of Civil War securities, and to baffle the gamblers in gold. These latter, on "Black Friday" (Sept. 24, 1869), thought they had cornered the gold on the market and "fixed" the President by extending favors to his hangers-on (R. H. Fuller, *Jubilee Jim, The Life of Col. James Fisk, Jr.*, 1928, p. 361; *New York Herald*, Oct. 8, 1869; *House Report No. 31*, 41 Cong., 1 Sess.). Grant ruined their hopes by releasing from the treasury such a flood of gold that it broke the corner. The financial collapse of 1873 increased the difficulty of currency deflation, for it was easy to array the debtor classes against any measure tending to appreciate the currency. But Grant vetoed an inflation bill in the following spring (Apr. 22, 1874), and signed on Jan. 14, 1875, an act setting January 1879 as the date for the resumption of specie payments.

For almost the whole of Grant's term of office Hamilton Fish was secretary of state. The two men never developed a friendly intimacy, yet Grant in general supported Fish in a firm and wise foreign policy. The attempt to annex the Dominican Republic in 1869, which produced a disastrous breach with Charles Sumner, was Grant's own venture, though it may have been the idea of political profiteers. He never receded from a belief in its wisdom, beaten though he was. Controversies with the British were cleared, after the surrender of the latter on the *Alabama* claims, in the Treaty of Washington,

May 8, 1871. Neutrality was maintained in spite of provocation given by Spain during her suppression of the Ten Years' War in Cuba.

The enforcement of the Fourteenth Amendment was attempted only half-heartedly and without success. Northern opinion reached its crest of militancy against the South in the spring of 1868. After the failure of the impeachment proceedings against Johnson there was never again adequate backing for a comprehensive interference with the gradual reëstablishment of home rule at the South. Midway in Grant's first term began the terrorism of the Negro electorate that deterred the Negroes from exercising their right to vote. Despite the Force Acts of 1870–71, the Southern states elected white officers and advanced along the process of consolidation in Democratic ranks that ended in a Solid South by 1876. Grant came, by 1880, to fear the election as president of one of the Confederate leaders who had tried to wreck the Union, but as president himself he saw the impossibility of permanent coercion.

Out of the Western and Northern moderate opinion there developed a Liberal Republican movement based on a belief in the unwisdom of Reconstruction and a demand for a reform in the administration of the national government. Its first objective, which was unattainable, was the defeat of Grant for renomination and reelection in 1872. Horace Greeley, who received incongruous nominations from both the Liberal Republicans and the Democrats, was easily defeated. Grant again stayed out of the canvass. "I am no speaker," he wrote, "and don't want to be beaten" (A. R. Conkling, *Life and Letters of Roscoe Conkling*, 1889, p. 435). The storm of scandal broke around his head before he was reëlected, and panic soon followed. A conviction was being driven home that as president he was a failure. "What wretched work. . . . They are tearing the government to pieces," Gideon Welles had written (*Americana*, April 1912, p. 403); "Can you really believe that the maker of the first Grant Cabinet . . . is fit for a President? I cannot," asserted Greeley before he was himself nominated (W. B. Parker, *The Life and Public Services of Justin Smith Morrill*, 1924, p. 239). The *New York Tribune* (July 24, 1885) at Grant's death still believed that "the greatest mistake of his life was acceptance of the presidency." "The crisis came," said the *Nation* (Mar. 9, 1876), "when an ignorant soldier, coarse in his taste and blunt in his perceptions, fond of money and material enjoyment and of low company, was put in the Presidential Chair."

The personal criticisms of Grant during his second term were galling to him, for he knew no way of dramatizing a simple personal honesty, and his power of speech and pen was totally inadequate in a fight with fluent and impassioned reformers. He sometimes replied to opposition with destruction. Sumner denounced the Dominican project and prevented the ratification of the treaty; whereupon Grant forced his deposition as chairman of the Senate committee on foreign relations (R. Cortissoz, *Life of Whitelaw Reid,* 1921, I, 190; S. Welles, *Naboth's Vineyard,* 1928, I, 392) and recalled his friend Motley from the post of minister of Great Britain. Grant was capable of letting go without a word the most dependable of his advisers— Hoar, Jewell, Bristow. Yet, craving association, he had room in his entourage for Conkling, the Camerons, and Zach Chandler. He believed the prosecution of his private secretary, Orville F. Babcock, was only a disguised attack upon himself, and did not lose confidence in Babcock's integrity until long after most other Americans. Conkling, to whom among others he offered the chief justiceship after Chase died, had a nicer sense of the needs of the office than did Grant and declined it. Yet the final choice, Morrison R. Waite, was good. Grant's critics long alleged that he packed the Supreme Court after its first legal-tenders decision (*Hepburn* vs. *Griswold,* Feb. 7, 1870, 8 *Wallace,* 603) by appointing Bradley and Strong, thus procuring a reversal in the second legal-tenders case, but the evidence for this seems unconvincing (C. Warren, *The Supreme Court in United States History,* 1922, III, 238; *American Historical Review,* April 1929, p. 532).

The breath of personal scandal has not touched Grant in any plausible form, but it struck so close to him and so frequently as to necessitate the vindication of his honor by admitting his bad taste in the choice of associates. Babcock was under suspicion of improper interest in the Dominican matter (S. Welles, *Naboth's Vineyard,* 1928, I, 400) long before he was smirched by his connection with the whiskey ring. Grant allowed himself to appear in public as the guest of Jim Fisk. Belknap, his secretary of war, was proved to have accepted graft money from a post trader; and Grant by letting him resign protected him from the consequences of a successful impeachment. The accumulating criticisms that Grant incurred threw him into the arms of those who did not criticize, and these were not the best leaders in the nation or the party.

As the second term approached its end there was suggestion of a third. Grant, in a somewhat cryptic letter (*New York Herald,* May 31, 1875), declined to be a candidate. He could not see why his fellow citizens did not desire him to continue in the presidency, and his wife resented the fact that they did not; but he accepted retirement without complaint. He had some achievements, after all. He had inherited a situation with Great Britain that was full of threat, and left it with American esteem satisfied and Anglo-American relations more harmonious than they had ever been. He had brought the United States through the factional hazards that followed the attempt to remove a president, through the financial and moral uneasiness of a period of deflation and the panic of 1873, and through the uncertainties of an electoral contest that might have blossomed into another civil war (A. Badeau, *Grant in Peace,* 1887, p. 256). There were trying days during the electoral count. It was uncertain until a few hours before Mar. 4, 1877, whether Grant would have a successor, and there was a possibility that he would be called upon to face a new crisis. The conviction that he would not have any hand in a *coup d'état* helped to prevent one.

Grant left office with a few thousand dollars saved from his salary and a craving to see Europe. With a family party, he sailed from Philadelphia in May 1877 for Liverpool and the foreign world. He embarked as a private citizen, but he landed as a world figure with whom the chamberlains of the European courts were uncertain how to act; for to treat him as a simple commoner would be grotesque, whereas he had no rank that would establish him in any rigid sequence of court precedence. It was left for his son Jesse to put Queen Victoria in her place (J. R. Grant, *In the Days of My Father General Grant,* 1925, pp. 224–27), but it took a long time for the European governments to assimilate ex-presidents with their own ex-royalties. For more than two years the Grants went from capital to capital, with an increasing baggage train of gifts and souvenirs, and in increasing need for a Fortunatus purse (J. R. Young, *Around the World with General Grant,* 1879). As the tour approached its end, a longing for home stimulated its progress, to Grant's political disadvantage.

Hayes had failed to get along with his party, and neither sought nor could have obtained a renomination. The friends of Grant were desirous for a return of the "good old days." The murmurings of labor presaged to the nervous a possible industrial revolt, and there was clamor, much of it inspired, for a "strong" man at the helm of state. The political advisers of Grant urged him to delay his return until the eve of the campaign of 1880, when his renomination might be accomplished on a wave of friendly publicity. He came back, instead, in the autumn of 1879, and the spreading third-term boom excited a stronger wave of opposition. At the Chicago convention in

1880 the faithful old guard, 306 strong, stood firm for Grant, and later struck off a medal to celebrate their loyalty; but they did him no good, for a coalition of his opponents defeated him by agreeing upon Garfield as the candidate.

The last phase of Grant's life was saddened by lack of means, by positive misfortune, by calumny, and at last by sickness until death. He took up his residence in a house in East Sixty-sixth St., New York, in August 1881, and lived with gratitude upon the income from a fund of $250,000 which some of his admirers placed in trust for him. The securities in which this was invested proved unreliable, and the income failed him (Woodward, *Meet General Grant*, 1928, pp. 476, 490). He went into business and was exploited. The failure of the brokerage firm of Grant & Ward (May 6, 1884) threw him into bankruptcy and humiliation. He had earlier used his swords and souvenirs as security for a loan which had been swallowed up. An attempt was made by his friends to care for him by reviving the office of general which he had vacated upon entrance to the presidency, but political opposition delayed this until it was almost too late. On his last day in office President Arthur signed the revival bill, and it was left to a Democratic president, Cleveland, to deliver the commission that carried a salary for life.

The life was short. A dangerous cancer of the throat was wearing Grant away, though he was fighting the disease in order to carry to completion the only civil task that he had learned how to do well. In 1884 he wrote for the publishers of the *Century Magazine* an article (February 1885) on the battle of Shiloh. This paid him handsomely and was an immediate success, whereupon was conceived another Cæsar's *Commentaries* to be written by the victor of the Civil War. He set to work upon the *Personal Memoirs,* writing in the sickroom and in the quiet of the house at Mount McGregor where he was taken to die. Mark Twain, then in business as a publisher of subscription books, waited for the copy, to put upon the market one of the most successful of American books. The family of Grant received nearly $450,000 from this literary endowment (A. B. Paine, *Mark Twain: A Biography*, 1912, II, 816); but he himself died, simply and greatly, before he could know of its triumph. He was buried at last in a great mausoleum of granite on Riverside Drive in New York City.

[Grant was not a bookish man, and he wrote as little as possible until he compiled the *Personal Memoirs of U. S. Grant* (2 vols., 1885–86). There is no considerable collection of his manuscripts, and the printed salvage from his letters is fragmentary: J. G. Cramer, ed., *Letters of Ulysses S. Grant to his Father and his Youngest Sister, 1857–1878* (1912); J. G. Wilson, ed., *General Grant's Letters to a Friend* [Elihu B. Washburne] *1861–1880* (1897). The many biographies are rarely more than compilations from his *Personal Memoirs*, enriched with fragments from the two works by his military aide, Adam Badeau, *Mil. Hist. of Ulysses S. Grant* (3 vols., 1868–81) and *Grant in Peace* (1887). The best of these biographies is W. E. Woodward, *Meet General Grant* (1928). Others not already listed in the previous bibliography are: J. S. C. Abbott, *The Life of Gen. Ulysses S. Grant* (1868); W. C. Church, *Ulysses S. Grant and the Period of Nat. Preservation and Reconstruction* (1897); Hamlin Garland, *Ulysses S. Grant. His Life and Character* (1898, new ed., 1920); Owen Wister, *Ulysses S. Grant* (1900); Chas. King, *The True Ulysses S. Grant* (1914). Better than any of the biographies for the period of his presidency are: J. F. Rhodes, *Hist. of the U. S.*, vols. VI–VII (1893); E. P. Oberholtzer, *A Hist. of the U. S. Since the Civil War* (3 vols., 1917–26); and C. G. Bowers, *The Tragic Era* (1920), a spirited brief for Andrew Johnson by an eloquent Democratic historian.]   F.L.P.

[SUPPLEMENTARY BIBLIOGRAPHY. The only recent broad interpretation of Grant is Bruce Catton, *U. S. Grant and the Am. Military Tradition* (1954). Horace Green, *General Grant's Last Stand: A Biography* (1936), is useful for new material about Grant's last days gathered from his physician's diary. A more general treatment is William E. Brooks, *Grant of Appomattox: A Study of the Man* (1942). Two studies of Grant's earlier life are Arthur L. Conger, *The Rise of U. S. Grant* (1931), and Lloyd Lewis, *Captain Sam Grant* (1950); the latter was continued by Bruce Catton in his *Grant Moves South* (1960). More specialized works dealing with Grant as a military man are: Robert R. McCormick, *Ulysses S. Grant, the Great Soldier of America* (1934); Clarence E. N. Macartney, *Grant and his Generals* (1953); Kenneth P. Williams, *Lincoln Finds a General*, vols. III and IV (1952–56); and Earl S. Miers, *The Web of Victory: Grant at Vicksburg* (1955). Comparative military studies include John F. C. Fuller, *Grant and Lee: A Study in Personality and Generalship* (1933), and Alfred H. Burne, *Lee, Grant, and Sherman: A Study in Leadership in the 1864–65 Campaign* (1939). A recently published memoir is Sylvanus Cadwallader, *Three Years with Grant*, ed. by Benjamin P. Thomas (1955). Major works covering the period of Grant's presidency are William B. Hesseltine, *Ulysses S. Grant, Politician* (1935), and Allan Nevins, *Hamilton Fish: The Inner Hist. of the Grant Administration* (1936).]

Woodrow Wilson

by

CHARLES SEYMOUR

WILSON, WOODROW (Dec. 28, 1856–Feb. 3, 1924), christened Thomas Woodrow, twenty-eighth president of the United States, was born in Staunton, Va. The Scotch strain was predominant in his ancestry. His mother, Janet (called Jessie) Woodrow, was born in Carlisle, England, close to the Scotch border, the daughter of a Scotch minister, descended from a long line of Presbyterians. His paternal grandfather, James Wilson, a genial, vigorous man of affairs, emigrated from Ulster. Grandparents on both sides came to the United States in the early nineteenth century. Joseph Ruggles Wilson, his father, himself a Presbyterian minister, was brought up in Ohio. Woodrow Wilson's immediate background in a family sense was that of the Middle West; in a literary sense, through his father's interests, it was English. Three years before his birth the family moved to Virginia, and in his second year to Augusta, Ga. His boyhood was thus of the South. In 1870 his father became professor in the theological seminary at Columbia, S. C., and pastor of the First Presbyterian Church. Four years later he moved to a pastorate in Wilmington, N. C. Woodrow Wilson's early years were thus colored by an atmosphere of academic interest and intense piety. The impressions of horror produced upon him by the Civil War were indelible. With an early-maturing mind and a keen delight in the personal and intellectual companionship of his father, he lived a youth largely separated from those of his own age and imbibed his learning at home. He spent a year (1873–74) at Davidson College, in North

Carolina, and in the autumn of 1875 entered the College of New Jersey (Princeton).

As an undergraduate he was a leader in debating, studied the art of public speaking, spent long hours over the lives of British statesmen. During his senior year he wrote an outstanding essay, published in the *International Review* in August 1879, entitled "Cabinet Government in the United States." His serious intellectual interests did not lead him to seek high marks in his classes. At graduation, in June 1879, his aspirations turned definitely to a career in public life. The natural path to it seemed to be the law, and he entered the school of the University of Virginia, where he was less interested in formal law courses than in British and American political history. In poor health he returned to Wilmington, N. C., in December 1880, and in 1882 set up in law practice with Edward Ireland Renick in Atlanta, Ga. The venture did not prosper. Wilson's intensity of intellectual interest in large political problems, his unwillingness to yield political convictions, his repugnance to the purely commercial practice of law, all unfitted him for success in the Atlanta courts. In the autumn of 1883 he gave up his almost clientless practice and entered the graduate school of the Johns Hopkins University.

He thus embarked upon a career for which he was ideally equipped and which in turn was to prepare him for public life. At Johns Hopkins under the training of Herbert Baxter Adams he found his creative literary powers actively stimulated. He rebelled against the German methods of post-graduate work and was disinclined to enter upon specialized research. A brilliant development of his favorite theme entitled "Committee or Cabinet Government" (published in *Overland Monthly,* Jan. 1884) secured for him a fellowship in the history department, and in January 1885 he published his first, perhaps his most important, book, *Congressional Government,* a clear, beautifully written analysis of American legislative practice with emphasis upon the evils that resulted from the separation of the legislative and executive branches of government and from the consequent power of congressional committees. With this as his thesis, in June 1886 he was awarded the Ph.D. degree by Johns Hopkins.

In the meantime he had married and secured a job. His marriage to Ellen Louise Axson took place on June 24, 1885. There thus came into his life its most important single influence, a woman capable of enduring the economic hardships that go with the life of a young teacher, appreciative of his capacity, and profoundly sympathetic with his ideals. Three daughters were born of this happy marriage: Margaret Wilson; Jessie Woodrow Wilson, who later married

Francis B. Sayre; Eleanor Randolph Wilson, who married William Gibbs McAdoo. In the autumn of 1885 Wilson began to teach history at Bryn Mawr College. He thus secured a living, although a bare one, and an opportunity to write. In 1888 he was called to Wesleyan University as professor of history and political economy, and for two years threw himself actively into faculty and undergraduate interests, wrote essays and book reviews, and published a comprehensive textbook in political science, *The State*. In 1890 his alma mater called him to her faculty as professor of jurisprudence and political economy.

Wilson came to the Princeton faculty as a young man not yet thirty-four, only eleven years out of college. He cared little for the scholarly distinction that comes from intensive research; but the breadth of his reading and the verve of his intellectual curiosity guaranteed his influence among faculty and undergraduates. Concerned not merely with the idea but with its effective expression, he labored incessantly over the art of literary expression, including that of epigrammatic phrase. By rigid self-criticism he learned to eschew the florid and unnecessary. "A man who wishes to make himself *by utterance* a force in the world," he wrote to a friend in 1897, "must—with as little love as possible, apply critical tests to himself" (Reid, *post*, p. 69). Twenty years later, as president of the United States, he was enabled, by this devotion to the art of expression, in his own phrase, to "wield the sword of penetrating speech." Distinguished and popular in the lecture hall, a leader of the younger liberals on the faculty, he was chosen in 1896 to make the principal address at the sesquicentennial celebration of the founding of the College. His experience broadened as he came into contact with literary circles and as he traveled through the West on lecture tours. His confidence increased as he perceived that he could interest and dominate audiences of a more general sort than those of the classroom. With delight he discovered that his professional field permitted him to develop in popular terms a philosophy of public life. On June 9, 1902, following the resignation of Francis Landey Patton, he was unanimously elected president of Princeton.

As professor, Wilson had already crystallized his ideas of necessary academic reform and he welcomed the presidency for the chance it gave to put them into effect. He was dissatisfied with the Princeton collegiate routine. His conviction that "the object of a University is simply and entirely intellectual" (Reid, p. 78) found little support in an undergraduate body dominated at the time by social and athletic ideals. Nor did Wilson believe that the Princeton course of study, chiefly characterized by the lecture system in which he himself so greatly excelled, provided adequate intellectual incentive. "From childhood up," his eldest daughter wrote (to E. M. House, Aug. 19, 1934, Yale House Collection), "I have heard him talk about the importance of developing the mind by using it rather than stuffing it, that the only value of books was their stimulating power—otherwise they were worse than useless." He meditated a thorough revolution in Princeton's attitude toward college life that would give to the serious scholar the prestige he had rightly earned and reduce the social and athletic "side shows" to a subordinate place (R. S. Baker, *Life*, II, 218).

Structural reorganization he believed to be essential. The principles of his plan were embodied in a double and interlocking scheme: the Preceptorial System and the Quad Plan. The first would provide opportunity for individual instruction; the second would coordinate the social and intellectual life of the college. Strongly impressed by his visits to Oxford and Cambridge, he realized the educational value of small groups, where the mind of the instructor could touch directly that of the student, and where he could help the student to correlate and assimilate the scattered information picked up in formal courses or reading. "He said," wrote his daughter, "that there ought to be in every university a professor to teach the relation of things. . . . The essence of the cultured mind was its capacity for relating knowledge" (to E. M. House, Aug. 19, 1934, Yale House Collection). In 1905 he called to the faculty a group of forty-seven young scholars whose first duty should be individual supervision of the students and the development of small discussion groups for the interchange of ideas. The principle of the plan was sound—it has since been adopted in the honors courses and tutorial work of leading colleges—and it was successfully applied.

Wilson was equally insistent that if the scholarly aspects of college were to dominate life in Princeton, they could not be divided from the social. The existing undergraduate organization of clubs was of a purely social character and because of their exclusive character brought no benefit to those very undergraduates who most needed it. In 1907 a committee of the trustees reported that the tendencies of the clubs were such that "the vital life of the place will be outside the University and in large part independent of it" (Reid, p. 103). Wilson's plan, again modeled upon English university organization, was to divide the university into colleges, developing the upper-class clubs themselves into colleges. "By a college I mean not merely a group of dormitories, but an eating hall as well with all its necessary appointments where all the residents of the college shall take their meals together. I would have over each college a master and two or three resident preceptors, and I would have these resident members of the faculty take their meals in hall with the undergraduates. . . . Each college would thus form a unit in itself, and largely a self-governing unit" (R. S. Baker, *Life,* II, 221).

The Quad Plan, so-called because each college was planned as a quadrangle around a central court, embodied Wilson's dislike of traditional privilege, his love of free opportunity, his hope of giving to the preceptorial system a social environment and thus facilitating contacts between cultured and immature minds. The Western alumni and a majority of the faculty, especially the younger members, approved it. But unlike the preceptorial system it touched vested interests. Clubmen of the alumni, especially in the East, protested, and some of the older members of the faculty wished to go slowly. The board of trustees, realizing the intensity of feeling in the opposing groups, voted to request the President to withdraw his proposal. The power of the clubs, Wilson bitterly remarked, proved to be greater than the interest of the University. This was merely another indication of his earlier conviction that "the side shows were swallowing up the circus" (R. S. Baker, *Life,* II, 218).

Ironically enough, this academic defeat brought Wilson before the American public and helped to open his path to politics. He was presented to the country as the champion of the underprivileged, as the supporter of democratic principles "so hateful to the old order at Princeton, to the bosses and politicians in state and nation" (Reid, p. 113). Nor has that defeat dimmed his academic prestige in the light of history. Twenty years later, Yale and Harvard in their College and House plans brought to realization the vision which he had opened up to the Princeton trustees. In this, as in his preceptorial system, Wilson proved himself the educational prophet, ahead of his time.

Another setback came to Wilson in the development of plans for the Graduate College. This he had conceived as the center of the intellectual life of the University, to be placed in the physical center. Dean West, of the Graduate College, preferred a more distant site and with the Wyman bequest for its building, he himself being an executor, persuaded the trustees to adopt his policy. Such defeats are the lot of a college president, but Wilson saw in them a blockade to the development of his ideal of a democratic coordinated university.

His disappointment was intensified by the growth of bitter personal feeling between his opponents and his supporters. He considered the possibility of resignation and a return to the literary life.

At this juncture fate opened to him an opportunity to carry on the struggle for democracy in a wider field. The tide of political discontent against Republican "standpatters" was running strong, and in 1910 the Democrats were seeking available candidates for the elections. In New Jersey Col. George B. M. Harvey, who in 1906 had spoken of Wilson for president, urged him upon the state organization as an ideal candidate for governor. Here was a man who "by utterance" could win popular support; a man, furthermore, who because of his fight against privilege in a university could be dramatized as the champion of the masses. Doubtful and puzzled, the machine leaders of New Jersey allowed themselves to be persuaded to nominate the Princeton President. Wilson himself hesitated as this vision of his early life again took form. Finally he agreed, stipulating that he be bound by no pledges of patronage. On Oct. 20, 1910, he resigned the presidency of Princeton and on Nov. 8 was elected governor of New Jersey.

The New Jersey governorship proved to be but a brief interlude in Wilson's career, as he himself had regarded it, a training school for a larger arena. But at no time did his qualities of leadership find clearer expression. Regarded by the machine politicians as a naïve theorist and suspected by the reformers as the tool of the machine, he speedily disillusioned both groups. The power and eloquence of his acceptance address and his campaign speeches provoked the enthusiasm of the mass of voters. The first trial of strength with the machine left him triumphant. He dared to fight James Smith, Democratic organization leader, in his contest for the Senate, and in the words of a political reporter "licked the gang to a frazzle" (R. S. Baker, *Life,* III, 127). Driving forward reform measures with vigor, by the end of the first session he secured the enactment of the most important proposals of his campaign: a primary election law, an invigorated public utilities act, a corrupt practices act, an employers' liability act.

Within a brief ten months New Jersey was studied by reformers as a practical example of the possibilities of reform, and Wilson himself began to attract the attention of national political leaders. Of these none was more sagacious than Col. E. M. House, the friend and adviser of successive governors of Texas. Wilson and House first met in the autumn of 1911, became friends immediately, and entered upon a relationship described by Sir Horace Plunkett as "the strangest and most fruitful personal alliance in human history" (*House Papers, post*, I, 44). House's liberal humanitarianism and his insistence upon a government responding to the needs of all classes were unshakable; he and Wilson never differed in principle. But his attitude was always tempered by his sense of what was immediately attainable. From the moment he met Wilson, House was convinced that here was the ideal president of the United States—a man of courage and imagination, a Democrat untouched by "Bryanesque heresies," an Eastern reformer of unmatched eloquence who would sacrifice personal success to principle. He set himself to work for the nomination of the New Jersey Governor, whose formal campaign was managed by William F. McCombs. House exercised his influence in Texas to win the forty votes of that state in the nominating convention. Bryan, who suspected Wilson of being the tool of Harvey and the New York interests, was next brought through House into a less distrustful attitude. In the meantime Wilson's reputation as a forceful and eloquent speaker was steadily developed through a series of widely delivered addresses.

At the Baltimore convention in June 1912, Bryan's influence was dominant. Of the four leading candidates, Champ Clark, Oscar W. Underwood, Judson Harmon, and Wilson, he favored the first. But he was primarily interested in pledging the convention to a repudiation of Tammany Hall as offensive to all liberals. Voting reached a deadlock. The issue was decided by Bryan, who declared that he would support no one who was supported by Tammany. Clark equivocated. Disregarding the advice of McCombs, Wilson stated flatly that he would not accept the nomination if it depended upon the Tammany vote. Bryan, already half won to Wilson, released the Nebraska delegates from their pledges and cast his own vote for him. From that moment the tide turned in Wilson's favor. On the forty-sixth ballot he was nominated by the necessary two-thirds majority.

In 1912, because of the personal quarrel between Roosevelt and Taft and the political split between Republican progressives and conservatives, the Democratic nomination was tantamount to election. On Nov. 5 Wilson was elected president with 435 electoral votes as against 88 for Roosevelt and 8 for Taft. It was the largest electoral majority in the history of the American presidency up to that time, although it represented a popular minority. Wilson entered the White House the champion of what he called the "New Freedom," a conservative reformer, eager to return to the common people equality of privilege threatened by the "interests" of industry, finance, and commerce. Distrustful of radical remedies such as the recall of judicial decisions, he had profound confidence in the Gladstonian philosophy of live and let live, and believed that the first essential to government at Washington was to render it sensitively responsive to public opinion. Such principles he expounded in general terms in his campaign speeches, a series of magnificent manifestoes which in a few months established him as the unquestioned leader of American liberalism.

The most serious difficulty faced by the President resulted from the inexperience of Democratic leaders in the conduct of government, for sixteen years had passed since the last Democratic administration. The cabinet as finally selected proved to be of more than adequate administrative ability. Bryan, who was appointed secretary of state, was a necessity in the cabinet. For sixteen years he had been party leader and still wielded tremendous influence in the country and in Congress. If Wilson was to lead the enormous Democratic majority successfully through the mazes of tariff and currency reform, he needed Bryan's political influence behind him. The new President was determined at the outset to rectify what he regarded as the great flaw in the American form of government by establishing a close working connection between the executive and the legislature. On Apr. 8, 1913, he appeared before the two houses of Congress to deliver his first message, thus reviving a custom that had lapsed since Jefferson discontinued it and one that gave him opportunity to exercise his persuasive rhetorical powers. Resolved to push through fundamental reforms in the tariff and in banking, he utilized the large Democratic majority to achieve extraordinary legislative triumphs. Of these, the most important were the Underwood Tariff and the Federal Reserve Act. The first, providing for notably lowered tariff schedules and a federal income tax, was passed in October. The second, designed to facilitate the flow of capital through twelve reserve banks, under the direction of a federal board, met strong objections from conservative bankers and radical currency reformers. It was nevertheless passed in December. The third major aspect of Wilson's program took form in the creation of the Federal Trade Commission and in the Clayton Anti-Trust Act designed to prevent interlocking directorates and declaring that labor organizations should not "be held or construed to be illegal combinations in restraint of trade." These bills were passed in the early autumn of 1914.

The principle of this legislation, in Wilson's mind, was to liberalize the industrial system, to eliminate special privilege, "to make men in a small way of business as free to succeed as men in a big way . . . to destroy monopoly and maintain competition as the only effectual instrument of business liberty" (R. S. Baker, *Life*, IV, 374). He had to meet the opposition of influential industrialists and to control the wilder reformers in his own party. Much of his success was due to the fact that Congress itself was young, political patronage only partly distributed, and as a consequence the Democratic majority, after many years in the wilderness, obedient to party discipline. It was due also to the readiness of public opinion to respond to reform measures, for the spirit of progressiveness was still alive. The chief factor in Wilson's early legislative success was his own genius for leading public opinion, for clarifying the larger political aspects of the issues involved, and his capacity for building in the country a fire behind opposition. For a year and a half he was irresistible. By the middle of 1914, however, he began to encounter the criticism that harassed him at Princeton and in the second year of his New Jersey governorship: that he was too restless and wanted to go too fast. The feeling was intensified by the industrial depression of 1913–14.

Fate was in an ironical mood in decreeing that Wilson, primarily interested in the domestic problems that touched the freedom of the individual, should be forced to give his major attention to international affairs just as he, the determined pacifist, was later compelled to lead his country in the greatest war of history. Philosophically his conception of foreign policy was akin to that of Gladstone. He was opposed intellectually and temperamentally to an imperialism fostered by private commercial interests, and believed intensely in the political wisdom and moral necessity of utilizing the national strength in foreign affairs with careful restraint. "It is a very perilous thing," he said in his most important early speech on foreign affairs, at Mobile, Oct. 27, 1913, "to determine the foreign policy of a nation in the terms of material interest." And he added: "I want to take this occasion to say that the United States will never again seek one additional foot of territory by conquest" (Baker and Dodd, *Public Papers, The New Democracy, post,* I, 67).

Upon such a policy of restraint Wilson hoped to base relations with Latin America, which for the first sixteen months of his administration formed the most important aspect of American diplomacy. He set for himself the task of creating an atmosphere of good will and of eliminating traditional jealousy of the North American Republic. The problem was made more difficult by conditions in Haiti, Central America, and especially in Mexico, where revolution produced political chaos and threatened American investments. The Mexican imbroglio with its irritating and almost explosive consequences harassed Wilson for three years. How could he help to restore order and promote justice? The simple method of supporting General Huerta, who had seized power through the assassination of his predecessor, he discarded immediately. "We have no sympathy with those who seek to seize the power of government to advance their own personal interests" (Mar. 12, 1913, *American Journal of International Law,* Apr. 1913, p. 331). He steadily resisted pressure based upon the doctrine that Huerta's régime promised at least the restoration of order. A moral issue was involved in non-recognition. In the meantime he would take no action beyond lifting, in February 1914, the arms embargo put on in 1913. "We can afford to exercise the self-restraint of a really great nation which realizes its own strength and scorns to misuse it" (*New Democracy,* I, 49).

Events soon tested the spirit of patience inherent in this policy of "watchful waiting." In April 1914, following the arrest of American sailors at Tampico, Admiral Mayo demanded an apology and salute which Huerta refused. On Apr. 21, American marines and blue-jackets seized the terminal facilities at Vera Cruz in order to prevent the landing of munitions from a German ship. American lives were lost. Wilson himself, the determined pacifist, almost despaired. "I do not see what other course was open to us or how we could have avoided taking such steps as we have taken. The next move is for Huerta. It depends upon him how far this thing shall go. I sincerely pray God it may not have to go to the length of definite war" (R. S. Baker, *Life,* IV, 332). Fortunately, at the moment of deepest gloom, on Apr. 25, the three chief states of South America, Argentina, Brazil, and Chile, offered mediation. The proposal was immediately accepted. As Wilson wrote privately, it presented an exit from a blind alley.

The results of the mediation conference by no means cleared the Mexican situation. War was averted and Huerta's resignation was hastened. Disorder continued, however, and the raids of the guerrilla leader Villa even threatened the American border. In the spring of 1916 Wilson was forced to dispatch a small force under General Pershing across the border in pursuit of Villa. A clash with Carranza's troops at Carrizal in June resulted in the capture of American cavalrymen. The national guard had to be mobilized for the protection of the border. To the end of his administration the President was plagued by Mexican anarchy.

Wilson's cooperation with the A. B. C. Powers had the advantage of creating confidence in him among the South American countries, thus enabling him to undertake a comprehensive Pan-American policy of understanding and peace. In the autumn of 1914, at the suggestion of House, he sketched the essential articles of an agreement to provide for international security in the Western Hemisphere. The first article carried the essence of the plan and forecasted clearly the later Covenant of the League of Nations: "Mutual guaranties of political independence under republican form of government and mutual guaranties of territorial integrity" (*House Papers,* I, 209–10). The agreement was actively discussed with the ambassadors of the A. B. C. Powers, who at first hailed it with enthusiasm. It was destined, however, after the entrance of the United States into the World War, to be merged in Wilson's more comprehensive plan for a world organization built upon a similar model.

The Mexican problem and its attendant negotiations had the effect of bringing Wilson into close diplomatic relations with Great Britain. British interests tended to support Huerta and a direct clash with the British Foreign Office was avoided chiefly because of the restraint displayed by the foreign secretary, Sir Edward Grey. His confidence in Wilson, whose Mexican policy was well represented at St. James's by Ambassador Page, was strengthened by the President's successful determination to secure repeal of the Panama Tolls Act. It was deepened, in December 1913, by the visit of Grey's secretary, Sir William Tyrrell, which led to a return visit to England by Colonel House in the spring of 1914. Their conversations raised the possibility of a close Anglo-American understanding which, in the mind of House, could be developed by the inclusion of Germany to end the mutual distrust of Triple Alliance and Triple Entente and assure world peace. In May 1914, Wilson sent House to Berlin, where the latter laid the suggestion before the Kaiser in a private interview. The British, hoping to discover a method of ending the naval race with Germany, expressed cordial but cautious interest. Events moved too fast, and the outbreak of the World War put an end to the plan.

American intervention in the European war was dreamed of by very few persons during the first nine months of the struggle. From Wilson's private papers we can discover that he shared the general prepossession in favor of the Allies that characterized the Eastern states and equally that he was determined that this should in no way affect a policy of complete neutrality. At the very beginning of the war he warned the nation against entertaining any feeling of partisanship; he was himself so far successful that he was brutally abused by each side as being favorable to the other. But the problem of neutrality involved a good deal more than simply minding one's own business. Both the Allied regulation of neutral maritime trade and the German submarine campaign infringed American rights and interests. Could the neutral position of America be adequately protected from the one side or the other without endangering the principle of peaceable negotiation to which, on both philosophical and emotional grounds, he had dedicated his policy?

During the first six months of the war the issue lay almost entirely with the Allies, who refused to accept the Declaration of London as a code of maritime operations without modifications that denatured it. They extended the contraband lists, brought neutral ships into harbor for search, detained cargoes, applied the doctrine of continuous voyage to conditional contraband. On Dec. 26, 1914, the United States issued a formal and comprehensive protest against Allied methods of maritime control. But the sharpness of this diplomatic conflict was at once alleviated by the German decree of Feb. 4, 1915, declaring the waters around the British Isles a war zone, threatening to sink all belligerent merchant ships met within that zone, and giving warning that neutral ships might also be sunk.

The German declaration changed the whole character of relations between the United States and Germany, and at once threw the quarrel with the Allies into the background. Wilson stressed the fact that the submarine warfare, necessarily based upon the method of sinking without warning, involved the blind destruction of neutral property, whether contraband or not, and perhaps of the lives of non-combatants. Without hesitation he drew a distinction between property and lives, between interference with material rights for which later compensation could be made, and destruction of American lives for which no adequate compensation could be made. On Feb. 10, he sent to Germany a warning that laid the basis of his whole policy toward submarine warfare. Destruction of the American vessel or American lives would, he stated, be regarded as "an indefensible violation of neutral rights" and the United States would be constrained to hold the German Government "to a strict accountability for such acts" (*Foreign Relations 1915 Supplement,* pp. 98–100).

The German submarine commanders were instructed to avoid sinking neutral ships, so far as possible. But the series of dreaded "accidents" began to appear. On May 7 the *Lusitania* was sunk and over a thousand persons drowned, among them 128 Americans. From this moment the issue was finally clarified in Wilson's mind. The

Germans must not use the submarine against merchant ships except according to recognized rules of warning, with due provisions for the safety of passengers and crew. The firmness with which he demanded that Germany give up the "ruthless" submarine campaign led in June to the resignation of Bryan, who saw in Wilson's insistence upon the preservation of traditional neutral rights the danger of war with Germany. The patience which the President displayed aroused bitter resentment on the American seaboard, where, as the submarine campaign continued, popular feeling demanded a diplomatic rupture with Germany. But the combination of Wilson's patience and firmness finally triumphed, at least temporarily. Following the sinking of the *Arabic* in August 1915, the German ambassador, Bernstorff, announced the promise of his Government that "liners" would not be attacked without warning. In the spring of 1916 Wilson finally drew from Berlin, following the sinking of the *Sussex,* the more comprehensive agreement to abandon the ruthless submarine warfare altogether.

This promise was extracted by the definite threat of a diplomatic rupture. Unless Germany should "effect an abandonment of its present methods of submarine warfare against passenger and freight-carrying vessels, The Government of the United States can have no choice but to sever diplomatic relations with the German Empire altogether" *(Foreign Relations 1916 Supplement,* p. 234). Such a rupture, in Bernstorff's opinion, would lead inevitably to active American intervention. There was no longer any doubt in Berlin, Bernstorff records, "that persistence . . . would bring about a break with the United States" (Bernstorff, *post,* p. 213).

In meeting what he regarded as a series of outrageous affronts by Germany, Wilson never permitted his sense of responsibility to be overclouded by natural emotion. "The country is undoubtedly back of me," he wrote privately on Sept. 20, 1915, "and I feel myself under bonds to it to show patience to the utmost. My chief puzzle is to determine where patience ceases to be a virtue" (to House, Yale House Collection). Always he held to the double principle he formulated at the moment he was smarting under the news of the sinking of the *Arabic:* "1. The people of this country count on me to keep them out of the war; 2. It would be a calamity to the world at large if we should be actively drawn into the conflict and so deprived of all disinterested influence over the settlement" (to House, Aug. 21, 1915, Yale House Collection).

On the other hand, Wilson made it clear that whereas the trade dispute with the Allies could form a subject of negotiation, there could be no compromise with Germany over the unrestricted submarine campaign. He yielded no legal right to the Allies and by his protests built up a case for damages; in the meantime immediate commercial interests were largely protected by private arrangements between American shippers and the British government. But the unrestricted use of the submarine, he insisted, struck directly at basic American rights in a way that precluded later compensation, rights which if once surrendered could not be regained. The sinking of American ships and the drowning of American citizens, whether passengers or sailors, he regarded as an attack upon national sovereignty. The right of Americans to travel freely on the high seas he would not yield. "For my own part," he wrote to Senator Stone, who advocated an evasion of the issue, "I cannot consent to any abridgement of the rights of American citizens in any respect. . . . We covet peace and shall preserve it at any cost but the loss of honor. . . . What we are contending for in this matter is of the very essence of the things which have made America a sovereign nation" (*Foreign Relations 1916 Supplement,* p. 177).

There was thus a limit to Wilson's patience. He publicly set it at the line where admitted neutral rights were infringed after protracted warning, and he made it a point of national self-respect and honor to defend those rights. "I know that you are depending upon me to keep this Nation out of the war," he said in January 1916. "So far I have done so and I pledge you my word that, God helping me, I will if it is possible. But you have laid another duty upon me. You have bidden me see to it that nothing stains or impairs the honor of the United States, and that is a matter not within my control; that depends upon what others do, not upon what the Government of the United States does. Therefore there may at any moment come a time when I cannot preserve both the honor and the peace of the United States. Do not exact of me an impossible and contradictory thing" (Speech of Jan. 31, 1916, *New Democracy,* II, 48).

Wilson's policy toward Germany received striking confirmation from Congress, which voted in March 1916 to table the Gore-McLemore resolutions designed to warn American citizens not to travel on belligerent ships. He received equal support for his ultimatum of Germany following the sinking of the *Sussex.* Still further confirmation came in the national election of 1916. During the summer and early autumn it was clear that in the Northeast the Democrats must expect decided defeats at the polls, partly because of dislike of Wilson's reform legislation, largely because after Roosevelt's desertion of the Progressives normal Republican majorities would control the election in those regions. In the Middle West Wilson was strong, chiefly because of his progressive leadership. German-Americans were on the whole opposed to him, but he could count on the pacifist vote. "He has kept us out of war," was the most powerful argument west of the Mississippi. The result of the election was so close that for twelve hours it was generally conceded that the Republican candidate, Charles E. Hughes, had been elected. Wilson himself went to bed believing that his term of office was ended. He had decided to resign immediately, after appointing Hughes secretary of state, so that, following the vice-president's resignation, Hughes would automatically take up the presidential office without having to wait until the following March. Only when the returns from the West came in was it seen that the Republican majorities in the East had been wiped out and that Wilson was reëlected by 277 votes to 254 for Hughes.

Wilson's victory was generally ascribed to the pacifists. He lost no time in preparing to justify their confidence by a determined move for peace. Since the early autumn of 1914 he had never ceased to explore possible avenues of mediation but had met constant rebuffs. Each side counted on peace terms that precluded negotiation. In the autumn of 1915 the President approved a plan suggested by House whereby mediation might be enforced through a threat to join the side which refused it. Another trip to Berlin convinced House that the Germans expected impossible terms. In London he received more encouragement and was able to draft with Grey a memorandum promising that Wilson would call a peace conference, setting forth certain terms, and indicating that if Germany refused either the conference or the terms the United States would enter the war to stop it. Wilson approved the memorandum. But all through the spring and summer the Allies refused any sign of willingness to enter a conference.

After the election, Wilson decided to issue a public call to the belligerents. He had received clear intimation from Germany that unless peace negotiations were started the submarine war would be resumed. The Germans without waiting for Wilson issued on Dec. 12 a statement of their willingness to enter a conference but in such a tone as to discourage any hope of terms that the Allies would consider. On Dec. 18 Wilson published his own note, requesting the belligerents to state their war aims: "an interchange of views would clear the way at least for conference" (*Foreign Relations 1916 Supplement,* pp. 98–99). Neither the German nor the Wilson suggestion produced any effect upon the Allies. The Germans immediately began to plan resumption of unrestricted submarine warfare, even though realizing that it would array the United States against them.

Conscious of the danger, Wilson worked desperately to stave it off by pushing forward his plans for a peace conference. On Jan. 4, 1917, in reply to House's suggestion of the need of military preparation "in the event of war," he insisted: "There will be no war. This country does not intend to become involved in this war. We are the only one of the great white nations that is free from war today, and it would be a crime against civilization for us to go in" (*House Papers*, II, 412). Anxiously he urged on Bernstorff the need of securing from Germany specific conditions of peace, armed with which he might go to the Allies. On Jan. 22, 1917, he delivered before the Senate a speech designed to serve as the basis for a negotiated peace, a settlement that would leave neither the one side nor the other crushed and revengeful, "a peace without victory."

Had Germany then held her hand it is possible that Wilson might have been able to start negotiations. The Allies were nearing the end of their financial resources. Given a little time the President might have exercised strong pressure upon them. The warning given to American investors by the Federal Reserve Board against Allied short-term credits, in the preceding November, indicated clearly the method by which pressure could be applied. But whatever chance of negotiations existed was spoiled by Germany. On Jan. 9 the decision approving the resumption of unrestricted submarine warfare was taken. On Jan. 31 it was announced to the United States that the pledges given after the *Sussex* ultimatum would no longer be observed. Wilson did not hesitate. His hopes of peace negotiations suddenly dashed, he decided immediately to give the German Ambassador his passports. "From that time henceforward," writes Bernstorff, "there can be no question of any earlier period, because up to that moment he had been in constant negotiation with us—he regarded the Imperial Government as morally condemned. . . . After the 31st January, 1917, Wilson himself was a different man. Our rejection of his proposal to mediate, by our announcement of the unrestricted U-boat war, which was to him utterly incomprehensible, turned him into an embittered enemy of the Imperial Government" (Bernstorff, p. 385).

Wilson still refused to believe that the diplomatic rupture meant war. "Only actual overt acts" would persuade him that the Germans would carry their threats into effect. He was willing to negotiate everything except the right to sink passenger and merchant ships without warning. But the Germans showed no sign of weakening.

"If Wilson wants war," wrote the Kaiser, "let him make it, and let him then have it" (*Official German Documents, post*, II, 1336). Given such determination on each side, American participation became merely a matter of time. Opinion in the United States was infuriated by the virtual blockade of cargoes in American ports; yet more by the publication of the Zimmermann note suggesting a German-Mexican-Japanese alliance and the Mexican reconquest of Texas, New Mexico, and Arizona. Still the President waited. He was not going to be forced into war by any material interest or emotional wave.

Finally, on Mar. 27, following the sinking of four American ships, he made the decision. On the eve of his war message he pondered the misery that would come. "For nights, he said, he'd been lying awake going over the whole situation. . . . He said he couldn't see any alternative, that he had tried every way he knew to avoid war . . . had considered every loophole of escape and as fast as they were discovered Germany deliberately blocked them with some new outrage . . . it was just a choice of evils" (J. L. Heaton, comp., *Cobb of "the World,"* 1924, pp. 268–70). On Apr. 2, 1917, he appeared before Congress to ask a declaration that a state of war existed with Germany. On Apr. 6, the resolution was voted by overwhelming majorities.

The declaration of war represented the all but unanimous sentiment of the American people. The anti-German feeling, at first characteristic of only the Atlantic seaboard, had spread westward, and with it the feeling that the Allies represented the cause of democracy and justice. The intimate financial and economic relations of the United States with Great Britain and France combined with an intellectual sympathy to foster a tendency to condone Allied infractions of neutral rights and to condemn as barbarism every German infraction. Pro-Ally feeling would not have been sufficient of itself to bring the United States into the war. But it created a state of mind which made the German declaration of the submarine war zone, followed by the Zimmermann telegram and the sinking of American ships, appear to Americans as a direct attack. Wilson was certainly never touched by any commercial or financial interest. Much more than the average American he was determined to avoid war. But he was not immune from the general pressure of opinion created by a variety of factors, and when he finally asked for the declaration of war he shared the conviction that imperial Germany was an international criminal.

Once in the war, Wilson was determined that the full strength of the nation should be concentrated on victory. The task of transforming a non-military industrial population of one hundred million souls into a belligerent machine involved one of the most wholesale transformations of history. There had been little preparation. For this the President must bear his share of responsibility, for he had been slow to admit the possibility of armed intervention by the United States. By the end of 1915 he came to the belief that steps should be taken to improve the efficiency and size of the military establishment and navy. In August 1916 he approved the creation of the Council of National Defense, charged with the "coordination of industries and resources for the national security and welfare." Preparation for war, however, had not gone very far. Wilson perceived the possibility of American participation, as his speeches and private papers of 1916 indicate; but at no time until the final break did he grasp emotionally its imminence.

But with the declaration of war. Wilson recognized that every interest must be subordinated to the attainment of victory. His leadership was distinguished in two respects. First, he created a national consciousness of common effort, made the people feel that this was a people's war and one in which every citizen must be glad to make his individual sacrifice. In the second place, the President, having selected for the vital military and administrative posts the men to carry through the technical details of organization and operation, never interfered with them and supported them unreservedly. These two aspects of Wilson's leadership made it possible for the nation to accept the emergency measures, very distasteful to American instincts but essential to victory: the army draft, the supervision and control exercised by the War Industries Board, the food and fuel control, the national administration of railways. They facilitated the national response to the appeal for a popular financing of the war effort through the Liberty Loans. They guaranteed to the military and administrative leaders an authority which, despite many mistakes, finally built up a fighting machine capable of coordinating the efforts of the home front with those of the fighting front in France. The steady support he gave to the secretary of war, Newton D. Baker, enabled him, in the face of sniping criticism, to proceed methodically and with ultimate success to the organization of a national service of supply that met the needs of an overseas force which finally numbered two million men. In France, General Pershing was guaranteed the full authority necessary to develop this force into a unified army. In no other war ever waged by the United

States was the opportunity for dishonest profit so largely eliminated and partisan political influence so thoroughly eradicated.

Wilson expressed a willingness to go to all lengths to achieve effective coordination with the Allies without surrendering the independence of American policy. He insisted that the United States was not an allied but an "associated" power, and never admitted the right of the European associates to speak for America in matters of policy. But he demanded the creation of machinery that would enable the United States to supply the necessities of those associates as rapidly and effectively as possible. This demand resulted in the American war mission of November 1917 which gave strong support to the plan for a Supreme War Council, and in combination with the British and French, successfully organized the various boards of interallied coordination.

The President's supreme contribution to victory lay in his formulation of war aims. He gave to the American and Allied peoples a consciousness that they were fighting for a peace worthy of the effort and sacrifice; and he doubtless weakened the enemy's "will to victory" by unfolding the vision of a new world organization that offered a better chance of ultimate happiness than any German triumph. The basis of permanent peace, he believed, must consist in the confidence of each nation that it would not be attacked, a confidence which could be achieved only through a system of international cooperation for security. This had been the principle of his Mobile speech and his Pan-American policy, and it underlay the House mission of 1914. Stimulated by the suggestions of Sir Edward Grey, as early as Dec. 24, 1915, he set down as an essential guarantee "a league of nations to secure each nation against aggression and maintain the absolute freedom of the seas" (Yale House Collection). Public expression of such a program formed the culmination of the speech of May 27, 1916, his very words suggesting at once an extension of the projected Pan-American Pact to the entire world and forecasting Article X of the League of Nations Covenant: "a virtual guarantee of territorial integrity and political independence" (*New Democracy*, II, 188).

Thus almost a year before American participation in the war, Wilson outlined certain principles which would justify American cooperation in world affairs. He elaborated them in his address to the Senate of Jan. 22, 1917, when he set forth the terms of a desirable peace upon which the belligerents might agree, insisting upon the principle of the Monroe Doctrine for the entire world, and demanding a concert of Powers capable of maintaining international tranquillity and the right of small nations. These principles he took for his text on Apr. 2, 1917, when he asked Congress to declare that a state of war existed with Germany. It is true that he now insisted upon the absolute defeat of the Imperial Government. It was no longer to be a "peace without victory." But the elevated purpose of the war and the final utilization of victory must not be forgotten in the heat of the struggle, and the ideals of peace time must be kept alive.

There was implicit in this program a conflict with the several war aims of the Allies, at least as set forth in the various treaties of 1915 and 1916. Wilson came to realize the fact. Later he testified before a Senate committee that "the whole series of understandings among the Allies was first disclosed" to him at the Peace Conference. But he had been informed of the most important of them by Mr. Balfour in April 1917, in some detail (*House Papers*, III, 61). This he may have later forgotten. He certainly recognized their general tenor. Writing to House on July 21, 1917, he said: "England and France have not the same views with regard to peace that we have by any means. When the war is over we can force them to our way of thinking, because by that time they will among other things be financially in our hands" (Yale House Collection).

Avoidance of acute difference with the Allies was achieved during the summer and autumn of 1917 by stressing the attack upon German autocracy and not pressing for any general agreement upon ultimate war aims. Wilson's hand, however, was forced by the Russian Revolution and the insistent public demand for a restatement of war aims. Allied leaders found it impossible to agree upon any general formula, far less upon any concrete statement of terms. House returned to the United States to tell Wilson that in order to maintain the morale of liberal and labor forces in the Allied countries he must make a comprehensive statement himself. On Jan. 8, 1918, the President delivered before the Congress the speech of the Fourteen Points. This was not designated as a public international charter but as a diplomatic weapon, to meet the Bolshevik drive for peace and to strengthen the morale of the Allied liberals. The six general points repeated ideals already enunciated by Wilson: open diplomacy, freedom of the seas, removal of trade barriers, reduction of armaments, impartial adjustment of colonial claims, a league of nations. The eight special points, dealing with immediate political and territorial problems, were not so far apart from the purposes declared by Lloyd George three days previously. The address was of particular significance in American policy for the reason that for the first time Wilson regarded territorial terms as America's business and laid down territorial conditions as a prerequisite of American cooperation. By the speech Wilson committed himself not merely to full participation in the general world problem of preserving the peace, but to an interest in the local problems peculiar to Europe that might disturb the peace.

The ultimate significance of the speech of the Fourteen Points lay in the fact that when the Germans in the early autumn of 1918 recognized the inevitability of defeat, they seized upon it as a general basis of peace negotiations. In the spring of that year, after the imposition of the peace of Brest-Litovsk upon Russia and with the peril of German victory in France imminent, the President refused any suggestion of compromise. But as the German armies, facing disaster, began their retreat, Wilson hoped to hasten their surrender by promising Germany protection against political or economic annihilation and the just treatment to which every nation has a claim. To him, therefore, the Germans turned in early October as to a savior from the destructiveness of Allied wrath.

Public sentiment in the United States was strongly against any negotiation with the Germans. Among the Allied leaders there was irritation that the appeal had been made to Wilson. It is reasonably clear that if it had been made to the Allies as a whole it would have been refused forthwith. The Germans would then have girded themselves for the last-ditch defense planned by Ludendorff and Prince Max; the fighting would have continued, in the words of Marshal Foch, "maybe three, maybe four or five months. Who knows?" (*House Papers*, IV, 91). By his interchange of notes with the Germans, Wilson gave the demand for peace in Germany an opportunity to gain force; once started, the peace flood could not be stemmed. Thus on Oct. 23 he was able to hand to the Allies Germany's acceptance of an armistice ensuring to them "the unrestricted power to safeguard and enforce the details of the peace to which the German Government has agreed" (*Foreign Relations 1918 Supplement*, no. 1, vol. I, p. 382).

There were complaints at the time that Wilson, by his handling of the negotiations, saved Germany from invasion and an unconditional surrender. Actually what Wilson offered the Allies was not peace but merely the opportunity to make it. They were still free to refuse if they chose. Naturally they accepted the opportunity. Wilson's diplomacy resulted in complete victory and also saved several months' fighting. More serious is the criticism that Wilson lured the

Germans into peace and the overthrow of the imperial régime by the promise of conditions which he did not intend or was unable to make good. It is a favorite German theme. It will not withstand critical analysis. When the German government proposed the Fourteen Points as the basis of peace, they might have insisted upon a clarification, reserving specific rights. Prince Max knew and stated that the Fourteen Points meant that Germany would doubtless lose important territory, Alsace-Lorraine, the Polish corridor, the colonies. He wished to send to Wilson a memorandum asking for definite guarantees. But he was not allowed to make any reservations lest the negotiations be broken off. The representative of the Supreme Command, Haeften, declared that "the definition of the Fourteen Points would endanger the whole armistice action" (*The Memoirs of Prince Max of Baden*, 1928, II, 39). Germany, with her armies still in the field, preferred to take her chance on the Fourteen Points undefined, rather than lose the chance of peace. There is in all this no question of being "lured into a trap."

Wilson had also to carry on a diplomatic contest with the Allies. Until the armistice negotiations they had not taken the Fourteen Points seriously. Clemenceau had not even read them. The general disposition in the Supreme War Council was to assume that their acceptance or refusal should be left to the Peace Conference. Colonel House, acting as Wilson's representative on the Council, insisted that Allied approval of the Fourteen Points must be a condition precedent to any armistice. Otherwise there would be no guarantee whatever against terms totally inconsonant with the whole Wilsonian program. The Allied leaders for a time refused to give formal or informal approval to the Fourteen Points. House responded with the threat that lacking such approval Wilson would be forced to tell Germany that the Allies refused the basic conditions, and would then ask the American Congress whether the war should continue in order to enforce European terms, although the American terms had been accepted by Germany. The threat proved sufficient. The Allies accepted the Fourteen Points and later speeches of Wilson as the basis of the peace, with one elucidation defining the meaning of "restoration," and one reservation providing for later discussion of "freedom of the seas." Wilson accepted both, and by his note of Nov. 5 transmitted to Germany the qualified acceptance by the Allies of the basic conditions of peace. Thus was completed the so-called Pre-armistice Agreement. On Nov. 11, the German and Allied delegates signed the armistice.

Wilson was at the height of his influence. The quondam college professor had become the greatest single personal force in the world. He had led the United States to victory in the greatest war of history. He had imposed his will upon defeated and triumphant Europeans. He was hailed as savior by the populations of Central Europe, freed from Hapsburg and Hohenzollern rule; he was the apostle of British liberals, French artisans, and Italian peasants. Allied leaders confessed their recognition of his power by their anxiety as to how he might use it. But the difficulties of capitalizing victory were far greater than those involved in winning it. During four years the mind of the world had been turned to war, and it was impossible to create an atmosphere favorable to permanent peace. The sense of common interest forced by the danger of a German victory evaporated when the danger disappeared. The political ideals of Wilson could not easily be transplanted to Europe; when applied to specific problems they might or might not prove practicable; and they involved principles which were bound to contradict each other.

At this critical moment Wilson made three mistakes, the bearing of which was only later perceived. He was regarded by Europe as politically supreme in the United States, and the belief accounted for much of his influence abroad. But in the November elections he publicly made of Democratic success at the polls a question of personal confidence, asking the voters to choose Democrats as an indication of personal trust. He thus abdicated his national leadership to assume the rôle of party leader. Democratic defeats in that election gave the appearance of a national repudiation, and threw control of the Senate foreign relations committee into the hands of his personal enemies. A second mistake lay in his choice of a peace commission. No member of the Commission really represented either the Republican party or the Senate. Wilson lost thereby the chance of winning support from his domestic opponents and stimulated partisan opposition. His supreme mistake lay in his decision to go to the Peace Conference in person. "He was the *God on the Mountain*," writes Colonel House, "and his decisions regarding international matters were practically final. When he came to Europe and sat in conference with the Prime Ministers and representatives of other states, he gradually lost his place as first citizen of the world" (Seymour, *American Diplomacy, post,* p. 399). Apart from these mistakes Wilson faced detailed difficulties. Delays in the calling of the Conference, resulting from domestic political problems in Europe, permitted the cooling of idealistic aspirations and the development of national particularism. The political leaders, himself included, failed to realize the vital importance of a definite program and a carefully studied organization of the Conference. The American commission was ill-organized, American delegates on the various commissions received no regular instructions, and the American program was never considered and developed comprehensively.

In spite of errors and difficulties Wilson achieved his main triumph at the very beginning of the Conference by forcing acceptance of the League of Nations Covenant as an integral part of the treaty of peace. He was equally successful in leading the commission chosen to draft the Covenant through a series of meetings which culminated in unanimous approval of a version, which on Feb. 14, 1919, he read to a plenary session of the Conference. When he sailed for the United States on the 15th he felt that his main work had been accomplished.

He returned a month later to find in Paris a definitely unfavorable atmosphere. When general principles were applied to specific questions it became clear that many of the Wilsonian ideals were impracticable. It was not so much a conflict between obvious right and wrong as between contradictory rights. Above all the discussion hung the cloud of industrial unrest and social revolution, making it vitally important that decisions should be rapidly reached and uncertainty dispelled. Was it not better to make an inconsistent decision, trusting to the League of Nations to rectify it, rather than to leave the world in chaos?

To discover that in their application his principles were at variance with each other, to adjust himself to the necessity of compromise, produced in Wilson a violent nervous shock. It was the worse because of a severe attack of influenza that struck him during the most important of the April negotiations. For a moment he considered the advisability of deserting the Conference and leaving Europe to settle her own problems. He ordered the *George Washington* to be in readiness to take him home. But such a desertion would do nothing to improve the state of Europe, quite the contrary, and would mean the end of the League. If he stayed on and refused to accept compromise, even though he might compel Clemenceau, Orlando, and Lloyd George to accept his own detailed solutions, it would mean the overthrow of their governments and the appearance at the Conference of more bitter reactionaries. When he tried an appeal to the people, over the heads of the delegates, as in his Fiume appeal to Italy, he was openly rebuffed by Italian public opinion and the unity of the Conference shaken. A firm stand against the Japanese meant their departure from the Conference; and who was to enforce the decisions of the Conference against them in the Far East?

Thus Wilson was forced to agree to a series of compromises which left liberals disappointed and Germans bitter. Yet the necessity of the compromises is apparent from the fact that the nationalists in both France and Italy were equally disappointed. The Fourteen Points were certainly disfigured, but without them and Wilson the treaties would have been far less liberal. Wilson agreed that Germans must pay in addition to direct damages the cost of pensions, but he saved them from total war costs. At the price of promising American aid to France in case of German aggression, in conjunction with Great Britain, he prevented the separation of the Rhine lands from Germany. He prevented the annexation of the Saar by France and made possible its ultimate return to Germany. He forced the system of mandates for the German colonies. He extracted from Japan the informal promise to return Shantung to China (*House Papers,* IV, 453, 455). Above all he secured the adoption of the League of Nations Covenant, with its provision for open diplomacy through the registration of treaties, progressive limitation of armament, an international court, and the avoidance of war. Wilson's failures did not lie in the terms of the Versailles Treaty, which was destined never to be applied as designed. His failure came later in America when his defeat by the Senate removed the essential basis of that treaty.

Neither Wilson himself nor those Americans who accompanied him, as they returned after the signing of the Versailles Treaty, felt that he had been defeated. They believed, rather, that in view of the difficulties of the situation he had accomplished a larger part of his program than might have been expected. There remained only the problem of winning the approval of the United States Senate. Properly handled that problem was far less difficult than many solved by Wilson in Europe. Public opinion generally favored the League and cared little about the details of the treaties. The League was supported by outstanding public figures such as Taft and Root. In the Senate itself Wilson could count on the support of all but a few Democrats and on the majority of the Republicans. His chief opponent, Senator Lodge, hoped to add some amendments or reservations, but not to defeat the Treaty and the Covenant. The balance of power was held by a group of moderates, led by Kellogg and McCumber, who desired "mild" reservations that would not touch the significance of the Covenant. A few concilatory gestures by the President would have sufficed to win the two-thirds vote necessary to ratification.

Wilson's attitude was not conciliatory. He intimated to the Senate committee on foreign relations that he would permit no changes in

Covenant or Treaty. As opposition developed, his tone became more unyielding. The issue shifted from the merits of the Covenant to the question of authority between President and Senate, even to a personal quarrel between Wilson and Lodge, chairman of the committee. In the hope of winning popular support Wilson set forth on Sept. 3 on a country-wide tour in the course of which he made some thirty speeches. It ended suddenly. On Sept. 25, at Pueblo, physically and emotionally exhausted, he was threatened with a complete nervous collapse, and he was hastily brought back to Washington. For three days he seemed not so ill, but on the morning of Oct. 2 Dr. Grayson, hurriedly called to the White House, found Wilson physically helpless. "The President is paralyzed" (Hoover, *post*, p. 101). His life was saved, but for weeks that followed he was incapable of transacting official business. Nor for months could he undertake any effort, physical or mental, that required initiative.

Wilson's illness was a hammer-blow of fate. Had he died, it seems certain that his successor would have made the compromises with the Senate necessary to ratification of the Covenant. Had he recovered sufficiently to receive the advice of those in touch with political realities, it is possible that he might himself have perceived the necessity of compromise. But completely isolated from the political situation he could do no more than maintain his earlier position: the Covenant must be ratified without essential changes; the reservations introduced by Senator Lodge, in his opinion, would nullify it. The supporters of the Covenant were divided between those who stood behind Wilson and the "mild reservationists." It was impossible to find a two-thirds majority for any resolution of ratification.

In the winter, hope for the Covenant again appeared. Viscount Grey, whose eloquent letters in 1915 had seriously influenced Wilson in favor of a League, was sent to the United States as special ambassador. For weeks he waited, hoping for an interview with the sick President. This was denied him. But on his return to England, he published a letter in which he stated that the success of the League demanded the adherence of the United States; if such adherence depended upon the inclusion of the Lodge reservations in the act of ratification, they ought to be accepted by Europe. It was a suggestion to Wilson that, in the circumstances, compromise with Lodge was wise. The suggestion was not followed. When the Treaty and Covenant were once more introduced into the Senate, Wilson maintained his objections to the Lodge reservations. He advised his supporters to vote against the resolution of ratification in company with the bitter-end opponents of any league whatsoever. Even so, the two-thirds necessary to ratification lacked only seven votes. So close was the United States to entering the League. Thus ironically did fate ordain that the nation should be kept out of the League at the orders of the man who had done more than any other to create it.

Wilson's statesmanship cannot be fairly adjudged on the basis of the handling of the Treaty in the Senate. His nervous and physical collapse was complete. From the time of his April illness in Paris there were many indications of a progressive breakdown certain to affect his political judgment and his personal dealings with men. After October, he lived in a sick-room, emerging merely for simple recreation or purely formal tasks which taxed his strength to a point that left no opportunity for reasoned consideration of difficult questions. The President was thus divorced from political realities. Even Colonel House was excluded, though there was no personal quarrel. Wilson may have known nothing of House's letters to him; they remained unanswered. "I feel that had not illness overtaken the President, all would have been well," wrote Ike Hoover, who had watched closely the relations between the two men since Wilson entered the White House. "He needed Colonel House, and in a way, fully realized the fact. But this illness changed the entire aspect of things" (Hoover, p. 95). The political effects of the separation were tremendous.

For three years after the end of his term of office, Wilson led a retired life in Washington. He formed a law partnership with Bainbridge Colby, but his physical condition permitted no active work. He was seen in public on few occasions. The reaction against the idealism of his own administration which followed the Republican victory of 1920 left him wrapped in dignified silence. His mind was clear and reasonably active but the physical machine was broken. Tired out, no longer able to influence opinion as prophet of higher political aspirations, he confessed that he was "tired of swimming upstream" (*Ibid.*, p. 108). On Sunday, Feb. 3, 1924, he died in his sleep.

Wilson was propelled into public affairs by his natural qualities and his sense of responsibility for their use. By taste and inheritance he was designed for a circumscribed, quiet life, and he was probably happiest while still a college professor. His personal feelings lay close under the skin. He was always dependent upon the help and encouragement he received from his domestic circle; his craving for feminine sympathy is revealed in his correspondence with Mrs. Reid and Mrs. Peck, friends from whom he constantly sought a purely intellectual understanding. His first wife died in the midst of the

European War crisis of August 1914. He was married for a second time, on Dec. 18, 1915, to Edith Bolling Galt, who survived him.

Qualified by personal and intellectual gifts for the public life, he never capitalized them fully. Of rather more than middle height, carefully dressed, erect, with square features and powerful jaw, eyes that shifted suddenly from merriment to severity, in appearance he was impressive and attractive. To those who worked closely with him he displayed a magnetism of personality—genial, humorous, considerate—and an expansive wealth of mental quality; and from them he evoked admiration and affection. But in dealing with men whom he did not like or did not trust Wilson would not call such advantages to his service. He was equipped by intellectual stature, by oratorical capacity, and by sincerity of emotion to lead a nation or the world; but he was handicapped in meeting the simplest problem of political tactics because he carried into public life the attitude of a private citizen. Simple in his pleasures, naturally averse to heterogeneous gatherings, interested in people because of what they were rather than because of what they could do to help or hinder, he refused many of the sacrifices of exacting taste demanded by the rough game of politics.

Wilson's prejudices were strong, often ill-founded, and he would not yield them to political exigencies. Because of them he alienated important leaders in the world of business and of journalism. At the close of his public career he was generally pictured in the public mind as a self-willed and arbitrary egoist, and the picture doubtless accounts for his personal unpopularity after the Peace Conference. Most of the bitter criticism was entirely undeserved. In the sense that he was always acutely interested in his own reactions to life, he might be termed an egoist, although the term would be entirely misleading if it implied selfishness, for no one was more considerate of the feelings and interests of those around him. But he matched himself constantly against his duties and his opportunities, and was unsparing in self-criticism. Sharply sensitive to the sympathies and advice of those for whom he cared, he had little respect for the arguments of personal or political enemies.

As lecturer and writer Wilson had a genius for simplification, for the clarification of the complex and the explanation of the relation of things. These qualities he carried into his political speeches and they account in part, at least, for the effect he exercised upon men's minds through his oratory; as he would say, "by utterance." He never sought the favor either of undergraduates or the public by condescending to cheapness of tone. But he labored incessantly to manufacture the phrase that would make the idea appealing. Popular approval he regarded as the ultimate test. Without it lectures, articles, or speeches were in vain, and policies, however justifiable, futile. By personal taste an aristocrat, he put his faith in the common man and accepted the democratic verdict as final.

The public force of Wilson's speeches resulted only in part from clarity of expression and piquancy of phrase; they were equally characterized by strong and effective moral fervor. His religious feeling was never separated from any aspect of his life; he strove consciously to measure everything by spiritual rather than material values. Publicly as well as privately he was not afraid to make an absolute distinction between right and wrong. Many of his speeches are political sermons. Not a few of his listeners and readers were irritated by the apparent dogmatism with which he laid down judgments, and contended that, like his favorite Gladstone, he claimed an intimacy with the designs of Providence that could scarcely be justified. But for the masses there was a strong appeal in the obvious sincerity of his conviction that a policy should be adjudged according to its morality, that the more power an individual or a nation possessed the greater was the obligation to avoid wrongdoing.

Wilson's political philosophy was simple. He was a liberal individualist, insistent upon the right of unprivileged persons and small nations to be freed from the control of more powerful groups. The principles of the New Freedom as applied to tariff and currency reform or labor legislation, and the doctrine of self-determination for oppressed nationalities spring from the same source. He looked upon his policies as primarily policies of emancipation. He had a good deal of eighteenth-century confidence in the virtues of the natural man; a feeling that if the latter-day abuses of privilege and despotism could be wiped out, both domestic and international problems could be set on the road to solution. Nor did he admit any real contradiction between the idea of freedom and the restraint of law, between national self-determination and international control. Just as the liberty of the individual is assured by the Constitution, so the independence of nations can be guaranteed by a "concert of free peoples." Thus he was able to speak of the League of Nations as "a disentangling alliance."

The extraordinary success of his program up to a certain point, whether domestic or international, was facilitated by the threatened bankruptcy of the industrial system and the completed bankruptcy of the diplomatic system. His legislation of 1913–14 rode on the

wave of the 1912 reform movement. His plea for international security, reflecting plans already sponsored by Roosevelt, Taft, Root,
and Grey, was driven home to the hearts of the people by the tragic
lessons of the World War. It was Wilson, however, who by his qualities and not merely because of his office, capitalized the opportunity
and wakened the world to a great vision. He was not able to transform the dream into fact. But just as it is certain that the nations
will pursue the hope of establishing an international organization
for the guarantee of peace, so it is certain that Wilson will remain
historically the eminent prophet of that better world.

[REVISED BIBLIOGRAPHY. A program for the collection and publication of all
Wilson papers, from both public depositories and private collections, has been
sponsored by the Woodrow Wilson Foundation and is now in active progress.
This definitive edition, under the editorship of Arthur S. Link with John W.
Davidson as associate editor and David W. Hirst as assistant editor, will make
available in approximately forty volumes an unrivaled source for the study of
Wilson's personal life and political career. The most important body of manuscripts now open to research is the Wilson Papers in the Lib. of Cong.; the
library also has important related collections. Other documentary sources are
in the State Dept. files in the Nat. Archives and in the N. J. State Lib. Voluminous unpublished material on Wilson is also available in a number of university
libraries, notably the Edward M. House Collection at Yale, the Hoover Institution on War, Revolution, and Peace at Stanford, the Houghton Lib. at Harvard,
and the Princeton Univ. Lib. Other pertinent collections are at Johns Hopkins,
Bryn Mawr, the Univ. of Va., Duke, and the Univ. of N. C. The most important
of Wilson's published writings are: *Congressional Government: A Study in Am.
Politics* (1885); *The State: Elements of Historical and Practical Politics* (1889);
Division and Reunion, 1829–1889 (1893); *An Old Master, and Other Political
Essays* (1893); *Mere Literature, and Other Essays* (1896); *George Washington*
(1896); *A Hist. of the Am. People* (5 vols., 1902); *Constitutional Government in
the U. S.* (1908); *On Being Human* (1916); *International Ideals* (1919); and
Leaders of Men (ed. by T. H. V. Motter, 1952). The standard edition of Wilson's
state papers and addresses is *The Public Papers of Woodrow Wilson*, ed. by
Ray Stannard Baker and William E. Dodd (6 vols., 1925–27). The campaign
speeches of 1912 establishing the principles of the New Freedom have been
skillfully reconstructed and brilliantly edited by John W. Davidson in *A Cross-
roads of Freedom* (1956). See also August Heckscher, ed., *The Politics of Woodrow Wilson: Selections from his Speeches and Writings* (1956); and Eleanor
Wilson McAdoo, ed., *The Priceless Gift: The Love Letters of Woodrow Wilson
and Ellen Axson Wilson* (1962).

The standard biography covering all aspects of Wilson's personal and public life is Arthur Walworth's *Woodrow Wilson* (2 vols., 1958). It is thoroughly documented with all the manuscript and printed sources now available, as well as the personal recollections of the President's family and associates, and is admirably balanced in its presentation of the varied and controversial aspects of Wilson's life and activities. Arthur S. Link's *Wilson: The Road to the White House* (1947), *Wilson: The New Freedom* (1956), and *Wilson: The Struggle for Neutrality* (1960) form the three opening volumes of an imposing biography of the highest scholarly quality, encyclopedic in concept and execution. These volumes carry the narrative to the close of 1915. Also by Link is a survey of the early presidency in the New American Nation series: *Woodrow Wilson and the Progressive Era, 1910–1917* (1954). Ray Stannard Baker's *Woodrow Wilson, Life and Letters* (1929–39) is in eight volumes, of which the last two are essentially a chronological summary; it concludes with the armistice of November 1918. The author was a friend in whom the President confided, and the book glows with Wilson's idealistic fervor and views him through the mist of hero worship. Herbert C. F. Bell's *Woodrow Wilson and the People* (1945) is a brief over-all survey, objective and critically sympathetic. Two recent interpretive studies are John M. Blum, *Woodrow Wilson and the Politics of Morality* (1956), and John A. Garraty, *Woodrow Wilson: A Great Life in Brief* (1956); see also Richard Hofstadter's chapter on Wilson in his *The Am. Political Tradition* (1948). A more specialized study is William Diamond, *The Economic Thought of Woodrow Wilson* (1943).

Memoirs and biographical interpretations of Wilson by contemporaries and associates are numerous and essential to an understanding of the man and his times. Among these are: Newton D. Baker, *How Woodrow Wilson Met Domestic Questions* (pamphlet, 1926); Ray Stannard Baker, *Am. Chronicle* (1945); Bernard M. Baruch, *Baruch: My Own Story* (1957); Josephus Daniels, *The Wilson Era* (2 vols., 1944–46); Mary B. Bryan, ed., *The Memoirs of William Jennings Bryan* (1925); Carter Glass, *An Adventure in Constructive Finance* (1927); Rear Adm. Cary T. Grayson, *Woodrow Wilson: An Intimate Memoir* (1960); Herbert Hoover, *Memoirs*, vol. I (1951), and *The Ordeal of Woodrow Wilson* (1958); Irwin H. Hoover, *Forty-two Years in the White House* (1934); David F. Houston, *Eight Years with Wilson's Cabinet* (2 vols., 1926); Charles Seymour, ed., *The Intimate Papers of Colonel House* (4 vols., 1926–28); Mary A. Hulbert, *The Story of Mrs. Peck: An Autobiography* (1933); J. J. Jusserand, *Le Sentiment Américain pendant la Guerre* (1931); James Kerney, *The Political Education of Woodrow Wilson* (1926); H. H. Kohlsaat, *From McKinley to Harding* (1923); Anne W. Lane and Louise H. Wall, eds., *The Letters of Franklin K. Lane* (1922); Robert Lansing, *War Memoirs* (1935); Eleanor Wilson McAdoo, *The Woodrow Wilsons* (1937); William F. McCombs, *Making Woodrow Wilson President* (1921); William G. McAdoo, *Crowded Years* (1931); Thomas R. Marshall, *Recollections* (1925); Henry Morgenthau, *Ambassador Morgenthau's Story* (1918); William Starr Myers, ed., *Woodrow Wilson: Some Princeton Memories* (1946); Thomas Nelson Page, *Italy and the World War* (1920); Burton J. Hendrick, *The Life and Letters of Walter H. Page* (3 vols., 1922–25); Bliss Perry, *And*

Gladly Teach (1935); Edith G. Reid, *Woodrow Wilson: The Caricature, the Myth and the Man* (1934); Stephen Gwynn, ed., *The Letters and Friendships of Sir Cecil Spring Rice* (2 vols., 1929); Joseph P. Tumulty, *Woodrow Wilson as I Know Him* (1921); and Edith Bolling Wilson, *My Memoir* (1939). Biographical studies of contemporaries include: Frederick Palmer's *Newton D. Baker: America at War* (2 vols., 1931), and his *Bliss, Peacemaker: The Life and Letters of Gen. Tasker Howard Bliss* (1934); John M. Blum, *Joe Tumulty and the Wilson Era* (1951); Margaret L. Coit, *Mr. Baruch* (1957); John A. Garraty, *Henry Cabot Lodge: A Biography* (1953); Alexander and Juliette George, *Woodrow Wilson and Colonel House* (1956); Alpheus T. Mason, *Brandeis, A Free Man's Life* (1946); A. D. Howden Smith, *Mr. House of Texas* (1940); and George S. Viereck, *The Strangest Friendship in History: Woodrow Wilson and Colonel House* (1932).

For the study of Wilson's foreign policy, official sources are available in U. S. Dept. of State, *Papers Relating to the Foreign Relations of the U. S.*, supplements on *The World War*, 1914–18 (9 vols., 1928–33) and on *Russia*, 1918–19 (4 vols., 1931–37). The official correspondence requires illumination from Wilson's private letters, of which those to Colonel House are the most revealing. Studies and memoirs relating to foreign affairs of the period are numerous: Edward H. Buehrig, *Woodrow Wilson and the Balance of Power* (1955); Buehrig, ed., *Woodrow Wilson's Foreign Policy in Perspective* (1957); Johann von Bernstorff, *My Three Years in America* (1920); Roy W. Curry, *Woodrow Wilson and Far Eastern Policy, 1913–1921* (1957); Constantin Dumba, *Memoirs of a Diplomat* (1932); Russell H. Fifield, *Woodrow Wilson and the Far East: The Diplomacy of the Shantung Question* (1952); James W. Gerard, *My Four Years in Germany* (1917); Louis L. Gerson, *Woodrow Wilson and the Rebirth of Poland, 1914–1920* (1953); George F. Kennan, *Soviet-American Relations, 1917–1920:* vol. I: *Russia Leaves the War* (1956), vol. II: *The Decision to Intervene* (1958); Tien-yi Li, *Woodrow Wilson's China Policy, 1913–1917* (1952); Arthur S. Link, *Wilson, the Diplomatist* (1957); Ernest R. May, *The World War and Am. Isolation, 1914–1917* (1959); Arno J. Mayer, *Political Origins of the New Diplomacy, 1917–1918* (1959); Harley Notter, *The Origins of the Foreign Policy of Woodrow Wilson* (1937); Charles Seymour, *Woodrow Wilson and the World War* (1921), *Am. Diplomacy during the World War* (1934), and *Am. Neutrality, 1914–1917* (1935); Daniel M. Smith, *Robert Lansing and Am. Neutrality, 1914–1917* (1958); Charles C. Tansill, *America Goes to War* (1938); Betty Miller Unterberger, *America's Siberian Expedition, 1918–1920* (1956); Arthur Willert, *The Road to Safety* (1953).

For the Peace Conference and its aftermath the continued Dept. of State *Papers Relating to the Foreign Relations of the U. S.* form the fundamental source: *The Paris Peace Conference* (13 vols., 1942–47); *The Lansing Papers, 1914–20* (2 vols., 1939). The most useful collection of documents, foreign as well as American, is in David Hunter Miller, *My Diary at the Conference of Paris* (privately printed, 21 vols., 1924). Paul Mantoux, *Les Délibérations du Conseil des Quatre* (2 vols., 1955), forms an invaluable supplement to the official minutes. Ray Stannard Baker, *Woodrow Wilson and World Settlement* (3 vols.,

1922) is valuable as expressing Wilson's personal feelings on the various issues, but is marred by the author's failure to understand European conditions. Other works include: Clarence A. Berdahl, *The Policy of the U. S. with Respect to the League of Nations* (1932); Bernard M. Baruch, *The Making of the Reparation and Economic Sections of the Treaty* (1920); Thomas A. Bailey, *Woodrow Wilson and the Lost Peace* (1944) and *Woodrow Wilson and the Great Betrayal* (1945); Georges Clemenceau, *Grandeur and Misery of Victory* (1930); Bainbridge Colby, *The Close of Woodrow Wilson's Administration* (1930); Edward M. House and Charles Seymour, eds., *What Really Happened at Paris* (1921); J. M. Keynes, *The Economic Consequences of the Peace* (1920); Robert Lansing, *The Big Four and Others of the Peace Conference* (1921), and *The Peace Negotiations, A Personal Narrative* (1921); Henry Cabot Lodge, *The Senate and the League of Nations* (1925); David Hunter Miller, *The Drafting of the Covenant* (2 vols., 1928); Harold Nicolson, *Peacemaking, 1919* (1933); Allan Nevins, *Henry White: Thirty Years of Am. Diplomacy* (1930); George B. Noble, *Policies and Opinions at Paris, 1919* (1935); Charles Seymour, *La Politique de Wilson et le Sénat* (1925); André Tardieu, *The Truth about the Treaty* (1921).

The hundredth anniversary of Wilson's birth called forth a variety of essays, among them those contained in: *Lectures and Seminar at the Univ. of Chicago . . . in Celebration of the Centennial of Woodrow Wilson* (1956); Em Bowles Alsop, ed., *The Greatness of Woodrow Wilson* (1956); and the Wilson centennial number of the *Va. Quart. Rev.*, Autumn 1956. For further references see Laura S. Turnbull, *Woodrow Wilson: A Selected Bibliography* (1948); Arthur S. Link's "Essay on Sources" in his *Woodrow Wilson and the Progressive Era;* and Richard L. Watson, Jr., "Woodrow Wilson and his Interpreters, 1947–1957," *Miss. Valley Hist. Rev.*, Sept. 1957.]

Theodore Roosevelt

by

FREDERIC LOGAN PAXSON

ROOSEVELT, THEODORE (Oct. 27, 1858–Jan. 6, 1919), twenty-sixth president of the United States, was born at No. 28 East 20th St., New York City, the son of Theodore and Martha (Bulloch) Roosevelt. Of the four children, Anna was older, and Elliott and Corinne were younger than he. In his *Autobiography* he stated that his ancestor, Klaes Martensen van Roosevelt, came from Holland to New Amsterdam as a "settler" about 1644; in various genealogies the name appears as Claes Martenszen van Rosenvelt and the date as 1649 (Whittlesey, Clemens, Johnson, *post*). Thereafter, six generations of Roosevelts before his own were identified with Manhattan, and the more recent of them were well-to-do. Robert Barnwell Roosevelt, civic reformer, anti-Tammany Democrat, and wildlife conservationist, was his uncle. His mother, the daughter of James Stephens Bulloch of Roswell, Ga., and a descendant of Archibald Bulloch, first president of the Provincial Congress of Georgia, was of the aristocracy of the Old South. His parents maintained in their brownstone residence a home of dignity, culture, and restraint; they were established in, though not highly valuing, the society of New York. Handicapped in childhood by asthma, and always by defective eyesight, Theodore rebuilt his body from sheer determination, teaching himself to ride, shoot, and box, though his early interests were more in natural history than sport. His parents gave him tutors and travel as a child and sent him to Harvard. He made Phi Beta Kappa there, but was not thrilled by academic opportunity, and was graduated in 1880, lacking a career but free to choose one.

Law, which he undertook to read, failed to interest him; so he turned to the history of the United States, beginning, with the publication in 1882 of *The Naval War of 1812; or, the History of the United States Navy During the Last War with Great Britain,* a literary and historical career of which he never tired. A free-lance historian, he later dreaded the possibility that he might be forced to enlist among "these small men who do most of the historic teaching in the colleges" (Bishop, *post,* II, 140). Chance, however, saved him from this fate, for a local Republican boss needed an eminently respectable candidate for the 21st Assembly district. Roosevelt was sent to Albany for three sessions, 1882–84, and won acceptance as a leader on his merit. Here his freedom served him well. Irritating to his seniors, he was attractive to reporters in search of news. He attacked misbehavior as he chose, saw to it that the newspapers had his side of every story, and supported with zest laws for the relief of the workingmen and for the better government of New York City. His associates saw him as "a light-footed, agile, nervous yet prompt boy, with light-brown, slightly curling hair, blue eyes and an eye-glass, and ready to rise and speak with a clear, sharp, boyish voice" (*Frank Leslie's Illustrated Newspaper,* May 10, 1884, p. 183).

His father had died in 1878. Beginning late in 1883, Roosevelt risked more than $50,000 of his patrimony in ranch lands in Dakota Territory, which he retained until 1887 (Hermann Hagedorn, *Roosevelt in the Bad Lands,* 1921). He lost most of his investment, but gained far more in access to the open air, in valuable experience in the ways of men and cattle, and in solace after the death of his young wife. On Oct. 27, 1880, he had married Alice Hathaway Lee, daughter of George C. Lee of Chestnut Hill, Mass. She died on Feb. 14, 1884, shortly after the birth of their daughter Alice Lee (later Mrs. Nicholas Longworth), and only a few hours after the death of Roosevelt's own mother. These tragic events darkened the year of his last fight in the legislature at Albany and his earnest effort to block the nomination of James G. Blaine for the presidency. Still under twenty-six, he won place as delegate at large to the Chicago Republican National Convention, where he stood by George F. Edmunds until the end. The ranch occupied his summer. He was discouraged by the nomination of Blaine and Logan, but came east at last to engage in what was described as a "most remarkable performance in the crow-eating line" (New York *World,* Oct. 19, 1884). He supported the ticket and always despised the Mugwumps. In quick succession he wrote *Hunting Trips of a Ranchman* (1885); *Thomas Hart Benton* (1886); *Gouverneur Morris* (1888); *Ranch*

Life and the Hunting-Trail (1888); *Essays on Practical Politics* (1888); and the first two volumes of *The Winning of the West* (1889). He returned to practical politics in 1886, when he entered a thankless contest to run against Abram S. Hewitt and Henry George for mayor of New York. After finishing third in this election he hastened to London where, on Dec. 2, 1886, he was married to Edith Kermit Carow, in St. George's Church, Hanover Square (S. L. Gwynn, *The Letters and Friendships of Sir Cecil Spring Rice*, 1929, vol. I, p. 48). In 1888 he supported a winning presidential ticket and stood in line for a minor reward in national politics.

Harrison made him a civil-service commissioner in May 1889, and Roosevelt was soon convinced that the spoilsmen were alarmed at his arrival in Washington. There was some reason to fear that civil-service reform had died aborning, for politicians tried to evade the specific requirements of the Pendleton Act of 1883. The commissioners were inconspicuous until Roosevelt brought a glare of happy publicity into his petty office. For six years he lived in and learned his Washington. The Roosevelts kept simple but open house on a side street, the Adams-Hay circle accepted them, Lodge and Spring Rice were in and out. The mysteries of high policy and "backstage" intrigue were open before their eyes. Already set to the notion that in ethics lay the cure of politics, Roosevelt wrote and spoke as a lay evangelist, and applied great energy to the task of keeping out the crooks and protecting the competent. This philosophy remained with him for life (*American Ideals and Other Essays, Social and Political*, 1897). The personal conflicts that were its consequence made good news stories in which he was generally as right as he always looked (*The Strenuous Life; Essays and Addresses*, 1900).

The municipal election of 1894 brought him back to New York the following year, still with no fixed career, but with *The Wilderness Hunter* (1893) added to his list, and *The Winning of the West* (vols. III, IV, 1894–96) nearly done. Writing at the same time and following in the tracks of Frederick J. Turner, he missed the point that Turner raised in *The Significance of the Frontier in American History* (published separately in 1894), and remained of the school of Francis Parkman, ever interested in heroic events and literary narrative. As president of the American Historical Association in 1912, he expounded his theory at length (*History as Literature, and Other Essays*, 1913). In New York a reform mayor, William L. Strong, organized a non-political administration in 1895. Roosevelt took the presidency of the board of police commissioners, and for two years learned to command men. He was doubtless overzealous and accomplished relatively little, but, with Jacob A. Riis as his Boswell (J. A. Riis, *Theodore Roosevelt, the Citizen,* 1904), he penetrated the lowest levels of slum life, observed an unholy alliance of graft, politics, and crime, and again by his ability to turn his daily routine into pungent news brought public attention to a focus on the cesspool.

He envied the career of his friend Henry Cabot Lodge, while Lodge was more than willing to assist him into one. There was chance of this after the election of McKinley in 1896, but it took laborious wire-pulling before McKinley could be persuaded to offer Roosevelt a place as assistant secretary of the navy. Roosevelt took this gladly, for it brought him back to Washington and to official society. In the Navy Department, with an easy-going chief, John D. Long, he was as jingo as Lodge, and hoped with Leonard Wood that war would come out of Cuba. He burned the naval appropriations in target practice, and showed the ambitious Dewey how to let politics aid merit (*Autobiography of George Dewey, Admiral of the Navy,* 1913, pp. 167–68). On an afternoon (Feb. 25, 1898) when Secretary Long was out of town he, as acting secretary, cabled Dewey in the event of war to "see that the Spanish squadron does not leave the Asiatic coast, and then offensive operations in Philippine Islands" (*Ibid.,* p. 179). Roosevelt, resigning on May 6, turned to active service in the field. Wood and he organized the first volunteer and cavalry regiment, procured its equipment, and secured its inclusion in the expeditionary force mobilizing at Tampa. The Rough Riders, dismounted of necessity, fulfilled his expectations. In the fighting before Santiago they took Kettle Hill (July 1, 1898); and when Wood was promoted to higher rank Roosevelt became their colonel. Richard Harding Davis chronicled their glory, as did Roosevelt himself in *The Rough Riders* (1899). For the rest of his life he attended reunions of his men, found them jobs, and occasionally kept them out of jail. With no army career to risk, Roosevelt took a lead in the "round robin" of July, directing public attention to the precarious situation of the troops in the tropics, because of health and sanitary conditions. This insubordination caused acute irritation in the War Department; but most of the army was evacuated in August for hospitalization at Montauk Point, and he, now "Teddy" to everybody in spite of his intense dislike of the nickname, came home an authentic hero of the war. His sudden popularity, and his expansive grin beneath his spectacles and army hat, upset the plans of Thomas Collier Platt for the approaching campaign. Platt yielded gracefully to his nomination for the governorship. Roosevelt took his escort of Rough Riders up and down the state and was elected over Augustus Van Wyck by a small majority. He was inaugurated in January 1899.

He would have been less than human if he had not now suspected that even higher place might come within his reach. He advanced practical reform as much as seemed possible without breaking with Platt, the most important contribution, in his own opinion, being a tax on corporation franchises. The abundant testimony (displayed in the libel suit of William Barnes in 1915) leaves it still uncertain whether he or Platt was boss; but there is no doubt that after two years of Roosevelt in Albany, Platt was ready for his promotion to any office outside the state. Roosevelt feared that he would be sidetracked as vice-president, but it suited Platt to encourage the boom; and the fact that Roosevelt was unacceptable to McKinley and Hanna was good reason for his indorsement by Quay. He was soon torn between his judgment that the vice-presidency was destructive of a future, and his desire to prove that he could not be kept off the ticket. He was nominated at Philadelphia in June 1900, with no negative voice but his own, and with McKinley prudently keeping hands off. His canvass matched that of Bryan in vivacity, making it possible for McKinley to remain at home in both dignity and safety. But when elected Roosevelt despaired of the future, talked of reading law under Justice White (Thayer, *post*, p. 153), and looked with reluctance to the tame life of president of the Senate. Just before his forty-third birthday, through the assassination of William McKinley, he became twenty-sixth president of the United States.

He took his oath of office in Buffalo, Sept. 14, 1901, pledging himself "to continue, absolutely unbroken, the policy of President McKinley for the peace, the prosperity, and the honor of our beloved country"; and suspecting that there were many who feared for the office in the hands of "this crazy man" (Thomas Beer, *Hanna*, 1929, p. 236). Since the basic pledges of the Republican party had been fulfilled, and since McKinley had given no more than a suggestion of a future course, this pledge was less informing than comforting to timid minds. Roosevelt might well have followed his urge as a reformer, exercising his great skill as an administrator, without breaking with the business statesmen. Yet there were new philosophies abroad, calling for more than an ethical approach to government. A younger generation of political leaders, among whom Robert M. La Follette was best known, were leading crusades for fair play and governmental control, and were using the ideas of Populism which were now becoming respectable since there was no danger that the People's party would establish them. Roosevelt disliked the technical detail now at the bottom of reform, but there was a chance for a flexible president to place himself at the head of a national movement for the reorganization of the American pattern. For his first term he kept McKinley's advisers in his cabinet, and announced no change in doctrine. Yet from the moment that he moved his family into the White House, with Alice and the five younger children— Theodore, Kermit, Ethel, Archibald, and Quentin—there was a new virility in the Executive Mansion and a new technique in the office of the president.

Quick administration was one of the changes. Roosevelt trusted his subordinates and cleared his desk, thus saving time to play where his predecessors felt forced to labor over bundles of official papers. He played beyond the speed of his secretarial advisers and soon surrounded himself with a group of agile companions—the "tennis cabinet"—for hikes, or rides, or games. Toward the end of his presidency, when the army complained of an order to keep physically fit, he rode (Jan. 13, 1909) one hundred miles over rough Virginia roads to shame it. From his playmates of the open he obtained a view of the workings of the government that was obscured by red tape from their superiors. At his hospitable table he sampled with insatiable curiosity the wit of the procession of visitors to Washington, meeting prize-fighter or royalty with equal ease. There was new dignity and formality in White House life, after the residence of several simpler predecessors; the paragraphers smiled at the cockades and livery on the White House coachmen. Decisions flowed from his desk, more often right than wrong, but always swiftly. Washington, under his eye and hand, turned into a world capital, with new monumental beauty and fresh, if somewhat disturbing, importance. There were changes in the diplomatic corps as Europe realized this fact. The French appreciated his tastes, and sent him Jusserand, who could both talk and tramp with him. The British fumbled after the death of Pauncefote, but in 1907 found him James Bryce, a mountain climber whose knowledge of American life was nearly as encyclopedic as his own. The Foreign Office also allowed Cecil Spring Rice, who was an honorary member of the Roosevelt household, to slip in and out of Washington and to maintain a revealing contact with the Roosevelt mind. The Germans, after Von Holleben, gave him his old friend Speck von Sternburg, with whom he had been intimate in Washington as a young man. Through these experiences, Roosevelt sat, mobile and watchful, rarely holding to a lesser advantage at the cost of a greater one, and bringing informed opportunism to a new level of national dignity.

He took over the presidency in the midst of readjustments caused by the war with Spain. Hay had nearly completed a new isthmian canal treaty with Great Britain, allowing the United States a free hand. This superseded both the old Clayton-Bulwer Treaty (1850) and Hay's own first agreement with Lord Pauncefote, which the Senate had wrecked in 1900. Roosevelt, then governor, had opposed it; but he approved the new treaty, signed Nov. 13, 1901, and the Senate gave assent within a month. In the following June, Congress, by passing the Spooner Act, approved the Panama route for the canal, if an agreement could be made in "a reasonable time" with Colombia; otherwise, the canal was to be built in Nicaragua. Under Roosevelt's immediate direction the Hay-Herran Treaty was soon negotiated; it was ratified by the United States Senate on Mar. 17, 1903, but on Aug. 2 was rejected by Colombia. The Colombians objected to certain limitations upon their sovereignty and sought more money, though it would appear that they expected this to come out of the payment of $40,000,000 from the United States to the New Panama Canal Company rather than from the Treasury itself. Roosevelt, enraged at the "inefficient bandits," apparently did not consider turning to Nicaragua, and regretted that in his official position he could not stir up secession in Panama. Representatives of the New Panama Canal Company, who had long been active propagandists for the Panama route, did the necessary stirring. Roosevelt was prepared to interpret an old treaty of 1846 with New Granada (now Colombia) as warranting the preservation of peace on the isthmus by the United States, even against Colombia when trying to put down insurrection. Panama seceded Nov. 3, 1903, received prompt recognition from the United States, and within the month negotiated in its own name the treaty that Colombia had rejected. "I took the canal zone and let Congress debate, and while the debate goes on the canal does also," said Roosevelt later, on one of the many occasions when he felt prodded to defend the summary action (*New York Times*, Mar. 24, 1911). He guided every step in the construction of the canal (J. B. and Farnham Bishop, *Goethals, Genius of the Panama Canal*, 1930). On Apr. 20, 1921, in the administration of Harding, the Senate ratified a treaty with Colombia, whereby $25,000,000 was paid that aggrieved republic though without the formal apology that Wilson had favored. (On the entire affair, see Bishop, I, chs. xxiv, xxv, xxxv; Hill, *post*, ch. iii; Pringle, *post*, pp. 301–38, and the references cited there.)

Panama was only one among Roosevelt's problems. China was in disorder; and so near to China lay the Philippines that the safety of the islands was involved. Hay continued to press discreetly for the extension of the doctrine of the "Open Door." The Latin-American republics were troubled by the consequences of economic penetration and their own recklessness, and, in the United States, capital was for the first time showing serious desire for the profits to be obtained in the exploitation of backward economic nations. In 1902 there was European intervention in Venezuela that bore on both the Monroe Doctrine and canal strategy. Roosevelt had announced that the Monroe Doctrine did not guarantee the Latin republics immunity from punishment after misbehavior, but it was no accident that Dewey was in Caribbean waters at the end of 1902 when intervention began with a "pacific blockade." Later, Roosevelt remembered an informal verbal "ultimatum" to Von Holleben which has not been corroborated (Hill, pp. 123–25; Bishop, I, 222–24). The Venezuelan claims were compromised or submitted to arbitration, and the blockade was lifted, but the dilemma remained. Should the Monroe Doctrine be abandoned, or should the United States permit the doctrine to protect defaulters and assume, itself, their liabilities? When in 1904 the Dominican Republic was threatened with intervention Roosevelt persuaded it to invite him to set up a financial receivership, with an American comptroller to collect and disburse its revenues. The Roosevelt corollary to the Monroe Doctrine, now advanced, asserted the interest of the United States in so guiding the affairs of weaker neighbors that they might avoid clashes likely otherwise to involve the Monroe Doctrine. Roosevelt's Dominican convention, submitted in February 1905, lacked Senate confirmation for two years (until February 1907) but his comptroller began work at once. The Senate resented but could not block his action.

He settled the old Alaskan boundary dispute on his own terms, by an adjudication under a convention signed on Jan. 24, 1903; and he recognized no American limits to American interests, but took a hand with Germany and France at Algeciras (S. B. Fay, *The Origins of the World War*, 1930, vol. I, 185, 189, 191). His cautious and friendly pressure upon Russia and Japan resulted in the Peace of Portsmouth, Sept. 5, 1905 (Dennett, *post*). Behind this diplomatic play the defenses of the United States were being modernized. Roosevelt had no confidence in arbitration as a substitute for preparedness. Elihu Root, as secretary of war, continued the army reforms of the McKinley administration, set up a general staff (1903), and returned to law in New York. The navy, new for the war with Spain, became newer each year until it could assemble a battle fleet of sixteen units. It was most likely to be tested in the Orient. Japan was sensitive, feeling its new strength, and finding the position of Orientals in the United States humiliating to them and at the same time unacceptable to American labor interests and Pacific Coast opinion. San Francisco, in 1906, engaged in discussions over the proper status of adult Japanese in attendance with American children in the lower grades of the schools, until Roosevelt was drawn into the discussion because of Japanese protest. Openly he soothed Japan, procured a "gentlemen's agreement" to prevent the emigration of Japanese laborers, and exercised coercive pressure on the San Francisco schoolboard; privately he was uneasy lest Japan might have overt action in mind. Against this background, and because no one yet knew how effective any fleet could be in long-range operations, he sent the whole fleet to the Pacific, and then around the world, on a practice cruise. He asked no permission for the demonstration, and left Congress no option but to pay the bills. The tour was a triumph of accurate administration. The fleet kept to its schedule, was greeted with enthusiastic hospitality in Japan, and, on Feb. 22, 1909, was welcomed back at the Capes of the Chesapeake, whence Roosevelt had dispatched it Dec. 16, 1907. "Speak softly," he liked to say, "and carry a big stick, you will go far" (Roosevelt to Henry L. Sprague, Jan. 26, 1900, Pringle, p. 214).

But the embarrassments due to too big a stick, or to one too often displayed, were visible in Latin America, where recent events seemed to set a pattern of North American aggression inconsistent with the altruistic promise of the Monroe Doctrine. South American jurists insisted that their own courts ought to be final over aliens, and Drago of Argentina had recently added a protest against the forcible collection of debts. These matters were scheduled for debate by the third Pan-American conference to be held at Rio de Janeiro in July–August 1906, and were likely to want a hearing at The Hague in 1907. To explain away the illusion of a North American menace, Root, now secretary of state after the death of Hay, was sent on tour among the southern neighbors.

Roosevelt's freedom of action in foreign affairs was in sharp contrast to presidential limitations at home, where the industrial revolution was remaking American society. He had need of such a technique as would recognize the existence of Congress, of the courts, and of a public opinion faster than which it was hazardous to go. This technique he never found. He threw aside obstacles until, by their mere accumulation, they jammed his progress. Always a boxer, he clung to his maxim: "Don't hit at all if it is honorably possible to avoid hitting; but *never* hit soft" (Bishop, II, 437). He knew that the best defense is to hit one's adversary first; but this sometimes made it hard for his friends to work with him, and embittered his enemies more than was necessary. He maintained that no utterance purporting to be from him was true unless he authorized as well as uttered it. He contradicted many who tried to interpret him; and from denial passed easily to the lie direct. The cartoonists recalled the biblical story of Ananias and devised a club to which none was eligible until he had been called a liar by Theodore Roosevelt. As the membership grew, it included some who were merely indiscreet or inconvenient. E. H. Harriman and the Bellamy Storers, Alton B. Parker, "Ben" Tillman and William E. Chandler, Delavan Smith, George Harvey, Thomas Collier Platt, William J. Long, Poultney Bigelow were added to the list of the Ananias Club, until unseemly altercation became a jest rather than a discredit. Yet behind these costly quarrels lay the fact that Roosevelt was trying to dominate a government of checks and balances in which the coordinate branches were as constitutional as was the President himself. No President since Thomas Jefferson had ranged his mind over so broad a field. None since Andrew Jackson had been so certain that he had a special mandate.

The domestic wrangle grew steadily more acrimonious, with the direction of Roosevelt swerving cautiously towards the left. Republicans of the school of McKinley sensed this, and feared and fought him. Radical aspirants tried to steal his glory. The fight involved a new hypothesis of the control of industrial society in order to save individual economic freedom. Through the four Congresses of his presidency the Republican party controlled the federal government. There was no effective Democratic opposition. But the key positions were held by conservative leaders, who were more apt to distrust Roosevelt's applications of the "square deal" than to cooperate with him. Joseph G. Cannon, speaker in the last three of his Congresses, was "stand-pat" and unashamed. Nelson W. Aldrich, and his elderly and seasoned coadjutors in the Senate, made no pretense of favoring a new theory of government. Furthermore, Roosevelt's relations with those who saw with him were hindered by the roughness of his technique.

Though president by accident, Roosevelt assumed headship of the Republican party in 1901. Before he moved into the White House he was in contact with Booker T. Washington on the problem of Negro appointments; and shortly thereafter he slipped into the political error of inviting the Negro educator to a meal in the White House (Oct. 16, 1901). This undermined his effort to break the Solid South by annoying the white South. He annoyed the

Negroes by summary dismissal of Negro soldiers after the Browns-ville, Tex., riot (Aug. 13–14, 1906), which also brought the fiery Foraker upon his trail (J. B. Foraker, *Notes of a Busy Life*, 1916, vol. II). But he kept to his task; occasional Negroes received federal appointment, while he held the Southern white Republicans as well, so that the votes of their delegations to national conventions in 1904 and 1908 were at his disposal. He had greater difficulty with Senator Marcus A. Hanna, who was chairman of the Republican National Committee and understood both business men and or-ganized labor. In 1903 Roosevelt took from the Ohio convention an indorsement of himself over Hanna's undisguised opposition, on the ground of impropriety. But Hanna was ill; he died in 1904, leav-ing to conservative Republicans no possible leader. His supporters were ready for peace, and Roosevelt was willing to pay something for an undivided front in a campaign in which he hoped for elec-tion in his own right. His fear of missing this was far greater than any of the obstacles. Nominated at Chicago without opposition, he put the national committee in its place, appointing a member of his cabinet, George B. Cortelyou, as chairman. The canvass against Judge Alton B. Parker, choice of the anti-Bryan Democrats, was without clear issue. The easy victory gained, Roosevelt issued on election night, Nov. 8, 1904, a disclaimer of a third term for himself, holding to the merit of the two-term tradition and conceding that for its purpose his fractional term constituted a first term. He later regretted the pledge, but it gave him freedom.

Among the specific domestic problems that confronted him in both terms, the tariff was a vexatious embarrassment. From the lib-eral western Republicans came the "Iowa idea" that the tariff made life too easy for the trusts and needed to be revised. This was anathema to protectionists, and though Roosevelt approved it the time never seemed ripe for action. The sharp fight that delayed his Cuban reciprocity bill (Dec. 17, 1903) indicated the risk that would be run in a general revision. As his second term ended, this revision was indicated as the first thankless task for his successor.

The trusts, however, were fair game. The Republican party had no official policy respecting them, while there was enthusiastic pub-lic approval for every exposure of their bad behavior. The "muck-rakers" were raging, but Roosevelt had preceded them, demanding at Pittsburgh, July 4, 1902, that trusts be subjected to public con-trol in the public interest. His speeches were popular in both parties, revealing a cleavage that cut across party lines. They had political value in covering the threatened tariff defection in the West, where

Speaker David B. Henderson (Sept. 16, 1902) declined even to submit his record to his Iowa district, and left politics. Through Attorney-General Philander C. Knox, Roosevelt attacked the Northern Securities Company as a conspiracy in restraint of trade, and on Mar. 14, 1904, procured its dissolution by the Supreme Court (*Northern Securities Company* vs. the *United States*, 193 *U. S.*, 197), so that he was a "trust-buster" in time for the campaign. He urged, and Congress added to the cabinet in 1903, a secretary of commerce and labor, whose bureau of corporations was to be the eye of the government in matters of business. The Elkins Law (Feb. 19, 1903) forbade one form of vicious favoritism, the rebate of freight rates. The expedition act (Feb. 11, 1903) gave the government power to hasten to trial its prosecutions under the interstate commerce and anti-trust acts. But there was more enthusiasm than certainty in trust control. Most efforts were based on resentment rather than understanding, and politicians were impatient of the scientific harness with which economists were likely to hamper their freedom of action. The guides to sound decisions lagged behind the desire for correction. But in 1906 the interstate commerce act was strengthened; while the unpopularity of business, increased by the "muckrakers," made possible sweeping laws for the protection of the consumer of food and drugs. So violently did the orgy of exposure and denunciation proceed that when David Graham Phillips launched his series on "The Treason of the Senate" in Hearst's *Cosmopolitan Magazine,* March 1906, Roosevelt himself tried to call a halt. First in the privacy of the Gridiron Club, Mar. 17, 1906, then publicly, Apr. 14, 1906, he spoke to the text of "The Man with the Muck Rake," and emphasized the need for constructive law. The "muckrake" period gradually died out, but he was left unpopular with business and the party stalwarts. A financial reverse in Wall Street in 1907, caused by gross speculation, was termed the Roosevelt panic, and he was described as an enemy of business and of his class. But he was on his way to another extension of government control, this time over natural resources.

More than most presidents, Roosevelt knew the West. In 1902 he approved the Newlands Act for a reclamation service, and the conviction grew on him that the national endowment had been squandered. To call attention to the problem, and to the inadequacy of existing law, he made enlargements of the forest reserves, withdrawing land from entry whether suitable for forests or not when he had reason to think that a useful resource lay within its area. He named a public lands commission in 1903, drafting civilian experts who knew the land, and placing at their service the clerical staff of the government ("Report of the Public Lands Commission," 1905, 58 Cong., 3 Sess., *Senate Document No. 189*). There was a similar inland waterways commission in 1907 ("Preliminary Report," 60 Cong., 1 Sess., *Senate Document No. 325*). On May 13, 1908, he assembled at the White House a conference of governors of most of the states, and elder statesmen of every persuasion, to discuss the inclusive theme of natural resources; and in June he named a conservation commission with Gifford Pinchot at its head. The report of this body in three volumes (60 Cong., 2 Sess., *Senate Document No. 676*) roused resentment because of its intrusion upon a field of action that Congress had left untouched. Congress forbade its wide circulation as a public document and rebuked Roosevelt by prohibiting further use of public funds upon any investigation not authorized in advance by law. Roosevelt avowed in retort that he was free to do as he pleased in that "twilight zone" lying between the prohibitions of the law and duties required by specific enactments. His presidency ended in open defiance on the part of Congress, which restricted the secret-service appropriations lest they be used to trail congressmen.

Blocked though Roosevelt was, the "Roosevelt policies" gained repute, and the question of a third term died hard. His decision to sponsor actively the candidacy of his secretary of war, William Howard Taft, seems to have been due to his desire to quiet suspicions of his own intentions. By the use of traditional methods, which four years later Roosevelt condemned, the nomination of Taft was effected. Roosevelt was happy in the hope that his administrative team would be held together. He had in both terms escaped the ineptitudes of a cabinet made for politics. His official family had worked well in harness. Taft, after his election in 1908, preferred to select his own cabinet, and Roosevelt left office somewhat disappointed, it may be, but still cordial.

The activities of the presidency, many as they were, could not keep Roosevelt busy. He had continued to write. He had traveled much, breaking a precedent when he left the country to visit the canal in 1906; and breaking it still more by reading Milton and Tacitus in odd moments. His letters were voluminous, and his talk was incessant. His enemies called him "quack," "demagogue," and "liar"; and even "drunkard" until he quieted this by a libel action at Marquette, Mich., in 1913. But his intimates loved him with an unreasoning devotion (L. F. Abbott, ed., *The Letters of Archie Butt*, 1924; *Taft and Roosevelt. The Intimate Letters of Archie Butt, Military Aide,*

2 vols., 1930). To the ordinary voter he had become the prophet of the "square deal."

Out of office in 1909, he had to find work. His comfortable estate (probated at under a million) yielded less income than he required. He took a post with the *Outlook* as contributing editor, sold literary work to the *Metropolitan Magazine* and the *Kansas City Star,* and received generous royalties from the publishers of his books, describing himself as "an elderly literary man of pronounced domestic tastes." But before taking up letters as an ex-President he arranged a hunt (*African Game Trails: An Account of the African Wanderings of an American Hunter-Naturalist,* 1910). There were only occasional echoes from the jungle while he was buried in it; but on his emergence at Khartum, Mar. 14, 1910, there began a progress of unexpected sparkle. He discussed intimate problems of colonial government with a pungency that made men gasp (*African and European Addresses,* 1910); visited the Kaiser to tell him that he alone among European sovereigns could carry his ward in New York; rebuked the Vatican and snubbed its critics; lectured formally at the Sorbonne, at Oxford, and at Christiania in return for his Nobel Prize; counted the birds in New Forest with Sir Edward Grey; and represented the United States at the funeral of Edward VII, where he had the time of his life. On June 18, 1910, he returned home to a triumphant reception (*New York Times,* June 19, 1910).

Already he had learned of the growing breach between the conservative and insurgent groups in the Republican party, and tales told on Taft were reaching him. He said that all he wanted was privacy, but it was not in his nature to abstain from political activity. He soon entered the unsuccessful fight for a direct primary law in New York and made it clear that in state affairs he would support the progressives (*New York Times,* June 30, Aug. 17, 1930). In the late summer he began a speaking tour in the West. On Aug. 31, at Ossawatomie, Kan., he declared that "property shall be the servant and not the master," and that the Constitution if too rigid to conform to the needs of life must be amended (*New York Tribune,* Sept. 1, 1910; Roosevelt, *The New Nationalism,* 1910). In the autumn he did more speaking, and asserted his leadership in New York, where he was elected temporary chairman of the Republican state convention and brought about the nomination of Henry L. Stimson for the governorship, though he was unable to bring about his election in November. His meetings with Taft had been unsatisfactory (Pringle, pp. 536, 538). By the summer or early autumn of 1911 the unhappy estrangement of the two friends had become complete. Roosevelt might have forced the nomination of La Follette, the most conspicuous member of the progressive group that was seeking to block the renomination of Taft in 1912, but he did not believe that La Follette could command the movement and allowed himself to be persuaded that the "Roosevelt policies" were lost unless he reëntered politics. His reëntry was staged to follow an appeal from seven Republican governors (Howland, *post*, pp. 212–13); he declared to a reporter that his hat was in the ring (*New York Times*, Feb. 23, 1912) and on Feb. 25 released his acceptance of the memorial (*Ibid.*, Feb. 26, 1912). Taking the aggressive by advocating direct primaries instead of conventions, he rolled up majorities wherever he could enter primary contests and demonstrated that he was the choice of the Republican rank and file. By his advocacy of the initiative, referendum, and recall, however, he had alienated the conservative leaders, among them his old friend Henry Cabot Lodge; and the administration controlled the party machinery, as it had four years before. Elihu Root steered the convention that seated Taft delegates in disputed cases and renominated him. In vain Roosevelt shouted "naked theft!" His delegation became the nucleus of the Progressive party which met Aug. 5, 1912, to nominate him for president and Gov. Hiram Johnson of California for vice-president on a platform that embraced most of the programs of liberal reform. He led Taft in November, but only succeeded in opening the breach through which Woodrow Wilson marched to victory as minority president. (For the entire campaign and its controversies, see Pringle, pp. 525–71, and references.)

Shot by a fanatic in Milwaukee, Oct. 14, Roosevelt recovered in time to finish his canvass, but the days of his youth were gone. In 1914 he tried one more major expedition, and one too many. Visiting the republics of La Plata he plunged into the blank spaces of the map (*Through the Brazilian Wilderness*, 1914), where he found the "River of Doubt," but whence he narrowly escaped with his life. He never recovered from the tropical infections, and was already blind in one eye, the consequence of a boxing accident while in the White House. He returned to his desk (*A Book-Lover's Holidays in the Open*, 1916) to watch the world at war. Roosevelt was a neutral until his old suspicions of Germany were revived, his sympathies with the Allies aroused, and he had persuaded himself that had he been president he would have stopped the war. The diplomatic course of President Wilson was generally offensive to him. Army officers told him stories, he supported the National Security League, and with tongue and pen sought to arouse the country (*America and the World War,* 1915; *Fear God and Take Your Own Part,* 1916; *The Foes of Our Own Household,* 1917). He was convinced that the Progressive party was dead and in 1916 he had a moment of hope that the Republican breach might be healed behind him, again a candidate. Between Hughes and Wilson he had to support Hughes, though each time he spoke he alienated the German vote which Hughes must gain to win.

When war came at last, his four sons were soon at the front while he besieged the War Department and overcame aversion to besiege the White House for permission to raise a volunteer division and to command one of its brigades. Despite the incumbrances of age, accident, disease, and the lack of professional military training, he found no justice in the refusal to accept his service. Bitter, he stayed at home to talk and write (*The Great Adventure; Present-Day Studies in American Nationalism,* 1918), until in January 1918, he rushed to Washington "to tell the truth and speed up the war." It may be that the way was being paved for his return as the presidential candidate of a united party in 1920. But, on Jan. 6, 1919, he died peacefully in his sleep. His career had personalized the American recognition of a changing world. His flaws were on the surface and undisguised; his human values were timeless.

[His official biography, J. B. Bishop, *Theodore Roosevelt and his Time Shown in his Own Letters* (2 vols., 1920), was begun under his direction and is in fact largely autobiographical; it supplements *Theodore Roosevelt: An Autobiography* (1913). All of his writings, cited above, are highly personal, and his earlier biographers found it easier to accept his estimate of himself than to reconstruct events from the evidence of working documents. His books, articles, journalistic releases, speeches, letters, and state papers are so numerous as to have defied complete collection; but selections from his works began to be assembled as early as the *Sagamore Ed.* (15 vols., 1900) and *Executive Ed.* (14 vols., 1901); among subsequent but incomplete collections are the *Elkhorn Ed.* (28 vols., 1906–20), and *National Ed.* (20 vols., 1926), in which the Roosevelt Memorial Asso., Hermann Hagedorn, ed., cooperated with the publishers. Roosevelt's letter files are in the Lib. of Cong. J. H. Wheelock, *A Bibliography of Theodore Roosevelt* (1920), is reasonably complete to its date. Tyler Dennett, *Roosevelt and the Russo-Japanese War* (1925); A. L. P. Dennis, *Adventures in Am. Diplomacy, 1896–1906* (1928); and H. C. Hill, *Roosevelt and the Caribbean* (1927), have made careful use of his papers in correcting part of the record. H. F. Pringle, *Theodore Roosevelt; A Biography* (1931), is a thoroughly judicious work with an excellent bibliography. W. F. McCaleb, *Theodore Roosevelt* (1931), has used the manuscripts but is inaccurate and shows bias. Roosevelt's presidency was lived under the observation of J. F. Rhodes, who covered it inadequately in *The McKinley and Roosevelt Administrations, 1897–1909* (1922); and under the admiring gaze of Mark Sullivan, *Our Times* (vols. II–V, 1927–33). Among the genealogies are W. M. Clemens, *The Ancestry of Theodore Roosevelt; A Genealogical Record from 1649* (1914); F. M. Smith, *Roosevelt Arms and Family History* (1909); C. B. Whittlesey, *The Roosevelt Genealogy, 1649–1902* (1902); A. P. Johnson, *Franklin D. Roosevelt's Colonial Ancestors* (1933).

The biographies that appeared during his life are little more than compilations of the growing newspaper legend, tinctured often with uncritical hero-worship: T. W. Handford, *Theodore Roosevelt, the Pride of the Rough Riders, an Ideal American* (1897); Murat Halstead, *The Life of Theodore Roosevelt* (1902); R. C. V. Meyers, *Theodore Roosevelt, Patriot and Statesman* (1901); F. E. Leupp, *The Man Roosevelt, A Portrait Sketch* (1904); J. A. Riis, *Theodore Roosevelt the Citizen* (1904); James Morgan, *Theodore Roosevelt, the Boy and the Man* (1907); Sydney Brooks, *Theodore Roosevelt* (1910); Max Kullnick, *From Rough Rider to President* (1911); C. G. Washburn, *Theodore Roosevelt; the Logic of his Career* (1916). A more useful group of works followed his death: L. F. Abbott, *Impressions of Theodore Roosevelt* (1919); H. C. Lodge, *Theodore Roosevelt* (1919); W. D. Lewis, *The Life of Theodore Roosevelt* (1919); W. R. Thayer, *Theodore Roosevelt, An Intimate Biography* (1919); J. B. Bishop, ed., *Theodore Roosevelt's Letters to His Children* (1919); W. A. White, *Political Adventures of Theodore and Me* (1920); H. J. Howland, *Theodore Roosevelt and his Times; A Chronicle of the Progressive Movement* (1921); Corinne R. Robinson, *My Brother, Theodore Roosevelt* (1921); Anna R. Cowles, ed., *Letters from Theodore Roosevelt to Anna Roosevelt Cowles 1870–1918* (1924); *Selections from the Correspondence of Theodore Roosevelt and Henry Cabot Lodge* (2 vols., 1925); Earle Looker, *The White House Gang* (1929), *Colonel Roosevelt, Private Citizen* (1932); L. D. Einstein, *Roosevelt, his Mind in Action* (1930); Owen Wister, *Roosevelt, The Story of a Friendship, 1880–1919* (1930). Among the journalists who enjoyed his friendship and recorded his *dicta* are: A. W. Dunn, *Gridiron Nights* (1915); J. J. Leary, *Talks with T. R.* (1920); H. H. Kohlsaat, *From McKinley to Harding; Personal Recollections of our Presidents* (1923); O. K. Davis, *Released for Publication; Some Inside Political History of Theodore Roosevelt and his Times, 1898–1918* (1925); C. W. Thompson, *Presidents I've Known and Two Near Presidents* (1929). An interesting collection of cartoons is Raymond Gros, ed., *T. R. in Cartoon* (1910).]

[SUPPLEMENTARY BIBLIOGRAPHY. A major contribution to Roosevelt scholarship is *The Letters of Theodore Roosevelt* (8 vols., 1951–54), ed. by Elting E. Morison, with John M. Blum as associate editor and Alfred D. Chandler, Jr., as assistant editor. Carleton Putnam, *Theodore Roosevelt: The Formative Years, 1858–1886* (1958), is the first volume of a projected full-length biography. An important interpretive study is John M. Blum, *The Republican Roosevelt* (1954); see also

Richard Hofstadter's chapter on Roosevelt in his *The Am. Political Tradition* (1948). Other recent biographical treatments are Edward Wagenknecht, *The Seven Worlds of Theodore Roosevelt* (1958), and William H. Harbaugh, *Power and Responsibility: The Life and Times of Theodore Roosevelt* (1961). Stefan Lorant, *The Life and Times of Theodore Roosevelt* (1959), offers a pictorial biography. On family matters, see Hermann Hagedorn, *The Roosevelt Family of Sagamore Hill* (1954), and Will Irwin, ed., *Letters to Kermit from Theodore Roosevelt, 1902–1908* (1946). Recent specialized studies include: Howard L. Hurwitz, *Theodore Roosevelt and Labor in N. Y. State, 1880–1900* (1943); George E. Mowry, *Theodore Roosevelt and the Progressive Movement* (1946); Gordon C. O'Gara, *Theodore Roosevelt and the Rise of the Modern Navy* (1943); Paul R. Cutright, *Theodore Roosevelt, the Naturalist* (1956); Thomas A. Bailey, *Theodore Roosevelt and the Japanese-American Crises* (1934); and Howard K. Beale, *Theodore Roosevelt and the Rise of America to World Power* (1956). Among recent biographies of Roosevelt's associates, two of the most pertinent are Philip C. Jessup, *Elihu Root* (2 vols., 1938), and Henry F. Pringle, *The Life and Times of William Howard Taft* (2 vols., 1939). George E. Mowry's volume in the New American Nation series, *The Era of Theodore Roosevelt, 1900–1912* (1958), provides a broad picture and a comprehensive bibliography. The Roosevelt Memorial Asso. Collection at Harvard Univ. is an unusually rich source, including books, clippings, and some manuscript materials, together with microfilm copies of Roosevelt's letters in the Lib. of Cong. and elsewhere as assembled by the editors of the published *Letters.*]

Oliver Wendell Holmes

by

FELIX FRANKFURTER

HOLMES, OLIVER WENDELL (Mar. 8, 1841–Mar. 6, 1935), jurist, was born at 8 Montgomery Place, now Bosworth Place, Boston, the son of Oliver Wendell Holmes, physician, poet, and essayist, and the grandson of Abiel Holmes, clergyman and historian. His mother was Amelia Lee Jackson, daughter of Charles Jackson, associate justice of the supreme judicial court of Massachusetts. "All my three names," he once wrote, "designate families from which I am descended. A long pedigree of Olivers and Wendells may be found in the book called 'Memorials of the Dead—King's Chapel Burying Ground.' . . . Some of my ancestors have fought in the Revolution; among the great grandmothers of the family were Dorothy Quincy and Anne Bradstreet ('the tenth muse'); and so on; . . . Our family has been in the habit of receiving a college education and I came of course in my turn, as my grandfathers, fathers and uncles before me. I've always lived in Boston and went first to a woman's school there, then to Rev. T. R. Sullivan's, then to E. S. Dixwell's (Private Latin School) and then to College" (O. W. Holmes, Jr.'s College Autobiography, quoted in F. C. Fiechter, "The Preparation of an American Aristocrat," *New England Quarterly*, March 1933).

Holmes was thus rooted in the Puritan tradition and his personal attachment to its meaning and environment went deep. "I love every brick and shingle of the old Massachusetts towns where once they worked and prayed," he said of his Puritan ancestors in one of his frequent references to them, "and I think it a noble and pious thing to do whatever we may by written word and moulded bronze and sculptured stone to keep our memories, our reverence and our love alive and to hand them on to new generations all too ready to forget" ("Ipswich—At the Unveiling of Memorial Tablets," July 31, 1902, *Speeches*, 1913, p. 92). After leaving Boston, he regularly returned to its nearby North Shore to enjoy each year its dunes and rocks and barberry bushes with refreshing devotion. But even as a college student he was a Bostonian apart. Very early his curiosities far transcended his emotional attachments. His own crowd in Boston, though fascinated, were quizzical about him for reasons that were implied in the remark of a leading lawyer who had been a boyhood friend: "I wish Wendell wouldn't play with his mind." From the time—before he was twenty—that he learned from Emerson the lesson of intellectual independence, his quest for understanding was hemmed in neither by geography nor by personal preferences. So whole-souled was his love of country that only fools could misunderstand when he said, "I do not pin my dreams for the future to my country or even to my race. . . . I think it not improbable that man, like the grub that prepares a chamber for the winged thing it never has seen but is to be—that man may have cosmic destinies that he does not understand" ("Law and the Court," *Collected Legal Papers*, 1920, p. 296). New Englander of New Englanders in his feelings all his life, Holmes disciplined himself against any kind of parochialism in his thinking. Because he so completely rid himself of it, he is a significant figure in the history of civilization and not merely a commanding American figure.

As a truth-seeking Puritan, then, he entered Harvard in the fall of 1857. But before he was graduated came the Civil War and Lincoln's call for men. In April 1861 Holmes, just turned twenty, joined the 4th Battalion of Infantry stationed at Fort Independence. On July 10—having in the meantime written and delivered his class poem and been graduated—he was commissioned second lieutenant and on Sept. 4 he started South with his beloved regiment, the 20th Massachusetts, part of the Army of the Potomac, to share, except when disabled, in its notable history (G. A. Bruce, *The Twentieth Regiment of Massachusetts Volunteer Infantry*, 1906). Three times he was put out of action, and his war experiences are the stuff of heroic tales. Not unnaturally could his great friend, Sir Frederick Pollock, sixty years later chaffingly suggest to Holmes that he could reinforce his argument "as to the contra-natural selection of war by the example of a certain stray bullet whose deviation by a fraction of an inch would have deprived" the world of all that Holmes's lucky escape gave it (*Holmes-Pollock Letters,* II, 43). His own recital (*Who's Who in America*) gives Holmes's war record with austere completeness: "Served 3 yrs. with 20th Mass. Volunteers, lieutenant to lieutenant colonel; wounded in breast at Ball's Bluff, Oct. 21, 1861, in neck at Antietam, Sept. 17, 1862, in foot at Marye's Hill, Fredericksburg, May 3, 1863; a.-d.-c. on staff Gen. H. G. Wright, Jan. 29, 1864, until mustered out July 17, 1864, with rank of captain."

On his return to Boston invalided from the front, his personal distinction and his war record irresistibly combined to make of him a military hero. Bishop William Lawrence gives the contemporary picture: "I saw him, a young officer, marching off to the front. . . . I watched his record, for we boys were alert to the heroes of those days, and as he was brought back wounded again and again . . . he was seen on the streets in Boston, a handsome invalid, to the great delectation of the girls of the city. He was a romantic hero, built for it" (address of Bishop Lawrence at presentation of portrait of Mr. Justice Holmes, Mar. 20, 1930, *Harvard Alumni Bulletin,* Mar. 27, 1930). What he called a "flamboyant" piece (*Holmes-Pollock Letters,* II, 270) in *Harper's Weekly* of Nov. 9, 1861, and Dr. Holmes's famous but too stylized *Atlantic Monthly* (December 1862) account of the Antietam episode, "My Hunt after 'the Captain,'" extended young Holmes's martial reputation much beyond the confines of Boston. He himself harbored no romantic notions about war. He saw too much of it. Indeed, he shocked patriotic sentimentalists by speaking of war as an "organized bore," just as later he was to offend those whom he regarded as social sentimentalists by his insistence that war is merely a phase of that permanent struggle which is the law of life. "War, when you are at it, is horrible and dull. It is only when time has passed that you see that its message was divine. I hope it may be long before we are called again to sit at that master's feet. But some teacher of the kind we all need. In this smug, over-safe corner of the world we need it, that we may realize that our comfortable routine is no eternal necessity of things, but merely a little space of calm in the midst of the tempestuous untamed streaming of the world, and in order that we may be ready for danger. We need it in this time of individualist negations, with its literature of French and American humor, revolting at discipline, loving fleshpots, and denying that anything is worthy of reverence,—in order that we may remember all that buffoons forget. We need it everywhere and at all times" ("The Soldier's Faith," a Memorial Day address, May 31, 1895, *Speeches,* pp. 62–63).

These are the convictions he took out of the Civil War. These were the convictions that dominated him for the long years to come. For the Civil War probably cut more deeply than any other influence in his life. If it did not generate it certainly fixed his conception of man's destiny. "I care not very much for the form if in some way he has learned that he cannot set himself over against the universe as a rival god, to criticize it, or to shake his fist at the skies, but that his meaning is its meaning, his only worth is as a part of it, as a humble instrument of the universal power" (*Collected Legal Papers*, p. 166). "Life is a roar of bargain and battle, but in the very heart of it there rises a mystic spiritual tone that gives meaning to the whole" (*Speeches*, p. 97). "It is enough for us that the universe has produced us and has within it, as less than it, all that we believe and love. If we think of our existence not as that of a little god outside, but as that of a ganglion within, we have the infinite behind us. It gives us our only but our adequate significance. . . . If our imagination is strong enough to accept the vision of ourselves as parts inseverable from the rest, and to extend our final interest beyond the boundary of our skins, it justifies the sacrifice even of our lives for ends outside of ourselves" (*Collected Legal Papers*, p. 316).

This faith he expressed as a returning soldier and he repeated it, in enduring phrases endlessly varied, for seventy years—in talk, in letters, in speeches, in opinions. But his "Soldier's Faith" was not merely an eloquent avowal of his philosophic beliefs regarding man's destiny, nor was it a gifted man's expression, in emotionally charged phrases, of what seemed to him "the key to intellectual salvation" as well as "the key to happiness" (*Collected Legal Papers*, p. 166). Holmes lived his faith. It would be difficult to conceive a life more self-conscious of its directions and more loyal in action to the faith which it espoused. His faith determined the very few personal choices he was called upon to make after he left the army; it was translated into concreteness in the multifarious cases that came before him for judgment for half a century.

He left the army because his term was up. In later life he said that if he had to do it again he would have stayed through the war. Instead, in the fall of 1864, he began the study of law. On graduating from the Harvard Law School in 1866, he made the first of his numerous visits to England. He had of course easy access to eminent Britishers but he won his way among them, even in his twenties, on his own intellectual distinction. Thus he met some of the great figures of the day—John Stuart Mill, Sir Henry Maine, Benjamin Jowett, the Master of Balliol—and in course of time formed friendships with Leslie Stephen, James Bryce, A. V. Dicey, and Sir Frederick Pollock and with gifted women like Mrs. J. R. Green, Mrs. W. K. Clifford, and Miss Beatrice Chamberlain. That a gay, handsome young man with a brilliant tongue—"that lanky talker of a Wendell Holmes" was the way an old servant in a Beacon Hill household described him—moved easily in English fashionable society is not surprising. Much more significant is the tender friendship that grew between him and an Irish parish priest, Canon Sheehan, whom he met on one of his English visits. Indeed, his last trip to England, in 1913, was made largely to see his friend, who was a-dying. Canon Sheehan, he wrote, "was a dear friend of mine—odd as it seems that a saint and a Catholic should take up with a heathen like me" (unpublished MS., May 19, 1917; see H. J. Heuser, *Canon Sheehan of Doneraile*, 1917). The most intimate of his English ties came to be with Sir Frederick Pollock. Their friendship was maintained by a steady exchange of letters over nearly sixty years. These, happily, were preserved, and their publication, thanks to the careful editing of Mark DeWolfe Howe, furnishes a cultural document of first importance for its era (*Holmes-Pollock Letters: The Correspondence of Mr. Justice Holmes and Sir Frederick Pollock, 1874–1932*, 2 vols., 1941).

England had a strong pull for Holmes. "I value everything that shows the quiet unmelodramatic power to stand and take it in your people," wrote Holmes to Pollock early in the First World War (*supra,* I, 222). But he could be sharp in detecting any tendency toward condescension or insensitiveness. He was a proud American who had no sympathy with suggestions of inadequacy of the American environment for finer sensibilities. Thus he thought that "there was a touch of underbreeding" in Henry James's "recurrence to the problem of the social relations of Americans to the old world" (*Ibid.,* II, 41).

After his fling in England, Holmes settled down to the serious business of law. He entered it with strong misgivings and not for years were they quieted. The magnetic disturbance was philosophy. But in 1886, to students whom his old anxieties might beset, he was able to say "no longer with any doubt—that a man may live greatly in the law as elsewhere; that there as well as elsewhere his thought may find its unity in an infinite perspective; that there as well as elsewhere he may wreak himself upon life, may drink the bitter cup of heroism, may wear his heart out after the unattainable" ("The Profession of the Law," *Speeches,* p. 23). Toward the end, when he was past ninety, he put the wisdom of his choice more pungently: "I rather was shoved than went [into the law] when I hankered for philosophy. I am glad now, and even then I had a guess that perhaps one got more from philosophy on the quarter than dead astern" (unpublished letter, June 11, 1931).

In 1867 he was admitted to the bar and practised his profession in Boston, first as an apprentice of Robert M. Morse, then in the office of Chandler, Shattuck & Thayer, and later with George O. Shattuck and William A. Munroe, as a member of the firm of Shattuck, Holmes & Munroe. With fierce assiduity he set himself to become master of his calling. "I should think Wendell worked too hard," wrote William James, in 1869, and the theme recurs in the correspondence of the James family. Holmes never made a fetish of long hours, however; indeed, he believed that what he called work —really creative labor—could not be pursued for more than four hours a day. But he worked with almost feverish intensity. For three years (1870–73), as editor of the *American Law Review,* he ranged the gamut of legal literature—reports, digests, casebooks, revisions of old texts, new treatises, lectures, and essays—and made his own the entire kingdom of law (see *American Law Review,* vols. V–VII, and bibliography in *Harvard Law Review,* March 1931). During the same period he worked indefatigably to bring Kent's *Commentaries* "down through the quarter of a century which has elapsed" since Chancellor Kent's death, and thereby gave new and enduring significance to the most important survey of the earlier American law (see James Kent, *Commentaries on American Law,* 12th ed., 1873). Holmes thus soaked himself in the details of the law. When he began "the law presented itself as a ragbag of details. . . . It was not without anguish that one asked oneself whether the subject was worthy of the interest of an intelligent man" (*Collected Legal Papers,* p. 301). But his imaginative and philosophic faculties imparted life and meaning to dry details. Where others found only discrete instances he saw organic connection. Thus it was true of him, as he said of another, that his knowledge "was converted into the organic tissue of wisdom" (appreciation of John Chipman Gray, reprinted in H. C. Shriver, *Oliver Wendell Holmes: His Book Notices and Uncollected Letters and Papers,* 1936, p. 135). At this time he also lectured on law at Harvard.

During all these years he was in active practice and getting desirable glimpses into actualities. In particular, what it meant to him to be associated with his senior partner, George Otis Shattuck, a leader among Massachusetts lawyers, is the theme of one of his memorable utterances (*Speeches,* pp. 70–74). His temperament being what it was, scholarly pursuits, though a side-line, doubtless enlisted his deepest interests. He would have welcomed appointment to the United States District Court for the greater intellectual freedom it would have afforded him ("The place . . . would enable me to work in the way I want and so I should like it—although it would cost me a severe pang to leave my partners," *Holmes-Pollock Letters*, I, 10). But destiny had other plans for him.

The early writings of Holmes canvassed issues which, howsoever formulated or disguised, are vital to a society devoted to justice according to law. What are the sources of law and what are its sanctions? What is appropriate lawmaking by courts and what should be left to legislation? What are the ingredients, conscious or unconscious, of adjudication? What are the wise demands of precedent and when should the judicial process feel unbound by its past? Such were the inquiries that guided Holmes's investigations at a time when law was generally treated as a body of settled doctrines from which answers to the new problems of a rapidly industrialized society were to be derived by a process of logical deduction. But in rejecting a view of law which regarded it as a merely logical unfolding Holmes had nothing in common with later tendencies toward a retreat from reason. By disproving formal logic as the organon of social wisdom he did not embrace antirationalism. Quite the contrary. His faith was in reason and in motives not confined to material or instinctive desires. He refused to believe the theory "that the Constitution primarily represents the triumph of the money power over democratic agrarianism & individualism. . . . I shall believe until compelled to think otherwise that they [the leaders in establishing the Union] wanted to make a nation and invested (bet) on the belief that they would make one, not that they wanted a powerful government because they had invested. Belittling arguments always have a force of their own, but you and I believe that high-mindedness is not impossible to man" (*Ibid.*, II, 222–23). Equally so, while fully aware of the clash of interests in society and of law's mediating function, Holmes had nothing in common with the crude notion according to which law is merely the verbalization of prevailing force and appetites.

But at a time when judges boasted a want of philosophy, Holmes realized that decisions are functions of some juristic philosophy, and that awareness of the considerations that move beneath the surface of logical form is the prime requisite of a civilized system of law. In his analysis of judicial psychology, he was conscious of the rôle of the unconscious more than a generation before Freud began to influence modern psychology. Again, exploration of the meaning of the meaning of law was attempted by Holmes half a century before C. K. Ogden and I. A. Richards wrote *The Meaning of Meaning* (1927).

These pioneer contributions, however, though they had organic unity, were made in seemingly disconnected and fugitive writings. An invitation to deliver a series of lectures at the Lowell Institute in Boston happily led him to systematize his ideas into "a connected treatise" and in 1881, before he had crossed forty—a goal he had fiercely set for himself—he published *The Common Law*. The book marks an epoch for law and learning. Together with half a dozen of his essays, *The Common Law* gave the most powerful direction to legal science. The way in which he conceived law and its judicial development was out of the current of the period. He reoriented legal inquiry. The book is a classic in the sense that its stock of ideas has been absorbed and become part of common juristic thought. A few of its opening sentences will give its drift. They represent the thought of today more truly than the temper of the time in which they were written. More than sixty years ago they placed law in a perspective which legal scholarship ever since has merely confirmed. "The life of the law has not been logic: it has been experience. The felt necessities of the time, the prevalent moral and political theories, intuitions of public policy, avowed or unconscious, even the prejudices which judges share with their fellow-men, have had a good deal more to do than the syllogism in determining the rules by which men should be governed. The law embodies the story of a nation's development through many centuries, and it cannot be dealt with as if it contained only the axioms and corollaries of a book of mathematics. In order to know what it is, we must know what it has been, and what it tends to become. We must alternately consult history and existing theories of legislation. But the most difficult labor will be to understand the combination of the two into new products at every stage. The substance of the law at any given time pretty nearly corresponds, so far as it goes, with what is then understood to be convenient; but its form and machinery, and the degree to which it is able to work out desired results, depend very much upon its past."

A work of such seminal scholarship as *The Common Law* makes its way only slowly in affecting the mode of thought of practitioners and judges; but it achieved prompt recognition from the learned world. Its immediate result was a call to Holmes from the Harvard Law School. Largely through the efforts of Louis D. Brandeis, as secretary of the then recently organized Harvard Law School Alumni

Association, a new chair was established for him, and in January 1882, he became Weld Professor of Law, accepting the position with the explicit understanding that he was free to accept a judgeship, should it come his way. On Dec. 5, 1882, Gov. John D. Long appointed him to the supreme judicial court of Massachusetts and on Jan. 3, 1883, Holmes took his seat as an associate justice on that bench. This, he used to say, was "a stroke of lightning which changed all the course of my life." Why did Holmes leave the chair for the bench? His aims were never for external power—always his striving was only for "the secret isolated joy of the thinker, who knows that, a hundred years after he is dead and forgotten, men who never heard of him will be moving to the measure of his thought . . ." (*Speeches*, pp. 24–25). But the Civil War evidently influenced him permanently against sheltered thinking. "To think under fire" was his test of most responsible thought. "It is one thing to utter a happy phrase from a protected cloister; another to think under fire—to think for action upon which great interests depend" ("George Otis Shattuck," *Speeches*, p. 73).

While at the bar, on June 17, 1872, he married Fanny Bowditch Dixwell, eldest daughter of his Latin school headmaster, Epes Sargent Dixwell, and grand-daughter of Nathaniel Bowditch, the mathematician. Without some reference to her influence in the Justice's life no sufficiently discerning biography of him is possible. We get an early glimpse of her in several letters from William James. "I have made the acquaintance of . . . Miss (Fanny) Dixwell of Cambridge, lately. She is about as fine as they make 'em. That villain Wendell Holmes has been keeping her all to himself at Cambridge for the last eight years; but I hope I may enjoy her acquaintance now. She is A1, if anyone ever was" (R. B. Perry, *The Thought and Character of William James*, 1935, I, 228; see also *The Letters of William James*, 1920, I, 76, II, 156). One who knew both well for much of their lives, and respected the reserves of both, wrote: "Her quick and vivid perception, her keen wit and vigorous judgment, and the originality and charm of her character cannot be forgotten by anyone who knew her. It is impossible to think of Justice Holmes without thinking of her also. Her effect on his life and career can neither be omitted nor measured in any account of him" (A. D. Hill, in *Harvard Graduates' Magazine*, March 1931, p. 268). She "was in many ways," according to another, "as extraordinary a personality as the Justice himself." She died on Apr. 30, 1929, and to Pollock he wrote: "We have had our share. For sixty years she made life poetry for me . . ."(*Letters*, II, 243).

The stream of litigation that flowed through such an important tribunal as the supreme judicial court of Massachusetts during the twenty years of his incumbency enabled Holmes to fertilize the whole vast field of law. Although questions came before him in the unpremeditated order of litigation, his Massachusetts opinions—nearly 1300—would, if appropriately brought together, constitute the most comprehensive and philosophic body of American law for any period of its history. Except for a synoptic table of his opinions (*Harvard Law Review*, March 1931, pp. 799–819) and a small selection from them (H. C. Shriver, *The Judicial Opinions of Oliver Wendell Holmes*, 1940), they remain scattered in fifty forbidding volumes of law reports. For him they had the painful inadequacy of one whose aim was the unattainable. "I look into my book in which I keep a docket of the decisions of the full court which fall to me to write, and find about a thousand cases. A thousand cases, many of them upon trifling or transitory matters, to represent nearly half a lifetime! A thousand cases, when one would have liked to study to the bottom and to say his say on every question which the law has ever presented, and then to go on and invent new problems which should be the test of doctrine, and then to generalize it all and write it in continuous, logical, philosophic exposition, setting forth the whole corpus with its roots in history and its justifications of expedience real or supposed!" (*Collected Legal Papers*, p. 245).

Such standards were doubtless stimulating to a bar, but were hardly calculated to leave it at ease in Zion. We have a trustworthy view of him as he appeared to lawyers who came before him in Massachusetts: "Nobody who sat on this Court in my time had quite such a daunting personality,—to a young lawyer at least. He was entirely courteous, but his mind was so extraordinarily quick and incisive, he was such an alert and sharply attentive listener, his questions went so to the root of the case, that it was rather an ordeal to appear before him. In arguing a case you felt that when your sentence was half done he had seen the end of it, and before the argument was a third finished that he had seen the whole course of reasoning and was wondering whether it was sound" (unpublished remarks of United States Circuit Judge James M. Morton, Jr., at the exercises in memory of Mr. Justice Holmes before the supreme judicial court of Massachusetts, Oct. 9, 1937). He hated long-windedness and recommended to the gentlemen of the bar the reading of French novels to cultivate the art of innuendo. He expressed himself, however, with sufficient explicitness in some labor cases to be deemed "dangerous" in important circles in Boston. Such was the direction of thought at the time that a dissenting opinion which has since established itself as a great landmark in legal analysis on both sides of the Atlantic (*Vegelahn* vs. *Guntner,* 167 *Mass.,* 92, 104) was seriously felt to be a bar to his judicial promotion. He had simply adhered to his detached view of the law and refused to translate fear of "socialism" "into doctrines that had no proper place in the Constitution or the common law" (*Collected Legal Papers,* p. 295).

He did become chief justice of Massachusetts, on Aug. 5, 1899; and the very opinions which disturbed the conservatism of Boston were in part the influences that led President Theodore Roosevelt to look in Holmes's direction when the resignation of Mr. Justice Horace Gray created a vacancy on the Supreme Bench. Gray was from Massachusetts, and it was natural to turn to Massachusetts for a successor. But the circumstances of Holmes's appointment illustrate what fortuitous elements determine Supreme Court choices. The near approach of the end of Justice Gray's service had been foreshadowed before President McKinley's assassination, and the nomination of Alfred Hemenway, a leading Boston lawyer and partner of McKinley's secretary of the navy, John D. Long, had been decided upon by McKinley. Before it could be made, Theodore Roosevelt had become President and "he did not feel himself bound by the informal arrangement which his predecessor had made with Mr. Hemenway" (unpublished remarks of Judge James M. Morton, Jr., *supra*). Roosevelt hesitated not a little about appointing Holmes. A letter to Senator Henry Cabot Lodge gives a full disclosure of Roosevelt's mind on the subject (*Selections from the Correspondence of Theodore Roosevelt and Henry Cabot Lodge,* 1925, I, 517–19). Holmes himself, to a friend, wrote of the curious doubt that troubled Roosevelt, as well as the circumstance that soon stirred his disappointment in Holmes: ". . . he was uneasy about appointing me because he thought I didn't appreciate Marshall. I thought it rather comic. I have no doubt that later he heartily repented over his choice when I didn't do what he wanted in the Northern Securities Case [*Northern Securities Co.* vs. *United States,* 193 *U. S.,* 197]. . . . Long afterwards, at a dinner at the White House to some labor leaders, I said to one of them who had been spouting about the Judges: What you want is favor—not justice. But when I am on my job I don't care a damn what you want or what Mr. Roosevelt wants— and then repeated my remarks to him. You may think that a trifle crude—but I didn't like to say it behind his back and not to his face, and the fact had justified it—I thought and think" (unpublished letter, dated Apr. 1, 1928).

Holmes took his seat on Dec. 8, 1902. He came to the Court at a time when vigorous legislative activity reflected changing social conceptions, which in turn were stimulated by vast technological development. What was in the air is well epitomized by the observation that Theodore Roosevelt "was the first President of the United States who openly proposed to use the powers of political government for the purpose of affecting the distribution of wealth in the interest of the golden mean" (C. A. and Mary R. Beard, *The Rise of American Civilization*, 1927, II, 597).

Though formally the product of ordinary lawsuits, constitutional law differs profoundly from ordinary law. For constitutional law is the body of doctrines by which the Supreme Court marks the boundaries between national and state action and by means of which it mediates between citizen and government. The Court thus exercises functions that determine vital arrangements in the government of the American people. These adjustments are based, for the most part, on very broad provisions of the Constitution. Words like "liberty" and phrases like "due process of law" and "regulate commerce . . . among the several States," furnish the text for judgment upon the validity of governmental action directed toward the infinite variety of social and economic facts. But these are words and phrases of "convenient vagueness." They unavoidably give wide judicial latitude in determining the undefined and ever-shifting boundaries between state and nation, between freedom and authority. Even as to these broad provisions of the Constitution distinctions must be observed. In a federated nation, especially one as vast in its territory and varied in its interests as the United States, the power must be somewhere to make the necessary accommodation between the central government and the states. "I do not think the United States would come to an end," said Mr. Justice Holmes, "if we lost our power to declare an Act of Congress void. I do think the Union would be imperilled if we could not make that declaration as to the laws of the several states. For one in my place sees how often a local policy prevails with those who are not trained to national views and how often action is taken that embodies what the Commerce Clause was meant to end" (*Collected Legal Papers*, pp. 295–296). The agency, moreover, must be one not subject to the vicissitudes and pressures under which the political branches of government rest. The Supreme Court is that ultimate arbiter.

Two major issues affecting the whole scheme of government have been the dominant concern of the Supreme Court throughout its history. The Court has had to decide in the most variegated situations from what lawmaking the states are excluded and what legislative domain Congress may enter. And as to both state and national authority it rests with the Court to determine under what circumstances society may intervene and when the individual is to be left unrestricted. But while the Supreme Court thus moves in the perilous sphere of government it does not itself carry the burdens of governing. The Court is merely the brake on other men's actions. Determination of policy—what taxes to impose, how to regulate business, when to restrict freedom—rests with legislatures and executives. The nature of the Court's task thus raises a crucial problem in our constitutional system in that its successful working calls for rare intellectual detachment and penetration, lest limitations in personal experience are transmuted into limitations of the Constitution.

His profound analysis of the sources of our law before he became a judge left in Holmes an abiding awareness of the limited validity of legal principles. He never forgot that circumstances had shaped the law in the past, and that the shaping of future law is primarily the business of legislatures. He was therefore keenly sensitive to the subtle forces that are involved in the process of reviewing the judgment of others not as to its wisdom but as to the reasonableness of their belief in its wisdom. As society became more and more complicated and individual experience correspondingly narrower, tolerance and humility in passing judgment on the experience and beliefs expressed by those entrusted with the duty of legislating, emerge as the decisive factors in constitutional adjudication. No judge could be more aware than Holmes of these subtle aspects of the business of deciding constitutional cases. He read omnivorously to "multiply my scepticisms" (unpublished letter). His imagination and humility, rigorously cultivated, enabled him to transcend the narrowness of his immediate experience. Probably no man who ever sat on the Court was by temperament and discipline freer from emotional commitments compelling him to translate his own economic or social views into constitutional commands. He did not read merely his own mind to discover the powers that may be exercised by a great nation. His personal views often ran counter to legislation which came before him for judgment. He privately distrusted attempts at improving society by what he deemed futile if not mischievous economic tinkering. But that was not his business. It was not for him to prescribe for society or to deny it the right of experimentation within very wide limits. That was to be left for contest by the political forces in the state. The duty of the Court was to keep the ring free. He reached the democratic result by the philosophic route of scepticism

—by his disbelief in ultimate answers to social questions. Thereby he exhibited the judicial function at its purest.

He gave such ample scope to legislative judgment on economic policy because he knew so well to what great extent social arrangements are conditioned by time and circumstances. He also knew that we have "few scientifically certain criteria of legislation, and as it often is difficult to mark the line where what is called the police power of the States is limited by the Constitution of the United States, judges should be slow to read into the latter a *nolumnus mutare* as against the law-making power" (*Noble State Bank* vs. *Haskell,* 219 *U. S.,* 104, 110). But social development is an effective process of trial and error only if there is the fullest possible opportunity for the free play of the mind. He therefore attributed very different legal significance to those liberties which history has attested as the indispensable conditions of a free society from that which he attached to liberties which derived merely from shifting economic arrangements. Even freedom of speech, however, he did not erect into a dogma of absolute validity nor did he enforce it to doctrinaire limits.

For him the Constitution was not a literary document but an instrument of government. As such it was to be regarded not as an occasion for juggling with words but as a means for ordering the life of a people. It had its roots in the past—"historic continuity with the past," he reminded his hearers, "is not a duty, it is only a necessity"—but it was also designed for the unknown future. This conception of the Constitution was the background against which he projected every inquiry into the scope of a specific power or specific limitation. That the Constitution is a framework of great governmental powers to be exercised for great public ends was for him not a pale intellectual concept. It dominated his process of constitutional adjudication. His opinions, composed in harmony with his dominating attitude toward the Constitution, recognized an organism within which the dynamic life of a free society can unfold and flourish. From his constitutional opinions there emerges the conception of a nation adequate to its national and international tasks, whose federated states, though subordinate to central authority for national purposes, have ample power for their divers local needs. He was mindful of the Union which he helped to preserve at Ball's Bluff, Antietam, and Fredericksburg. He was equally alert to assure scope for the states in matters peculiarly theirs because not within the reach of Congress.

The nation was nearly deprived of one of its great men because President Theodore Roosevelt resented that Holmes, in his estimate

of John Marshall, should have subordinated the intellectual originality of the Chief Justice to his political significance. It was to be
expected, therefore, that on the Supreme Court he would be left un-
impressed by what are called great cases. What he cared about was
transforming thought. "My keenest interest is excited, not by what
are called great questions and great cases, but by little decisions
which the common run of selectors would pass by because they did
not deal with the Constitution or a telephone company, yet which
have in them the germ of some wider theory, and therefore of some
profound interstitial change in the very tissue of the law" (*Collected
Legal Papers*, p. 269). Judged by conventional standards, therefore,
his opinions not infrequently appeared to dispose rather cavalierly
of controversies that were complicated in their facts and far-reaching
in their immediate consequences. "This brief summary of the plead-
ings" he wrote of a litigation in which the record filled a five-foot
shelf, "is enough to show the gravity and importance of the case. It
concerns the expenditure of great sums and the welfare of millions
of men. But cost and importance, while they add to the solemnity of
our duty, do not increase the difficulty of decision except as they
induce argument upon matters that with less mighty interests no
one would venture to dispute" (*Sanitary District* vs. *United States*,
266 *U. S.*, 405, 425). With his vast learning he combined extraordinary rapidity of decision. His opinions were felicitous distillates
of these faculties. His genius—put to service by rigorous self-
discipline and deep learning—was to go for the essentials and express them with stinging brevity. He was impatient with laboring
the obvious as a form of looseness, for looseness and stuffiness equally
bored him. He genially suggested that judges need not be heavy
to be weighty. ". . . our reports were dull because we had the notion
that judicial dignity required solemn fluffy speech, as, when I grew
up, everybody wore black frock coats and black cravats . . ." (*Letters*, II, 132).

In his opinions the thinker and the artist are superbly fused. In
deciding cases, his aim was "to try to strike the jugular." His opinions appear effortless—birds of brilliant plumage pulled from the
magician's sleeves. But his correspondence gives glimpses of the great
effort that lay behind the seemingly easy achievement. "Of course in
letters one simply lets oneself go without thinking of form but in my
legal writing I do try to make it decent and I have come fully
to agree with Flaubert. He speaks of writing French, but to write any
language is enormously hard. To avoid vulgar errors and pitfalls
ahead is a job. To arrange the thoughts so that one springs naturally

from that which precedes it and to express them with a singing variety is the devil and all." And again: "The eternal effort of art, even the art of writing legal decisions, is to omit all but the essentials. The 'point of contact' is the formula, the place where the boy got his finger pinched; the rest of the machinery doesn't matter."

Whenever he disagreed with the majority of his brethren he was reluctant to express his dissenting views and did not often do so. In Massachusetts the number of his dissents is less than one per cent of all his opinions. On the Supreme Court of the United States the expression of dissenting views on constitutional issues has, from the beginning, been deemed almost obligatory. In Washington, therefore, they came from Justice Holmes's pen more frequently and sometimes were written with "cold Puritan passion." He gave a public hint of the forces that clashed in the Supreme Court in the decorous form of a mere lawsuit when he said "we are very quiet there, but it is the quiet of a storm centre . . ." (*Collected Legal Papers*, p. 292). In a letter to Pollock he gave more than a hint of the inevitable conflicts within the Court: "Today I am stirred about a case that I can't mention yet to which I have sent round a dissent that was prepared to be ready as soon as the opinion was circulated. I feel sure that the majority will very highly disapprove of my saying what I think, but as yet it seems to me my duty. No doubt I shall hear about it on Saturday at our conference and perhaps be persuaded to shut up, but I don't expect it" (*Letters*, II, 29). Some of his weightiest utterances are dissents, but they are dissents that have shaped history. (See *Adair* vs. *United States*, 208 *U. S.*, 161, 190; *Hammer* vs. *Dagenhart*, 247 *U. S.*, 251, 277; *Abrams* vs. *United States*, 250 *U. S.*, 616, 624; *Evans* vs. *Gore*, 253 *U. S.*, 245, 264; *Adkins* vs. *Children's Hospital*, 261 *U. S.* 525, 567; *Tyson & Bro.* vs. *Banton*, 273 *U. S.*, 418, 445; *United States* vs. *Schwimmer*, 279 *U. S.*, 644, 653; *Baldwin* vs. *Missouri*, 281 *U. S.*, 586, 595.) Disproportionate significance has been attached to his dissents, however; they are merely a part of a much larger, organic whole.

After his retirement he played briefly with the suggestion that he put his ultimate thoughts on law between the covers of a small book, but all his life he had been driven by the lash of some duty undone and at last he revelled in the joy of having no unfinished business. Moreover, he felt strongly that he had had his say in the way in which he most cared to express his reflections—scattered in his more than two thousand opinions and in his lean but weighty collection of occasional writings. "I am being happily idle," he wrote to Pollock, "and persuading myself that 91 has outlived duty. I can imagine a book on the law, getting rid of all talk of duties and rights—beginning with the definition of law in the lawyer's sense as a statement of the circumstances in which the public force will be brought to bear upon a man through the Courts, and expounding rights as a hypostasis of a prophecy—in short, systematizing some of my old chestnuts. But I don't mean to do it . . ." (*Letters,* II, 307). He was no believer in systems. These, he felt, were heavy elaborations of a few insights—*aperçus,* to use his recurring word. Systems die; insights remain, he reiterated. Therefore, a few of his own *aperçus* will give the best clues to his philosophy of law and to his judicial technique in the most important field of his labors.

". . . the provisions of the Constitution are not mathematical formulas having their essence in their form; they are organic living institutions transplanted from English soil. Their significance is vital not formal; it is to be gathered not simply by taking the words and a dictionary, but by considering their origin and the line of their growth" (*Gompers* vs. *United States, 233 U. S.,* 604, 610).

". . . when we are dealing with words that also are a constituent act, like the Constitution of the United States, we must realize that they have called into life a being the development of which could not have been foreseen completely by the most gifted of its begetters. It was enough for them to realize or to hope that they had created an organism; it has taken a century and has cost their successors much sweat and blood to prove that they created a nation. The case before us must be considered in the light of our whole experience and not merely in that of what was said a hundred years ago" (*Missouri* vs. *Holland, 252 U. S.,* 416, 433).

"Great constitutional provisions must be administered with caution. Some play must be allowed for the joints of the machine, and it must be remembered that legislatures are ultimate guardians of the liberties and welfare of the people in quite as great a degree as the courts" (*Missouri, Kansas & Texas Ry. Co.* vs. *May,* 194 *U. S.,* 267, 270).

"While the courts must exercise a judgment of their own, it by no means is true that every law is void which may seem to the judges who pass upon it excessive, unsuited to its ostensible end, or based upon conceptions of morality with which they disagree. Considerable latitude must be allowed for differences of view as well as for possible peculiar conditions which this court can know but imperfectly, if at all. Otherwise a constitution, instead of embodying only relatively fundamental rules of right, as generally understood by all English-speaking communities, would become the partisan of a particular set of ethical or economical opinions, which by no means are held *semper ubique et ab omnibus*" (*Otis* vs. *Parker,* 187 *U. S.,* 606, 608–09).

". . . I should not dream of asking where the line can be drawn, since the great body of the law consists in drawing such lines, yet when you realize that you are dealing with a matter of degree you must realize that reasonable men may differ widely as to the place where the line should fall" (*Schlesinger* vs. *Wisconsin,* 270 *U. S.,* 230, 241).

It is futile to try to account for genius; and the term is not inaptly used for one whom so qualified an appraiser as Mr. Justice Cardozo deemed probably the greatest legal intellect in the history of the English-speaking judiciary. Holmes simply heeded his own deepest impulses. He was born to probe beyond the surface of things, to cut beneath the skin of formulas, however respectable. In his formative years he found most congenial the company of speculative minds like William James and Charles S. Peirce and Chauncey Wright. All his life his pastime was not courtroom gossip but "twisting the tail of the cosmos" (Perry, *The Thought and Character of William James,* I, 504–19). Although native bent was powerfully reinforced by his Civil War experience, the deeper ferment of his time also worked in him. He came to maturity when Darwin began to disturb ancient beliefs. If Genesis had to be "reinterpreted" no texts of the law, however authoritative, could claim sanctity. By whatever combination of native disposition and outside influences it came to pass, however, the result was that Holmes early rejected legal principles as absolutes. He looked beneath their decorous formulations and saw them for what they usually are—sententious expressions of overlapping or conflicting social policies. The vital judicial issue is apt, therefore, to be their accommodation. Decisions thus become essentially a matter of drawing lines. Again and again he adverted to that necessity, which he once summed up as follows: "I do not think we need trouble ourselves with the thought that my view depends upon differences of degree. The whole law does so as soon as it is civilized. . . . Negligence is all degree—that of the defendant here degree of the nicest sort; and between the variations according to distance that I suppose to exist and the simple universality of the rules in the Twelve Tables or the Leges Barbarorum, there lies the culture of two thousand years" (*LeRoy Fibre Co.* vs. *Chicago, Milwaukee & St. Paul Ry.,* 232 *U. S.,* 340, 354). Such a view of law of course implies the exercise of choice. But judicial judgment precluded the notion of capricious choice. It assumes judgment between defined claims, each of recognized validity and with a cultural pedigree of its own, but all of which necessarily cannot be completely satisfied. This process of adjustment is bound increasingly to fall to the legislature as interests and activities in society become more and more interdependent. The considerations which thus prompt legislation and the intricate, dubious materials out of which laws are written bring into sharp focus the duty of deference to legislative determinations demanded from the revisory process called adjudicative. In a thousand instances Holmes was loyal to that philosophy. Thereby he resolved into comprehending larger truths the conflicting claims of state and nation, of liberty and authority, of individual and society.

"It is right and proper that in the reading room of the Harvard Law School the portrait of Holmes should face in equal honor the portrait of Marshall" (A. D. Hill, *Harvard Graduates' Magazine, supra,* p. 284). There fell to Marshall, as Holmes took occasion to say, "perhaps the greatest place that ever was filled by a judge" (*Collected Legal Papers,* p. 270). That Marshall seized it, the rôle of the Supreme Court in American history bears witness. Holmes's claim to preëminence has a different basis. He is unsurpassed in the depth of his penetration into the nature of the judicial process and in the originality of its exposition. His conception of the Constitution cannot be severed from his conception of a judge's function in applying it; and his views of the judge's function derive from his intellectual presuppositions, that is, from his loyal adherence in judicial practice to his philosophic scepticism. His approach to judicial problems was inseparable from his consciously wrought notions of his relations to the universe. These abstractions appear far removed from the particular cases that came before him. But the clarity with which a specific controversy is seen, in the context of the larger intellectual issues beneath the formal surface of litigation, and the disinterestedness with which such analysis guides decision and opinion, are the ultimate determinants of American public law.

After a major operation in the summer of 1922, Holmes showed signs of age—he was then in his eighty-second year; but his marvelous physique gradually reasserted itself, though he strictly conserved his energy for his work. Some of his most powerful opinions were written in his ninth decade. Until near the end of his tenure he usually wrote more than his share of opinions. He was nearly eighty-nine when the illness and death of Chief Justice Taft cast upon Holmes for a considerable period the heavy burden of presiding in

Court and the still more difficult task of guiding its deliberations at conferences. He did both, in the language of Mr. Justice Brandeis,. "as to the manner born."

The machinery was running down, however, and on Jan. 12, 1932,. he sent his resignation, in his own beautiful script, to the President— "the time has come and I bow to the inevitable." He continued his serene life, in Washington and in the summers at Beverly Farms, reading and being read to, enjoying the simple and familiar things of nature that had always refreshed him and the devoted attention of friends, especially the young. He had become a very old man but his faculties were never impaired. He had grown almost wistful in his gentleness. The fire of his exciting personality was dying down and on the morning of Mar. 6, 1935, came the end.

With the sure response of the mass of men—given enough time— to goodness and gallantry of spirit, Holmes, the fundamentally soli-- tary thinker, had become a pervasive and intimate national posses- sion. His death elicited an outpouring of feeling throughout the country. But of all the moving things that were said he would prob- ably have most liked the few words of his old friend and his closest colleague for fifteen years, Mr. Justice Brandeis, when the news was brought him: "And so the great man is gone." On his ninety-fourth birthday—a raw March day with snow gently falling—he was buried with due military honors, in the Arlington National Cemetery, alongside his wife and near his companions, known and unknown,. of the Army of the Potomac.

Without accompanying explanation, he left the bulk of his sub- stantial estate to the nation, the largest unrestricted gift ever made to it. Congress established a Holmes Fund Memorial Commission,. whose proposals, interrupted by the Second World War, await the consideration of Congress.* In a message to that body recommend-- ing an appropriate use of the bequest, President Franklin Roose- velt thus interpreted Holmes's intention: "It is the gift of one who,. in war and in peace, devoted his life to its [his country's] service. Clearly he thereby sought, with a generous emphasis, to mark the full measure of his faith in those principles of freedom which the country was founded to preserve." And the President expressed what he deemed to be the country's desire that Congress "translate this gift into a form that may serve as a permanent impulse for the main-

---

* By an act of Congress approved on Aug. 5. 1955, a Permanent Committee for the Oliver Wendell Holmes Devise was created, to supervise the prepara- tion and publication of a history of the Supreme Court, and, in its discretion,. to support an annual lecture or series of lectures and a memorial volume con- taining selections from the writings of Mr. Justice Holmes.

tenance of the deepest tradition that Mr. Justice Holmes embodied."
That tradition, wrote President Roosevelt, "was a faith in the creative possibilities of the law. For him law was an instrument of just
relations between man and man. With an insight into its history that
no American scholar has surpassed; with a capacity to mold ancient
principles to present needs, unique in range and remarkable in
prophetic power; with a grasp of its significance as the basis upon
which the purposes of men are shaped, Mr. Justice Holmes sought to
make the jurisprudence of the United States fulfill the great ends
our nation was established to accomplish" (President's Message to
Congress, Apr. 25, 1935).

[Holmes's Massachusetts opinions may be found in *Mass. Reports*, vols. 134–82;
for analytical table see *Harvard Law Rev.*, Mar. 1931, for chronological, H. C.
Shriver, *Judicial Opinions of Oliver Wendell Holmes* (1940). His Supreme Court
opinions are in *U. S. Reports*, vols. 187–284, and an analytical table is in *Harvard
Law Rev.*, supra. Alfred Lief, *Dissenting Opinions of Mr. Justice Holmes* (1929)
and *Representative Opinions of Mr. Justice Holmes* (1931), give selections. For
bibliography of early writings and selections see *Harvard Law Rev.*, supra;
these and others are reprinted in Shriver, *Justice Oliver Wendell Holmes: His
Book Notices and Uncollected Letters and Papers* (1936). *The Common Law*
(1881, 1938) has been translated into several foreign languages. His *Speeches*
(1891), with additions, was reprinted in 1913 and 1938. H. J. Laski, ed., *Collected
Legal Papers* (1920), contains speeches and essays. Only two full series of his
correspondence have thus far been published—M. DeW. Howe, *Holmes-Pollock
Letters* (2 vols., 1941), and letters to J. C. H. Wu, published in *T'ien Hsia
Monthly*, Oct. 1935, and reprinted in Shriver, *Book Notices*. R. B. Perry, *The
Thought and Character of William James* (1935), contains correspondence
between James and Holmes. Other collections are in the Lib. of Cong., the
Harvard Law School Lib., and private possession. Critical and biographical
material may be found in *Mr. Justice Holmes, a Collection of Essays* (1931),
ed. by Felix Frankfurter; Silas Bent, *Justice Oliver Wendell Holmes* (1932);
Felix Frankfurter, *Mr. Justice Holmes and the Supreme Court* (1939); Francis
Biddle, *Mr. Justice Holmes* (1924); Max Lerner, *The Mind and Faith of Justice
Holmes* (1943); Catherine D. Bowen, *Yankee from Olympus* (1943.)]

[SUPPLEMENTARY BIBLIOGRAPHY. Several collections of Holmes's writings have
appeared in recent years: *Touched with Fire: Civil War Letters and Diary of
Oliver Wendell Holmes, Jr., 1861–1864* (1946) and *Holmes-Laski Letters: The
Correspondence of Mr. Justice Holmes and Harold J. Laski, 1916–1935* (2 vols.,

1953), both ed. by Mark DeW. Howe; and "The Holmes-Cohen Correspondence," ed. by Felix S. Cohen, *Jour. of the Hist. of Ideas*, Jan. 1948. *The Occasional Speeches of Justice Oliver Wendell Holmes* (1962), compiled by Mark DeW. Howe, supplants and expands the earlier *Speeches*. New biographical and critical treatments include: Mark DeW. Howe, *Justice Oliver Wendell Holmes: The Shaping Years, 1840–1870* (1957) and *Justice Oliver Wendell Holmes: The Proving Years, 1870–1882* (1963); Francis Biddle, *Justice Holmes, Natural Law, and the Supreme Court* (1961); Samuel J. Konefsky, *The Legacy of Holmes and Brandeis: A Study in the Influence of Ideas* (1956); and Edmund Wilson, *Patriotic Gore: Studies in the Literature of the Am. Civil War* (1962), ch. XVI.]

William Howard Taft

by

HENRY F. PRINGLE

TAFT, WILLIAM HOWARD (Sept. 15, 1857–Mar. 8, 1930), president and chief justice of the United States, was of the third generation in his family to follow the law. His grandfather, Peter Rawson Taft, was a judge of the probate and county courts of Windham County, Vt.; and his father, Alphonso Taft, served two terms on the superior court in Cincinnati, Ohio. Though born and brought up in Cincinnati, William Howard Taft belonged to New England rather than the Middle West. Beginning with Robert Taft, his ancestors on his father's side had dwelt in Massachusetts and Vermont since the seventeenth century. His mother was Louisa Maria Torrey (she signed herself Louise), the second wife of Alphonso Taft. Her ancestor, William Torrey of Combe St. Nicholas, Somersetshire, England, emigrated to America in 1640, settled at Weymouth, Mass., and served as a clerk of the Massachusetts House of Deputies, a magistrate, and a captain of the militia. His descendant, Samuel Davenport Torrey, born at Mendon, Mass., on Apr. 14, 1779, married as his second wife Susan Holman, who was the mother of Louisa Maria Torrey (born Sept. 11, 1827).

William Howard had two half-brothers, Charles Phelps and Peter Rawson; there were two younger brothers, Henry Waters and Horace Dutton, and a sister, Fanny Louise. At twelve he was at the head of his class, at thirteen he entered the Woodward High School in Cincinnati, and at seventeen he was ready for Yale, where he matriculated in the fall of 1874. Taft did well at Yale. He delivered the class oration on his graduation in 1878, and was second in a class of 121. Then turning his face westward, he went back to Cincinnati where, in 1880, he received his law degree from the Cincinnati Law School and was admitted to the Ohio bar. He was a large, too good-natured young man with a tendency toward sloth which worried his father and his youngest brother, Horace. Thus he was rebuked by the former in the summer of 1879 for being at a boat race when he might have been handling a minor law suit. "As usual," wrote Horace to his mother, "he put the thing off until he had only two or three days to prepare in" (Apr. 19, 1885). This weakness for procrastination never really left Taft. He was constantly complaining, when in the White House, that he had not yet had time to prepare some speech and would have to get it in shape in too brief a time. On the other hand, the law was a rather casual mistress in the eighties. While studying, he also had time to serve as a court reporter for the *Cincinnati Commercial*.

Taft's first participation in politics also occurred in 1880 when, encouraged by his father to develop himself as a speaker, he did some spell-binding for the Republican state committee. That he was to follow his father into that party was, of course, foreordained. The next year he campaigned for Miller Outcault, candidate for prosecuting attorney of Hamilton County; his reward, when Outcault was elected, was a post as assistant. This was his first public office. In 1882 he learned that politics had an unsavory side. Appointed collector of internal revenue for Cincinnati in March, he was promptly subjected to demands that he oust four or five office holders, "the best men in the service." Their removal, he wrote his father, "will cause a very big stink," and he declined to do such "dirty work" (July 24, 1882). He resigned several months later, resumed the practice of law, and toured Europe. He took an active part in the campaigns of 1884, although he shared his father's disappointment in the nomination of James G. Blaine. By now he was a partisan, although not a machine, Republican. The Mugwump movement did not penetrate Ohio to any extent. So William and Charles Taft, possibly because they knew that their father's diplomatic career would terminate unless Blaine won, did their best for the Republican nominee. In addition, William was chief supervisor of the election in Cincinnati. "You must have had a hard struggle to keep . . . the Kentuckians from voting at our polls," wrote his father from St. Petersburg (Nov. 3, 1884). Taft had an interest greater than the campaign. This was a disbarment case against Tom Campbell, a local politician-lawyer (Duffy, *post*, pp. 9–12). Taft was appointed to the staff which conducted the case against Campbell in the summer of 1884. In January 1885 he made the opening address and spoke, according to his admiring young brother, for over four hours during which "the life, the interest, the logic, the facts and the eloquence did not fail for one minute" (Horace to Alphonso Taft, Jan. 11, 1885). In May he became engaged to Helen Herron, the daughter of John W. Herron of Cincinnati, "a woman who is willing to take me as I am, for better or for worse." They were married on June 19, 1886, and in the course of time had three children, Robert Alphonso, Helen, and Charles Phelps.

Taft ascended the bench, the place beyond all others where he was happy, for the first time in March 1887. Gov. Joseph B. Foraker appointed him to the superior court of Ohio for the unfinished term of Judge Judson Harmon, who had resigned. In April 1888 he was elected for a five-year term; this was the only office save the presidency which he achieved by popular vote. Few of the youthful judge's opinions were of legal importance. Then, as later, he had a weakness for verbosity in writing. His most important case, perhaps, was *Moores & Company* vs. *The Bricklayers' Union, No. 1, W. H. Stephenson, et al.* Moores & Company, building supply dealers, boycotted by the union, had been awarded $2,250 damages by a jury in the lower court. Taft wrote an exhaustive opinion in which he declared the boycott illegal and confirmed the damage award (*Weekly Law Bulletin and Ohio Law Journal*, Jan. 20, 1890). The ruling attracted wide attention and was one of the factors which caused labor so bitterly to oppose him in later years.

The star of Taft was rising. It was a placid star, not a comet, against the judicial and political sky. In 1889, although but thirty-two, he was discussed for associate justice of the Supreme Court, but refused to share "the very roseate view" of those who thought he might be appointed. "My chances of going to the moon and of donning a silk gown at the hands of President Harrison," he wrote his father, "are about equal" (Aug. 24, 1889). He received, instead, a post as solicitor-general at Harrison's hands and the stage of his activity was enlarged to include Washington, D. C., where he assumed office on Feb. 4, 1890. Apprehensive about his ability, he wrote his father that he had had no experience in the federal statutes, and that the prospect was "rather overwhelming." But he did well. Within a year he could report that he had argued eighteen cases in the Supreme Court and won fifteen (to Alphonso Taft, Feb. 9, 1891). In March 1891 Congress created a new judgeship for each circuit of the federal circuit court and Taft was mentioned for an appointment to the sixth, which covered Kentucky, Ohio, Michigan, and Tennessee. Mrs. Taft was opposed. "If you get your heart's desire," she wrote him that summer, "it will put an end to all your opportunities . . . of being thrown with big-wigs" (July 18, 1891). But Taft had small taste for big-wigs. Clearly, he was less ambitious than other members of the family. He did not mind being poor, he said, for people with small incomes were as happy as those with fortunes. For eight years, from Mar. 17, 1892, he served on the circuit court.

For a man of judicial tastes, who was also becoming a profound legal scholar, the appointment was ideal. Noting that there was "only one higher judicial position in the country," Taft continued to keep an eye on the Supreme Court. Meanwhile, the work was absorbing. Many decisions related to labor, and Taft was to de damned for these in 1908 and 1912. The man and the jurist must be kept distinct in any attempt accurately to portray Taft's views on labor. A large element of conservative public opinion was exceedingly alarmed over the state of the nation in 1892. The Haymarket bombing of 1886 was still all too vivid. The Homestead riots were in a few months to make crimson the muddy Ohio River. Financial panic and breadlines were to follow in a year. That Taft, as a private citizen, shared the alarm of the respectable people is clear. In July 1894 the Pullman strike was raging in Chicago. "It will be necessary for the military to kill some of the mob before the trouble can be stayed," he wrote his wife. "They have only killed six . . . as yet. This is hardly enough to make an impression" (July 8, 1894).

His first major labor case as circuit judge was when P. M. Arthur, grand chief of the Brotherhood of Locomotive Engineers, ruled that the members of the organization would refuse to handle freight of the Toledo, Ann Arbor & North Michigan Railway, which had declined to raise wages. They were to refuse, that is, even if they worked only on connecting lines. Taft upheld a temporary injunction previously issued by himself against this order and was criticized, unjustly, on the mistaken theory that he had ruled against strikes (54 *Federal Reporter*, 730; Duffy, pp. 35–36). In the case of Frank M. Phelan, a lieutenant of Eugene Debs, he made his viewpoint clear. Phelan, during the Pullman strike, urged the employees of the Cincinnati Southern Railroad, in receivership and therefore under the jurisdiction of the federal court, to cease work. He was enjoined. When he violated the injunction he was sentenced by Taft to six months' imprisonment (62 *Federal Reporter*, 803). "I shall find him . . . guilty on [sic] conspiring unlawfully to tie up the road by a boycott" (W. H. Taft to Helen Herron Taft, July 11, 1894). The decision was handed down on July 13, 1894. At the same moment when, as a private citizen, Taft was voicing approval of Chicago bloodshed he declared, as a judge, that the employees of the Cincinnati Southern had a right to organize, join a union, conspire to strike, and conduct a strike. "They have labor to sell," he said. "If they stand together, they are often able . . . to command better prices . . . than when dealing singly with rich employers" (62 *Federal Reporter*, 817). But he felt that the employees of the Cincinnati Southern had, in this instance, no grievance. Phelan was part of a combination which was illegal. The boycott he sought was illegal (Duffy, pp. 39–45). Actually, Taft's position on the right of labor to organize was definitely in advance of the existing legal opinion of the day. He gave further evidence of his sympathy for the workingman in his decision (on which he was reversed by the Supreme Court) that an employer could not relieve himself from negligence in accident cases by requiring employees to agree to nonliability (79 *Federal Reporter*, 561; see also 176 *United States*, 498). In another case (96 *Federal Reporter*, 298) he ruled that employers could not plead contributory negligence on the part of employees where statutory safety provisions had been violated. While on the circuit bench, Taft also strengthened the Sherman anti-trust law. In 1898 he decided, in the Addyston Pipe Case, that a combination of manufacturers of cast-iron pipe was in restraint of trade and issued an injunction (85 *Federal Reporter*, 271; Duffy, pp. 49–51).

In 1899 Taft was asked by the "liberal element" of the Yale Corporation to consider election to the presidency of the university (H. W. Taft to W. H. Taft, Jan. 14, 1899). He answered that "two insuperable objections" made this impossible. The first was that he was a Unitarian and this would "shock the conservative element" of the alumni. The second was that he did not feel qualified for the post (W. H. Taft to H. W. Taft, Jan. 21, 1899). A far different assignment lay ahead. On Mar. 15, 1900, he resigned from the bench, at the instance of President McKinley, to become president of the Philippine Commission. For the first time he was to be an executive and administrator. The reputation he earned did much to advance him toward the presidency. Emotionally, he grew very much attached to the little brown inhabitants of the Philippine Islands and their welfare always remained close to his heart.

On his arrival early in June 1900, Taft concluded that "the back of the rebellion" was broken and that the first immediate necessity was to end military rule in the islands. He was not a sentimentalist; the Filipinos who persisted in lawlessness were, when caught, to be "either hung or banished in Guam" (W. H. Taft to B. I. Wheeler, Oct. 17, 1900). Executions were not necessary. Education, pacification of still rebellious natives, and settlement of the perplexing issue of the friars' lands were the immediate objectives of the Philippine Commission. Taft directed his efforts to these as soon as he had relegated the military command of the islands to a secondary position. The Philippines, under Spain, had to a large extent been ruled by friars. That they had abused their authority was, when Taft arrived, a firm conviction of the Filipinos. Many of the friars had been slain in the insurrections prior to the war with Spain. Their lands had been confiscated by the Philippine Congress. Taft concluded that this was "a political and not a religious question" (W. H. Taft to J. J. Hooker, Jan. 7, 1901). Most of the surviving friars had fled the islands and Taft's conviction was that the Roman Catholic hierarchy must not insist on their return. A specific part of the problem was settlement for the 400,000 acres of land owned by the friars and, until the insurrection, rented to the natives. Taft desired to purchase these lands and sell them to the natives at fair prices (Duffy, p. 109). After prolonged negotiations, which included a journey to Rome and conferences, in June 1902, with Pope Leo XIII, an agreement was reached. Ultimately, the United States paid $7,200,000 for the friars' lands. Meanwhile, in July 1901, Taft had been made civil governor of the islands. Until January 1904, when President Roosevelt called him back to become secretary of war, he devoted himself with great energy to improving the economic status of the Philippines, to the building of roads and harbors, toward establishing limited self-government.

On two occasions while Taft was in the Philippines he was offered an appointment to the Supreme Court by President Roosevelt. He declined because he felt that his task had not been completed. He accepted the post of secretary of war on the ground that he could continue his supervision of the affairs of the islands. But this was only part of his work. Taking office on Feb. 1, 1904, he soon became a close adviser to the President. Roosevelt and Taft made an excellent team; the latter's easy-going conservatism counteracted the President's impulsive qualities. Taft became, in effect, the "trouble shooter" of the administration. He took on his too-broad shoulders the task of starting actual construction of the Panama Canal and hurried to the Canal Zone for that purpose. When Roosevelt left Washington for a vacation he made his secretary of war, to all purposes, secretary of state as well. Everything was all right, the President said, with Taft "sitting on the lid." In September 1906, Taft was rushed to Cuba to effect peace when a revolution threatened. Clearly, Taft had been revealing unusual talents as an administrator and even more as a conciliator. Soon after Roosevelt's declaration in 1904 that he would not run again, the name of Taft as a successor came to the front. His private letters show that he had no taste for the office, that he believed himself disqualified because of his labor decisions when on the bench. But Mrs. Taft and his brothers desired that he stand for the nomination (Pringle, p. 498). His private letters of protest grew weaker as 1905 advanced. Late in 1907 he received definite word that he was the chosen candidate of the President. He ran as Roosevelt's man. He was elected in November 1908 over Bryan by an electoral vote of 321 to 162 and a popular plurality of more than a million. He took office in March 1909. He was troubled, bothered, and harassed almost from the start.

With Roosevelt's cordial assent, Taft chose his own cabinet. Secretary of State Philander C. Knox, Attorney-General George W. Wickersham, and, to a degree, Charles Nagel, secretary of commerce and labor, were the members on whom Taft was to lean most. His advisory board was not distinguished for its strength. Like most such bodies, it represented compromise. It included no member of the insurgent wing of the Republican party and to that degree was reactionary. But it was not a "Wall Street" cabinet, either. Wickersham was to annoy the financial interests in New York by his trust prosecutions. Taft began his presidency with a divided party, although technically he had both houses of Congress behind him. His fatal error of political thought, as distinct from specific mistakes, was his belief that the Republican party could be continued in power without giving ground to its more liberal wing. At the start and on the specific advice of Roosevelt, he declined to join in the fight of the House insurgents on the autocratic powers of Speaker Joseph G. Cannon (W. H. Taft to W. A. White, Mar. 12, 1909). His real difficulty, of course, was that he did not possess his predecessor's great genius for guiding, sometimes confusing, public opinion. His honesty of purpose was stolid and plodding. He could not magnify minor issues. "There is no use trying to be William Howard Taft with Roosevelt's ways," he said, ". . . our ways are different" (Butt, *post,* I, 236). Roosevelt had zealously refrained from attempting tariff revision, thus avoiding an issue fraught with death to presidents. Taft promptly plunged into it.

Tariff revision was part of the general demand, more vocal in the Middle West and the West than in the East, for a more equal distribution of wealth. Roosevelt had stilled the outcry only partially.

Now, in 1909, a wide segment of public opinion insisted that tariff revision downward would further control the trusts. So Taft called a special session of Congress. The House schedules, while not revolutionary, marked real reductions. But the Senate, with Nelson W. Aldrich as the extreme high-tariff advocate, amended the bill almost beyond recognition. Taft effected many compromises and said, in a detailed explanatory letter of June 27, 1909, to his brother Horace, that "the Payne bill was a genuine effort in the right direction." "I am not a high-tariff man; I am a low-tariff man," he insisted (W. H. Taft to W. D. Foulke, July 15, 1909). Shortly afterward he wrote his wife that he would either beat the bill or get what he wanted. After the Payne-Aldrich bill was passed, the President felt that it was a distinct step forward, "the best bill that the party has ever passed" (W. H. Taft to R. M. Wanamaker, Nov. 24, 1909). This was not wholly untrue; the Payne-Aldrich act was of slight economic importance, but it did mark a recession of the Republican urge toward higher and higher duties. Taft agreed that he "could make a lot of cheap popularity by vetoing the bill" (W. H. Taft to Horace Taft, June 27, 1910). Instead, he made himself its defender, praised it too lavishly, and so reaped the unpopularity which the act itself received.

"I have had a hard time . . . I have been conscientiously trying to carry out your policies but my method of doing so has not worked smoothly," wrote Taft to Roosevelt as the latter prepared to return from his African jaunt (May 26, 1910). Taft's cup of woe was brimming. On the one hand, in his own party, he faced such insurgents as Senators La Follette, Cummins, Dolliver, Bristow, Borah, Clapp, and Beveridge. On the other, he was threatened by the growing strength of the Democratic party, which was to take over the House in November 1910, and the imponderable strength of Woodrow Wilson as a possible Democratic nominee. Worse than all was the friction with Roosevelt, to whom the insurgents were appealing and who disapproved of Taft's action in dismissing Gifford Pinchot because of his charges against the secretary of the interior, Richard A. Ballinger. Yet there were many accomplishments to which Taft might have pointed with pride had he been more of a political leader and less judicial. By means of the Tariff Board he started the first scientific investigation of rates. He created the postal savings system. He was a sincere friend of conservation, despite subsequent accusations from the Progressives. He negotiated an agreement with Canada which meant relatively free trade between that country and the United States. He then secured ratification by Congress only to have Canada, at first enthusiastic for the measure, ultimately reject it. Deeply interested in international peace, he attempted to arrange treaties of arbitration with Great Britain and France. They were so amended by the Senate that Taft discontinued the effort to secure senatorial concurrence. Under Attorney-General Wickersham a series of vigorous prosecutions against trusts were started; as a "trust-buster" President Taft was, in fact, more active than Roosevelt. Among his other accomplishments were efforts toward economy and efficiency in government, the first step toward a federal budget; the appointment of a commission to investigate the question of additional safety and workmen's compensation legislation; the admission of New Mexico and Arizona as states.

The Roosevelt-Taft "break," so-called, was inevitable from the time that Taft's predecessor returned from Europe in the summer of 1910. But there is no specific incident from which it can be dated. In general, it was due to the complete antithesis between the two men. Taft believed in a government of laws, not of men. Roosevelt held the law lightly; he believed in a government of men or, more accurately, of a single man—himself. Roosevelt was a consummate politician, in contrast to Taft. He enjoyed the presidency. Taft's four years in the White House were probably the unhappiest of his life. He was not such a misfit as Roosevelt came to believe, but he had no taste for politics. His private letters reveal that he was discouraged early in his administration and did not believe he would be reelected. On Sept. 6, 1911, he confessed to his brother Charles: "I am not very happy in this renomination and reelection business. I have to set my teeth and go through with it. . . . But I shall be willing to retire and let another take the burden." He grew more conservative as the years passed, leaning more and more on such men as Aldrich. Roosevelt, in evolving his New Nationalism, grew more radical. Finally, he called for the initiative and referendum and for the recall of judicial decisions. The last, in particular, made Taft recoil. The two men drifted; Taft toward the nomination which he had to accept from his party whether he wanted it or not, and Roosevelt toward a contest for that nomination. At the Republican National Convention in Chicago in June 1912, Taft was renominated by routine steam-roller methods and was accused by Roosevelt of having "stolen" the convention. Roosevelt organized the Bull Moose Party and the campaign, the most bitter since that of 1876, began. Taft's defeat was inevitable. "As a leader, I had to have confidence and hope, but in my heart I have long been making plans for my future," he wrote when it was over (W. H. Taft to C. H. Clark, Nov.

9, 1912). He received only 8 electoral votes against 88 for Roosevelt and 435 for Wilson. He was condemned by contemporary historians as one of the most lamentable of White House failures, a greater failure even than Grant. The appraisal was not sound. Taft would under no conditions have been a great president, but the political situation between 1909 and 1913 was such that no Republican, even Roosevelt, could have been successful. Taft was unique in that he did not want the office and surrendered it gladly. "Politics makes me sick" is a phrase which beats like a minor refrain through his private letters when he was president. The office brought out all his worst traits: vacillation, irritability, a complete inability to lead. It obscured very real gifts: an excellent judicial mind, an integrity which was never clouded, great talent as an administrator, a wide and broad sympathy for human problems.

He retired in March 1913 to the campus of his beloved Yale as Kent Professor of Constitutional Law. During the World War he served as joint-chairman of the National War Labor Board. Then, on June 30, 1921, President Harding gratified his heart's desire by naming him chief justice of the United States. It is not impossible that his work as administrator of the nation's highest court was more important than his decisions. He found himself, in 1921, on a bench which was badly divided; out of 180 opinions handed down in 1921–22, dissents were expressed in forty-five cases—exactly one-fourth of the total. Moreover, the Court was behind in its work. Taft's private letters disclose his concern, in the matter of new appointments to the Supreme Court, that the number of dissents be cut down. Regarding one candidate he wrote that the jurist "is rather an off horse and dissents a good deal" (W. H. Taft to C. D. Hilles, Dec. 1, 1922). "It would be too bad," he continued, "if we had another on the bench who would herd with Brandeis . . . as Brandeis is usually against the Court." The Chief Justice, in this instance, was not objecting to the liberal views of Associate Justice Brandeis, but to the frequency of his dissents, whether liberal or conservative. This is not an implication, on the other hand, that Taft was not, on the whole, conservative in his interpretation of the law.

As president he had been "to a unique degree . . . interested in the effective working of the judicial machinery and conversant with the details of judicial administration" (see Frankfurter and Landis, *post*, pp. 156–58). As chief justice he immediately interested himself in finding some relief from the mass of litigation which was swamping the Supreme Court and the lower federal courts.

His first accomplishment was authorization by Congress in 1922 for the creation of a conference of senior circuit judges, with the chief justice as its head. This introduced the first degree of coordination into the federal judicial system (*Ibid.*, pp. 241–54). Even more important was his part in effecting the passage of the act of Feb. 13, 1925. This was known as the Judges' Bill and, stripped of technicalities, it gave the Supreme Court a greatly increased discretion over the cases which came before it. It terminated certain classes of appeals as matters of right and made them reviewable only through the discretionary writ of certiorari. The Supreme Court now had time to give prompt action on questions of constitutionality and other cases of national significance (*Ibid.*, pp. 261–86). When he retired in February 1930, the business of the court was practically current.

The reputation of Taft for conservatism came, in part, from the so-called Child Labor Case and the Coronado Coal Company Case. The former (*Bailey* vs. *Drexel Furniture Co.; 259 U. S.*, 20) resulted from an attempt of Congress to control child labor by the imposition of a tax imposed on interstate products manufactured through its aid. This, Taft wrote, was an infringement on the rights of the states and not a proper use of the power to tax; "to give such magic to the word 'tax,'" he held, "would be to break down all constitutional limitation of the powers of Congress and completely wipe out the sovereignty of the States." The Coronado case (*United Mine Workers of America* vs. *Coronado Coal Co.; 259 U. S.*, 344) grew out of a strike in the Prairie Creek field in Arkansas in 1914. Property of the Coronado Coal Company was destroyed and action for damages against the United Mine Workers had resulted in a verdict for the company in a lower court. Taft wrote the opinion, denying federal jurisdiction since coal-mining was not interstate commerce, but holding that the union, even though unincorporated, could be sued under the anti-trust laws; its funds, accumulated for conducting strikes, were subject to execution for unlawful acts committed during a strike. "The circumstances are such," said he, "as to awaken regret that, in our view of the federal jurisdiction, we can not affirm the judgment" (*259 U. S.*, 413).

The most important dissent by Taft was against the majority opinion of Justice Sutherland invalidating the law of 1918 which fixed a minimum wage for women in the District of Columbia (*Adkins* vs. *Children's Hospital; 261 U. S.*, 525). The majority of the Court held that the act did not deal with any business charged with the public interest or with any temporary emergency. But the

Chief Justice held that a minimum wage law for women was constitutional because sweatshop wages did just as much to impair their health and morals as did long hours (see C. E. Hughes, *The Supreme Court of the United States,* 1928, pp. 209–10). Taft did not fulfill, however, this promise of leading the Court toward an increasingly liberal view in social and labor questions. It is clear that his duties as administrative officer of the Court gave him, as a general thing, no desire to dissent.

In so far as Taft sanctioned the control of commerce and industry he believed, his decisions show, that supervision by the federal government was superior to that by the states. He agreed with the Court in nullifying the Kansas law creating a court of industrial relations, on the ground that the industries it proposed to control —and the act gave extraordinary powers to the court of industrial relations—were not affected with the public interest. It had never been supposed, he said "that the business of the butcher or the baker, the tailor, the woodchopper . . . was clothed with such a public interest that the price of his product or his wages could be fixed by State regulation" (Hughes, pp. 211, 221–22). But he was, in contrast, an advocate of broad federal powers under the commerce clause of the Constitution. The Supreme Court had already refused to limit the power of Congress; in 1905 Associate Justice Holmes had held that the packers were engaged in interstate commerce even though their actual business might be limited to the stockyards of Chicago. Taft extended this doctrine when he wrote the opinion upholding the stockyards act (*Stafford* vs. *Wallace; 258 U. S., 495*). The packing and stockyards industry, he said, was national in scope and susceptible to federal regulation even to the point of letting the secretary of agriculture fix brokers' prices. Several other cases might be cited in which he further amplified this view. In the case of *Myers* vs. *United States* (272 *U. S.,* 52), the Supreme Court settled an ancient controversy by sustaining the presidential power to remove executive officers. Taft's opinion, it has been said, "will probably rank as one of his most important contributions to constitutional law" (*Proceedings of the Bar and Officers of the Supreme Court of the United States in Memory of William Howard Taft,* 1931, p. 37).

Yet Taft, a coordinator and conciliator all of his life rather than an advocate, was not a leader of judicial thought in the sense that Justice Holmes was a leader—or Justice Brandeis or Cardozo. The new Supreme Court building will remain as a permanent monument to his constructive talents; he was largely responsible for the congressional act under which it was built. On Feb. 3, 1930, bad health, due chiefly to heart disease, forced his retirement from the bench. He died in Washington on Mar. 8, 1930, and was buried in the Arlington National Cemetery.

Taft's published writings, outside of his legal opinions, were not important. Most of them were revised from public lectures. Among them might be mentioned: *Popular Government* (1913); *The Anti-Trust Act and the Supreme Court* (1914); *Ethics in Service* (1915); *Our Chief Magistrate and His Powers* (1916). Taft was not the type who would contribute very much to contemporary thought by his pen. He blazed few new trails, even in the law. He was thorough rather than original in his mental processes. The final decade of his life, as chief justice, was beyond any doubt the happiest. During it he was doing the work he loved. He was filling the post to which he had always aspired. Before he died, it is a safe assumption, his quadrennium in the presidency had faded like an evil dream into those mists which memory no longer penetrates.

[This sketch is based very largely on the William Howard Taft papers at the Lib. of Cong., which are open to students under certain restrictions. A critical biography is under preparation by Henry F. Pringle, who has had free access to them. For Taft's decisions as superior court judge of Ohio see the files of *The Weekly Law Bull. and Ohio Law Jour.* (1887–90). An adequate analysis of his services on the U. S. Circuit Court is in H. S. Duffy, *William Howard Taft* (1930); the cases can be found in *Federal Reporter*, vols. LI–CI. The Taft papers are voluminous for his periods as governor of the Philippine Islands, secretary of war, and president. They contain much source material on the campaign of 1912. His services in the reorganization of the Supreme Court are described in Felix Frankfurter and J. M. Landis, *The Business of the Supreme Court* (1928). His labor decisions are discussed by A. T. Mason, in *Univ. of Pa. Law Rev.*, Mar. 1930. Secondary sources of value include: A. W. Butt, *Taft and Roosevelt: The Intimate Letters of Archie Butt* (2 vols., 1930); H. H. Kohlsaat, *From McKinley to Harding* (1923); Mrs. W. H. Taft, *Recollections of Full Years* (1914); C. W. Thompson, *Presidents I've Known and Two Near Presidents* (1929); W. A. White, *Masks in a Pageant* (1928); N. W. Stephenson, *Nelson W. Aldrich, A Leader in Am. Politics* (1930); H. L. Stoddard, *As I Knew Them* (1927); Samuel Gompers, *Seventy Years of Life and Labor* (2 vols., 1925); L. White Busbey, *Uncle Joe Cannon* (1927); C. M. Depew, *My Memories of Eighty Years* (1922); J. B. Foraker, *Notes of a Busy Life* (2 vols., 1916); *La Follette's Autobiography* (1913); T. B. Mott, *Myron T. Herrick, Friend of France* (1929); Harvey W. Wiley, *An Autobiography* (1930); H. F. Pringle, *Theodore Roosevelt, A*

Biography (1931). For genealogy and other personal details, see Mabel T. R. Washburn, *Ancestry of William Howard Taft* (1908); "The Ancestry of William Howard Taft," in *Genealogy*, Apr. 13, 1912; *Quarter-Centenary Record of the Class of 1878, Yale Univ.* (1905); *Obit. Record of Grads. of Yale Univ.*, 1929–30, pp. 69–72.]

[SUPPLEMENTARY BIBLIOGRAPHY. Henry F. Pringle's two-volume *The Life and Times of William Howard Taft* was published in 1939. A popular interpretation is Edward H. Cotton's *William Howard Taft, a Character Study* (1932). Recent works which treat aspects of Taft's life are Frederick C. Hicks, *William Howard Taft, Yale Professor of Law and New Haven Citizen* (1945), and Charles E. Barker, *With President Taft in the White House: Memories of William Howard Taft* (1947).]